Hobbies

*Leisure and the
Culture of Work in America*

Steven M. Gelber

COLUMBIA UNIVERSITY PRESS   NEW YORK

Columbia University Press
Publishers Since 1893
New York   Chichester, West Sussex

Library of Congress Cataloging-in-Publication Data

Gelber, Steven M.
   Hobbies : leisure and the culture of work in America / Steven M.
  Gelber.
     p. cm.
  Includes bibliographical references and index.
  ISBN 0-231-11392-7 (cloth : alk. paper). — ISBN 0-231-11393-5
(pbk. : alk. paper)
    1. Hobbies—Social aspects—United States. 2. Leisure—Social
aspects—United States. 3. Hobbies—United States—History.
4. Industries—Social aspects—United States—History. 5. Social
change—United States. I. Title.
GV1201.38.G45   1999
306.4'812—dc21   98-48421

Chapter 1, "Here's a Job You Can't Lose," first appeared as "A Job You Can't Lose:
Work and Hobbies in the Great Depression," *Journal of Social History* 24 (summer
1991): 741–766.

Chapter 4, "Stamp Collecting: Commodifying the Ephemeral," first appeared as
"Free Market Metaphor: The Historical Dynamics of Stamp Collecting,"
Comparative Studies in Society and History 34 (October 1992): 742–769.

Parts of chapter 10 (and parts of other chapters) first appeared as "Do-It-Yourself:
Constructing, Repairing and Maintaining Domestic Masculinity," *American
Quarterly* 49 (March 1997): 66–112.

To my sons,
Jesse and Gideon

Contents

Preface

This book examines the history of two categories of hobbies, collecting and crafts, but does so in somewhat different ways. Collecting is treated more topically, whereas crafts are examined roughly chronologically. The different approaches have been dictated by the nature of the hobbies themselves. The structure of collecting has remained essentially constant over the last century and a half, but the nature of crafts has gone through a series of fairly distinct changes. Therefore, I have chosen to view collecting as a set of issues that have to do with the collector and the object, whereas I have written about crafts as changing form from the Victorian to the postwar eras. I stop the story at the end of the 1950s because that decade marked the maturation of the do-it-yourself trend, on the one hand, and the kit assembly craze, on the other. The 1960s brought a rebirth of interest in serious crafting. The counterculture sparked a new arts and crafts movement that, like its Progressive Era predecessor, gave rise to a cohort of professional artisans and a generation of highly skilled hobbyists. To do this movement justice, particularly given its overtly anti-industrial and often anticapitalist ideology, would have taken up more space than practicable.

On a more personal level, this book grew out of my own transition from the 1950s to the 1960s. Growing up on suburban Long Island in the 1950s, I watched and sometimes helped my father work around the house. He showed me the sense of satisfaction that comes from planning and successfully executing a project. Then in 1961 I went off to college, where the tidy package of values I had grown up with came undone. The change in the way I understood the world came less from the political and social turmoil in the streets of Ithaca and Madison than from several undergraduate classes I took with Paul E. Breer at Cornell. Those classes did for me what all of us who teach hope to do with at least some of our students, they made me reconsider my assumptions about the nature of society. Not only did Breer introduce me to the sociology of knowledge, he showed me how it functioned in the real world, and I have spent much of the succeeding thirty years trying to apply the ideas I learned in those classes to aspects of America's past.

I have written about art, religion, baseball, and now hobbies. The topics have been diverse but the object of the search has been consistent: how are our beliefs and values related to the work we do for a living, and how do we express them in areas outside of work? In this book I have chosen to explore the meaning of hobbies because of the particularly dramatic way in which they express workplace values. As an academic, my own workplace is as much at home as it is in my school office, and in that sense I approximate a preindustrial life of integrated work and leisure. Furthermore, as a fully socialized member of my socioeconomic caste, I have been reluctant to admit, even to myself, that I have any hobbies. After all, with an office at home, there is no excuse for spending time doing anything but scholarly work, which is supposed to be inherently enjoyable. Indeed, I am writing this preface on a national holiday!

Yet the truth is I have always had hobbies, and so when I explore why Americans have pursued hobbies for the past 150 years, I am also writing a history of things with which I am intimately familiar. I went through the obligatory collecting phase when I was ten or eleven, although neither my stamp nor baseball card collection ever amounted to very much, and as an adult I have steered away from any serious collecting to avoid anything that would feed my historian's compulsiveness. As a teenager I took up photography and pursued it into adulthood until I realized one day that I really did not like working in the darkroom; since my photographs had little recommend them aesthetically, I quit. I continue to find a leisure-time sense of accomplishment taking up where my father left off when he moved back to the city, with woodworking and household do-it-yourself, both of which I do only slightly better than photography but enjoy much more. The home repair and maintenance are done as needed, but the woodworking, like most people's hobbies, is something I spend more time planning than executing. Although I do not build furniture as often as I would like, the knowledge that I can provides me with a theoretical escape from my regular work and with a sense of achievement when I actually do it. The fact (according to the thesis of this book) that my own productive leisure reproduces a dominant ideology about which I have grave reservations does not overly disturb me because of my undergraduate realization that while I may be able to influence my environment, I can never escape it. I can, however, try to understand it.

Although this is a history of American hobbies, I have used British sources from time to time. Most of those can stand in for domestic material because they were either republished in this country by American presses or distributed here. And they make it clear that the patterns in the United States were not unique. Most of the broad trends discussed here repeated themselves throughout Great Britain and the Continent, and, as my section on stamp collecting makes clear, the United States both borrowed and exported hobby trends. Given my emphasis on cultural values, cross-cultural analyses, or at least analyses of other societies, could test to what extent the ideology I discuss was the product of capitalism and to what extent it came from other, more peculiarly American social patterns.

Finally, I stress that this is not a technical history of either collecting or crafts. As I discuss in detail later, hobbies generate expertise, much of which is passed on in printed form. There are scores of narrowly focused hobby books that provide both how-to information and, in the case of collecting, highly detailed histories of the collected objects. What I have tried to do here is explain how and why hobbies emerged as a category of leisure activity in the nineteenth century and why they have continued to hold such a prominent place in the menu of leisure activities that we all choose from. I hope that readers will find my argument about the meaning of hobbies persuasive but that the pleasures of productive leisure will survive the stripping away of some of its mystery.

Portions of this study have previously appeared in articles in scholarly journals. Part of my discussion of the history of hobbies in the depression was first published in the *Journal of Social History* 24 (summer 1991). Sections of the chapter on stamp collecting originally appeared in *Comparative Studies in Society and History* 34 (July 1992), and some of the analysis of men and do-it-yourself came out first in the *American Quarterly* 49 (March 1997).

I am deeply indebted to numerous libraries and their staffs for the generous help they have provided me in doing the research for this book. In particular I thank the archivists and librarians at the Strong Museum in Rochester, New York; the Henry Ford Museum in Dearborn, Michigan; the National Museum of American History in Washington, D.C., and the Cooper-Hewitt Museum in New York City, both part of the Smithsonian Institution; the American Numismatic Society, the Collectors' Club (stamp collecting), and the Grollier Club (book collecting), all in New York City; and Cynthia Bradley of Orradre Library at Santa Clara University, for their generous assistance. Friends and colleagues have provided both sympathetic and critical feedback, but no one has been a more supportive friend or stern analyst than my colleague (and wife) Catherine Bell.

Hobbies

Introduction: Context and Theory

How doth the little busy bee
Improve each shining hour,
And gather honey all the day
From every opening flower!

In works of labour or of skill,
I would be busy too;
For Satan finds some mischief still
for idle hands to do.
—Issac Watts, *Horae Lyricae and Divine Songs*

Nearly three centuries after it was written, Isaac Watts's admonitory poem "Against Idleness and Mischief" persists as an epigraph for hobbies. The poem articulates the disquiet that motivated generations of teachers, parents, and self-appointed experts to promote productive leisure, such as collecting and handicrafts, as an antidote to the dangers of destructive pastimes. Industrialism quarantined work from leisure in a way that made employment more worklike and nonwork more problematic. Isolated from each other's moderating influences, work and leisure became increasingly oppositional as they competed for finite hours. The fluidity of preindustrial time gave way to discrete blocks of commodified time that could be sold for work or withheld for leisure, which led guardians of public morals to fear that time spent not working would be time spent getting into trouble. Watts's warning that Satan would appropriate idle hands for his own use is the locus classicus of an image that rapidly became part of the folk wisdom of capitalism. Subsequent iterations of Watts's admonition would often alter the original formulation so that "hands" became "minds." The inadvertent substitution expressed the belief that leisure was not only a behavioral threat but also an ideological one; it led to both delinquent activity and deviant ideas.

Americans responded to the threat posed by leisure in two ways. First, reformers attempted to remove the source of contagion by eliminating or restricting access to inappropriate activity. Second, they sought to encourage benign pastimes. Hobbies have been among the most prominent of such socially approved leisure activities. In this study I attempt to explain how hobbies emerged in the nineteenth century as a "good thing" to do, and why these curious, homebound, solitary, and sometimes wasteful activities became so beloved of those who wished to shield the public from the temptations of idleness.

Twenty years ago John Kasson suggested that at the end of the nineteenth century Coney Island turned recreation into a "fantastic replication" of urban-industrial life and by doing so "served to affirm the existing culture." The amusement parks that Kasson wrote about were factory analogs, large commercial enterprises where people could spend their earnings in a frenetic burlesque of their everyday world. In contrast, the home was supposed to be a refuge from both the competitive business environment and from the temptations of commercial amusement. In truth, however life was not so easily bifurcated. Work and home may have been separated by industrialism, but workplace attitudes, values, and behaviors could not be completely compartmentalized. Despite the rhetoric of domestic sanctuary, a man did not shed his business experience when he opened the front door, and conversely, his wife could not completely isolate herself from the culture of the workplace by shutting it. The ideology of the workplace infiltrated the home in the form of productive leisure.[1]

Hobbies developed as a category of socially valued leisure activity in the nineteenth century because they bridged the worlds of work and home. They allowed women to practice, and therefore to understand, worklike activities, and they allowed men to create a business-like space for themselves inside the female-dominated house. As leisure, hobbies provided a respite from the normal demands of work, but as a particular form of *productive* leisure they expressed the deeper meaning of the work ethic and the free market. Hobbies gained wide acceptance because they could condemn depersonalized factory and office work by compensating for its deficits while simultaneously replicating both the skills and values of the workplace, a process I refer to as "disguised affirmation."

Disguised affirmation allows participants to think about an activity as leisure-time recreation while it functions as a form of ideological re-creation. The capacity of hobbies to act simultaneously as resistance and accommodation serves to remind us that we have to examine *all* the meanings of leisure if we are to understand any of them. There has been a tendency in the past twenty years or so for scholars to stress the ways in which members of disempowered subcultures manipulate elements of the dominant culture to their own ends. Historians, sociologists, and cultural theorists have all celebrated the ability of the working class to exert autonomy on the job and in the marketplace. These scholars have demonstrated how people bound within a society controlled by others could still carve out personal, ethnic, class, gender, and other particularistic meanings from even the most monolithic products of mass culture. Their studies of the grassroots resistance to prescribed forms has quite usefully directed our attention to previously unacknowledged diversity.[2]

The scholarly emphasis on opposition, however, has been so pervasive that it is easy to forget that beyond subcultural differences there is still the cultural commonality. Powerful ideas, symbols, and objects continue to knit the society together because they are accepted by both the strong and the weak. The dominant culture dominates not because it is imposed but because it is embraced. Bits and pieces may be appropriated by subcultures for their own purposes, but the fundamental structure retains the capacity to reproduce itself in the everyday life of the society. Indeed, as I attempt to show here, one of the great strengths of mass culture is its remarkable ability to respond to popular disaffection in ways that acknowledge the discontent while defusing it. Hobbies are important because they combine critical and affirmative elements in a single category. Teachers, recreation directors, journalists, and other voices of authority have felt free to encourage the autonomy and creativity of hobbies because even if they sensed that hobbies could critique regular work, they also recognized that hobbies' triumph over idleness was a victory for the values of a market economy.

The first section of the book explains how productive home leisure came to be recognized as a distinct category of leisure that appropriated the existing term "hobbies" and in doing so changed the meaning of that word from negative to positive. Before about 1880 a hobby was a dangerous obsession. After that date it became a productive use of free time. Two forms of hobbies, collecting and handicrafts, were almost universally recognized as members of this new class of pastimes, and they are the hobbies examined in this book. Several other leisure activities have also been widely acknowledged as hobbies and could certainly be explored in the same way. They include husbandry (gardening and pets), amateurism (including music, dancing, theater, and participatory sports), and perhaps volunteerism.

While the forms of collecting and crafts may have changed somewhat over the last 150 years, their meaning has not. A stamp collector in the 1860s and a phone card collector in the 1990s pursue their pastimes in essentially similar ways. Likewise, a fret sawyer in the 1870s and a contemporary kit assembler both make small decorative objects for what appear to be similar reasons. The dramatic changes that have taken place in the structure of the market and the workplace have been less important than the continuity in the values that underlie the system. Indeed, the attitudes and values reproduced in hobbies arose not with industrialism but with capitalism. Hobbies originated as a category in response to the industrially induced bifurcation of work and leisure, but the values they reproduced were mercantile as well as industrial. It is true that hobbies changed along with the society (people collected radios as well as spoons, built airplanes as well as sailing ships, and worked in plastic as well as wood), but the meaning of collecting and crafting behavior has been surprisingly constant over time. Hobbies have been a way to confirm the verities of work and the free market inside the home so long as remunerative employment has remained elsewhere.

The second section of the book examines collecting, which by the early twentieth century had become so closely identified with hobbies that "collecting" and "hobbies" were often used synonymously. Industrialism allowed the elite occupation of collecting art and fine antiques to become the popular hobby of collecting everyday items. Beginning with printing, mass production democratized collecting by creating objects whose very commonness assured they would become scarce because they were usually made to be thrown away. Hobby collectors rescued objects from the trash heap and created value by inventing sets into which to fit them. The collection became the sum that created the value of its parts, bestowing singularity not only on often mundane items but also, by extension, on the collector as well.

At the turn of the century, child psychologists discovered that more than 80 percent of children pass through a "collecting stage" in their preteen years and that females focus on the aesthetic and sentimental aspects of collected objects, while males stress their economic value. That distinction expressed itself in some surprising forms. Male stamp collectors, for example, created a subculture that affirmed the ideology of the free market in a most proper and gentlemanly way. Antique collectors, however, developed a freewheeling pastime that celebrated behavior that would be considered unethical in almost any other commercial transaction. Women, as well as men, practiced a form of pitiless capitalism that turned objects from the American past into trophies of marketplace expertise.

If collectors have been the white-collar "financiers" of leisure, then handicrafters have been the blue-collar producers, and their activities are described in the third part of this study. There is no financial conjuring when crafters use their skill and labor to transform raw materials into finished products. The crafted object is a straightforward confirmation of the work ethic; idle hands have been put to good use. It is not entirely clear whether the use of class designations like white- and blue-collar are more than metaphorical. Socioeconomic data on contemporary hobbyists is thin enough to preclude any definitive conclusions; information about the past is even rarer. Collecting does appear to have been more popular among white-collar workers, and blue-collar workers have been somewhat more likely to be crafters than have office workers, but both hobbies have been remarkable more for their class inclusiveness than their exclusiveness. Money can buy high-priced collectibles and fancy tools, but those are differences of scale rather than of meaning. Ultimately, hobbies have transcended class much more easily than gender.

Both middle-class and working-class men were supposed to find work in a market-driven economy intrinsically rewarding. Thus they could embrace the meaning of collecting and crafts as part of their worldview. Women, on the other hand, were sheltered from the rough-and-tumble of the economic world (except as consumers), so that for them hobbies did not replicate work-place values but provided a socially approved way to practice those ideals modified in gender-appropriate ways. As the new leisure class of industrial society, middle-class women first laid claim to crafting in the nineteenth century when they began to transform sewing from a duty into a pastime and took up light handicrafting as a way to productively pass the time. Women's craft items were often sold at charity bazaars, which functioned as pseudo-markets where social ritual was as important for determining price as supply and demand.

Victorian husbands avoided manual activities altogether. Only the jigsaw fad of the last quarter of the nineteenth century broke the mold and set the stage for the arts and crafts movement, which legitimated a broad spectrum of crafts for both genders. The masculinized manual pastimes of the arts and crafts movement allowed men to exercise a new "domestic masculinity" by using tools around the house, a trend that expanded steadily from World War I through the great do-it-yourself boom of the 1950s. Blue-collar men, who were both poorer and more familiar with tools then their white-collar brothers, may have been more likely to undertake household projects out of necessity, but both they and middle-class men saw do-it-yourself as a hobby as well as a chore. Despite their experience in taking over home mainte-nance during the war, women continued to play a secondary role after 1945, conceding a sphere of domestic masculinity to men.

There is a certain academic arrogance in attributing a particular meaning to avocations engaged in by millions of people over more than a century. Decades differ, subcultures differ, and individuals differ. An antebellum woman who sewed Berlinwork while she waited for her husband to return from the office did not derive exactly the same meanings from her activity as a middle-class office worker making a coffee table in a postwar tract house. Where I found evidence to distinguish meaning among groups and over time, I have tried to do so. Gender distinctions are clear and constitute a major theme in this book. Differences between social classes are murkier, not only because of the nature of my sources but also because the meaning of hobbies appears to have surmounted class. Other commonly recognized group identities, such as race, ethnicity, and geographic location, are invisible in the historic record as I found it. Perhaps future scholars of productive leisure will be able to tease out variances I missed. Certainly, there must have been some differences among such groups, and maybe there were more changes over time than I have found, but to me, the continuity in meaning has been much more striking than the variations in practice. For well over a century, the productive leisure of hobbies has operated as a form of disguised affirmation, helping to sustain the overarching ideology of capitalism by serving up its ideas in the palatable form of domestic leisure.

The Concept of Leisure

Readers uninterested in the social sciences may be tempted to ignore the remainder of this introduction, and if they do, the rest of the book will still make sense. By skipping ahead, however, the reader will miss much of the contemporary scientific grounding for the historical analysis in the main body of the book. There I have tried to read the past through the lens of social science. I have not ignored the more fashionable cultural theorists, but their speculative interpretations strike me as less useful than the more rigorous explorations of sociologists, anthropologists, and psychologists. My conclusions about the meaning of hobbies in the nineteenth and twentieth centuries draw from the findings of a wide variety of scholars whose work is too often ignored by historians. Even those who do not read the rest of the introduction will not escape entirely, since recent social science studies are incorporated sporadically throughout the book. It is these theories that explain how hobbies function as the oxymoron "productive leisure."

The contradiction derives from the general understanding that leisure is the opposite of work. Although there are those, like sociologist John Kelly, who despair of formulating a single description of leisure, finding it "pluralistic in its varied and combined meanings, its forms, its locales, and, to a lesser extent, its associations," most academic (and popular) discussions make three fundamental assumptions about the nature of leisure activities. First, leisure activities take place in time that is free from work, and in this context, "work" includes those personal, familial, and home care activities necessary for life maintenance. Second, leisure activities are voluntarily undertaken. Third, they are pleasurable. It is not what, but why and when something is done that make it leisure. Therefore, one person's livelihood can be another person's pastime—and vice versa. Amateur car mechanics on the one hand and professional "sex workers" on the other invert the usual meaning of those activities.[3]

Voltaire is reputed to have said that every man may choose his choice, but no man may choose his choices. The aphorism explains why the psychology of making a choice cannot be divorced from the sociology of available choices. Both the psychological and sociological are integral to the common understanding of leisure: viz., leisure is pleasurable activity, voluntarily undertaken in nonwork time. Pleasure is psychological; motivation can be either sociological or psychological; and work is socially defined. Each is necessary, but none is sufficient to define an activity as leisure. For example, activities that are understood as work (including nonremunerated labor such as family care or schoolwork), no matter how pleasurable, are not leisure, although time "stolen" from work for on-the-job relief might be. Nor for that matter, are unpleasant voluntary activities undertaken out of a sense of civic or religious obligation, but similar activities that were enjoyable might be thought of as leisure depending on the extent of obligation involved. Conversely, not all leisure activities are enjoyable in the same way, and some involve elements of drudgery and even pain. Yet none could be fundamentally disagreeable to the participants or else they would not do it voluntarily. Mark Twain used this principle to explain why Tom Sawyer's friends were willing to pay him to let them paint his Aunt Polly's fence: "Work consists of whatever a body is *obliged* to do, and Play consists of whatever a body is not obliged to do."[4]

Faced with this hodgepodge of conflicting elements, it is not necessary, as some scholars have suggested, to abandon separate work and leisure categories.[5] People's willingness to do things in their spare time that are analogous or even identical to what other people do for a living is a testament to the underlying importance of motivation. A variety of studies have shown that from the participants' points of view the single most important element in defining leisure activity is not what they are doing but how freely they have chosen to do it.[6] Soccer players and gardeners who actually did the same thing for both work and leisure said the most important distinction between them was not that they were paid for the work but that they could choose the leisure.[7]

People dislike work to the extent that it is obligatory, extrinsically rewarded, structured, and repetitive. The worst-case job described by this definition
is completely unfree. It must be done; the individual has no say in how it is
done; there is no inherent joy in doing it; and its rewards are determined by
others. The best-case leisure by contrast is completely free. The individual
determines how and when to do it, and the rewards for participating are
inherent in the activity itself. What is done is irrelevant so long as it gives the
participant pleasure, which is why attempts to define leisure by describing
activity have invariably been stymied. Roger Caillois made an important
effort at categorizing play by identifying its component parts, but play is only
one kind of leisure and takes pleasure and voluntary participation for granted.[8] Very few scholars have attempted to extend the Caillois model from the
narrow area of play to the wider domain of leisure as a whole, probably
because as complex as play and games may be, they are the essence of simplicity compared to other forms of leisure.[9]

In order to accommodate the multivariate meaning of leisure, sociologists
have tended to use the approach exemplified by John R. Kelly or John
Neulinger who have constructed separate models that take into account that
both work and leisure can be more or less free and more or less pleasurable.
Any given activity could contain a mixture of worklike and leisurelike elements. Which predominates—and to what extent—depends on the perception of the participants, and other investigators have sought to construct patterns of leisure that derive from the participants' own understanding of what
they are doing. Unfortunately, the results can obscure as much as they
reveal. For example, scholars using this approach have variously labeled as
leisure watching television "friendship and relaxation," "intellectual stimulation," and "family pleasure." This diversity serves as a valuable reminder that
leisure has multiple meanings.[10]

However varied the meanings of pastimes may be, all analysts agree, and
often take for granted, that pleasure is the one indisputable element in
leisure. Curiously, however, few scholars try to understand the sources of
that pleasure. Perhaps because they have a hard enough time achieving
anything resembling a consensus when they use the participants' own explanations, they are reluctant to complicate matters further by adding another
layer of analysis. Psychologist Mihaly Csikszentmihayli justifies this conservative approach by arguing that while chess players may actually want to
symbolically kill their fathers and mountain climbers may in fact be
expressing latent homosexuality or a death wish, the question still remains
as to why such subconscious urges are expressed on a checkered board or on
a granite cliff. The explanation, he argues, should not be sought in the subconscious motivation but in the experience of the act itself. In other words,

investigators should take participants' description of pleasure at face value.[11]

By placing the self-reporting individual at the center of the definition of leisure, this approach strips away not only the subconscious but also the sociological and ideological elements; it makes the individual's conscious state of mind the most important determinate in identifying leisure.[12] As a mountain climber, Csikszentmihayli initially wondered why people like himself found pleasure in admittedly dangerous activities. He concluded that types of activities that he calls "autotelic" (self-directed) give certain kinds of people, also called autotelic, a special form of pleasure called "flow." Flow, he says, is the sense of euphoric concentration experienced by people when they are successfully using their skills to the utmost. A person in a state of flow feels in control, knows the moves necessary to reach an unambiguous goal, and acts more or less automatically. The optimal conditions for a state of flow occur when the participant is challenged but not overwhelmed by the activity.[13]

Flow is a transcendent experience. It occurs only occasionally and only in some people, and for that reason is not a very useful tool for describing most kinds of leisure. It turns out, however, that flow is not limited to leisure since Csikszentmihayli and Judith LeFevre found that "flowlike situations occurred more than three times as often in work as in leisure." The authors express surprise at their findings, but when we consider that flow takes place when there is an optimal relationship between challenge and skill, and that most leisure activities in our culture (perhaps in all cultures) are nonchallenging, there is no reason to expect flow in most pastimes. Work, on the other hand, is much more likely to be difficult. Even routine blue-collar jobs require greater concentration and a higher level of involvement than the most popular pastime, watching television. In fact, to the extent that people do seek flowlike emotions from their leisure, they have to continually make their leisure more challenging, which is to say more worklike, always safe in the knowledge that they can quit if the pain overwhelms the pleasure.[14]

Even if pleasure at work does not make it leisure nor labor at leisure make it work, the problem of explaining why people engage in leisure that involves worklike behavior remains. Since it is so intense, the flow state is not experienced by most people most of the time. However, less extreme feelings, such as pride, satisfaction, and achievement, can come from both work and leisure activities. These positive emotions do not appear spontaneously but are conditioned responses to socially valued accomplishments. To understand why both work and worklike leisure induce these kinds of feelings, we need to examine how culture generates an ideology that censures idleness.

Work, Leisure, and Ideology

A group of scholars, usually labeled cultural theorists, have integrated ideas from both anthropology and sociology to develop several useful descriptions of the role leisure plays in contemporary culture. Most assume that individual leisure activities make sense only in the context of a society dominated by power relationships based on wealth and social control, and that leisure, like every other cultural institution, is an expression of the underlying economic structure that rewards some and exploits others. Some theorists emphasize the role of ideology specifically, while others are more general, but all of them recognize that leisure is part of a system made up of people with diverse and often conflicting interests who are nevertheless tied together by a set of shared beliefs and values, their ideology. It is this ideology that underlies emotions such as achievement, pride, and satisfaction that are vital to understanding how worklike leisure functions in the modern capitalist world.[15]

This basic argument assumes, of course, that there is a common ideology in industrial society. Cultural theorists on the left (which is to say almost all of them) refer to this as the "dominant ideology" although they differ on the extent of its grip. One group, whom sociologist John Clarke has called "pessimists," seeks to show how business dominates every aspect of life, including leisure, by creating a world both on and off the job that reproduces the ideology of market capitalism. Whereas classic functionalist anthropology assumes that all cultural institutions operate to maintain a benignly homeostatic society, this pessimistic version attributes malign intent to the powerful property-owning classes who retain their status, wealth, and power by perpetuating the status quo. In this interpretation the poorer classes are powerless participants in behavior and unthinking believers in an ideology that ensures their continued domination.[16]

Members of the second, and recently much more prominent, group, whom Clarke calls "populists," accept the essence of the first position but are unwilling to write off weaker groups and individuals as impotent in the face of hegemonic capitalism. Instead they acknowledge the ability of the oppressed individual to fight back, no matter how modestly, against the encroaching power of the dominant culture and thus to preserve a sense of individual agency. Perhaps as important as their emphasis on the preservation of some seed of autonomy is the populists' understanding that the process of internalizing an ideology is as much one of appropriation as domination. Far from being passive recipients of received values, individuals interpret and express the ideology in uniquely personal ways. Therefore every time the dominant ideological paradigm is absorbed or expressed by individuals it is altered, creating a dynamic system in which the dominator is changed by the act of domination.[17]

Interesting as it is, the debate between the pessimists and the optimists tends to divert attention from the larger truth: pastimes are part and parcel of an integrated fabric of institutions that are mutually compatible and reinforcing. Leisure, no less than church, state, family, education, and work, is constituted in a way that generates and reproduces the structure of society. All the various relationships that form the social structure—including class, race, gender, and age—express themselves in leisure activity, and even activities that critique the dominant mode are determined by it. While resistance may not be futile, ultimately there is no escape, and leisure is part of the cultural scaffolding that has been constructed to hold up Western free-market capitalism.

Citizens who wish to avoid being ground up by the system have to learn its rules and regulations; they have to internalize its values so that what they do to survive makes sense to themselves. Perhaps the single most acknowledged character trait necessary for success in a capitalist system is the belief, originally identified by Max Weber, that work is good for its own sake. Usually called the "work ethic," employers encouraged it among their employees and, although they resisted at first, workers too ultimately embraced and internalized the idea that work was a positive good and, as its opposite, leisure was suspect. Since the work ethic explicitly privileges work over leisure, it has been the wellspring of antileisure attitudes in Western society. Adherents find life's meaning and purpose, if not necessarily life's pleasures, intimately bound up with work and perceive the failure to work long and hard as a moral deficiency. Since leisure in the industrial world exists in time that might otherwise be used for work, its very existence is a threat to this core value. The point is not that people who espouse the work ethic find work more enjoyable than leisure but that they find it morally superior.[18]

The work ethic may be hostile to leisure, but it can coexist with pleasure as long as the pleasure comes from work or from worklike leisure. John Clarke and Chas Crichter have dubbed the desire to avoid idleness and engage in productive leisure, the "Protestant leisure ethic." The phenomenon of finding pleasure in work explains why people with a strong work ethic seek similar satisfactions from worklike leisure such as hobbies. Because hobbies have almost all the characteristics that give people pleasure at work, they can provide the satisfactions of a "career" and confirm the legitimacy of the work ethic even for people with unpleasant jobs. As a form of what sociologist Robert Stebbins calls "serious leisure," hobbies develop specialized skills, reward perseverance, integrate participants into a specialized subculture, and provide them with benchmarks by which they can measure their achievements.[19]

Achievement-generated pleasure from worklike leisure reinforces the participants' beliefs they are doing something that is good. In leisure, as in work, a difficult task done well is a source of pride. The most common passive forms of leisure cannot generate a sense of accomplishment. There is no pride in watching television, reading popular fiction, drunkenly cheering in a sports bar, or chatting over coffee with a friend. However, serious leisure such as helping others as a volunteer, creating something in a hobby, or producing professional results as an amateur are all activities designed to generate feelings of achievement. Indeed, almost all pastimes that are held up for social approbation, with the possible exception of serious reading, are activities that induce pride based on personal effort. Such leisure is socially valorized precisely because it produces feelings of satisfaction with something that looks very much like work but that is done for its own sake.

Leisure is only one of a variety of sources for values. Family and friends, church and school, mass media, private cogitation, and of course, work also contribute to the interlocking beliefs that make up ideology.[20] Starting in the mid-1950s, a number of studies attempted to describe how work molds workers' values in a way that affects them on and off the job and in their postworking life as well. Sociologist Theodore Caplow was among the first to recognize that work experiences affect nonjob lifestyles when he developed the concept of "occupational ideologies." Such ideologies, he claimed, influence everything from patterns of consumption, dress, and decorum to family mores. This idea was expanded by Harold Wilensky who argued that actual experience on the job determines behavior off the job. Wilensky did not deny that complex occupational codes of behavior influence nonwork activities, but he also hinted that something linked directly to specific occupational behavior influences how workers interact with their communities.[21]

Neither Caplow nor Wilensky attempted to explain how actual work might function as the source of ideology, but in 1965 sociologists Paul Breer and Edwin Locke specifically described how jobs generate values. Despite an unfortunate lack of confirming studies, Breer and Locke's analysis is so suggestive that it could well serve as the keystone for a general theory of ideological origins. Breer and Locke do not deny there are multiple sources for values, but they do argue that jobs ("task experiences") are a primary source of basic beliefs. "It is our thesis," they state, "that in working on a task an individual develops certain beliefs, values, and preferences specific to the task itself which over time are generalized to other areas of life." They were able to demonstrate this process experimentally by varying task reward systems and measuring the resulting shifts in subjects' values. They generalized their laboratory experience by suggesting that task-based attitudes are developed through a process in which workers initially become aware that certain ways of doing the job are more successful than others. Workers then adopt those patterns of behavior and perceive them as good (and their opposites as bad). Finally, they formulate norms that define the good form of behavior as that which is expected for all task participants. Even more dramatically, Breer and Locke found that attitudes developed through task experience are generalized from the specific to the abstract. So the self-directed worker will not only believe that other real-life problems can best be solved through individual action but also that autonomous individualism is an absolute good regardless of the immediate context. In this way the job experience of the individual generates beliefs and values that are elevated to the level of ideology.[22]

The link between on-the-job and off-the-job values is not a one-way street. There is evidence, for example, that participation in solitary hobbies may help build an ideology of individualism that produces resistance to non-leisure activities that would reinforce collectivity. To the extent that hobbies function like work, this actually reinforces the Breer and Locke thesis. It is also likely that ideology itself influences how certain tasks are accomplished or even what tasks are made available. Yet in the final analysis, Breer and Locke were able to demonstrate experimentally that people's abstract values can be significantly shifted through relatively brief task experiences. When experimenters can manipulate how people feel about "the individual's relationship to society, the exercise of authority, the relationship between man and God, time orientation, achievement, luck, control, and man's relationship to nature" in a few hours in the laboratory, then the significance of a lifetime of work must be taken very seriously indeed.[23]

If work is a major source of the values that make up ideology, then work-like leisure should be a significant expression of that ideology. And in fact there is ample evidence that some pastimes have an ideological meaning far out of proportion to the amount of time and money spent on them. The symbolically representational nature of certain leisure activities has led anthropologist Clifford Geertz to refer to them as "deep play." These expressive forms of leisure take up certain cultural themes, organize them, and then present them in a way that represents their essential nature. They remind us, notes one scholar, "of the social order and our place within it."[24]

Play, of course, is almost universally recognized as the way children learn and practice their roles in society. Psychologist Erik Erikson's description of the progressive stages that infants and children go through to gain knowledge and mastery of their environments is probably the best known model of this widely observed phenomenon. The essence of Erikson's approach has been expanded from the individual to the collective level by anthropologists John M. Roberts, Brian Sutton-Smith, and a variety of collaborators into what they call the "conflict-enculturation hypothesis." Roberts and Sutton-

Smith start with the assumption that the socialization process creates stress and conflict for individuals faced with the prospect of learning all the unspoken rules that govern social behavior. They then suggest that "games and other expressive models . . . provide buffered learning or enculturation important to both the players and their societies."[25] They do not claim that the games reduce or resolve the conflict; the games are not a catharsis. Rather, they are a way of "increasing the confidence of the players in analogous competitive processes," and thus "the fun of the game derives from an exercise in competence rather than an exercise in tension assuagement."[26]

Roberts and Sutton-Smith's singular contribution to the understanding of leisure is their explanation of how games of skill, chance, or strategy each express the socioeconomic structures of particular societies. Like Breer and Locke, Roberts and Sutton-Smith demonstrate how the requirements of workaday life mold attitudes that are projected into spheres distinct from the world of work. They find, for example, that both tribal peoples and modern unskilled workers who lack control over major life decisions share a predilection for gambling, a leisure expression of fatalism that confirms their belief that they have relatively little power over their own future. The Breer and Locke and the Roberts and Sutton-Smith studies establish an empirical confirmation of the common assumption among scholars that class or national character influences choices in leisure activity and, in turn, that activity "maintains or reinforces the ideological heritage of a social system."[27]

Jay Mechling, in his sophisticated analysis of the contradictory meanings of three group games played at a Boy Scout camp, has demonstrated how leisure can express the dominant ideology. The first game was very popular with the Scouts because it rewarded perseverance and skill, and was unambiguously consonant with the work ethic. The second game, also rewarded cooperation and hard work but introduced an element of chance. Mechling suggests the Scouts liked this game too, despite the risk that their work could go unrewarded, because it modeled the unsureness of real life. The third game was a farrago of obscure and conflicting rules, hated by the campers because, according to Mechling, it was ideologically subversive. It implied that the merit system of badges and ranks was false and that success was random rather than rational. The two agreeable Scout games confirm the Roberts and Sutton-Smith hypothesis by serving as devices to help the boys understand conflicts and contradictions in their society. Furthermore, the boys' resistance to the third game is an apt illustration of the Breer and Locke thesis. The game was incompatible with the official Scout ideology and with the day-to-day task experiences of camp life. It neither grew out of nor reflected back on the Scouts' experience, and they resisted participating. When leisure activity was compatible with the beliefs and values generated by their day-to-day "work," the Scouts embraced it, but when it conflicted with their basic ideology, they viewed it solely as an unpleasant task and tried to avoid it.[28]

The Relationship of Work and Leisure

If work generates ideology and leisure reflects it, then there should be a positive correlation between work and leisure. Like the Boy Scouts in Mechling's study, people should embrace leisure that reflects values that originate in their work and avoid activities that contradict those beliefs. This book is about the ways that they do. However, leisure's role as a relief from work frequently obscures this deeper meaning and creates the false dichotomy that has dominated the scholarly discussion of the work-leisure relationship for seventy years. Stressing the relief aspects of leisure, one school argues that leisure compensates people for desired qualities missing from work. A second group contends that the job experience is so powerful that it inevitably spills over into leisure activity.[29]

The scholarly discussion of the relationship between work and leisure began in the 1920s when prescriptive sociologists and educators concerned with the "right use of leisure" contended that leisure should contain elements missing from work as a form of compensation. Their fundamental assumption that leisure existed to restore "the balance of life" was called into question by psychologist Donald Super in a pioneering study published in 1940. Super found that different hobbies had different meanings for their participants. Some provided compensatory balance, but some replicated the hobbyists' regular work. Because Super's insight was ignored by other leisure scholars, the contemporary debate began not in 1940, but twenty years later with the work of sociologist Harold Wilensky, who originally coined the "compensation/spillover" terminology that continues to be used.[30]

Taking his lead from a classic piece by Frederick Engels, Wilensky sought to blame the destructive behavior of working-class leisure on the nature of industrial employment. Like Engels, Wilensky perceived leisure-time dissipation among workers as a form of "explosive compensation for the deadening rhythms of factory life." In contrast to this "compensatory model," "spillover leisure" extends workplace ennui into the workers' free time.[31] Wilensky's paradigm has been developed by sociologist Stanley R. Parker, who expands it to include white-collar as well as blue-collar workers and who attributes functionality to his categories, saying that leisure "serves society" by teaching individuals to play their roles in it, helping it achieve its collective goals, and maintaining group solidarity. Parker also hints at, but does not develop, the idea that work and leisure need to be ideologically consistent.[32]

Parker builds his theory on the assumption that self-reporting can be taken at face value as an accurate measure of people's reasons for engaging in given leisure behavior. One need not assume that responses on questionnaires are lies to conclude that the respondents may not be aware of or understand how their leisure satisfies deeper needs. Thus consciously compensatory pleasures could coexist with subconscious elements of ideological spillover. Yet even at a conscious level, people often look for leisure that allows them to carry over job skills, habits, and values into their leisure. It is, therefore, quite possible that compensation and spillover can function at the same time in the same activity. Both the copyeditor who writes novels and the assembly line worker who builds a boat may be compensating for lack of creativity on the job and spilling over their job-related skills.[33]

Despite a few studies that indicate otherwise, the majority of investigators believe there is a direct causal relationship between work and leisure. They argue that pastimes compensate people for experiences and feelings they want, but do not find, on the job. The sense that leisure should compensate for workplace deficits derives in part from the historic separation of work and leisure into distinct categories; the yin of leisure is understood to balance the yang of work. To the extent that work is compulsory and leisure is voluntary, which they are by definition, all pastimes can be considered compensatory because they are exercises of the freedom that is lacking on the job. Beyond that, compensatory leisure would seem to be more likely to involve a conscious choice to do something that is different from, and that in some sense balances, experiences at work. When Welsh workers were asked, for example, why they engaged in leisure activities, they generally agreed that "the purpose of leisure is to let off steam after work, to do something completely and deliberately different."[34]

Taking participants at their word invariably produces a compensatory understanding of leisure. Might dispassionate observers, however, see some connection that participants overlooked? A study by Boris Kabanoff and Gordon O'Brien that used nonparticipants to judge job and leisure attributes also confirmed the compensatory role of leisure, but the study's criteria were so specific that complexities of motivation were lost. For example, the authors said that for professionals, stamp collecting is compensatory but playing football would be spillover. While ball playing might well be a spillover activity (I have argued precisely this elsewhere), so too is stamp collecting. As a market-based hobby, stamp collecting involves both behavioral and ideological elements that integrate participants into the capitalist system. But since these qualities did not fall into any of the authors' categories,

the ideological meaning of stamp collecting was lost. Just as taking participant feelings at face value overemphasizes the psychological meaning of
leisure, ignoring them completely leaves an analysis vulnerable to distortion
in the opposite direction.[35]

Two separate studies of mountain climbers have demonstrated how
obvious compensatory qualities can obscure underlying patterns. Since
most mountain climbers are desk workers, these analyses confirm what
many others have found: sedentary workers are more likely to engage in
active leisure than those with physically tiring jobs. The authors of both
studies stress the ways in which physical challenges of mountain climbing
contrast with the safe and inactive aspects of office jobs. However, when the
climbers described the meaning of their sport, they spoke about goals and
challenges, about testing themselves and focusing on the task at hand; they
also noted that mountain climbing requires training, planning, and competition against the environment and one's own limitations. The authors'
emphasis on compensation obscures an obvious subtext. Granting that
mountaineers were looking for the physical risk and excitement they
missed in their employment, they still structured their leisure using worklike concepts such as goals, challenges, self-testing, and planning. The
compensatory risk took place in an ideological context that was completely
consonant with work.[36]

If the compensatory relationship between sedentary work and physically
active leisure overlays unseen ideological associations, then compensatory
explanations become even more complex when they are applied to psychological contrasts, such as the pervasive idea that leisure can provide a sense of
meaning or accomplishment missing in work. This idea is frequently, but
not exclusively, applied to serious leisure involving a high degree of personal
commitment.[37] In fact, several studies suggest that people identify physical
and abstract qualities in their leisure that are missing in their work. These
include a sense of achievement, exercise, creativity, status, competition, and
leadership. It is almost axiomatic to say that individuals focus on those
aspects of leisure that are different from work because it is those elements
that distinguish their leisure from their work. To not focus on them would be
to deny not only the differences but also the core reason for engaging in the
leisure. If the differences are not important, then the person might as well
continue working, which is, of course, exactly what many professionals do
who take their work home with them. Thus to say that leisure is compensatory is an undeniably true but incomplete explanation of the choices that are
made. The more central question is whether leisure participants seek out a
pastime that is structurally different from work, or are they attracted to an
activity because of underlying structural similarities to their work?[38]

Research indicates that when people are aware of a deficit in their work and have an opportunity to compensate for it in leisure, they do so, although those denied such opportunity will replicate work patterns in their spare time. To use David Banner's useful formulation, the compensation is deliberate, but the spillover is psychologically programmed. The conscious and the subconscious do not exclude each other. On the contrary, they coexist and interact in ways we do not fully understand. Our jobs mold us at multiple levels. They teach us physical and social skills, behavior patterns, and value systems that we seek to express beyond the workplace. It is what sociologist Martin Meissner calls "the long arm of the job" and it reaches into every part of our lives. The more people work the more they are formed by their work and the more strongly their work affects their leisure. All work, however, is not the same. White- and blue-collar workers have different work experiences, which result in distinctly different patterns of work-leisure congruence; white-collar workers more often engage in leisure that replicates attitudes and worldviews typical of their vocations.[39]

The straightforward extension of workplace skills into the leisure sphere is the most obvious form of behavioral spillover, which is perhaps why it has received so little attention. It is fairly obvious, however, that people who have developed manual, mental, or social dexterity on the job will often seek pastimes that showcase these same abilities. This is particularly true for skilled workers and professionals in technical fields whose expertise readily lends itself to leisure expression. By exercising their skills in a leisure context, skilled workers emphasize the pleasure that can be derived from worklike activities, which can then become a benchmark that makes the work itself more enjoyable. For example, more than a third of the surgeons interviewed in one study equated the satisfaction they got on the job to the pleasure received when "working with their hands on crafts or carpentry." It was, said one surgeon, "the gratification of taking an extremely difficult problem and making it go."[40]

For this surgeon the similarity between work and hobby transcends the common proficiency with tools to include the mental structure of the process. The surgeon has a sense of himself as a person who physically masters problems, and he expresses his self in both his work and leisure. Sociologist Joseph Harry has referred to these sorts of work-related values as "situational attitudes," and several studies have found them evinced in a variety of vocations. Just as the surgeon sees both his work and leisure as the application of particular skills to the abstract demands of problem solving, so outdoor workers, mechanics, and police officers extend their physical and relational skills into the leisure sphere in ways that reflect a generalized sense of activity appropriate to the values of their callings.[41]

French leisure theorist Joffre Dumazedier observed these relationships and took an important early step toward recognizing ideological spillover in 1967. Dumazedier speculated that for blue-collar workers whose meaningful jobs had been destroyed by industrialism, many forms of leisure, including fishing, gardening, and do-it-yourself activities, were not an escape from work but a return to traditional nonalienated forms of labor. In these leisure-time pseudo-occupations, the participants determine the form, set the pace, and are the sole beneficiaries of the fruits of their labor. However, rather than viewing such productive leisure activities as a return to a golden age of labor, it is perhaps more useful to view them as exercises that serve to ideologically integrate work and leisure by permitting workers to engage in worklike behavior in a noncoercive environment. In the words of another student of blue-collar workers, a hobby such as fishing, "allows the psychological mechanisms of busyness to go on."[42]

Working at leisure gives meaning to both work and leisure. In the first place, it legitimates the work ethic by allowing workers to exercise it freely and thus make it their own, not something forced upon them. Second, it legitimates leisure by filling some part of nonwork time with productive activity, diminishing the bifurcation between work time and leisure time. In this sense hobbies are a homeopathic reaction to the job, that is, a dilute form of work that can cure the alienation caused by industrialism. As such, hobbies actively confirm the ideology of the work ethic by providing a productive way to use leisure, and they passively condemn the work environment by offering a contrast to meaningless jobs.[43]

There are very few studies of ideological spillover, but those that exist point to a tendency to seek forms of work and leisure that express the same kinds of abstract values, such as freedom, creativity, and status. The workers in these studies transferred more than skills or even narrowly defined attitudes from work to leisure; they carried over a holistic sense of self and an outlook on life. Thus spillover leisure appears to take two distinct forms. In the first type, specific physical skills become part of the individual's sense of competence and are exercised in leisure-time activities in which the participant can set the goal and the pace. The second kind of spillover involves broader attitudes, values, or personality traits molded by the job. In these latter cases the leisure behavior may or may not involve analogous skills, but it will express the individual's sense of what is right and good, beliefs that have been affirmed by work. Both kinds of spillover can exist in conjunction with compensatory leisure. Compensatory elements give the leisure participant a sense of relief and change, but spillover elements give the leisure a sense of meaning.[44]

While sociology, anthropology, and psychology contribute a useful tool kit of ideas for studying the past, studying the past provides a way of understanding leisure that is often obscured by conflicting schools of modern interpretation. Specifically, the historical development of hobbies seems to indicate that the ongoing academic debate between those who argue that leisure compensates people for workplace deficits and those who say it replicates employment behavior may be a case of scholars talking past each other. There is strong historical evidence that serious leisure activities, such as hobbies, have done both. Rather than being mutually exclusive, compensation and spillover can coexist because they function at different levels of awareness. Compensation is, for the most part, self-conscious. People know what they do not like at work and choose the opposite in leisure. Spillover is often unintentional. Workers instinctively gravitate to leisure activities that allow them to use skills and attitudes that have brought them success on the job.

The preponderance of contemporary empirical evidence points toward a consistent pattern of skill and ideological spillover of work into leisure, especially for those serious pastimes that involve an investment of psychic energy. While all leisure needs to be viewed in the broader cultural context, some activities are more obviously consonant with the dominant ideology than others. In this sense, hobbies are among the most conservative possible pastimes. The rest of this book explains how, for 150 years, business, government, and education—society's most powerful defenders of the status quo— have promoted this form of productive leisure. All these groups have sensed that hobbies reinforce the dominant ideology, although they also frequently recognized that as leisure, hobbies provided relief from the unpleasant aspects of work. In this way, hobbies disguised their affirmation of capitalism and may have even contained a real element of critical resistance. The very fact that they functioned as "perfect jobs" reminded hobbyists that by contrast their regular jobs were less than perfect, but as "perfect jobs," collecting and handicrafts also confirmed the status quo by reproducing the core values of capitalism. The dual meanings of hobbies rendered them a form of leisure safe from the snares of idleness. Without rejecting the ways that hobbies may have functioned as a form of resistance, a careful analysis of the historical record upholds the conclusions that can be drawn from the social science literature: hobbies developed as a way to integrate the isolated home with the ideology of the workplace.

Section 1

Hobbies as a Category

1 Occupations for Free Time

Hobbies are a contradiction; they take work and turn it into leisure, and take leisure and turn it into work. Like work, hobbies require specialized knowledge and skills to produce a product that has marketplace value (even if there is no thought of selling it). Like leisure, hobbies are entered into voluntarily, and however hard people might work at them, hobbyists are never motivated by the need for income. Hobbies occupy the borderland that is beyond play but not yet employment. More than any other form of recreational activity, hobbies challenge the easy bifurcation of life's activities into work and leisure.

Work and leisure are bound together in a reciprocal relationship that is both obvious and obscure. Obvious, since in a commonsense way leisure is the opposite of work, which is to say that whatever else it may be, leisure is nonwork. Obscure, because by being nonwork leisure is defined in terms of work, cannot exist except in relation to work, and therefore is constantly changing in response to shifts in the work world. Since it is defined in terms of work, leisure is an integral part of the value system that people use to make sense of work. As leisure is not work, so work is not leisure, and what people think about each will affect what they think about the other. Since each category exists only in relation to its opposite, they are necessarily part of the same mental landscape.

There is, in other words, an ideology that people use to make sense of their activities and they engage in an ongoing process of adjusting that ideology to fit changing behavior and of adjusting behavior, where they can, to keep it consistent with the ideology. Since industrialism produced the greatest change in the nature of work in modern times, it also produced the greatest change in the nature of leisure. The relatively seamless preindustrial world of work and leisure, home and job was irrevocably rent by the rise of the office and factory. The value system that had grown up around mercantile capitalism still made sense in the new world of industrial capitalism but much less in the now separate world of the home. Just as there could be no significant leisure at work, there could be no significant work at home.

Industrialism bifurcated life into separate spheres of work and leisure: the space in which they were done, the time in which they were done, and the reasons for doing them.

The disentangling of work and leisure led not only to the commodification of labor but also to the commodification of time. By purchasing the workers' time rather than their skills, industrial employers endowed time with new meaning. Leisure came to represent freedom because it took place in time separate from work, and time in an industrial world could be used for either work or leisure (excluding the minimum necessary for individual maintenance). For this reason, industrial capitalism sharpened the West's ambivalent feelings about leisure. It was only when human labor could be put to productive use all the time (not just in certain seasons of the year) that time could be "wasted" and thus become a major social concern. In this sense, premodern people may have worked less than modern people, but they did not have more leisure because their work time was dictated by natural rhythms that precluded their working all the time even if they wanted to. The commodification of time was the ultimate step in removing the worker from an integrated life. While on the job, industrial workers may create periods of playful nonwork or take pleasure in the work task itself, but they can no longer experience the organic coherence of the preindustrial style of life.[1]

Leisure in the Victorian Household

Farmers and agricultural laborers, who were the majority of workers until approximately 1880, escaped the combined tyranny of clock and site, but the increasing centralization of both manufacturing and service industries meant that all classes of urban workers began to lead segmented lives with work very much the dominant segment. Packaging work in contiguous blocks of time initially led employers to increase the hours of work because workers were paid by the day not by the hour, so that extra hours of work cost the employer nothing. However even when the method of compensation switched to hourly pay or piece rate, the benefits of running machinery continuously put pressure on employers to maximize the daily hours of work. The low point in leisure time was reached around 1850 when, as economist Juliet Schor notes, working hours constituted "the most prodigious work effort in the entire history of humankind."[2]

Inevitably workers rebelled and demanded that the contiguous blocks of work time be reduced—and by the same token that the contiguous blocks of leisure time become larger. By demanding eight-hour days, five-day weeks, and multiweek vacations, organized workers succeeded in reducing the number of hours worked per year. Although the specific figures vary somewhat, most scholars agree that the approximate number of hours worked fell from sixty-five hours per week in 1850 to forty during the depression. They increased during World War II, but retreated to forty from 1948 to 1969, when they began to rise again.[3]

Employers resisted the rise in leisure time not only because it increased the cost of labor but also because it violated their sense of ideological propriety. Large blocks of unoccupied time were an affront to the core value of industrial capitalism, the work ethic. Leisure time was dangerous time because when they were not on the job both manager and factory hand were away from the controls imposed by a centralized workplace. Unlike preindustrial leisure that occurred in shorter periods and in close proximity to the workplace (which continued to be the model for women who worked at home), industrial leisure took place away from work under circumstances that precluded the imminent return to the job. Therefore the new leisure, even more than the old, was perceived as akin to idleness. Industrial workers were not taking a brief respite from which they would return refreshed to the job; they were off work with nothing to do.

As distinct nonwork time increased through the late nineteenth and twentieth centuries a variety of leisure activities arose to fill the empty hours. Taverns became saloons and proliferated in cities. Participatory sports and active leisure expanded but not nearly as fast as the passive consumption of commercially produced spectacle. Professional sports, live theater and vaudeville, amusement parks, movies, and mass-produced magazines catered to the tastes of people who had previously had much less discretionary income and time. With the exception of pulp reading, almost all the new leisure took place not only away from business but also away from the home. Even though women were eventually courted by theaters and amusement parks, most of these new recreations targeted men and thereby divided the family, which was supposed to stay at home, safely isolated from the aggressive culture of the workplace.

Advocates of increased leisure were acutely sensitive to the dangers of free time and couched their arguments in terms that stressed familial benefits not public recreational opportunities. In 1855 Catharine Beecher typically urged fathers to "subtract time from their business, to spend at home, in reading with their wives and children, and in domestic amusements which at once refresh and improve."[4] Hers was carefully hedged advice. While Beecher suggested that middle-class men work less, it was so they could spend time nurturing their children's love of home and family not enjoying leisure as an end in itself. Most commentators assumed that free time spent at home was superior to that spent at public amusements, and prescriptive literature favored useful domestic occupations as appropriate leisure activity.

Consequently, the Victorian period became a golden age for household entertainment. Amateur music making was ubiquitous, and when the family tired of playing and singing, there were parlor games. The rise of hobbies was part of this upwelling of home-based leisure, and it worked to reintegrate the divided spheres of work and leisure. When paid labor left the house, it had taken its values with it. While the house could and did become a major center for consumption, the ideals that attended production and finance had little application in the domestic life of women, children, and resting men. On one level, Victorians responded to this bifurcated world by creating a separate ideology for the home, the widely noted "cult of domesticity." The values that governed the workplace were, for the most part, left at the factory gate—but not entirely. One could avoid the temptations of idleness not only by working at work but also by working at home. "We were taught in boyhood's days never to whittle without making something," recalled a crafts author in 1877. "There is no need of idle hours," he explained, and argued that his hobby was not "mere work" because it was also art. When the Chicago *Current* recommended a series of productive pastimes in 1884 that men should pursue "earnestly and arduously," the paper assured its readers that despite the work-like effort that went into them, "they will prove recreative nevertheless."[5]

Victorian advice on home-based leisure struggled to reconcile several contradictions. The ideological imperative for useful pastimes conflicted with the general assumption that leisure should be recuperative while not distracting participants from work. Consequently people were counseled to pursue a useful hobby—but not too intensely. A painter who gave up his artistic career for a more practical business vocation in an 1880 short story used his leisure time for "reading and varied studies." He avoided painting out of fear that "if he plunged into the old work, it would prove too intoxicating for him." In the same spirit, the popular Victorian women's magazine *Godey's Lady's Book* (known as *Godey's*) cautioned those involved in mental work to avoid chess since it involved too much intellectual effort. Instead, suggested the magazine, such men should engage in "some lighter game, combining, if possible, physical and mental amusements." Leisure, in other words, functioned as a counterbalance that should not itself be unduly stimulating. "An innocent hobby" could act as "a safety-valve for the escape of nervous excitement," recommended the *New York Times*. Leisure was best when it was useful, that is, productive, but it was still supposed to create a relaxed state of mind.[6]

Until the early 1880s the term "hobby" was used to designate any preoccupation. "The Hobbies," a song published in Massachusetts in 1798, calls fees the hobbies of lawyers, husbands the hobbies of scolds, and women the hobbies of sailors. Samuel Johnson's 1823 dictionary defines hobby simply as "the person, thing, or occupation that pleases one most," and that definition remained virtually unaltered for the next sixty years. The term was usually, but not always, applied to nonwork activity, and was often cast in negative terms. The reverend B. F. Tefft warned his fellow Methodists in 1846 that "the Christian should have no religious hobby," that is, no unorthodox personal beliefs or practices.[7]

This vague and sometimes censorious use of the term "hobby" covered a multitude of activities. "We shall find a hobby in each house," noted *Arthur's Home Magazine* in 1856, and among the possibilities listed were homes, gardens, clothes, sports, politics, and church. This particular piece focused on the wood-turning hobby of a bank clerk, a classic form of handicrafts. Yet, in the same period and in the same magazine, an article about house cleaning was titled "Mrs. Niel's Hobby." There was no implication that Mrs. Niel's activity was leisure; on the contrary, "hobby" referred to her obsessive concern with keeping the house clean. The potential suitor of an inveterate needleworker in an 1867 short story referred to his own hobbies as "Character, Principle, Individuality," but did not apply the term to his female friend's fancywork.[8]

Intensity of involvement, which defined hobbies, was the source of both their benefits and dangers. On the positive side, it was clear that people engaged in hobbies were safe from the temptations of idleness. "Man, in the absence of some special object to engage his thoughts is almost sure to get into mischief," cautioned *Godey's* in 1876, therefore, "it is better for him to push ahead on any sort of hobby that is not vicious, than to lounge through life in a slipshod, desultory way, without definite aim or purpose." On the negative side, a deep involvement could become an unhealthy preoccupation. Women's hair, Negro rights, inventions, gymnastics, the Constitution, temperance, children, auctions, the parlor, religion, and Turkish baths were all, at one time or another, called hobbies in the mid-nineteenth century. Their common denominator was that each could become a fixation. The *Catholic World* reminded its readers in 1876 that "every enthusiasm, from the most exalted moral self-forgetfulness to the most ludicrous extravagance, has been in turn called folly and ridiculed as a hobby."[9]

Since the term hobby originally applied to an Irish pony, discussions of hobbies were frequently couched in equestrian metaphors, and the problem, to paraphrase Thoreau, was not so much that people rode hobbies but that the hobbies might ride them.[10] At the very least, such a preoccupation could be a drain on funds. "A hobby is apt to be an expensive palfrey," cautioned *Godey's.* "It sometimes costs piles of money to groom and run him, and he

seldom wins purses and cups enough to pay for his keep and entrance fees."
At their worst hobbyists could become compulsive, driven, and monomania-
cal. Obsessive behavior might be forgiven at work, but hobbies were not
work, and people ridiculed hobbyists who pursued them as if they were.
Thus an eccentric amateur scientist who suffered from the delusion that he
would someday become famous was said to be "riding his hobby to the
death." By the same token, people took offense when their deeply held pursuits were dismissed as hobbies. "Can't get away from your hobby, I see," a
friend said to a temperance advocate, "Well, every one must have something
to ride, if only for amusement." The teetotaler demurred, insisting that his
concerns were not a hobby, they were serious.[11]

As late as 1876 hobbies could still imply obsessive preoccupation, and parents were cautioned that they were inappropriate for the young. Adults, however, were another matter. "Every man should have a hobby," advised a collecting expert in 1871; "it does not take him away from home; it diverts him,"
and keeps his regular work on track. In the same vein, an article on stamp
collecting benignly defined hobbies as "a favorite pastime out of the ordinary
routine of daily occupation."[12] A transition was underway. The older broadly
negative meaning of hobbies was being replaced by a newer more circum-
scribed and often more benign usage. Indeed, the same author who warned
against hobbies for young people, noted that "hobbies and collections are
somehow related; at least the mind is used to coupling them together."[13] The
change in usage was not deliberate, and it went unrecognized at the time.
Nevertheless, after 1885 or so hobbies were generally understood to be
wholesome activities, most of which involved solitary productive activity that
took place at home.[14]

Historian Stephen Constantine has argued that the English middle class
began to engage in gardening during this period because gardening, often
referred to as a hobby, was a productive use of leisure time. He also believes
that the authorities, recognizing the conservative implications of gardening,
aggressively and successfully promoted it among the working class. Constantine's point is equally valid for collecting and crafts in the United States. It
would be a mistake, however, to view hobbies as a deliberately imposed
instrument of false consciousness. Rather, they were an unplanned, unorga-
nized, and undirected accommodation to industrial capitalism by all classes.
The historical emergence of hobbies as a socially recognized category of
leisure was an organic process in which people spontaneously changed the
meaning of the word in order to reflect new realities. Popular language was
evolving what linguists call a "basic level" category.[15]

Linguists hold that people begin to organize their understanding of the
world with basic level categories at which things "are perceived holistically

as a single gestalt." Basic level categories are neither so broad that they contain too many different types of items nor so narrow that they exclude functionally similar items. Thus "chair" would be a basic level category, narrower than "furniture" but broader than "throne" or "rocking chair." "Superordinate" categories are comprised of related basic level things and "subordinate" categories are the components of the basic level classification. This linguistic approach to classification runs counter to the scientific taxonomic paradigm in two ways. First, it starts in the middle rather than at the bottom. While the end result is still a system ascending from the specific to the general, it grows not from the essential component but from the most typical. Second, since the conceptual system originates with the basic level category, it makes no pretense at being anything but culturally derived.[16]

The linguistic classification system assumes that people who share a culture will instinctively recognize a basic level category in relation to the greater and lesser parts of the organizational scheme. Thus, people in the late Victorian Era began to use to term "hobby" to refer to a group of leisure activities. Leisure was the superordinate category, and specific hobbies such as collecting and handicrafts were the subordinates. In the linguistic model, items are included in a basic category according to how closely they approximate a prototype, but an item does not have to contain all the elements of the prototype to be a member of the set.[17] Assuming that collecting and handicrafts are prototypical hobbies, then a hobby involves voluntarily working alone at home with a few relatively simple tools to make an object (which in the case of collectors is the collection itself) that has economic value. Gardening clearly fits the pattern, and other pastimes such as playing a musical instrument or raising pets come very close. The point here is not to exclude certain activities but to describe how collecting and crafts became central to the popular understanding of hobbies as a leisure category.

This linguistic mutation in the meaning of the word "hobbies" was dramatically demonstrated in two essays published in Charles Dickens's magazine *All the Year Round*. In 1865 a piece entitled "Hobby Horses" leaned heavily on the equestrian metaphor to poke gentle fun at a vast variety of adult activities. It discussed hobbies as generally harmless but often oddball recreations, which included re-creating historic battles with toy soldiers; fishing; fox hunting; collecting art, china, and bric-a-brac; nature study; gardening; friendship; moral philosophy; physiology, phrenology, and all the other 'ologies; sickness and health; self-pity; homeopathy; social reform; religious fanaticism; punning; talking about dreams; and giving parties. It was a random list with a strong sense that most hobbyists were eccentric at best and in many cases positively daft.[18]

Twenty-five years later, in 1890, the magazine published a second essay, "About Hobbies," which abandoned both the equestrian metaphor and the condescending tone of the first article. No longer were hobbies the obsessions of amusing cranks; they were now highly desirable "antidotes to ennui" that would forestall the mischief that Satan found for idle hands. The journal had become such a supporter that it advocated "a central office for the recommendation and distribution of hobbies to all kinds of people." In the meantime, it took upon itself to promote hobbies as beneficial for children, working adults, and retired people. Although it mentioned sports, cards, nature study, and gardening as useful hobbies, most of the article focused on collecting. Collecting, it argued, was the best example of this new category of leisure, and the best example of collecting was philately. Both the general philosophy and specific language of the second article would appear time and again over the next forty years in other writers' commentaries on leisure. The wide adoption on both sides of the Atlantic of this position makes "About Hobbies" the de facto manifesto of the new home leisure.[19]

The older notion that a hobby could be anything that caught one's fancy had changed to a new one in which hobbies were leisure and therefore in explicit opposition to work. Thus after 1880 there was a growing sense of hobbies as not only as a source of interest for hobbyists but also as a compensatory form of relief. Work was hard and could hurt workers; hobbies were fun and could heal them. "Before you fill the boiler and build the fire, provide the safety-valve," cautioned the Boston Youth's Companion in 1879. Yet at the same time, observers began to recognize that what they called "light home occupations" also had deep similarities to "heavy" workplace occupations.[20]

For hobbies to function both as an extension of and a buffer to industrialism, they had to perform two roles. As an extension they needed to reproduce the beliefs and behaviors necessary for the continuation of capitalism. As a buffer they needed to give participants a sense of relief and perhaps empowerment in the face of centralized production. Not only were these two functions far from incompatible, they were virtually two sides of the same coin. Since the hobby was done at home in free time, it was under the complete control of the hobbyist. It was, in other words, a reembracing of preindustrial labor, a re-creation of the world of the yeoman, artisan, and independent merchant. By the same token, because it was the re-creation of a thoroughly capitalist world, the underlying values of that world—from market economics to the work ethic—were colonizing the home. As disguised affirmation, hobbies were a Trojan horse that brought the ideology of the factory and office into the parlor.

The Meaning of Hobbies

The full extent of the hobby infiltration is unclear. A recent survey of leisure activity, for instance, claims that people spend more time on their hobbies than any other form of active leisure; yet it also quotes findings that only 12 percent of men and an improbable zero percent of women have hobbies.[21] Such contradictions are legion in studies of hobbies because there is no common definition of what constitutes a hobby and no agreed upon way to measure frequency of participation. Bearing this imprecision in mind, the proportion of adults with hobbies seems to be in the neighborhood of 10 to 15 percent.[22] Crafts are twice as popular as collecting, and there is some indication that blue-collar workers prefer house and car care, while white-collar workers are more attracted to collecting and handicrafts.[23] The significance of such a small percentage of participants is further reduced by the fact that hobbies involve only about 2 percent of people's free time, with do-it-yourself taking up another 4 to 5 percent. Television, in contrast, occupies a full third.[24]

Nevertheless, even if only a relatively few people spend only a small portion of their free time pursuing hobbies, these pastimes are fraught with importance well beyond that usually attributed to leisure activity. In this sense, hobbies are like sex, the amount of time spent thinking about the activity is probably a better measure of its importance than the amount of time spent doing it, and even those who are not doing it wish they could or think they should. Hobbies do not just happen; they are planned, executed, and reviewed. They involve a great deal of intellectual energy and therefore have more significant psychological meaning than do casual activities that may actually take up more of the individual's free time. This assessment is affirmed by sociologist John R. Kelly, whose own research found people ranking hobbies low on a list of preferences, but who nevertheless concluded that adults most valued "expressive activity in which they have invested considerable effort in gaining competence." While they "may spend more time watching television," he concludes, "they define themselves by and invest themselves in more intense engagement."[25]

In a series of articles written during World War II, psychiatrist William Menninger suggested some of the ways that adult hobbies might in fact be linked to sex. Menninger asserted that hobbies differ from other forms of leisure because they demand an investment of interest and energy, and they differ from work because they are pursued for intrinsic rather than extrinsic rewards. One of those intrinsic rewards, he continued, is the legitimate subliminal expression of infantile sexual pleasures suppressed by parents and society. At the same time, however, he found that the ardent pursuit of a

hobby often produces feelings of guilt because the hobby is symbolic masturbation or defecation, and the guilt is augmented by the shame of indulging
in what most adults consider a child's pastime.[26]

Without the support of any empirical or even clinical evidence, Menninger burdened hobbies with a heavy load of psychological freight. His suggestion that crafts are an adult extension of the creative pleasure of defecation, while collecting represents the sense of power that comes with bowel
control, remains speculative. Whether or not the source of their satisfaction
is psychosexual, studies have shown that people consider hobbies the most
meaningful form of leisure. This is what Mihaly Csikszentmihayli discovered when he asked people to list the sources of their enjoyable experiences.
The one thing they found more meaningful than hobbies was work, which
Menninger and most other impressionistic observers thought lacked the
intrinsic satisfaction of hobbies.[27]

Scholars have assumed that hobbies could be satisfying in the same way
that work should be but never seem to imagine that work could be satisfying
in the same way hobbies are. In 1961 sociologist Georges Friedmann and
leisure historian Roger Caillois both argued that the average worker in industrial society turned to craft hobbies for, in Friedmann's words, the "sense of
achievement denied to him in his work," and more recent leisure experts
have hewed to the same line. There is, however, a fair amount of evidence
that hobbies are more than compensatory; they can also act in concert with
jobs to provide a familiar worklike set of satisfactions in the nonwork areas of
life.[28] Several studies show that, with the exception of pay, people give
remarkably similar reasons for working and for taking part in active pastimes
like hobbies. In fact, one study has actually demonstrated that professional
woodworkers find more satisfaction on the job than amateur woodworkers
get from their hobby.[29] Far from compensating for workplace deficits, the
evidence indicates that hobbies and other forms of active leisure are, for all
psychological intents and purposes, voluntary and unpaid forms of work
both before and after retirement.[30]

The parallel psychological meanings of work and hobbies derive, in no
small part, from the similar ideological underpinnings of both activities. Both
work and hobbies involve the focused application of skill and knowledge
toward the production of a specific product. Ideally in work, but always in hobbies, that product is the source of pride in a job well done, which is the essence
of the work ethic. Hobbyists may bask in the approbation of others, but what
satisfies them most is their personal sense of accomplishment. This is the point
missed by left-wing critics who have argued that workers use "hobbies and
crafts" to distance themselves from consumerized and professionalized leisure.
Distancing themselves from consumerism (which may be true for handi-

crafters but is certainly not true for collectors) is not the same thing as distancing themselves from the "capitalist mode of production," because the ideological superstructure of capitalism embraces much more territory than the commercial marketplace. Hobbyists may be rejecting some elements of the job and the marketplace, but they are affirming the principles of the system itself.[31]

In his historical study of the postwar hot rod subculture H. F. Moorhouse describes how these hobbyists expressed the work ethic at leisure rather than on the job. His conclusion is somewhat ambiguous. He sees how the hot-rodders are able to appropriate the dominant capitalist ideology for their own use and pleasure, but at the same time Moorhouse recognizes that by doing this, hot-rodders are making the work ethic "more psychologically meaningful for the bulk of the population." The tension in Moorhouse's conclusion is the essential tension of hobbies; they are at once the reappropriation of the job by workers and the colonization of the workers' leisure by the ideology of the job.[32]

Hobbyists, including Moorhouse's hot-rodders, often fantasize that they will someday earn a living from their hobbies, imagining that hobbies are the perfect job. Hobbies do indeed seem to embody almost every positive element of work except human interaction. Workers enjoy jobs that allow them to create something, permit them to use a skill, give them the opportunity to work wholeheartedly, and let them exercise initiative and responsibility. Conversely, hobbies have none of the elements that people dislike most about their jobs. Hobbies do not involve doing repetitive work, limit the worker to making only a small part of the whole, require doing useless tasks, create a sense of insecurity, or involve close supervision. Of all the scholars who have written about leisure, only historian Ross McKibbin seems to have recognized this pattern of hobbies as a form of perfect work and understood its implications. In an article that demolishes the fragile argument that hobbies undermine British workers' commitment to their jobs, McKibbin demonstrates how hobbies mirror work. He shows that even where the workers' hobbies did not involve specific work skills, they "had all the characteristics of work: indeed that is their fundamental quality."[33]

From their beginnings in the nineteenth century, American hobbies had a symbiotic relationship with capitalism. As leisure activities they had to disguise their affirmation of the work ethic in the clothing of pleasure and, for the most part, segregate it from the taint of commercialism. Nevertheless, even when it appeared to be critical of the industrial process, the hobbies discourse built ideological consensus. For example, writing in 1955, hobby author Horace Coon acknowledged the stultifying nature of contemporary work and wrote that hobbies could "be an escape from your boring job." Calling crafters "rebels" against industrialism, Coon described the dehuman-

izing impact of modern work and urged his readers to act in small but explicitly critical ways to free their souls from hegemonic industrialism. His critical
comments, however, must be viewed in the context of the book as a whole, a
book entitled *Hobbies for Pleasure and Profit*. Coon revels in consumption,
suggesting that a woman who feels her husband is spending too much
money on his hobby could "always retaliate by a much more extravagant
hobby of her own," and he goes into great detail describing how hobbyists
could turn their avocations into money-making propositions. The final result
is a book whose criticisms of industrialism are more than balanced by its celebration of market capitalism and the work ethic.[34]

The inherently conservative meaning of hobbies struck a particularly
responsive chord in the cold war environment of the 1950s. In 1954 commentator Russell Kirk, one of the leading intellectuals of the postwar right,
believed that in order to reduce "the menace of the proletariat," working
people should pursue leisure that upheld traditional family values. Although
he did not call his ideal workers' leisure "hobbies," he did say that "one form
of leisure is to turn from our accustomed work to another sort of work, equally productive, but less monotonous and employing individual skills." Kirk
the right-wing ideologue advocated virtually the same vision as Coon the
hobby expert. For both of them hobbies were compensatory work, but congruent ideology.[35]

From the perspective of the hobbyists, who are seldom aware of the ideological implications of their pastimes, hobbies can be either an extension of a
favorable work experience into the leisure sphere or compensation for a
sense of unfulfilled needs. Separate surveys of workers and managers have
concluded that workers perceive their avocations as "compensatory-recuper-
ative," but managers see their hobbies as closely related to their work. There
is little sense of what workers actually mean when they tell investigators that
their hobbies are or are not related to their work, but Simon Bronner's
impressionistic analysis of wooden chain-carvers may help put the social science studies into a more human framework. "Unlike the factory, it was the
task, not the time, that mattered here," observed one of Bronner's infor-
mants. Bronner saw his chain-carvers as "old men crafting meaning," and the
meaning they were crafting was the meaning of work. Many of them were
professional woodworkers whose factory jobs deprived them of the opportunity to complete an entire piece, but at their work benches, free of the time
clock, they could choose their own projects and work unsupervised from
beginning to end. "Chain carving is hard work, all right," says one, "but it is
work you want to do."[36]

If a hobby is a job you want to do, then it would seem natural for hobbyists
to dream about turning their pastimes into their jobs. The long tradition of

published advice on how people can transform their avocations into vocations is explored in some detail later in the book. There is, however, also a certain amount of tension between the hobby as leisure and the hobby as work. Hobbies may reinforce the culture of capitalism, but they are not work because they are voluntary and not normally a source of income. Once collectors subordinate the meaning or beauty of an object to its value, or crafters begin to measure their projects by the price they will fetch when sold, they compromise their hobbies' purity by making them too businesslike and undermining the sense of freedom that distinguishes work from leisure. Unlike passive leisure, which has no end-product, productive leisure generates the seeds of its own destruction. To remain hobbies, productive pastimes must produce items of value whose value remains secondary.

The "Threat of Leisure": Hobbies in the New Century

Despite the dramatic growth of commercial entertainment after the turn of the century, active home-based leisure flourished. Hobbies were able to grow in part because they were not competing with other forms of leisure for a fixed block of free time. The expansion of leisure activities was the direct result of a decrease in work hours. Although the United States lagged behind other industrial nations in the pace of workweek reductions, typical industrial workers had eight hours more free time per week in 1920 than they did in 1900. The Saturday half-holiday, which would not become widespread until the 1920s, made its first appearance in the Progressive Era, limited at first to the summertime, when it enabled workers to participate in newly popular outdoor activities.[37]

The broadening of leisure options was accompanied by a narrowing in the definition of "hobby," which increasingly took on the modern meaning of a productive pastime. Most commonly, collecting was considered a hobby, although handicrafts, gardening, animal raising, and music were also frequently mentioned. The older sense of the word, that is, as some 'ism or 'ology ridden compulsively by a "crank," made only an occasional appearance in the Progressive Era, such as the watch collector who defensively claimed in 1913 that his activity could "never be regarded as a mere idle hobby" since it was educational.[38]

Mocking hobbyists would prove to be a perennial amusement for outsiders, but after 1900 hobbyists began to poke fun at themselves. Thus the joking became gentler and took on an undercurrent of pride, tempered by a certain self-consciousness. Essayist Arthur C. Benson defended his own musical and artistic hobbies and others' craft hobbies by saying, "there is no reason why one should not amuse oneself by doing a thing badly, if one cannot do it better." The claim that productive hobbies were a good thing even if the end results were something less than expert could be made because people were beginning to realize that the public attitude toward hobbies had become generally positive. "Hobbyists, who may have nourished a sneaking suspicion that they were objects of mild raillery to the rest of mankind," noted the first annual report of the Hobby Club in 1912, "suddenly realized, through the columns of the newspapers, that their fads were regarded benevolently by their fellow citizens, were even endowed with a certain element of civic righteousness."[39]

The Hobby Club, which published this self-congratulatory assessment of the public mood, was a short-lived organization composed of approximately forty-five upper-class New Yorkers who were engaging in something of a self-fulfilling prophecy. First they generated news coverage of their events, then they used those stories as proof of their own acceptance as hobbyists. Like other men's clubs of the period, the Hobby Club was a purely social organization, but in this case formed around the common interest in collecting. Members met together at occasional formal dinners where one of their number would give a talk on his avocation. In 1912 the *New York Times* gave the Hobby Club an illustrated two-page spread in its magazine, headlined "Well-Known Men with Hobbies—And Proud of It." The headline reflected the undercurrent of ambivalence toward hobbies, but this type of spotlight gave them the legitimacy that could only be bestowed by financiers, corporate presidents, and Columbia University professors.[40]

William Schnitzer, the treasurer of the club and a Wall Street broker, felt the country was in the grip of a "hobby mania," and it was his belief that every boy and every businessman should have a hobby. He had less hope for women, noting that "it is a singular fact that comparatively few women have been successful hobby riders."[41] However, Schnitzer overestimated the extent of the "mania" just as he underestimated the participation of women. Hobbies do not appear to have made any significant inroads among blue-collar workers whose leisure time was still quite limited nor, from the limited data available, among the population in general.[42] And his dismissal of women ignores the central role they had in the development of craft hobbies from at least the 1830s. Nevertheless by equating the growth of hobbies with the growth of collecting among businessmen, Schnitzer was indicating how hobbies were becoming socially approved by those who controlled cultural definitions of appropriateness.

To become an appropriate pastime for businessmen, hobbies had to shed the old stigma of eccentricity and define themselves as consonant with the attitudes and behavior expected of middle-class men. In doing so, the hobbyists of the Progressive Era constructed an argument that yoked, however uncomfortably, the apparently contradictory concepts of leisure and the work ethic. As leisure, hobbies were perceived as compensatory and supposed to provide surcease from work. "What, you have no hobby?" asked the author of a 1913 article. "In these days of drive, push and worry how can you recreate yourself without the aid of a hobby?" These rhetorical questions were based on the premise that hobbies literally restored energy depleted by the job.[43]

Similar arguments could, of course, be made for almost any pastime, so hobby advocates needed to distinguish between the revitalization that came from pursuing hobbies and that which might proceed from some other leisure activity. Reading the newspaper and attending the theater were no match for hobbies in reducing stress because thoughts of business could easily intrude in those activities, explained a 1909 editorial in the *Independent*, but since a hobby was an activity that really interested its participant, the mind focused on it exclusively. This refocusing of interests, explained the writer, "takes the blood away from that portion of the brain usually occupied with business cares and by transferring it to another set of cells gives the first set a thorough opportunity to rest." In other words, the hobby was an active rather than passive form of leisure that helped overcome "morbid subjectivism," the root cause of neurasthenia and psychasthenia brought on by "the sufferer thinking far too much about himself, and particularly about his mental states."[44]

These arguments, couched in the psychotherapeutic language of the period, recognized that hobbies involved mental activity that was analogous to work but directed to a different end.[45] The hobby was refreshing not so much because it was different from all work but because it was different from the hobbyist's usual work. In fact, hobbies might even be remunerative, and in any case would always be enriching and uplifting.[46] It was true, admitted a hobby enthusiast in 1907, that hobbies deprived one of leisure, but those whom the gods hate, he reminded his readers "lead a long life of leisure."[47] The new role of hobbies as work-leisure was neatly captured by the Scottish commentator Samuel Smiles who observed, "Hobbies evoke industry of a certain kind and at least provide agreeable occupation. . . . Even a routine mechanical employment is felt to be a relief by minds acting under high pressure: it is an intermission of labour— a rest—a relaxation, the pleasure consisting in the work itself rather than in the result."[48]

Once recognized, the worklike elements of hobbies contributed to their continued inroads among businessmen in the 1920s. Prohibition America liked to think of itself as a land of sobriety, hard work, and the free market, and without the influence of alcohol, warned one hobby advocate, Americans would look at their meaningless leisure and "know unmistakably when we are bored." Sober, and perhaps bored, businessmen were told they needed to supplement their regular work with leisure that provided balance without dissipation. "The businessman who after a hard day at his office steps into a small, well appointed carpenter shop at the rear of his house and wields a hammer and saw is maintaining a healthful equilibrium," explained a health magazine. Hobbies "are recommended by psychiatrists as a cure for nerves, or whatever it is that makes the patient bored with himself and the world," noted the *New York Times,* and a commercial journal said that "one good hobby is worth several pounds of pills so far as the health of the business man is concerned."[49]

Another group of hobby advocates argued that since factory jobs had stripped work of importance, leisure was the only way to produce meaning in life. They relocated the job-centered work ethic to free time and announced a new "leisure ethic" that made self-fulfilling leisure an end in itself rather than a balance to work.[50] Perhaps more damningly, there were those who cast doubt on the meaningfulness of white-collar and even entrepreneurial work. The author of the first general hobby book for adults said that "the average day at business . . . lacks the mental stimulus to keep a man going full speed ahead." But, he concluded, all traces of ennui disappear when the man enters his workshop. Promoters of the leisure ethic, however, were a minority, and even liberal commentators reminded their readers that the qualities promoted by leisure "cannot take the place of others, equally desirable, which can be secured through work activities alone."[51]

Work was still too central to most people's lives to take a backseat to leisure as a central life interest, even if it did seem less meaningful than it once was. Hobbies were one way to bridge the gap by bringing the ideology of work into the area of leisure. It was probably true, observed Henry Ford, "that the Devil finds work for idle hands to do" but, he said that men who spent their weekends working constructively around the house returned to work refreshed not dissipated. Hobby advocates like Ford recognized that productive leisure not only balanced work but reinforced it. A hobby, explained a letter writer to the *New York Times,* could be "idealistic and spiritual" in the sense that it allowed the participant to enjoy the sense of accomplishment that came from making progress toward a self-determined goal. Advising against studying at home after work, an author in *Harper's* recommended instead that lawyers and businessmen "learn to do one modest little hobby well" and thus become an expert "without losing the amateur touch." Hobbies were the happy medium that acknowledged the work ethic without corrupting free time with real work like studying.[52]

The 1920s also witnessed a widespread use of "celebrity endorsements" to promote hobbies. Continuing the pattern begun by the society gentlemen of the Hobby Club before World War I, well-known businessmen and heads of state were used as examples to help scrub away any residue of disrepute that may have clung to people who invested too much time, energy, and money in something other than their work. Not everybody got the word, however, and some people continued to be embarrassed about their hobbies, likening them, in the words of sociologists Robert and Helen Lynd, to "an heretical opinion, something to be kept concealed from the eyes of the world."[53]

Where the burghers of Muncie may have seen heresy, others saw opportunity. Once they had achieved a position of social acceptability, hobbies could be used not only to relieve work but to enhance it. "It was not altogether by accident that, nearly a dozen years ago, I formulated a policy of encouraging every executive in our headquarters plant and branch offices to have hobbies," wrote one sales manager in 1926, and he then went on to explain how hobbies helped his salesmen build rapport with customers. Using hobbies to further business interests breached the wall between work and leisure, and advocates insisted it was "ethical to play on a prospects' hobbies" only if the discussion were genuine not manipulative. When salesmen could assume hobbies as an icebreaker with clients, fears of heresy do not seem very realistic. Hobbies had entered the mainstream.[54]

As early as 1883 the New York Times had approvingly reprinted a piece from the London Saturday Review that promoted collecting as a suitable occupation for retired businessmen. The article said collecting was a better pastime than playing cards because the hobbyist had to develop technical expertise and meet the challenge of completing sets. Problems of retirement would not become a major subject in the hobby literature until the depression, but an article in Nation's Business in 1928 acknowledged that the best retirement was not one in which the retiree did nothing but one in which he took on a new career. The writer suggested public service or hobbies, each of which was perceived to be a functional substitute for a job and essential to keeping the retired businessman mentally and physically sound. Otherwise he was in danger of emulating former president Calvin Coolidge who could think of nothing to do but sit in his basement and watch the handyman shovel coal into the furnace.[55]

The nascent discussion of retirement leisure reflected a broad concern with "the worthy use of leisure" that informed almost all analyses of free-time activities in the 1920s. Although the National Education Association had been concerned with "education for avocation" as early as 1908, it coined this particular catchphrase in 1918 when it drew up "seven cardinal principles of secondary education." Point number five, "education for the worthy use of leisure," became a dominant theme in educational thinking.[56] Shorter work hours prompted Columbia University president Nicholas Murray Butler to declare: "Guidance in the right use of leisure is vastly more important than what is now called vocational guidance." "Why waste time teaching city children how to work," asked Arthur Pound, a widely quoted prophet of automation and increased leisure, "when their chief need is to know how to live?" The caveat about Satan's use of idle hands was amplified in the 1920s by an ongoing criticism of commercial leisure. The world was a dangerous place to the child who was simply allowed to "run along and play." "The street playground with its menace of traffic, the vacant lot with its often vicious companionships, the roadhouse or the promiscuous movie or the news stand, with their degrading influences" were all waiting to snare the idle child.[57]

Since, as one educator stated in 1924, "all the wrong and sin of the world is committed during our leisure time," and conversely, "nobody gets into trouble when he is at work," the challenge was to keep children busy. Short of a return to child labor, the solution to keeping children (and adults) properly busy was to teach them to use their leisure time constructively. The police chief of San Francisco attributed an outbreak of crime in 1922 to the "wrong use of leisure." A growing chorus of leisure reformers called not only for more parks and playgrounds but also for more hobbies as a mischief-free use of spare time. "In education the hobby is encouraged where once it was frowned upon as a waste of time," reported the *New York Times*.[58] Fifty years earlier hobbies had been widely opposed as a waste of time; now they had become a panacea for the ills of the new leisure. Hobbies would serve a threefold purpose: "the useful employment of an otherwise idle hour, the acquisition of valuable knowledge, and [the creation] of worthwhile friendships."[59] Every discipline from the liberal arts and the sciences to the vocationally oriented manual arts began to justify itself as a source for hobbies in adult life. By the end of the decade industrial arts teachers began to complain that the rigorous technical skills once taught in general shop had degenerated into "recreational activity."[60]

Educators' preoccupation with the "threat of leisure" inevitably spread to the general population and proved to be a powerful tonic for the growth and acceptance of adult hobbies. It was their duty, said one earnest Texas educator, to teach "the working class to use their increased hours of leisure time in the betterment of home conditions and in the development of higher social and moral impulses." Pointing to the growing observance of a half-holiday on Saturday and the widespread adoption of a forty-four-hour week (and calls for a seven-hour day and five-day week) a teacher-preparation textbook of the period told its readers that modern industrial work was soul-deadening and that workers could only be restored through "the proper use of the leisure which our intense devotion to productive activities has made possible."[61]

Despite the effort of educators, hobbies did not achieve complete acceptance in the 1920s because the term itself remained ambiguous. It was used both as a synonym for any leisure activity and as a label for a particular kind of productive, solitary pastime.[62] Broad-based surveys, in which respondents were asked to name their hobbies, elicited a wide spectrum of leisure activities including literally hundreds of different pastimes and interests; passive leisure was always more popular than productive. "All hobbies are not laudable ones, nor beneficial to their possessors," wrote the *Literary Digest* in 1923, "vicious habits, wasteful pastimes, harmful indulgence, criminal wickedness may become a veritable hobby and lead to ultimate disaster." The article concluded that adults should make a hobby of their work and reserve leisure hobbies until retirement.[63]

"Here's a Job You Can't Lose"

The end of prosperity and the sudden, unwanted increase in forced leisure during the depression elevated hobbies from a casual pastime to a broadly sanctioned category of leisure activity crucial for preserving the work ethic in the absence of work. The economic crisis crystallized the concept of hobbies and produced a movement that gave them universal legitimacy as part of the repertoire of good-things-to-do when there was nothing to do. Municipalities, schools, and businesses sponsored hobby clubs. The media, including newspapers, magazines, and radio, regularly focused on hobby activity, and several national organizations emerged to promote them for children and adults.

Lacking even a crude estimate of hobby participation before the depression, we cannot compare participation in the 1930s with previous decades, and it is possible that the great hobby craze of the 1930s was as much the product of media hype as an actual reflection of changes in leisure activity. However, one extensive survey of five thousand people taken in 1933 found a sharp, self-reported increase in less-expensive home-based activities and a corresponding decrease in commercial leisure. In addition, this survey found that more people increased their participation in hobbies than in any other household leisure, and they did so more intensively. Despite the reported increase in hobby participation, however, this survey and others discovered that hobbies fell far down on both children's and adults' lists of favorite pastimes. Most people said they wanted physical pleasure and relaxation, not the mental stimulation of hobbies.[64] Although the figures are rough, it would appear that somewhere between 10 and 15 percent of children and adults regularly participated in hobbies (solitary, home-centered, productive leisure) during the depression, a figure that closely approximates estimates for more recent years.[65]

Rather than reflecting a broad shift in leisure patterns, the increased use of the term "hobby" was part of a strategy that bestowed authoritative approval on collecting and crafts. While "hobby" may have emerged as a natural linguistic category in the late nineteenth century, in the depression it became a fully developed ideological construct used to distinguish between "good" and "bad" pastimes. A group of self-professed experts surfaced in academia and journalism to join the hobbyists themselves in a lively discussion over the definition and merits of hobbies. The development of an animated discourse on hobbies by a group of people with a shared set of perceptions established a value-loaded vocabulary with which to frame the discussion. Even when they disagreed among themselves as to specific interpretations, their use of common themes delineated the parameters of the issues and thus helped to fix the meaning and privileged status of the category if not its contents.

In the depression, both the unemployed and the underemployed needed to fill the hours that had once been devoted to work. Those who had full-time jobs may not have had more leisure, but they usually had less money, so they too needed ways to occupy nonwork hours that were less expensive than commercial entertainment. The specter of idleness, problematic in the best of times, became deeply threatening in a nation with bonus marchers, Hoovervilles, and radical politics. Hobbies provided a safe way to absorb the sudden surplus of leisure, and hobby advocates made relatively little distinction between their advice to children and adults. They recommended hobbies for both groups for the same reasons—they allowed participants to use a variety of skills and attitudes that would make them more fulfilled and more productive. Like the work-relief programs favored by the New Deal, hobbies preserved and developed job skills and prowork values outside the private-sector job market. Even organized labor, which had spent the previous fifty years seeking to replace work time with free time, abandoned the drive for shorter hours in the 1930s in return for acknowledgment of the right to work. In this context, hobbies served to confirm the legitimacy of a worldview that favored more work over more leisure by turning leisure into work.[66]

"Here's a Job You Can't Lose," promised the title of a popular magazine article in 1933. The title declares that a hobby is a job and that, in some unstated way, a person engaging in a hobby is in fact working. Yet because the hobby is a job that can't be lost, it is a unique form of work from which the least desirable elements of a real job have been banished. In the depression, ironically, one of the worst aspects of work was the possibility that it might disappear. Hobbies avoided that risk and afforded their riders (the equestrian metaphor was still in wide use during the 1930s) the promise not of eternal leisure but of eternal work.[67]

Some hobby advocates in the depression recognized the intermediate quality of their pastimes and sought to define them as a golden mean that embodied the benefits of both work and play but without the drawbacks of either. Free of the compulsion of work, yet safe from the temptations of idleness, hobbies allowed one to be righteously leisured. Austen Fox Riggs, one of many new leisure experts, said a hobby "resembles work, but its spirit is that of play; it stands half-way, one might say, between the two and it may be the offspring of either." Rather than an offspring of either work or play, it is more accurate to view hobbies as an offspring of both; a child of two fathers who inherited the freedom of play and the discipline of work. A "true hobby" has to contrast with the hobbyist's regular work, has to produce some recognizable product, and has to have an element of difficulty, explained a physician at the end of the decade.[68] This sense that a hobby had to be compensatory and productive at the same time meant that when asked their hobbies people were more likely than in the past to single out productive leisure.[69]

Like a grim joke, experts had set up the "problem of leisure" during the prosperity of the 1920s only to have the punch line delivered by the Great Depression. Enforced leisure turned out to be the unwanted culmination of half a century of pressure for shorter working hours. "Yesterday belonged to the worker. Tomorrow belongs to the wise users of leisure," announced Columbia University professor Walter B. Pitkin, whose best-selling book *Life Begins at Forty* was a protracted attack on the work ethic. Even before Franklin D. Roosevelt took office, the *New York Times* was calling for increased cultivation of handicraft hobbies, to absorb free time.[70]

The establishment of the National Recovery Administration and its maximum-hour codes only increased the sense that leisure forced on people by the depression would be codified by the state. Leisure experts saw the universal five-day week as a precursor to a shorter work day, with the most optimistic predicting five- and even four-hour days.[71] The depression was a manifestation of overproduction, in the view of many contemporaries, and the solution lay not in increased consumption but in reduced production through less work. Unemployment was thus the unfortunately rude introduction to a new world of mandatory leisure for which people had to develop constructive pastimes.[72]

Leisure was deadly, cautioned the experts. So long as he was employed, wrote one white-collar worker, he was fine, but he had never learned to do anything productive in his nonwork hours. Now that he was out of work, he complained, "My life is dull and drab and always on the verge of becoming vicious. Would to God I had something creative to do." In a sense, the unemployed were prematurely retired, a fact not lost on the leisure experts who promoted hobbies as the best way to prepare for part-time leisure while working and for full-time leisure when unemployed or retired. The alternative to hobbies was death warned a widow whose husband had been driven to take his own life by the monotony of retirement.[73]

Hobbies became a compensatory panacea for both the mental and physical stresses of modern life. The National Safety Council advocated them as a way for people to retain their "mental balance" when "life or business seems to be going wrong."[74] Beset by pressure on the job and off, people needed a safety valve to save them from the otherwise inevitable explosion:

> A Professor wise with searching eyes
> And nine letters aft his name
> Says worldly toilers are but boilers
> In life's scheme-heating game.
> Our daily "pep" on which we step
> He likens unto steam
> But says this sage, we shun the gauge
> That shows a bursting seam.
> A pop-off spout, he's figured out,
> A thing unique and nobby,
> · Thru which to vent our steam unspent—
> He calls that thing a hobby.[75]

The proper pastime, doctors assured their patients, would make them "more mellow and contented" and thus lower their blood pressure. "Hobbies are better than pills for many ills of mind and body" wrote a physician, and they were touted as cures for "undesirable complexes," for "neurasthenia and psychasthenia," and for "Americanitis," the functional and nervous disorders that came with the intense American lifestyle. According to Dr. Josephine L. Rathbone of Columbia University, hobbies could cure the dread "curse of the age," residual neuromuscular hypertension that occurred when "fatigue toxins" accumulated faster than they could be slept off.[76]

Since most hobby activities were by their very nature solitary pursuits, one hobby advocate recommended them as a way to help isolated people forget their loneliness.[77] Nevertheless, proponents liked to stress that hobbyists would also be making themselves more interesting and joining a preexisting circle of friends when they took up their new avocations. Both arguments had their origins in the therapeutic model of hobbies. "Do you know a person who is so bubbling over with enthusiasm that everyone around him catches the kindling spark?" asked one article: "Have you noticed how interesting he is, how easily he attracts friends? Would you like to know his secret?" The secret, of course, was a hobby.[78]

In addition to touting hobbies as a cure for depression and loneliness, hobby advocates of the 1930s were unanimous in their contention that hobbies were an antidote for juvenile delinquency—and for adult crime as well. "You will rarely find a man who has a hobby getting into trouble," observed *Hobbies* magazine. In fact, it said that crime and gangsterism "could be reduced to a minimum and probably wiped out entirely, were every boy encouraged early in life to pursue some kind of hobby." A survey taken by the Welfare Council of New York in 1935 concluded that 80 percent of boys and 90 percent of girls had unsatisfactory leisure lives.[79] Continuing a theme begun in the 1920s, teachers sought to educate their students in the "worthy use of leisure time," arguing that it was not Latin and higher mathematics that children needed to learn; these had become the "real frills." "The essentials today," explained a professor of education, "are music, health education, industrial and fine arts and training in wholesome recreation, for these are demanded by the age of leisure."[80] Unable to find either full or part-time work, young people without hobbies spent their time "hanging around the corner drugstore, the pool-hall, and worse places."[81] With hobbies, however, the child would learn the rewards of hard work and the value of neatness, would develop special knowledge, and would keep out of mischief.[82]

It is difficult to know how widely schools heeded the call for teaching hobbies, although evidence indicates there was certainly an increased awareness of the issue. Schools and colleges opened "hobby halls," sponsored hobby clubs and shows, and included hobbies in their shop and home economics courses.[83] The support of the school system for hobby education was paralleled by an increasing focus on hobbies in various scouting organizations that sought to involve entire communities in the hobby movement.[84]

The drive to promote hobbies spread beyond the educational establishment to include municipal governments, business, and several private organizations, the combination of which gave the new movement unassailable legitimacy. The National Recreation and Playground Association, which had added "Recreation" to its name in 1911, dropped "Playground" in 1930 and as the National Recreation Association of America took an active role in advocating for adults the same kinds of leisure opportunities it had previously promoted for children. One of its basic principles held that "every man should be encouraged to find one or more hobbies." Under the association's influence some municipalities began to sponsor hobby clubs and other recreational activities for adults. In 1933, 430 cities had handicraft programs, more than any other form of recreation except sports. Municipal recreation commissions, school systems, and sometimes the federal government sponsored classes and clubs at "lighted schoolhouses" that adults could attend in the evening.[85]

While there were exceptions, businessmen in the 1930s were much less eager to show off their hobbies than they had been in the 1920s.[86] Rather than trumpeting their own activities, businessmen preferred to sponsor company hobby shows and encourage hobbies in company publications. Business hobby shows were often competitive in nature with the firm offering prizes for the best entries in various divisions.[87] Arguing that manual skill hobbies made better and more productive workers, the president of a Massachusetts steel company proposed the "intensive development and encouragement of home talent by putting it on a competitive basis." He suggested that company contests could be expanded to local, regional, and finally national hobby competitions.[88] Businessmen, like government and education leaders, understood the benign nature of hobbies and served as directors of hobby shows in the same way they might for any other noncontroversial charitable activity.[89]

Despite the misgivings of Otto C. Lightner, the conservative publisher who founded *Hobbies* magazine in 1931 and did not think unemployed people had earned the right to have hobbies, the unemployed were a major focus of hobby advocacy groups. The National Homeworkshop [sic] Guild was started in 1934 in Rockford, Illinois, as a local effort to have unemployed men with home workshops make toys for charitable organizations. By the end of 1935 more than 150 clubs throughout the country had joined the guild, although its original purpose had been set aside and it became an organization for home improvement hobbyists.[90] The most prominent of the depression-era hobby organizations was the Leisure League of America. Formed in 1934 in New York City, the Leisure League announced its intention to publish pamphlets on more than seven hundred different hobbies that would enable people to "bring out their submerged powers."[91] Lamenting the increase in passive leisure, the league sought to promote the productive use of the "new leisure" by flooding the country with its hobby publications, which included Earnest Elmo Calkins's influential introduction to a wide variety of pastimes *The Care and Feeding of Hobby Horses*.[92]

The Leisure League's publicity campaign contributed to a swelling host of prohobby advocacy groups that, by the end of the decade, had expanded from schools and businesses to the mass media and a hobby book club.[93] In 1934 William Randolph Hearst Jr. personally oversaw the establishment of a "hobby department" in his *New York American*. The editor of the new section, Marion Cole, subsequently became the host of a radio network show on which she interviewed famous people about their hobbies.[94] Despite Cole and an earlier radio show on NBC in 1933, the undisputed star of the genre was Dave Elman.[95] Out of work, deeply in debt, and grieving over the recent death of a young son, Elman began to search for a hobby that would divert him from his troubles and save his sanity. He became so intrigued with the hobbies he studied that he imagined a radio show to "tell the troubled world how to dispel gloom by making better use of its spare time." He sold his car, borrowed money, and launched his program, *Hobby Lobby*, in 1937 without commercial support. After a rocky start, he signed on a sponsor and by 1939 was reaching 155 stations with a weekly program that was still broadcasting in 1947.[96] Elman's emphasis on hobbies that could help other people may be the reason why social service and volunteerism appeared so frequently on hobby lists of the late 1930s and early 1940s.[97]

The broad-based depression-era support for the movement grew out of a widely shared sense that hobbies, particularly handicrafts and collecting, embodied socially sanctioned values. Nevertheless, the leisure aspects of hobbies still seemed to conflict with their worklike qualities and the instinctive assumption that leisure should balance work led to advice that emphasized the difference between the two. "A person engaged in any task needs relaxation of an opposite nature to the occupation for which he earns his bread and butter," suggested *Hobbies* magazine, while the *New York Times* proposed that "dramatists push wheel hoes, and farmers push fountain pens." Yet even as they were giving this compensatory advice, writers were suggesting that hobbies developed skills that made people more effective workers.[98]

The contradictory tone of the hobby literature arose because the hobby professionals were confused by the worklike nature of hobbies. Ultimately they surrendered to the obvious; the solution to meaningless work on the job is to find meaningful work off the job, explained the National Education Association. Men and women who learned hobbies, it reported, were given a new lease on life.[99] Hobbies were held out as the contemporary expression of that mythical golden age when all workers were independent artisans who took pride in the products of their labor. The final product might not be perfect, but the producer could be proud, hold it up and say, "An ill-favored thing, but mine own—and not so bad at that."[100]

Children and adults alike were told that their hobbies could train them for a job, no small promise in a time of unemployment.[101] "Parents need have no fear of hobbies as a waste of time," counseled a professional engineer, because children will only pursue those hobbies they enjoy and "it may be the start and guide to a successful life work." A survey of more than three hundred Iowa high school students found that 44 percent of them thought their hobbies might turn out to be their occupation.[102] While such expectations may have been unrealistic, they did indicate that, at least in the teenagers' minds, hobbies and jobs could be fused. Newspapers and magazines promoted the same belief by running profiles of people who had turned their hobbies into vocations. Show your wife this article about hobbies that grew into businesses "when she complains that you are wasting too much time with your stamp collection," suggested *Nation's Business*, the magazine of the U.S. Chamber of Commerce. "If you are bored with your job but in no position to tell the chief what you think of him and walk out," advised the magazine, "look around for a hobby [and] you may be able to grow an honorarium in your own back yard."[103]

Relatively few people were in a position to turn their hobbies into jobs, but many more could turn their job skills into hobbies. Hobby shows indicate, for example, that both architects and blue-collar workers were likely to have pastimes that were closely related to their regular jobs.[104] And the one genuinely systematic survey that compared hobbies and work concluded that men who held "constructional" jobs (i.e., made things with their hands) were more than twice as likely as men who held nonconstructional jobs to have constructional hobbies.[105] As an escape to the perfect job, hobbies could reproduce the skills as well as the attitudes and values of the workplace and provide an unexpected answer to the question posed in the old hobo and IWW song, "How the hell can I work when there's no work to do?"

Productive Leisure and Prosperity

Having no work to do was the least of anybody's problem during the full employment brought on by the war. Free time was at a premium and productive leisure surrendered to war production. Hobbyists conceded the preeminence of the war effort and fought a half-hearted rearguard action, reminding people that even in wartime it was okay to take some time out for leisure.[106] The decrease in free time may have reduced the necessity for and participation in hobbies, but the great hobby crusade of the 1930s had done its job too well for the fad to disappear with the end of the depression. The fundamentally conservative message of hobbies—set goals and work hard to achieve them—remained valid in both the civilian and military environment. Members of the armed forces appear to have received minimum support for their hobbies during the early part of the war, but toward the end, as discussed in more detail later, both the army and navy supported hobby programs for armed forces personnel and used them as part of their rehabilitation programs for wounded servicemen.[107]

Prewar dreams of a four-hour day in a four-day week vanished with postwar prosperity. Whatever their other differences, organized labor, the business community, and the federal government had forged a de facto alliance that rejected the surplus production explanation for the depression and instead focused on the need for more consumption, which called for more work and higher wages.[108] If the prewar predictions of vast new leisure were unfulfilled, the 1950s were nevertheless a decade of stable eight-hour days and five-day weeks, up roughly five hours a week from the depression low, but down about the same amount from the highest war years.[109] One could still find anachronistic voices predicting brave new worlds of leisure brought on by technological efficiency and worrying about the constructive use of leisure time, but the general tone of the 1950s was one of acceptance of the forty-hour week.[110]

Buoyed by military support at the end of the war and meshing easily with the conservative cultural environment of the 1950s, hobbies retained their image as socially acceptable leisure. Popular hobby writers sought to encourage participation with wild claims that two-thirds to three-quarters of teenagers had hobbies, or that virtually every adult had at least one and probably several hobbies. Scholarly interest in hobbies, however, decreased so we lack any systematic surveys of participation. *Popular Science* magazine declared photography, stamps, music, model making, and home workshops the five most popular hobbies in 1941. The magazine supplied neither definitions nor statistics to back up its assertion, so the claim is essentially another piece of anecdotal evidence for the centrality of collecting and crafts among those who pursued hobbies.[111]

Although the number of hobbyists does not appear to have changed after the war, there does seem to have been a further refinement of the meaning of the term in popular usage. While sometimes the word was used casually to refer to almost any pastime generally recognized as "wholesome," collecting and handicrafts continued to be the activities most commonly referred to as hobbies.[112] There is no reason to think that fewer people were participating in socially sanctioned pastimes such as athletics, amateur groups, and music, but by consensus usage, these activities were consigned to categories other than hobbies.[113] With the possible exception of gardening, the leisure category of hobbies had been functionally distilled to collecting and handicrafts.[114]

As prototypical hobbies, collecting and handicrafts were indisputably solitary pastimes. Hobbyists could, and to some extent did, form clubs where they could trade techniques or objects, but the primary activity took place at home. Even grandiose claims for hobbies' benefits to the family, community, and nation were predicated on their benefits to the individual.[115] Prime among these benefits was the compensatory balance hobbies provided to the stresses of everyday life. Psychiatrist William Menninger said that "successful professional men," should "set aside their cyclotrons, computations and compositions to take up manual work after hours." Academics agreed with practitioners that the yin and yang balance between work and hobbies had to be maintained. A University of Southern California sociologist wrote: "Quiet hobbies are needed for people living or working in noisy surroundings; outdoor hobbies for people working indoors, and vice versa; active hobbies for desk workers; lively hobbies for people working at routine tasks; varied-activity hobbies for people living a dull and monotonous life; headwork hobbies for people engaged in handwork, and vice versa." The American Medical Association recommended that men take up hobbies for high blood pressure and other ills caused by the daily pressures of business, and physicians prescribed them for menopausal women as a way to stay busy and young. The belief in the medical efficacy of hobbies was so deeply embedded that an otherwise objective academic observer could baldly state in 1952 that "a lack of hobbies is a very dangerous sign, and a man who loses all his hobbies should see a doctor about it."[116]

Hobbyists themselves accepted the idea that their avocations counterbalanced the stresses of work because they involved neither compulsion nor extrinsic review. An informal survey of sixty-four chemical industry executives in 1954, for example, found that while sixty of them either gardened or engaged in handicrafts, the executives perceived their pastimes in terms of contrast. As indoor white-collar workers, they explained that they sought outdoor and manual hobbies. Similarly, typical respondents in a 1952 survey said they enjoyed their hobbies: "because I'm not obligated in any way; I can start and stop when I wish," and "No responsibilities to worry about. Spontaneous interest in hobbies."[117]

Like fishing and golf, both of which can also be very serious forms of leisure, hobbies produced a genre of commentary that poked fun at the pastime, or more commonly poked fun at the hobbyist. In order to justify worklike leisure, hobby humor subverts its "workness" by denigrating the product. The humor applies business principles to leisure and finds that hobbies do not meet minimum marketplace standards; they lose money. Such self-deprecation affirms the underlying ideology. The hobbyists laugh at themselves because they do work that does not pay, but that is okay since hobbies are not really work and are not supposed to turn a profit. The difference between a hobby and work noted one hobbyist was that the outcome of the hobby had no profound consequences: "No reputation is at stake, the security of your livelihood is not threatened. You are not competing with anyone. Not even your dignity need suffer." He gave the example of a man who buys a thousand-dollar machinist's lathe and ultimately makes a fifteen-cent part to fix the washing machine: "Completely triumphant, you cover up the lathe, leave the mess to clean up later and leap youthfully up the stairs to announce that the washer is running again." Then, he said, "you announce, 'that machine just paid for itself again!' "[118]

The hobby humorists were defensively proud of their foolish activity, but nonhobbyists were defensively guilty about their lack of it. "Yoo-Hoo, Satan, I'm Idle," wrote Hildegarde Dolson in the *New Yorker* as she recounted a miserable visit to a friend who dragooned her into helping refinish a piece of furniture. The only consequence for her was a bad back that left her "burning up with occupational therapy." She admitted, however, that she suffered from a "guilt complex" because her leisure activities were reading mystery novels and returning old beer bottles. She understood that nonproductive pastimes did not carry much weight on the scales of ideology.[119]

Returning old beer bottles presumed emptying new ones, and in a social environment preoccupied with the issue of juvenile delinquency, hobbies retained a prophylactic reputation. Hobbies kept young people off the streets where they hung around unproductively "whistling at girls and making senseless remarks to passers-by."[120] Educators' rhetorical and programmatic dedication to hobbies remained undiminished in the postwar period, but students still preferred passive to active leisure, and sports to either collecting or crafts.[121] A study of high schoolers' participation in hobbies in Houston in 1948 found that only a third of the girls and less than a quarter of the boys had a hobby—and those elevated figures were reached only by including reading, dancing, and some sports in the definition of hobbies.[122] Undeterred by, or unaware of, their low level of success, hobby advocates maintained a steady stream of articles from the war through the early 1950s promising children an apparently unwanted opportunity for creativity and promising parents that the youngster with a hobby "would not be 'aimless' or 'underfoot' " since "hobbies teach and discipline." With that sort of agenda it is a wonder that any children at all took up hobbies.[123]

Schools and colleges continued previous commitments to hobbies by sponsoring clubs and courses, but the most highly visible expression of public support for the hobby movement was the large number of hobby shows that often featured both children and adults.[124] The phenomenon began in the depression, rose sharply in the early 1940s, and then tailed off in the mid-1950s. The tensions caused first by the depression and then by the war were collective in nature, and the interest in exhibits may have grown from hobbyists' desire for confirmation that their solitary pastimes were appropriate behavior. Sponsored by schools, businesses, and private organizations, hobby shows were a form of public display that linked the hermitic world of hobbyists with the outside world that legitimated it. Between 1941 and 1954 in New York City alone, large hobby shows were held under the auspices of the New York Stock Exchange, the Union League Club, various government agencies, the New York Real Estate Board, and the New York Medical College. Two organizations that have left little trace of themselves, the Hobby Guild of America and the American Hobby Federation, appear to have been instrumental in the hobby show movement. The Hobby Federation began sponsoring shows in New York City in 1935 and continued at least through 1954, and the Hobby Guild actively participated in other shows during the period and tried, without apparent success, to create a national federation of hobby clubs in 1952.[125]

The matter-of-fact language of published reports on hobby shows attests to their wide acceptance, although there was an understandable tendency to focus on the odd, rare, and extreme as a way to liven up the stories. Journalists seemed particularly fond of models constructed from multiple thousands of toothpicks. Ultimately, however, the hobby shows were demonstrations of the prosaic rather than the exotic. The great and the small created and collected not the great but the small. Executives and janitors, students and housewives showed off their own photographs and drawings, not fine art. They displayed collections of cigar bands, old bottles, and campaign buttons, not rare porcelains. Prizes were usually awarded for the best presentations, so the shows represented the competitive aspect of the business world, but at the same time they could dissolve the normal structure of authority so that the powerless could triumph over the powerful. It was reported that all employees of the Solar Aircraft Company in San Diego "enjoyed the joke" when for four years amateurs won photography awards and members of the firm's photography department "did not even rate an honorable mention." Nor did they care "if the supervisor's or the department head's wife happens to lose out to the stock clerk's daughter." With this *carnivale*-like quality hobby shows allowed an inversion of social roles that confirmed both the democratic and meritocratic elements of American society. If the clerk's daughter had sewn a better quilt than the manager's wife and won a prize for it, then by implication the manager had won his job over the clerk because he too was better at it. And where the genuinely amateur beat the professionals at their own game, a much rarer and more problematic situation, it was perceived as "a joke."[126]

Retirees played a prominent role in both the corporate sponsored shows and in a parallel series of senior citizen hobby shows.[127] The New York City welfare department featured displays of retired people who took part in a hobby program to give them "some activity to replace the loss of the work day." "I go to work to keep away from work," said one retired model builder at a New York hobby show. In a world where there were no established activities for older people, specialists latched onto the one form of work that even retired people could do.[128] "There can be no better bulwark against the tedium of nonemployment than the pursuit of some interest," advised the *Saturday Review* in a column advocating adult education for the elderly. The author suggested that the amateur scholar might "not only draw delight from his study . . . but may indeed well add to the sum of knowledge." By proposing that the retired hobbyist could add to the sum of knowledge, the author was stressing that retirement hobbies were not merely like work; they were work, with a measurable and valuable product. The product became a commodity when the elderly were told that they could use their hobbies to earn supplemental income. *Better Homes and Gardens* ran a story urging people to develop a hobby while they were working that would allow them to continue working after they retired. Such a hobby will make you feel and look younger, promised the article, "and if your pension will be small, a craft may augment your income."[129]

The campaign to involve retired people does not seem to have created a very large body of elderly hobbyists. A study in Indiana done at the end of the 1950s concluded that seniors (like working people and children) preferred passive and social activities to hobbies. Aside from gardening, which was done by 40 percent of the small sample, constructive hobbies (sewing and woodworking) were done by less than a quarter, while less than 10 percent collected. Nevertheless, their lack of hobbies was a major source of frustration for many retired people who did not do hobbies but wished they did.[130]

For Fun and Profit

Before World War II most hobbyists and hobby advocates had tiptoed around the awkward truth at the heart of their pastime: since hobbies were worklike, under the right circumstances they could become work and cease to be leisure. To be sure, there was a long tradition of amateur collectors drifting over into dealing and hard-pressed home crafters trying to sell their products, but it was only after 1945 that the control of hobbies passed from amateur to professional hands. The conceptual awkwardness of the past evaporated as the center of hobby activity shifted from education, government, and employee recreation programs to companies that made hobby supplies and hobby shops that sold them for a profit.[131] There were still large, even expanding, numbers of crafters who worked in the traditional mode, but what made the postwar hobby world new was the intense commodification of the process. As companies increasingly made profits from hobbyists, hobbyists felt increasingly comfortable making profits from their hobbies.[132]

The obvious commercial connections of postwar hobbies created an environment in which contemporary commentators could do what they had never done before, acknowledge the ways in which hobbies duplicated work. In 1953 *Harper's Magazine* editor Eric Larrabee was the first to point out that hobbies had developed in the nineteenth century in response to industrialism. The Protestant ethic required that leisure be both "pointless and productive. It had to be pointless," he said, "or it would be indistinguishable from work; it had to be productive," he continued, "or it would be bad for one's character." The two forms of hobbies that had most closely met these criteria in the past, he noted, were crafts, which developed manual skills, and collecting, which recapitulated the process of scientific discovery. In the postwar world, Larrabee argued, the "time-killing" quality had disappeared from hobbies and they had turned "deadly earnest." Some, like do-it-yourself, had a practical purpose; others, like golf and tennis, were extremely expensive. In either case they were too serious to be taken lightly and had more in common with work than with play.[133]

Larrabee described, as had no one before him, the common roots of work and hobbies. Prior to the 1950s, commentators often warned hobbyists away from exploiting their pastimes for monetary gain for fear of corrupting the leisure. After the war, however, the cat was out of the bag, and nobody seemed too terribly upset. "Let's not kid ourselves," wrote a management consultant in 1954, "the purposeful hobby is work; and it results from a viewpoint that considers this work worth-while." It was fine, she said, for work skills to spill over into hobbies, and she saw no problem if hobbies happened to make money so long as that was not their sole purpose.[134] Compensatory rhetoric fell away, and a new generation of hobbyists embraced work-leisure congruence right down to the retail level. *Profitable Hobbies* magazine, first published in 1945, marked the emergence of this new subset of hobbyists. Earlier concerns about the insidious influence of profit evaporated so completely that the phrase "for fun and profit" became an advertising cliché. This new group of hobbyists deemphasized freedom, the very essence of leisure, in favor of enjoyment, which became the major criterion by which hobbies were judged.[135] The participant was still a hobbyist first and an entrepreneur second, but there was no conflict between the roles. As one *Profitable Hobbies* author explained, "The person who has hit on something that makes money invariably finds life interesting, and the person who has found something that makes life interesting can usually figure out a way to profit financially from it."[136]

Hobbyists did not have to make money from their pastime, but publications such as *Profitable Hobbies Handbook* and *Handicraft Hobbies for Profit* increasingly focused on doing so.[137] While the activity might continue to be enjoyable, it stretched the definition of leisure to apply it to conduct that qualified as a business expense and that was not done voluntarily but because "you must now deliver the goods." Yet writers quite deliberately incorporated new "professional hobbyists" into their definitions. "If these people are doing such work for pleasure then you can call the activity a hobby," said one in 1955. The journalists and hobby apologists who were trying to have their cake and eat it too (or at least trying to sell the cake to a gullible public) wrote about making money from a hobby, but those who took their advice seriously quickly recognized the contradiction. A model railroad enthusiast who stopped assembling kits and started manufacturing them was extremely successful. However, he said, the decision to go commercial "was when a perfectly good hobby went out of the window. We soon found that there is no such thing as a hobby-business. To pay off, it has to be your business and the other fellow's hobby."[138]

The contradiction could be minimized by making the hobby-business part-time. If the hobbyist were not dependent on the income then some element of freedom could be maintained. Postwar magazines were full of display and classified advertisements that jumbled together hobbies and supplemental at-home businesses. The advertisements promised "big money in spare time," "make extra money, learn at home," and often let the hobbyist choose the objective: "make candles for a profitable business or fascinating hobby," "photography for pleasure or profit," "sewing for pleasure and profit." And, of course, there were ads for craft supplies and collectors items; those that did not mention profits ran side by side with those that did. The target audience of these magazines appears to have been working-class and lower-middle-class people who were either very unhappy with their regular jobs or who felt their living standard being eroded by inflation.[139]

Mixed in with the hobby-oriented advertisements were offers for making money at home by stuffing and addressing envelopes, raising hamsters, or breeding worms, all of which indicate that at one end of the spectrum the idea of hobbies blended smoothly into the shady world of schemes designed to enrich the promoters much more than the participants. Indeed, the classified advertising section of *Profitable Hobbies* magazine, optimistically called "The Hitching Post, Where Hobby Riders Tie Up for Profits," not only ran ads for people selling supplies and ideas to hobbyists but also ads from hobbyists who apparently could find no other outlet for their dolls, shell jewelry, pin cushions, paperweights, and recipes than to try to sell them to other hobbyists.[140]

The unrealistic expectation that hobbyists would buy each others' homemade wares indicates a much more limited market for hobby products than implied by the for-fun-and-profit literature. In fact, relatively few people actually tried to make a living from their hobbies. When *Profitable Hobbies* polled its readers in 1950, it discovered that only twenty-two of the fifteen hundred people who responded to the questionnaire pursued their hobbies exclusively for profit. Roughly two-thirds hoped to make some money, but a third had no such expectations even though they were subscribers to a magazine whose purpose was to promote money-making hobbies. The idea of profiting from hobbies seems to have appealed mostly to older, homebound people who wanted to earn a little "pin money." Although the percentage of people who made money from their hobbies was a minority, the popularity of the concept of profitable hobbies points to a further blurring of the line between work and hobbies in the postwar world.[141]

Earning income from a hobby confirmed its worklike nature and, by extension, the compatibility of hobbies with the dominant capitalist ethos. Those hobbyists who began to make their living from selling their products, from supplying other hobbyists with raw materials, or from teaching hobby skills to novices had obviously moved beyond even the most indulgent definition of hobbies as leisure. Nevertheless, some hobbyists clung to illusions of lost innocence, such as those in a Milwaukee hobby club who barred professional dealers, even while admitting as "bona fide hobbyist[s]" members who sold their wares.[142]

The commercial hobby culture of the 1950s may have made hobbies less pure in some sense by openly tying them to the marketplace, but hobbies had always traveled on a track parallel to work. The postwar environment gave participants the option to acknowledge the deeper meaning of productive leisure by making amateurs more of a mass market and making the products of leisure more obvious commodities. Functionally, the role of hobbies did not change. They remained a way to learn and confirm the basic work and market values of the dominant ideology; there was just a little less disguise in disguised affirmation.

Section 2

Collecting

2   The Collectible Object

The systematic accumulation of man-made objects simply to possess them may be as old as human manufacturing itself. Recent archeological evidence indicates that people made and collected nonfunctional stone tool points as early as 4000 B.C.[1] If this is the case, stone-age cultures had their own Franklin Mints producing objects that mimicked functional items but had no purpose other than to be collected. Assuming they were made to be bought, sold, and traded in the Neolithic marketplace, these precursors of the Christmas plate mark the beginning of the parallel collecting economy. Unlike the mainstream economy, which deals with goods and services that have some use in everyday life, the collectors' economy deals with items whose functionality, if any, is irrelevant.

There are, roughly speaking, three kinds of collections: primary collections made up of objects made to be collected such as baseball cards; secondary collections composed of items originally made for other purposes such as postage stamps; and intangible collections in which the things collected are not actually possessed such as bird-watchers' "life lists." Primary and secondary collectors, who are my main focus here, operate in the parallel economy. Intangible collectors do not. They may waste money, but they will never make any.[2] The parallel economy of object collecting mimics the real economy in both ideology and practice. Primary collectibles, which exist only in the parallel economy, are isolated from the world of everyday production and use. Unlike other collected objects, which have a life cycle discussed below, primary collectibles move directly from the maker's hands to the collector's, and from there into the hobby market where they are bought, sold, and traded. Most collectibles, however, are secondary, that is they pass through one or more intermediate stages before they become collector commodities. This is true for art, antiques, manuscripts and books, coins, stamps, autograph documents, and most dramatically for common manufactured items from buttons to beer cans. Even collectors of natural objects such as seashells produce collectibles by the act of collecting. Whether they collect primary or secondary, natural or manufactured goods, hobbyists often create a leisure world every bit as ruthless as the business marketplace.[3]

The Origins of Hobby Collecting

The collecting of art, antiques, coins, and books all have ancient origins, and the first U.S. collectors were either rich people emulating European patterns of conspicuous consumption or amateur scholars interested in objects for reasons divorced from their economic value. In both cases, their motivation and methods of collecting place them outside the hobby category in the sense I am using it here.[4]

The man who probably deserves the title of "first American hobby collector," William Buell Sprague, was in many ways a transitional figure between earlier amateur scholar collectors and later market-oriented hobbyists. A Presbyterian minister who eventually held pulpits in Connecticut, Massachusetts, and New York, Sprague collected autographs strictly as a hobby. In 1816, when he was twenty-one years old, Sprague met George Washington's nephew, Bushrod, who allowed him to take fifteen hundred of the first president's letters from the family papers. With that running start, Sprague launched his career as the original American autograph collector.[5]

Initially, with only one collector, there was no American autograph market. Sprague did not have to buy documents because nobody else wanted them. Most people seem to have been more than willing to provide this man of the cloth with samples of their own signatures and those of others for free. Starting about 1830, additional collectors began to appear, and eventually quite an active market developed for both historical and contemporary autographs. The number of dead people's autographs was fixed, and they could be obtained only through sale or trade. Cooperative live people, however, could produce a constant supply, and all through the second half of the nineteenth century "autographmaniacs" followed Sprague's lead by besieging important people for their signatures on letters and in autograph albums. Sprague, who amassed close to a hundred thousand autographs in his lifetime, never bought a single item and sold only two. He did, however, trade liberally with other collectors. Mostly he traded one document for another, but one fellow clergyman "glad to be rid of this bundle of old letters," procured a guest sermon in return. Thus Sprague participated in a barter market even as he eschewed cash transactions.[6]

Because he was the pioneer autograph collector there were no established structures for arranging U.S. autographs, and it fell to Sprague to develop a method for ordering his new hobby. It was he who conceived the autograph collectors' holy grail, the "signer set" of all the names on the Declaration of Independence, as well as signature sets of all the generals of the American Revolution, the framers of the Constitution, and so on for various other combinations of early American figures. Unlike primary collectibles, which are often deliberately created in sets, and many manufactured secondary collectibles, such as stamps and coins, which fall into obvious groupings, autograph sets require a greater leap of imagination on the part of the collector, and Sprague's approach set the pattern for future generations of collectors.[7]

Sprague's career as a collector embodies a number of themes that mark the collecting hobby as a whole. First and foremost, it was a "career," begun as a young man and continued through retirement; Sprague pursued it with the same dedication and enthusiasm as his regular profession. Coincidentally, but most appropriately, Sprague was a Calvinist minister, an ideological descendent of the divines who had established the fear of idleness. By making his leisure a career, Sprague could avoid any hint of idleness, and by collecting items of historical importance he could further justify his activities as educational and socially useful. Like any modern businessperson he brought structure and order to his activities; in his case actually creating the structures from scratch. Although Sprague avoided the cash market of the autograph commodities that he was instrumental in creating, he nevertheless actively competed and negotiated with fellow collectors in a most businesslike way. However, preaching not collecting was his business, and Sprague recognized that his love of collecting transcended the bounds of conventional behavior. It was, he said, a "mania" and a "ruling passion." As a man who collected almost a hundred thousand autographs, and close to that many early American religious pamphlets, Sprague was indeed obsessive. He donated the pamphlets to various libraries but could not bear to part with autographs during his own lifetime.[8]

While the objects that Sprague collected had little to do with the Industrial Revolution, his systematic, or "scientific," approach was the prototype of a pattern that would be adopted by others of his generation as they began to collect the emblems of industrialism. Stamp collecting, which is discussed in some detail below, was the first and most important of the collecting hobbies tied directly to intentionally insignificant manufactured products. Like Sprague, collectors of manufactured items developed expertise, created artificial sets that they then tried to complete, and by doing so constructed a secondary market for items originally created for another purpose.

Collecting and Mass Production

While stamps set the pattern for the collection of industrial ephemera and remained the long-term favorites, for about thirty years, from 1873 to the turn of the century, they were challenged in popularity by chromolithographs. In 1880 *Arthur's Home Magazine* suggested that "there is scarce a village into which this fashion has not penetrated—the fashion of collecting bright chromo cards, business or otherwise, and pasting them into a scrapbook." Chromos were full-color pictures printed on card stock and used as advertisements, premiums, and greeting cards. Collecting chromos became so popular that, like bubble gum cards of the next century, the premium became more important than the product it was promoting, and printers began producing them for direct sale. Taking their cue from the way people collected stamps, some distributors created sets so collectors would have to buy their products multiple times in order to fill a series.[9]

Collected mainly by children and women, chromos were valued mostly for their beauty and, like stamps, mounted in albums, or more specifically, in the scrapbooks that women had been making since the beginning of the nineteenth century. Unlike stamp albums, organization took second place to aesthetics and sentiment in scrapbooks. "Everybody possesses, or has possessed, a scrap-book of some kind or other," noted a hobby writer in 1883, and she lauded the pastime for the way it enabled the makers to reflect back on their personal histories. That was why, she said, "the genuine scrap-book has no legitimate arrangement. Into it goes promiscuously all that interests, amuses, or strikes us," so that jelly recipes and quotations from Tennyson would appear side by side. The scrapbooks were thus miniature museums of the collector, filled with personal odds and ends that appealed to the compiler's sense of beauty or sentiment. With an established tradition of mounting pressed flowers, leaves, watercolors, drawings, etchings, and other printed pictures in albums, it was natural that the new color chromos would become mainstays in late Victorian scrapbooks.[10]

In 1881 dialect author Kate Crombie described how rustic Aunt Ruth was bitten by the collecting bug. While visiting her cousin in town, she was impressed by a niece's album of four hundred "business cards" that included "floral cards, and pictures of little girls and boys, all dressed up as harnsome's dolls, and flowers and landscapes. . . . there was puzzle cards, and shadder cards, and comical cards of every description." "I had ketched the fever, sure enough and had got it bad, too," she admitted as she went off to buy soap flakes, coffee, ice cream, men's collars, starch polish, and a host of other unnecessary items to satisfy her collecting urge. Later, humiliated at having been so foolishly caught up in the craze, she wondered, "Is it possible t'any body else was ever sech a fool as I've ben to-day?" Her niece assured her she was not unusual, and admitted to having once spent fifteen dollars (more than an average worker's weekly wage) for unneeded items in order to get cards. On the last day of her stay, Aunt Ruth visited city hall to see a card show that featured collections of more than a thousand cards, where prizes were given for the largest and best collections.[11]

The chromos in Crombie's short story were not fully commodified collectibles because there was apparently no market for collectors to buy, sell, or swap them. They were, rather, quasi commodities that represented the real commodities whose sale they encouraged. Chromos were, however, the first example of primary collectibles, items with no practical value that were created in order to be collected. Souvenir spoons, a somewhat more expensive early version of the primary collectible, were popular from the early 1890s to about 1920. Chromos came free, yoked to some normally useful product. Souvenir spoons, on the other hand, were made to be sold outright. They had local scenes embossed on their handles and bowls, and were available in cities throughout the country. Places too small to warrant their own could buy spoons with generic scenes and engrave the town name locally. Traveling salesmen seem to have started the spoon collecting fad, and manufacturers capitalized on the idea by bringing out "apostle spoons" for Christmas and historical and literary commemorative spoons to appeal to nontraveling collectors.[12]

Unlike chromos and spoons, most Victorian collectibles were secondary, that is, they were manufactured for another purpose. For example, buttons, both older handmade and newer manufactured ones, were widely collected in this country perhaps as early as 1840. There is little evidence of a market among hobbyists for chromos, spoons, and buttons probably because women were major collectors and they generally tended to avoid the market elements of the pastime. The obvious exceptions were male-oriented chromo cards distributed in cigarette packages. The cigarette cards were avidly collected by boys and some men who bought, sold, and traded them, as they did several other tobacco-related products including cigar bands and the small metal or wax tags attached to tobacco tins and bags.[13]

Cigar bands, which like cards were printed by the chromolithograph process, were first used in the middle of the nineteenth century as a cigar decoration. The most elaborate were embossed and required as many as twenty-two separate printing runs to lay down all their colors, leading the *New York Sun* to comment in 1888 that the "label is often better than the cigar." The literal truth of this flip remark was confirmed a few years later when the collecting mania reached such proportions that the printers transformed the secondary to primary by selling unused bands directly to collectors. Author A. E. Hotchner remembered always carrying blotter paper in his pocket to preserve the cigar bands he found in the gutter as he made his boyhood rounds in depression-era St. Louis. Some of the bands were sufficiently rare to warrant following smoking men down the street

waiting for the opportunity to retrieve the precious decoration from a discarded butt.[14]

In one sense, the Victorian collecting craze was unexceptional since people were merely doing what they had always done. Whether for "instinctive"
or cultural reasons, patterns of collecting were deeply established in Western
society, and the availability of inexpensive industrially produced objects
made it easier for more people to participate. Yet the ubiquity and uniformity
of manufactured products distinguished them from intrinsically unique
objects like art or seashells, and collecting them signaled a new relationship
between people and things. In the preindustrial economy of scarcity there
was a simple logic to saving and even creating rare objects and then imbuing
them with value greater than their practicality. Whether jeweled Easter eggs
or Kwakiutl coppers, culturally privileged singular objects become signs of
wealth, status, and power. Saving the rare is commonsensical; saving the
common seems nonsensical. Even while the plethora of cheap goods undermined the traditional sentimental and economic worth of the individual
object for most people, it somehow made other people want to gather and
display some of the least intrinsically valuable products of the system, things
that were made to be given away or even things that people had thrown away.

The absurdity of collecting inherently low-value products disappeared
when collecting became a process that turned garbage into gold (or some
reasonable approximation thereof). This wonderful alchemy took place
through the magic of the marketplace, and for that reason collecting found
easy acceptance in an era that conflated God's law of hard work with nature's
law of survival of the fittest. Although its origins predated both industrialism
and capitalism, collecting came into its own in an industrial capitalist world.
Industrialism produced a multitude of objects to collect and capitalism created an ideology for doing so. The same cultural changes that underlay the
emergence of hobbies as a category of leisure made collecting the premiere
example of hobby activity. Collecting was productive leisure that satisfied the
need for free-time activities that emulated work both in form and meaning.

"Collecting stands midway between sport and trade," wrote book collector Gabriel Wells in 1920; "it is too serious for sport, and too playful for trade."
Wells's characterization of collecting captures the tension inherent in doing
something for fun that has the obvious characteristics of business. It was,
however, this tension that gave collecting its special appeal. Stamp collecting, explained the editor of a small collectors' journal, "offers ready escape
from the rush and worry of mundane existence, reveals historical, geographi-
cal, political, heraldic and zoological facts in an incomparably interesting
manner, and sometimes leads to the discovery of rare specimens and conse-
quent financial gain." It was the prefect pastime for a capitalist culture—fun,
educational, and potentially profitable.[15]

Markets and Museums

Collectibles transcend their commodity status because collectors consider them interesting objects in their own right; therefore people who collect for the intrinsic qualities of the object can exist outside the market. In the early 1950s, for example, Charles R. Lamb had more than six hundred bottles of sand, from as many different worldwide locations, neatly lined up in a special case in his study. Because he gathered sand systematically, Lamb was in a different category from the apocryphal pack rat who collected string in a box carefully labeled "too short to save." On the other hand, unlike William Sprague, whose pioneer autograph collecting led the way for others with whom he could trade, plain sand was unlikely to ever become part of a market system. The object of Lamb's collecting was too common and that of John and Donald List too rare. In the late 1930s, the Lists began collecting iron "pigs" (casts) from old stone blast furnaces in Ohio. Their carefully sorted and labeled collection won them local admiration, but nobody else followed them, so they remained outside the market system.[16]

The List brothers created a private museum, and in some sense most personal collections are private expressions of the public activity of museums. In both museums and private collections sets of objects are removed from circulation and displayed in specially constructed environments.[17] Museums privilege the aesthetic, the historic, or the associational characteristics of objects over their market value, but even museum objects have not been completely decommodified since they can still be deaccessioned for trade or cash. Whatever their personal motives for collecting in the first place, serious collectors acknowledge this bifurcation between commodity and collectible when they convert their private collections to public museums, giving up the right to reconvert their collections into money and opting instead to immortalize their names by binding them to the collection.

The very origins of museums lay in the collections of natural and historical "curiosities" by men and women in the Renaissance who stored them in "curiosity cabinets," many of which were built for display as well as preservation. Heterogeneous collecting retained a genteel legitimacy into the nineteenth century. An 1871 short story has a minister's daughter describe her collection "of fossils, and shells, and petrifactions, and curiosities, from all parts of the world." As late as 1912 a book of boys' hobbies included a section entitled "How to Form a Home Museum"; the museum would contain natural objects, exotic and historical human-made artifacts, and old prints.[18]

The shift from promiscuous accumulation to more systematic collecting of everyday objects did not reduce collectors' desire to show off their prizes. Household display cabinets were standard in collecting circles, and the more ambitious small-scale collectors turned their collections into tiny museums open to the general public. After World War II a growing interest in collections of manufactured items culminated in full-scale public museums like the Strong Museum in Rochester, New York, and the Lightner Museum in St. Augustine, Florida, where collections of shaving mugs and toys could receive the same kind of curatorial attention and public admiration that were once reserved for art and rare books. While such collections may be of greater historical than aesthetic interest, their enshrinement in major museums provides additional social legitimacy for the collector of ordinary objects and, of course, greater value to such objects.[19]

Until well into the twentieth century, the term "collector" was reserved for collectors of fine art, antiques, or rare books, which is to say for people of some wealth. In 1883 the London *Saturday Review* urged collectors to specialize, warning that no person could become an expert on all the things that could be collected, which included "ivories, bronzes, embroideries, Elzevirs [rare books], pictures, scarabs, gems, porcelains, coins, etchings, and so on." It seems unlikely that the "and so on" was meant to encompass manufactured everyday items. Thus when it commented on the "whimsical" holdings of American collectors in 1890, the *New York Times* focused on people who collected the then-unfashionable Baribzon School of French art. If buying Corot, Rousseau, and Millet were not amusing enough, the *Times* did throw in a few paragraphs about rare books and a couple of genuinely odd collections of historical hats, chairs, and architectural ornaments, but nothing manufactured.[20]

The collector's menu expanded a bit after 1900; nevertheless, stamps, coins, books, prints, Indian relics, and European antiques continued to be the norm.[21] Distinctions were somewhat arbitrary, and new items joined the list of legitimate collectibles piecemeal. By the late 1860s everybody had recognized the stamp collecting subculture, although collectors of chromos, postcards, and spoons were ignored until the twentieth century. If there were people collecting mass-produced items like porcelain toothpick holders, glass bottles, or streetcar transfers, they were not afforded the title "collector" until the 1920s at the earliest.[22] In a 1928 satire of antique collectors, Kenneth Roberts made fun of people who collected old scissors and iron thumb catches but completely dismissed the possibility that anybody might collect "old tin cans, old lobster buoys, and old egg crates." Yet within a generation even they had become fair game. By 1941 the concept of collecting had broadened sufficiently for a textbook on leisure to list more than 150 items, including a variety of nineteenth-century manufactured and printed ephemera, as appropriate targets for the would-be hobbyist.[23]

Even while the boundaries of collecting were expanding, there was, and continues to be, a distinction between the collecting of unique high culture objects and the popular hobby of collecting manufactured goods.[24] Matters of taste, class, and specialized knowledge of the collected object, what Pierre Bourdieu has called "cultural capital," all contribute a rough and shifting, but nevertheless clearly understood, status hierarchy among collectors.[25] Real as those distinctions may be, they are subsumed in the transcendent ideological similarity that binds both high and low collecting into a single category.

Just as stamp collecting paved the way for collecting all manner of mass-produced items, it also transformed the meaning of "collecting" from conspicuous consumption to hobby. By the time of the First World War, "hobby" and "collecting" were sometimes used as synonyms. The wealthy New York gentlemen who founded the Hobby Club in 1911, for example, were all collectors. Even though not one of them collected mass-produced items, not even stamps, they nevertheless embraced the hobby appellation. The identification of hobby with collecting deepened during the great hobby boom of the depression. In 1931 *St. Nicholas*, a children's magazine, wrote that there were "many boys and girls who have formed a taste for pursuing some kind of a hobby" and then went on to list a variety of items that could be collected; no other kind of hobby was even mentioned in passing. By the same token, O. C. Lightner's *Hobbies* magazine founded in 1931 was limited to collecting, as were the hobby shows the publisher underwrote in both Chicago and New York. Readers of another, more upscale depression-era hobby magazine, *Avocations*, showed a distinct preference for collecting over handicrafts.[26] While the wealthy continued to collect more traditional objects, the numerous hobby exhibits routinely displayed items that were, in the recent sense of the word, "collectibles," that is, odd objects of mass production such as keys, cigar bands, and campaign buttons.[27]

The only objective difference between traditional collecting and hobby collecting is the value of the collected objects, although a great many subjective differences flow from that. An object that is worth tens of thousands of dollars is going to be taken much more seriously than one worth tens of dollars. Value, of course, is established by the interaction of supply and demand, and the fact that art, the most traditional of collectibles, is handmade and therefore unique, means that the available quantity of any given object is one. There are exceptions to this rule such as limited edition prints or multiple casts of statues, but at some point an excessive supply reduces the value of an object enough to remove it from the category of art no matter how beautiful it is. When Joseph Alsop says that aesthetics are as important in collecting art as in creating it, he is condemning those who collect only for value. Alsop admires those "courageous and discerning collectors who have seen beauty where no others saw it and have therefore made aggressively unfashionable collections." Alsop's unacknowledged premise is that others will eventually recognize the courage and discernment of the collector, since the collection that remains forever unfashionable will be forever obscure. A collector's foresight in collecting the unfashionable is recognized only when the collection is no longer unfashionable, which is to say when it has become valuable.[28]

Because of its cost, traditional collecting was and is done only by the wealthy; it is inevitably an act of class distinction no matter how aesthetically motivated. Even the formalized exchange of valuable objects in an auction becomes a performance of class difference or what anthropologist Arjun Appadurai calls a "tournament of value." Appadurai stresses the gamelike quality of the auction in which the elite "define themselves as such by agnostic speculation upon a restricted corpus of signs."[29] It is, however, not so much the game as the price of admission that allows art auctions to define status. A rural auction of household goods is not fundamentally different from an auction at Sotheby's except that a Louis XV commode is going to command a much higher price than a side table from the 1950 Sears catalog. Each formalized, some might say ritualized, exchange of value takes place among a group of people who confirm their membership in a collecting subculture through their participation in the auction; the major difference is that the purchaser of the Sears table could not afford the French antique and the purchaser of the antique would not want an example of mass-produced furniture.

Collectibility and the Life Cycle of Things

Objects made to be collected such as chromos and Christmas plates have only limited rarity and thus only limited value, although that value can be enhanced by deliberately limiting the number of items produced. Once production has ceased, they become, like any other collectible, an artifact of the marketplace. The purchase of an item to add it to a collection is the act that creates the item's value. While the difference between spending ten dollars and ten thousand dollars is profoundly important in terms of creating social distance, it is of very little difference in terms of bestowing the quality of collectibility on the object itself. Generally speaking, a thing is collectible when there are fewer of them than are desired by people willing to pay for them, and when there is sufficient knowledge in the market so that multiple people can attempt to acquire them. "In any form of collecting," noted book collector Reginald Brewer in 1935, "it is obvious the thing you acquire must be both rare and desirable. Rarity alone is insufficient, for there must be others equally desirous of making it theirs."[30]

Thus before 1969 there were people scattered about the country who collected old beer cans, each of whom apparently thought he was the sole player in a one-man game. Such collectors could acquire their cans for free off the street, from dumpsters, landfills, and similar sources. Although they were being collected, the beer cans were not collectibles since even cans that were old, rare, or both had no market value. In this sense collectibles are like lawyers: some towns are too small for one, but no town is too small for two. The beer can collectors' world changed in 1969 when a St. Louis newspaper ran a story about a local collector, bringing him to the attention of five other men who had also collected in isolation. They formed the Beer Can Collectors of America in 1970 and in less than a decade had thirteen thousand members worldwide. The economic status of pre-1969 beer cans was that of any easily acquired object. This means that economically, although not psychologically, what young children and eccentrics do when they gather string or stones is not collecting. We impute economic value only to those things that we want and cannot have except through the exchange of something else of value.[31]

In the case of the beer cans, the unused object has a certain minimal value as a beverage container and once used has no value; it is literally and figuratively garbage. If, however, a sufficient number of people should desire to obtain this garbage, then the can once more acquires value. At that point the can has undergone two rather dramatic transformations: first, from being a low-value commodity to being no-value garbage, and second, from being no-value garbage to being a high-value (compared to its original worth) collectible. Or as Krzysztof Pomian puts it, the use-object has now become a sign. As a sign, the collectible's meaning has nothing to do with its original purpose; it now signifies particular metaphysical elements of the culture. In this sense, according to Jean Baudrillard, a thing cannot be both used and possessed. A *New York Times* writer grasped this essential principle in 1879 when he attacked violin collectors who bid up the prices of beautiful instruments just to keep them out of the hands of competing collectors. The end result, said the *Times*, was to deny them to "men of moderate means who need them for the purpose for which they were made." When is a Stradivarius not a violin? When it is a collectible.[32]

Anthropologist Igor Kopytoff refers to these kinds of transformations as part of the "cultural biography of things." A thing created for one purpose and having some value for that purpose becomes the desired object of collectors and thereby gains value as a commodity of a very different kind. The excess of demand over supply creates, in Kopytoff's terms, singularity. Kopytoff's description of the life cycle of a common-object collectible is strikingly similar to Joseph Alsop's discussion of the difference between patrons and collectors. A patron commissions an artist to paint a picture for a particular purpose, while a collector acquires available paintings. The commissioned painting is the first kind of commodity, that is, one produced for a specific use, while the collected painting is the second kind, one wanted for its singularity rather than its intended function. While paintings may not go through the "garbage" stage of life, the cycle of taste certainly will relegate many commissioned paintings to something very close. Consider, for example, the demand for thirty-year-old portraits of suburban families done by obscure and marginally talented artists, and then compare that with the demand for similar paintings done by even less technically skilled eighteenth-century limners. Self-serving portraits of unknown people from the mid-twentieth century can be bought cheaply by the square foot, but similar, if rarer, pictures that are two hundred years old, are highly prized and priced to match.[33]

There is, then, no single life path to the condition of collectibility. Most are secondary collectibles that started their lives as functional commodities, ranging from cheap beer cans to commissioned art, and are transformed into collectibles by the market. Some are primary collectibles, born to be collected. These too can range in value from trading cards to huge canvases by successful artists. But no matter what their origins, collectibles are ultimately the product of the market culture of capitalism. This is one example of the inexorable process of commodification that Kopytoff recognizes when he writes of the depersonalizing of objects under the onslaught of a money economy.[34]

The Object and Personal Identity

A collectible is an object that somebody wants for a collection. It is an object for which there is a market and, while collectors have regularly complained about the corrupting influence of the market, few reject it as a way to obtain objects. A numismatist argued in 1877 that misstrikes should not be collected because they were nothing but ugly errors. "Instead of looking for the beautiful, in fine clear impressions of specimens of the art," he complained, "much time and money seems to be spent in searching out poor and imperfect specimens" just because they were rare. Like the numismatist who wanted only beautiful and fine coins, the couple in a 1932 short story refused to sell a pornographic snuffbox they found in a recently purchased desk. "It is a funny, stupid business," the husband explains to his wife, "this being born a gentleman. Now I could buy this, I suppose, and be a patron of the arts without question. But imagine selling it, and getting bread and butter from the proceeds." They could not, and did not, violate their principles of good breeding for money but clearly had no objection to the principle of buying and selling collectibles.[35]

While they may vary in their emphasis, they are rare collectors indeed who do not take at least secret pride in the value of their collections. Since that which is costly is also socially significant, collectors identify with their collections, which is why the fictional couple could not sell that which they never would have bought; a pornographic snuffbox was not who they were. The common phenomenon of identifying with the collection transcends the market and yet is linked to it. For the living collector the collected thing is infused with importance by the market that in turn can make it harder to sell. Thus one book collector who had made a particularly astute purchase just before the depression could have sold it for a substantial, and very opportune, profit in the depths of bad times. Yet he found "the very fact that it had become so scarce and was in such great demand, clothed it with a desirability far greater than the temptings of a handsome profit."[36]

When they die, collectors can seek immortality by donating their collections to a library or museum and stipulating that the collection be kept together, an eternal proxy for its creator. Thomas Addis Emmet gave his collection of American autographs to the New York Public Library on the condition that his albums remain intact. Each was prefaced with his photograph, which he hoped would forever be "a silent pleader" of his wishes. Lest some future curator doubt his seriousness, the prefaces also contained the threat that should the collection be disturbed he would do whatever was in his power from the hereafter to "burden the conscience of the vandal who disregarded my wishes." Rather than preserving the corpus of the collection, book collector A. E. Newton sought to scatter his bibliographic genes widely. He expressly declined to consign them to "the cold tomb of a museum" and requested instead that "they shall all be dispersed under the hammer of the auctioneer, so that the pleasure which the acquiring of each one of them has given me shall be given again, in each case, to some inheritor of my own tastes."[37]

In 1897 Robert Chambers wrote a short story in which a butterfly collector identified so closely with his rarest specimen that he took on the insect's name, calling himself the Purple Emperor. The lepidopterist eventually murdered a rival who threatened his status by also acquiring a specimen of *Apatura iris*. A common variant of that tale has a collector discover that there is a second copy of an item he owns and thought unique. The collector searches for, finds, buys at great price, and then destroys the duplicate. The desire to be the possessor of a unique item is, in the opinion of many collectors, the underlying motivation for the hobby since it makes one the object of envy, and to be envied is a sign of success. It is not enough to merely have more money than others; money is, after all, undifferentiated. The money must be converted into something unique that others want. At the beginning of the depression, when many people were worrying about where their next meal might come from, book collector William Dana Orcutt suggested that "thrills are difficult to secure when a man is once a multimillionaire, but to become the owner of a rare literary item, coveted by all the world, perhaps supplies a something that is lacking even in the successful merger of great industrial organizations." Fellow bibliophile Reginald Brewer, also writing in the 1930s, concurred. "If we approach the matter with an honest heart and truthful tongue," he said, "we cannot avoid the admission that the desire to collect is founded on pure pride of ownership—the privilege of possessing something that your neighbor has not, or that you know is owned by only a few others in the world." The singularity of the collection bestows singular identity on the collector.[38]

Singularity and Sets

Singularity has two distinct but inseparable qualities. First, uniqueness makes the object valuable in the marketplace. Second, that monetary value gives the item the power to confer psychic value. Possession of the unique is every collector's dream because the singular object makes the collector unique, the object of envy, and the owner of an item of uncontested value. There are, however, two very different modes of singularity, each of which in turn has two subdivisions. The first kind of singularity is the most straightforward; the object is physically unique or extremely rare. Every handmade object is, to some extent, unique, and those handmade objects created as art or intended to express the personal vision of the creator are very deliberately different from all other items of the same genre, whether created by that artist or others working in the same style. Value for handmade objects is therefore additionally dependent on quality as judged by experts who help guide the market. Machine-manufactured objects, on the other hand, are functionally identical, and since they are mass-produced, uniqueness is an accident of history or occasionally an accident of production as in the case of misprinted stamps. While they are being produced there is no possibility of rarity for things that are being made by the thousands or even millions. Fortunately for the collector, mass-produced items are intentionally ephemeral. Even the most expensive manufactured products, like automobiles, are made to be discarded, so that while singularity is not built in as it is in art, scarcity is. Mass-produced items are supposed to become garbage; art items are not.

The second mode of singularity is more complicated because it has nothing to do with either the appearance or the number of the item extant, but rather has to do with the history, or provenance, of the collectible. The most common objects that have been owned by the great or famous sometimes command premium prices even when there would otherwise be no market at all for, say, an old baseball glove. Expert documentation is absolutely necessary to authenticate that the particular item was used by Babe Ruth, or to take an example suggested by Richard Mitchell, that a penny has indeed accompanied an astronaut to the moon, otherwise it is still just worth a penny. Even then, however, there is no guarantee of a market. In 1929 the *New York Times* puzzled over the fact that a first edition copy of a Dickens book, of which there were many, had sold for sixty-five hundred dollars while the actual desk on which Dickens had written it, of which there was only one, brought only twenty-five dollars. A second kind of historical value comes not from contact with the famous but from the personal history invested in an object, although such items are not collectible in the usual sense of the word since there is no market for them beyond the person for whom they have meaning. For you, the locket your mother wore at her wedding cannot be replaced by one exactly like it. For anybody else the two would be interchangeable—except, of course, if your mother were famous.[39]

As early as the sixteenth century, items owned by famous people found a special place in collectors' curiosity cabinets. Like the religious relics they emulate, these secular relics can take on varying degrees of importance so that even those items not directly used by the famous can attain a certain amount of associational value. An antique cup drew particular attention in 1913 because it "has come down to us from the hand that held the hand of Washington." By the same token an early collector of playbills explained in 1905 that it was not mere rarity that determined a bill's value but also its indirect association with a famous event. For example, a program distributed at an actor's last performance before his sudden death or accident or the last performance in a theater before it burned down would enhance the importance of the item.[40]

Even for those items that have no particularly exotic provenance, history plays an essential role in the creation of collectibility. Because of the different ways in which art objects and manufactured objects acquire singularity, each has a unique relationship to history. With the special-case exception of stamps and coins, manufacturing defects do not bestow collectibility on mass-produced items; only the erosion of supply that occurs with time can do that. Except for limited editions, no currently produced item can be collectible because it is readily available; therefore all manufactured collectibles are tokens of the past. In her perceptive theoretical analysis of objects, *On Longing*, Susan Stewart maintains that collections are given authenticity by the past. The collection, however, is not a prisoner of the past, she says, because it is able to transcend history with classification, which creates "order beyond the realm of temporality," and order is indeed the soul of collecting.[41]

In 1909 W. A. Laughlin wrote a poem for the *Collectors' Journal* in which he told of buying a pack of cigarettes and casually tossing its chromo card into the muddy street. Unmindful of the danger, a "dozen urchins" pounced on the picture, one of whom was run over by an oncoming carriage. The boy was rushed to the hospital where he remained unconscious for several days. Finally, he came out of his coma, and pulled the writer, who had been visiting him regularly, close to his bed and said:

> I found yer picture — my! 'twas wet,
> But just the kind that I collect;
> It's worth a broken leg to get
> A card that just makes up one's set.[42]

Completing a set is so closely identified with collecting that it stands as a virtual definition of the hobby. In 1932 educator Walter Durost explained that if an object "is valued primarily for the use, or purpose, or aesthetically pleasing quality, or other value inherent in the object . . . it is not a collection." On the other hand, if the object is valued because of its relationship to other objects "such as being one of a series, part of a whole, a specimen of a class, then it is the subject of a collection." Sets or series grow naturally out of the process of classification, which is the sine qua non of collecting. Classification is the process by which things are both distinguished from and linked to each other. Unless collectors are truly megalomaniacal, like Sir Thomas Phillipps who thought he could acquire one copy of every book in the world, they have to learn how the collectibles are similar and how they are different, sometimes down to the most minute distinctions such as watermarks or serial numbers.[43]

These distinguishing characteristics are what bind the collection to history; they do not, as Susan Stewart avows, allow the collection to transcend history. Stewart argues that placing objects in post hoc categories strips them of history. "Coins and stamps," she writes, "are naturalized by the erasure of labor and the erasure of context of production." While this argument might apply to the rare collectors who do not care about the origins of their items, most collections are built explicitly on categories constructed around historical qualities. When, where, why, how, out of what, and by whom an item was made determine its place in the collection. Far from being independent of or transcending history, classification is usually dependent on it. The examples of antiques that Stewart herself uses to demonstrate that it is "necessary to obliterate the object's context of origin" in order to construct what she calls a "narrative of interiority" are in fact distinguished by historical period and maker. They are handcrafted and may or may not have been made to look different from other members of their category. Thus they might be deliberately unique works of applied art, or they may have achieved their status by accident of survival, but in either case their history is vital to their collectibility.[44]

Even eclectic collectors are not anarchic accumulators. If they are collecting antiques, they are not collecting stamps, or books, or the signatures of famous people—or if they are they would certainly not consider those disparate objects parts of the same collection. Predicting in 1910 that "the day of the collector of more catholic taste is surely coming," a china collector recklessly kicked over the traces of convention and suggested that people could collect not only mugs or pepper boxes but both, or even teapots as well. In collecting circles, unbridled eclecticism can be narrow indeed. The very concept of eclecticism denotes deviance from a more widely agreed upon pattern. Collectors create categories and seek out only those objects defined by the categories; that is how collectors know they are collectors and not mere pack rats. "Things have an entity which constitute their identity," explained book collector Gabriel Wells in 1920, "and they have fringes which constitute their differentiate. It is these fringes which fasten themselves upon the fancy." By ordering these fringes, collectors make categories, which in turn make rarities. Except in the case of the hermitic collector of the otherwise uncollected object or the obstinately aesthetic collector who considers sets "an unfortunate confusion between what is rare and what is beautiful," categorization is an artifact of a market.[45]

In 1887 the New York Times observed that the French distinguished between collectors and "collectioners." The former had a pastime, the latter an obsession. For the Times writer, systematic organization and the making of sets was the hallmark of the obsessive form of collecting: "When the collector of buttons has given proof of his mania by gathering many buttons, and of method in his madness by making for his buttons a classification, scientific or empirical, he is by right a collectioner." The nominal subdividing of collectioners from collectors never took place in the United States, but the concept was ever present. Stamp collectors, in particular, created organizational taxonomies to demonstrate that theirs was a "scientific" pastime. Those, like a depression-era philatelist, who broke the canonical structure and collected by pictorial subject rather than country of origin, risked being read out of the fraternity of true collectors for assembling "a scrap-book rather than a stamp collection."[46]

The arbitrary imposition of structure gave the collector the basis on which to develop a "science," and creating a systematic taxonomy of sets was prerequisite to establishing rarity. Sets gave meaning to what might otherwise be a random accumulation, and serious collectors often sought an ever finer sieve with which to refine their sets. The novice print collector hopes to procure a complete set of a master artist, explained a collectors' journal in 1889. He does, but in the process realizes that there are run-of-the mill prints and proofs, so he decides that he must have a set of proofs, but then he discovers that there are first states and that some strikes are better than others and so forth and so on, creating for himself a series of ever rarer sets. Experts cautioned that real collectors needed to create sets even where it was difficult to do so, as with antiques. An antique collection "should indicate the purpose of the amateur to possess representative examples of different periods of factories, or the varying and progressive styles of the designers and makers," explained one such specialist in 1921.[47]

The set was the scorecard. Collectors had to impose some pattern on their acquisition so they could know not only what they had but also what they did not have. Creating an arbitrary series so that one could then fill it is, no doubt, odd behavior in the eyes of those who do not share the hobby, but it is how the game is played. Describing himself and other philatelists, psychiatrist William Menninger said that the "chief satisfaction" of a stamp collector is taking his "mass of unsorted, unarranged stamps" and arranging them in a systematic order. Menninger acknowledged that "the feeling common to many collectors that they must 'complete the set' " was "technically compulsive," but he found it harmless and admitted "most of us greatly enjoy the planning of our collection, its arrangement and rearrangement."[48]

Menninger found satisfaction in imposing order on a small corner of the chaotic world of manufactured goods. By doing so he symbolically affirmed continuing human mastery over factory production, and hobby collecting was, above all, a choreographed interaction with the artifacts of industrialism. The mode for this behavior was established by the first American hobby collector, William Sprague. Although Sprague's autographs were not manufactured objects, he treated them more like postage stamps than old masters. As industrialism democratized collecting through mass production, the organizational model established by Sprague was repeated with other objects. Machine-made collectibles became ubiquitous, both primary collectibles such as chromolithographs and secondary collectibles such as stamps could be organized into sets, traded in a marketplace, and be legitimated through public display. Because they were made to be discarded, manufactured goods could become secondary collectibles as their numbers decreased through attrition. The resulting singularity meant that even an everyday item could ultimately possess uniqueness—the ultimate desideratum of any collectible—and by owning this singular object the collector could share in the specialness of the collected object.

3 Collectors

Just as collectors create new meaning for objects by collecting rather than using them, objects can create new meanings for collectors by transforming them. Collectors are not merely people who accumulate objects, but those who accumulate them in a particular systematic way that necessitates the development of specialized knowledge. The application of that knowledge is what distinguishes collectors from noncollectors. Even though collecting is usually perceived as a beneficial activity when it is pursued in moderation, collectors are frequently viewed with suspicion by others because the desire for possessions often seems to take possession of the collectors themselves. Just as the chain that binds the slave to the slaveholder also binds the slaveholder to the slave, the relationship between object and owner is fraught with ambivalence, which make collectors one of the most complicated types of hobbyists.

Developing expertise is the almost inevitable first step in becoming a collector, and it is what gives the hobby its reputation as educational. Collecting, said one apologist in 1922, "presupposes some knowledge of the objects collected, some desire to know all one can about them." By concluding that "one might as well poke fun at a university as to poke fun at one who collects intelligently," he was explaining why parents and teachers were among collecting's most enthusiastic advocates. The process of dividing and then subdividing objects into collectible sets requires people who have developed the special knowledge that allows them to correctly categorize the objects and, by the same token, distinguish between the authentic and the counterfeit. In traditional areas of collecting, like art, experts may be formally educated professionals, but most collecting experts are either dealers (who often begin as collectors with surplus items) or experienced collectors who have accumulated their knowledge through practical experience. In 1864, for example, the process by which a pioneer collector of hymn books developed his specialty was held up as an example of the acquisition of all human knowledge: "Somebody is drawn by innate taste or outward accident toward some minute unknown specialty. He takes it up first, perhaps, as a whim, and follows it afterward as a solid pleasure and serious pursuit, and by and by the world gets the benefit of his researches."[1]

Since most collections start casually with a gift or an idle purchase that catches the buyer's fancy, the original set is broad and new objects are readily available. The novice collector quickly discovers, however, that finding additional examples is too easy and therefore no fun. To make the game challenging, the collector needs to learn increasingly more obscure subcategories. Writing in 1949, a glass collector said that the growth of the hobby had led some devotees to fear "that the field may soon be exhausted, and may not, in consequence, offer the same opportunities for pioneering." The fear seems to have been less that the supply of glass was becoming exhausted than that there was a decreasing opportunity to develop original expertise. "Many new patterns remain to be listed," wrote the author reassuringly, "many unclassified forms are yet to be uncovered." Collectors who became ever more deeply enmeshed in the technical minutiae of their hobby were indeed following the developmental path of academics, learning more and more about less and less; they might eventually reach the level of book collector Henry Bradshaw of whom it was said: "He never forgot a specimen of type which he had once examined; a single page, or even a tiny fragment of a page, would often enable him to name the book to which it belonged, its printer, and its date."[2]

Collectors who were developing expertise in an established field could consult books and attend meetings, but the pioneer had to be an autodidact. On a trip to Liverpool in 1894, an English traveler met an American who improbably claimed to have collected three tons of scissors, most of which had been owned by the crowned (and presumably well-shorn) heads of Europe. The American bragged that he was the only scissors collector in the world, a fact the Englishman earnestly hoped was true.[3] Assuming this eccentric Californian wished to collect his scissors systematically, he would have had to determine how many and what kinds were made, when, and by whom, as well as document whose royal hairs or needlework had been trimmed by them. Since there were no other scissors collectors, rarity would not have been correlated with value. Nevertheless, as a highly motivated solo collector he could amass enough expertise to define both technical (who made them, and how) and associational (who owned them) categories, and proceed in a career of lonely but highly systematic collecting.

There is a natural progression in the hobby careers of collectors toward specialization and its associated expertise, which leads to a much more rational, that is to say, business-like approach. Experts on Bakelite buttons or Victorian hair wreaths have the satisfaction that they have mastered an arcane body of knowledge that is an intellectual extension of the collection itself.

Humorist Michael Berry noted the prevalence of these self-taught experts who insist on giving you "a highly technical discourse on the history and the endless varieties of netsuke," assuring you that he or she "is one of the outstanding authorities in the field." Philippe Jullian has argued that collecting is "the revenge of wounded ambition," by which he means that frustrated middle-class people accumulate large collections as compensation for failures to be more successful in their regular work. This may be true, but it ignores the meaning of expert collecting for the successful person, and misses the ideological congruence altogether. Collectors like William Menninger did not use stamps as a substitute for career fulfillment. It was, rather, an example of work patterns colonizing leisure. To systematically, if voluntarily, study the minutiae of a subject and then apply that knowledge in a way that can measure success in dollars and cents is to work at play.[4]

The development of expertise confirms Robert Stebbins's observation that serious leisure participants are characterized by careerlike dedication to their pastimes; increasing knowledge is one of the differences between a career and a job. Psychiatrist Frederick Baekeland recounts the example of a highly focused businessman "for whom the demands of work take precedence over almost everything else except collecting, which seems to serve him as a vicarious emotional outlet." But at the same time he notes that the collector "has in effect, converted collecting into a second career." The businessman was pursuing his hobby with the same single-mindedness, and applying the same ideology, that he normally reserved for business. Baekeland wants to emphasize the ways in which collecting can provide creative alternatives to work and an outlet for individuality. Yet the examples he provides demonstrate surface distinctions built on structural similarities.[5]

The Joy of the Hunt

By establishing sets, collectors create rarity, and by creating rarity they establish the need for expertise. Expertise and sets are linked in a dynamic relationship, with more complex sets requiring a higher level of knowledge, which in turn allows for the creation of more arcane sets. The upward spiral of expertise and rarity feeds off the competitive joy of the hunt. Speaking of a fellow book collector in 1932, Holbrook Jackson said he "tracked down mighty tomes with the infallibility of a Red Indian hunter; he followed the scent of a lurking specimen of palaeotypography with the persistence of a bloodhound," and because he pursued his prey scientifically, "he added knowledge, observation and inference, to instinct, marking down his game before he started on the chase." Since they are experts, collectors know what they are looking for before they find it and suffer the letdown of success when they do. In 1926 Carolyn Wells described her search for the only book she needed to complete her set of Whitman's publications. She defined her series; she developed her expertise; and she tracked her quarry until she found it. Her elation, however, quickly turned to despair. "An incomplete collection is a thorn in my flesh," she lamented, "and a complete collection is a bore."[6]

Almost without exception, collectors embrace the hunting metaphor and acknowledge that pursuit is as important, and sometimes more important, than possession. In 1926 book collector John Winterich suggested that collecting had its origins "in the brain of that dim ancestor who one morning, in pursuit of the day's food supply, discovered a joy in the hunt itself which was something apart from consuming the quarry." A turn-of-the-century essayist who dismissed collections because "acquisition seems to rob most things of their intrinsic value" nevertheless accepted collecting because of the recreational value of seeking an object. Some years later a British collector-dealer made the same point when he wrote, "I would rather be a collector than the owner of a collection." He urged coin collectors to sell their collections, switch specialties, and begin the hunt anew: "I feel the chase is more worth while from at least the non-pecuniary point of view than the actual kill."[7]

The joy of the hunt is based on the emotional response elicited by the process of search and discovery. A lepidopterist described his "hot anxiety" when a new butterfly sailed into view: "the all but unbearable excitement when the longed-for quarry appears." Butterfly collecting is, of course, a form a real hunting with live prey, but the same author used similar language to describe the "intoxicating hours" he spent when he found an unexpected treasure trove of rare books in a widow's attic. Collecting chroniclers Douglas and Elizabeth Rigby characterize the collector about to achieve the object of his hunt as having "the glint in the eye of a savage about to spring upon his victim." "Your breath quickens, your heart misses a beat and you feel hot and cold all over," was how one book collector described the adrenaline rush of victory.[8]

The frequent and intense use of the hunting metaphor locates collecting in an established set of traditionally masculine images. Yet the language was frequently used by female collectors. It is not clear if they were simply borrowing the dominant vocabulary or if the hunting language was a way to emphasize that they could play the collecting game by the traditional male rules—at least where they were permitted to. Women were virtually excluded from some collecting communities, such as stamps, coins, and books, but seem to have outnumbered men in autograph collecting and dominated collecting of "female" objects such as dolls and dishes. In 1916, when Agnes Repplier described an autograph hound as "the wily hunter, stalking his game through coverts dim and mean" and concluded that "the pleasure of possession is prefaced by the keener pleasure of the chase and by the supreme joy of outwitting a stupid world," she used the masculine pronoun and decidedly masculine imagery but is as likely to have been referring to a woman as a man.[9]

Hunter-collectors of both genders saw themselves as playing a game, and they understood Grantland Rice's famous dictum: "It is not whether you win or lose, but how you play the game." However, like most players they preferred to win. Collecting prints "is as much sport as fishing, securing the prize more fun than owning it," noted collector John Ramsay in 1947. Ramsay, however, did not lose sight of the goal, "In the game of collecting, it is always fair to take advantage of the other fellow's mistake," he claimed, although he admitted "robbing widows and orphans is poor sportsmanship." Robbing widows and orphans is an activity traditionally ascribed to landlords and unscrupulous investment advisers, and by using that phrase he was combining the language of sports and business.[10]

Elaborating on the idea of competitive collecting, a 1915 essay in the London *Times* noted that while some people were solo collectors, most preferred to have at least one rival to defeat and even steal from. "Collecting is a game," the essayist said, "and stealing is not a breach of the rules." Even the most honest men are seduced by the game "so that they come to regard stealing as only a bold and skillful kind of collecting" (see fig. 3.1). The author goes on to describe the hobby as a simplified and reduced model of life in which the rules, and therefore the results, are clear, if morally ambiguous. In fact, ambiguity is the essence of the analysis. The piece calls collecting a game, yet says stealing and forging (cheating) are understood as parts of it. The author says it is easy to determine if you have won, but concedes that most people set the rules up so they can never win. By acknowledging the competitive aspect of the hunt, the essayist has grasped the deeper meaning of collecting. Like life, it is activity governed by a code of behavior; some rules are externally imposed and some come from within, but all are subject to change. Although it only obliquely alludes to the economic elements of collecting, the essay nevertheless sets up a classic description of a leisure activity as a form of ideological spillover.[11]

The collected object is the prey, but with very few exceptions, it is an inanimate object, incapable of defending itself against those who wish to possess it. The real opponent is not the prey but those who own it or would like to own it. In 1917 *Outlook* magazine explained that "the cautious bargaining with the dealer or the feverish competition of the auction sale" were the real joys of collecting since they could lead to "the pleasant feeling of

Picking up rare old bits of pewter for virtually nothing at a dealer's. By exercising great care the collector can add almost anything to his smaller pewters in this way.

FIGURE 3.1 A sardonic commentary on collecting ethics by Booth Tarkington shows a collector shoplifting antiques. (Reprinted from Kenneth L. Roberts, *Antiquamania* [Garden City, N.Y.: Doubleday, Doran, 1928], 229.)

superiority on discovering that some less well-informed collector has been taken in." Psychologist Ruth Formanek describes collecting as a search for prey in which the collected object is "a symbol of one's aggression and prowess." For men in particular, the image of the hunt as both a search for game and a form of game imbued collecting with an air of masculinity that legitimated it as an expression of superiority in a Darwinian world. The underlying aggression common to both hunting and competitive games is also, of course, an integral element in marketplace dealings. On a strictly economic level, buying low, with at least the option of selling high, is the primary measure of success in the free market.[12]

Psychiatrist Edmund Bergler has argued that male bargain hunters, who are commonly perceived as "passive-feminine" types, are in fact practicing a form of aggression in which they take pleasure in outwitting the dealer who is a surrogate for a "bad mother." Bergler's speculative Freudianism assumes this aggressive pattern is uniquely male, but a woman collector in 1926 explained "the joy of a collector is showing off his books to other collectors, hoping to make them green with envy." She had begun collecting only when she was told that all the most desirable editions of a particular author had already been bought up. She did not care about the soul of the book, she said, only the body. In fact, she did not even particularly care about the body; what she cared about was the challenge of finding books that others said could not be found and the pride of having done so.[13]

Collecting autographs from living people was one form of the hobby in which the prey could escape on its own. Although women were active autograph collectors, males appear to have been more aggressive. Seeking autographs was, in the title words of a 1925 reminiscence, "A Boy's Hunt for Big Game." Male collectors were extremely proud of the various postal ploys they used to pry signatures out of reluctant celebrities. When simple requests went unanswered, they turned to "invitations in which the RSVP loomed large, letters claiming kinship, threatening suit, sending gifts or newspaper clippings, [and] inquiring about allegedly mutual friends." Rebuffed five times by Vachel Lindsay, in his sixth request a collector challenged the poet's masculinity saying he "understood that his wife did not permit him to send his signature." Lindsay rose to the bait and sent his autograph. Six requests was a small-bore assault compared to the sixteen letters with which Seymour Halpern bombarded aviator Charles Lindberg, all to no avail until he enlisted the assistance of Lindberg's father-in-law, New Jersey senator Dwight Morrow. Unable to get Benito Mussolini's autograph, but successful in getting one from Pope Pius XI, Halpern challenged Il Duce to match the Pontiff's generosity, which Mussolini did only after an Italian attaché had authenticated the Pope's signature.[14]

Since the pleasure of collecting was more in the search than the seizure, collectors could make a sharp distinction between capturing the object directly and buying it in the marketplace, or worse yet, having it bought by an agent. As early as the 1880s famous people were charging autograph hounds for their signatures, causing one collector to conclude that once "a price is set upon an autograph, its value to the true collector is gone. It is the difficulty of acquisition that lends zest to the occupation, and directly that difficulty can be overcome by the mere exchange of dollars and cents it degenerates into a matter of trade." Yet even this collector acknowledged that no serious collector could avoid the marketplace altogether, but at the very least collectors were supposed to do their own negotiating.[15] In an extended bit of doggerel about car manufacturer Walter Chrysler's coin-bank collection, Norman Sherwood wrote:

> He hunted far, he hunted wide—
> He had me hunting—also you
> And the "big shots"—who run the Chrysler "outfit"
> He had them hunting too.[16]

If Chrysler indeed sent his minions out to find banks for him, it would have been a logical move for a man who sat at the apex of a large corporation all of whose employees existed to do the president's bidding. Moreover, he would have been acting in the tradition of wealthy collectors who used agents to collect art and antiquities. Nevertheless, Chrysler would also have been violating the spirit of the hunt as it was understood by most collecting hobbyists. The true book hunter "must hunt the books himself and not by proxy, must actually undergo the anxiety, the fatigue, and, so far as purse is concerned, the risks of the chase," explained Holbrook Jackson.[17]

The Shame of Collecting

Despite both its behavioral and ideological congruence with work, collecting among adults is not an unconflicted pastime. Warranted or not, collectors have cultivated a self-deprecating attitude of beleaguered victimization. In 1912 Adrian Hoffman Joline, a member of New York's exclusive Hobby Club, observed that "the hapless being who confesses that he is an autograph collector receives the most general condemnation." Joline said that if he collected "all the ill-natured and abusive things ever written or printed about autograph collectors," he would have to hire the Metropolitan Life Building to hold them. In fact, despite their self-mocking complaints, there has been surprisingly little serious criticism of collectors. A rare exam-ple in 1902 called collectors bores who were obsessed by their objects and riven with jealousy of other collectors. Most criticism of collecting, however, has its origins with the collectors, not with their critics. While Joline spoke of "confessing" that he was a collector, as though the hobby were a sin or a crime, the transgressions were mostly in his mind because he, like so many of his fellows, seems to have been burdened with a guilty conscience.[18]

Gardener Teall, a collector of art objects, wrote in 1920 that "your true collector may often maintain reticence" in order to remain "undisturbed by the merely idle curious" and avoid "the skepticism of those who measure the sanity of their fellows by the canons of their own irrevocable and undeviat-ing limitations." Teall's was a particularly arrogant expression of an other-wise widespread reluctance of collectors to go public. Sociologist A. D. Olmsted argues that the collectors' shame or embarrassment stems from their sense that they are violating cultural expectations about the rational, work-oriented use of time. His argument is a sociological version of psychia-trist William Menninger's observation that "many persons pursuing a hobby exhibit an unusual modesty or reticence in referring to it and may even pre-sent an apologetic or shamefaced attitude when questioned about it." Like Olmsted, Menninger attributed this reserve to the belief that "play and recreation are forbidden as a waste of time and demoralizing," although he locates the source of the guilt in the collector's parents not society. Men-ninger goes on to link the solitary vice of collecting with *the* solitary vice, masturbation. This connection seems deficient on two grounds. First, seri-ous collecting is much closer to rational, worklike behavior than most other forms of leisure and is more encouraged than discouraged both by parents and by society at large. Second, people have very few reservations about dis-cussing other much less rational and work-oriented leisure such as travel or watching television.[19]

No doubt much collectors' secrecy is no more complicated than experts' reluctance or inability to talk to the untutored about their areas of expertise. We assume that everyone understands sports or movies and feel free to open discussions about them, although the same might not be true for stamps or buttons. There is, in addition, the quality of solitariness that is part of the common understanding of a hobby.[20] If one goes about talking with people who have nothing to offer either in the way of objects or expertise, one is infringing on the solitude or sanctuary quality of the pastime.

Granting these two straightforward reasons for collector reticence, there is still too much anecdotal evidence of shame or guilt to be dismissed. Col-lectors do seem to feel some psychological discomfort with their hobby, which mirrors a sense of discomfort that members of the noncollecting public have with them. If collecting is actually more consonant with capitalist values than other forms of leisure, why should it generate this psychological tension in both participants and observers? Why should people feel ashamed or guilty about activities that emulate universally praised behavior and that, at the same time, reinforce the ideological underpinnings of that activity? It may be, as I discuss in greater detail later, that collecting emulates not only the approved but also the dubious aspects of market capitalism. Thus if the collectors or their critics see their activity not as educational and rational capital formation but as speculation, then collectors might feel embarrassed about partaking in an activity that produces wealth without producing social value. Olmsted seems to imply this when he calls the collecting of mundane objects like baseball cards controversial since they "have little use-value, but considerable exchange value." Whatever real function they may serve in the efficient allocation of resources, speculators are popularly seen as parasites, and that is a label most people would gladly forego.[21]

Additional discomfort may arise from the very fact that collecting is neither clearly work nor clearly leisure. It seems to cross categories, and as anthropologist Mary Douglas has explained, we are most uncomfortable with those things that violate our sense of categorical order.[22] Collecting is pretend work. It is work effort being applied to nonwork ends, and therefore neither collectors nor society can be quite sure if the collector is working hard or playing hard. In collecting, and perhaps in some other serious leisure activities as well, work has spilled out of its boundaries. It is no longer safely contained within the factory or office walls, bound by the clock to socially and legally prescribed hours. It threatens to take over the leisure sphere and thereby recolonize a part of life that has only recently been wrested from it. Thus the very aspects of collecting that make it popular and generally praised also set up a paradoxical fear of the hobby. It mimics business and it mocks business. It reinforces the ideological foundations of market capitalism and it threatens to undermine the foundations of leisure. This does not mean that every collector is going to be torn by unresolved psychological conflicts between commending capitalism and containing it, but it does explain why there may be ambivalence about those pastimes that promote the work ethic as well as those that negate it.

The Psychology of Collecting

So long as it is done by children, or in moderation by adults, collecting raises few objections and much support. When, however, collectors begin to focus the kind of attention on their hobby that is supposed be reserved for work, both the hobbyists and the public become uncomfortable. Serious collectors recognize that their hobby strikes outsiders as abnormal. "Crazy? Well, mebby I be; leastwise, if some folks that thinks so are sane, I'm willin' to be the other thing," an artifact collector argued defensively in 1910. Collectors and noncollectors alike acknowledged that taken too far the hobby became a disease. The main character in an 1876 Mark Twain short story makes the mistake of suggesting that his uncle take up a collecting hobby. The older man does so and is soon caught up in a "raging fever." The uncle quits work and turns an "elegant leisure into a rabid search for curious things." He creates a series of what he believes to be unique sets (cow bells, brickbats, flint hatchets, and stuffed whales) but each time discovers that there is one other collector who owns the last object he needs to fill his set and who will not sell at any price. Ultimately the older man exhausts his fortune and mortgages his estate to collect echoes. "The Canvasser's Tale" is not vintage Twain, but it does capture the fear that the benign hobby contains the germ of a dangerous disease.[23]

In 1906 John Walker Harrington wrote a light piece (the vast majority of references to collecting as a disease are humorous) that he titled "Postal Carditis and Some Allied Manias." In Harrington's pathology the ravages of "cranko-organisms" led to the "faddy degeneration of the brain." Likewise the *New York Times* described William M. Schnitzer, a founding officer of the Hobby Club, as having been "infected with the bacillus" of collecting. Identifying collecting with disease draws attention to the behavioral symptoms while absolving the collector of responsibility since a disease is not something one contracts voluntarily. Barton Currie, a book collector who wrote in the 1920s and 1930s, constantly referred to collectors as madmen whose disease was "beyond the reach of medicine, surgery, or even metaphysics." Currie said the germ of bibliomania was like the germ of love, it turned responsible people into victims of their emotions. It is not clear why any given collector preferred the negative and passive image of disease to the positive and active metaphor of hunting, but the two were never used together. E. R. Pennell recognized that she had a choice between viewing her cookbook collecting as a sport, which is what one expert she cited called it, or as a "peculiar malady," the characterization of another. She chose the second, concluding that her behavior had been the result of the "deadly germ."[24]

Collecting as a somatic malady brought on by a pathogen was a popular image for people spinning humorous stories of compulsive behavior. However, the idea that collecting was a psychological malady was both more widespread and sometimes more serious. Everyone understood that there was no collecting germ, but it was less obvious that there was no collecting mental illness. It took police and sanitation workers nineteen days in 1947 to dig through the refuse to find the bodies of Homer and Langley Collyer in their New York City apartment and an additional five months to clear out their twelve-ton collection of newspapers, pianos, toys, rugs, and auto parts. Linda Belle Titus Knox, a wealthy Chicago widow who married her gardener and with him proceeded to fill eight houses with Indian blankets, glass, books, china, antiques, pewter, copper, costumes, and beads was certainly eccentric and may have been crazy. But what of run-of-the-mill collectors? "He thought I was mad, of course," said a collector of ship models in a 1927 short story, "and as a matter of fact I was. Every collector is that and worse!"[25]

Exactly where self-indulgence ends and mental illness begins is not clear. Recently, psychiatrist Werner Muensterberger has suggested that serious collectors are attempting to compensate for an unquenchable desire. Like an opiate, each new acquisition brings real but temporary relief and thus primes the collector to seek yet another object to ease the pain. For the bibliophile who had become a bibliomaniac buying just one book was "like the first secret dram swallowed in the forenoon," the first step down the slippery slope to dissipation. Reformed addicts always remembered the thrill. In 1863 John Hill Burton described book collecting as a "malady" of youth that, like billiards and roulette, could be overcome but that the collector would always recall "with fond associations to the scenes of his dangerous indulgence." Another book collector in the 1930s confessed to having "repented, sinned, struggled, and fallen." To be sure, his language of sin, like the vocabulary of disease, was used playfully; yet underlying the humor was the deeper understanding that the collector was, in the words of a turn-of-the-century hobbyist, "frankly selfish, —not to say greedy," one of the seven deadly sins.[26]

On the more benign side, descriptions of collecting could fold together mental disease and sin and then praise the activity as beneficial, as the *New York Times* did in 1900 when it called collecting a "mania" complete with "symptoms" and "ravages." It then quoted a collector who used the biblical description of the road to perdition to describe her entry into the hobby: "Broad is the path and easy and pleasant is the way which leads to the state of a chronic collector." Nevertheless, the article presents the pastime as "delightful" and "educating" if somewhat preoccupying. Reflections on collecting danced along a fine line, mixing allusions to physical disease, mental disorder, and moral turpitude, usually but not always, in a spirit of playful good will. Beware of "the effect of antiques on the collector's mind," warned a character in a 1926 short story, "they ruin it . . . the morals go, too, and then all the rest." The analytic confusion arose from the fact that, more so than most hobbyists, collectors could and did go over the edge and there was always that large gray area of people who were probably too sane to be committed but not sane enough to be released.[27]

A depression-era psychiatrist who advised people to "be glad you're neurotic" noted that collecting hobbies allowed one to replicate the self-centeredness of infancy. Classic psychosexual theory sees the roots of collecting in the anal stage of infant development when children become aware of and then learn to control their excretory functions. The emotional satisfaction that is achieved in bowel control is transferred in later life to the accumulation and ordering of objects. "All collectors are anal-erotics," psychiatrist Ernest Jones claimed in 1912, "and the objects collected are nearly always typical copro-symbols." Jones thought coins, stamps, and books were substitute feces, as were birds' eggs, and less obviously, butterflies. Although not explicitly anal-erotic, Menninger also locates the origins of collecting in childhood experience when he suggests that resentment over being forced to share as part of the socialization process lies behind the adult's collecting activities. Unlike the child who has to share in order to earn parental love, the adult collector can "keep as part of himself, with full social approval, certain objects in which he can make an emotional investment," a feeling that itself might be related to anal retentiveness.[28]

Whether or not its origins lie in the frustrations and pleasures of toilet training, in a desire to exercise childish selfishness, or as discussed below, in the erotic possessiveness of adult males, there does appear to be a collecting personality type. Usually labeled "obsessive-compulsive," such people are orderly, methodical, systematic, thorough, conscientious, rigid, clean, uncertain—and have an inordinate fondness for collecting things.[29] The obsessive-compulsive label is so closely associated with collecting that there are those who make it the definition of a true collector. Psychologist William Cahill, for example, acknowledges that people might be motivated to collect for profit, aesthetics, historical appeal or even because they enjoy the social interaction with other collectors, but such people are not "true" collectors says Cahill. True collectors are "those who derive a sense of satisfaction from acquiring and possessing objects; they have a need for completeness, for closure; they pay a great deal of attention to details and they are quite systematic in their collecting activities; they are continually seeking to enlarge and improve their collections, and they feel somewhat compelled or driven in this quest."[30] Anecdotally this personality type is associated with stereotypically fussy bachelors who cannot bear to have anybody else sharing their space or their things.[31] The objects themselves become friends, if not lovers. Speaking in 1918 of an unmarried New York collector of antique furniture, glass, china, lacquered trays, silver, pewter, silhouettes, tinsel pictures, and tea caddies, a writer admiringly described them as "his friends and companions—companions who do not worry him with their troubles or with good advice about his health, but with which he holds constant and satisfying converse."[32]

Collectors may understand their activity as a hunting game but psychologists tend to see it as a search for love, although sometimes the two quests seem to merge in the analysts' minds. Frederick Baekeland says finding a wanted work of art is like falling in love. Freud himself argued that collecting was a way to substitute what one could get for that which was unobtainable: immortality or love. By saying "every collector is a substitute for a Don Juan Tenerio," Freud was excluding Don Juan from the circle of collectors of objects but tacitly acknowledging him as a collector of women. Pioneering psychoanalyst Karl Abraham was a bit less predatory, but his point was identical when he said that the value the collector places on the object "corresponds completely to the lover's overestimate of his sexual object," and he concludes that collecting among bachelors (in the 1920s) was a surrogate for sex and thus "a bachelor's keenness for collecting often diminishes after he has married."[33]

Perhaps the most elaborate and speculative psychological description of the collected item as an object of erotic desire comes from philosopher Jean Baudrillard, who has suggested that collecting "derives its fullest satisfaction from the prestige the object enjoys in the eyes of other people, and the fact that they cannot have it." This feeling in turn leads to a "powerful anal-sadistic impulse that tends to confine beauty in order to savor it in isolation." Assuming, like so many scholars, that only males collected, Baudrillard notes that a collector would no more lend a collectible than he would lend his wife. Then reversing the object's gender, he says the collector identifies sexually with it and that loss or damage would constitute symbolic castration. "When all is said and done," he concludes, "one never lends out one's phallus." There is, in Baudrillard's scheme, a cycle of jealousy. The collector is jealous of others who have what he wants, and he wants others to be jealous of what he has. It is not enough for him to be the dog in the manger, he must be the top dog in the manger who deprives all the others of access to the objects of their desires.[34]

Collectors speak of their love for their collections, but they want more love than can be provided by one lover or even by two or three. They collect love, not chastely and monogamously like Don Quixote, not even promiscuously and serially like Don Juan, but rather like a caliph with a harem of beautiful women that are all simultaneously his. The charm of a series, as Baudrillard has observed, lies in the fact that it is "bounded by intimacy [that is] bounded by seriality." Collecting actual women, however morally problematic, at least eliminates the conflict that so frequently arises when the collector finds he loves his collection more than his spouse. "More wives hate collections than say so," noted Arnold Bennett in 1924, because the collection had become an additional wife. "Sometimes," observed Bennett, "the woman is the principal wife; sometimes she comes second to the collection."[35]

This conflict is sardonically noted in a popular bumper sticker whose first line announces, "My wife said, 'it's either fishing or me!' " The second line resolves the crisis with only a touch of regret: "Damn, I'm going to miss that woman." Charles Dickens related just such a case in which a wife, driven to distraction by her husband's clock collection, gave him an ultimatum; it was either her or the clocks. He chose the clocks. In this case, however, the gentleman missed "that woman" so much that he agreed to leave most of his clocks unwound so she would return home. The great, and greatly eccentric, English book collector Thomas Phillipps inverted this situation by desperately searching for a second wife with an income large enough to support his compulsive book buying. And in the same vein once removed, in 1886 a wealthy collector agreed to his son's marriage only when her family gave him a ceramic piece he desired.[36]

In fiction as well as fact, males' collections regularly surpass wives as objects of affection. The eminent book collector A. S. W. Rosenbach wrote a short story in 1917 that used the language of adultery to describe a collector's attempts to hide his acquisitions from his wife. Despite his best efforts, he said his wife would regularly catch him "flagrante delicto as I would stealthily remove my beloved from its brown wrapping-paper; or catch me napping with a first edition that she was sure she had not seen before." He resolved to divorce her but could think of no grounds. She solved the problem by divorcing him "on the grounds of infidelity," because he loved his first folio of Shakespeare more than he did her.[37] As the poet Eugene Field observed, books were perfect wives, compliant and faithful:

> Prose for me when I wished for prose,
> Verse when to verse inclined, —
> Forever bringing sweet repose
> To body, heart and mind.
> Oh, I should bind this priceless prize
> In bindings full and fine,
> And keep her where no human eyes
> Should see her charm, but mine![38]

During the depression, novelist Radclyffe Hall wrote of a man who stole a Leonardo da Vinci statuette and willingly spent four years in prison, beggaring his family, for the pleasure of having briefly possessed it.[39] Hard times raised particular concerns about obsessive collectors who would sacrifice their families and even themselves for the inanimate love objects. Although collecting was one of the many hobbies promoted during the 1930s, commentators seemed acutely aware that collecting could become an end in itself and thus work against the very values it was thought to embody. Rather than promoting economy and savings, it could become the vehicle for financial ruin. Rather than cementing the family around home-based hobbies, it could tear the family apart emotionally while destroying it economically.

The warnings, like so much that dealt with the pathology of collecting, tended to be light hearted, but the pattern was nevertheless clear; the collectors (usually husbands, but sometimes wives) were in danger of putting their families at risk. Pearl Eley Seal complained in verse about her husband who ignored her, their children, the leaking roof and plumbing, as well as other family crises to spend all his spare hours on his gun collection. Grace Sharritt protested that her husband's hobbies were using up the money she needed for a new hat, and Kenneth Roberts wrote in 1930 that "as long as there are bills to be paid or children's clothes to be bought," wives will never be able "to sympathize whole-heartedly with the overwhelming emotion that fills their husbands' breasts when they are confronted by something rare and beautiful." On the other side of the gender divide in 1935 Frank Farrington discovered that despite a strict budget adopted to curb his wife's antique buying habit, she had been ignoring the butcher bills in order to surreptitiously fill their spare room with what he considered junk. Harriet Pinkham, a Minneapolis glass collector, wrote how she "cuts down on the groceries, electricity and gas, / Wears old clothes, darns her socks — to buy a piece of glass."[40]

The emphasis on displaced aggression and sexuality in the psychological commentary on collecting, along with its emphasis on male hobbyists, mirrored cultural assumptions about the business world. As long as those feelings remained under control, collecting was perceived as a positive activity. However, when they interfered with the family, or with business itself, what had been leisure became mental illness. Roy Tinney, a gun collector in the 1930s, described how gun cranks would cross the line, not only scrimping on personal expenses but also becoming too preoccupied with their hobby to take advantage of business opportunities. While collecting might model work, it could also interfere with it and thus move into the realm of the self-destructive behavior exhibited by a book dealer who was so obsessed with his volumes that he was happiest when a customer left his shop empty-handed.[41]

The Benefits of Collecting for Adults and Children

Because collecting can shade over so easily into deviant behavior, the snares of the hobby and the foibles of its followers have attracted considerably more comment than its benefits. Nevertheless, collecting never lost its reputation as a form of beneficial leisure, not the least, ironically, because it was thought to contribute to mental health. Of course, those who praised the mental health benefits of collecting had to take pains to distance themselves from the image of the obsessed collector. Writing in 1924 Arnold Bennett insisted that "the collecting instinct is not quite so unusual, abnormal, or absurd" as some critics claimed, and "still less is collecting usually a form of madness or mania which entitles its devotees to a place in a lunatic asylum."[42]

As an aid to psychological well-being, collecting was usually treated as a specific example of the generic good that came from having a hobby. Thus it was not so much that collectors were actively acquiring particular objects as a part of a series but that they were hobbyists spending their leisure time in a productive fashion that made the activity laudable. Addressing the Rochester Numismatic Association in 1914, Harry Earl Montgomery said that "a man with a hobby is too busy to be unhappy and has no time for ennui or the blues." "It will make no difference what hobby you adopt," he told his audience, "but a hobby you must have if you are to find health and happiness." Even a hobbyist who used the disease metaphor, calling collecting a "mania" that is "not only infectious but practically incurable," recommended it for "its healing way with nervous wrecks and despondent businessmen."[43]

Used to spending their time in a productive capacity that they found psychologically satisfying, businessmen and professionals became uneasy, that is to say bored, when they had time on their hands. Collecting struck many such people as an appropriate way to fill those leisure hours. Although they did not always make a clear connection between the activities and values of the hobby and those of work, the congruency was clearly implied. For example, magazine collector Harry Kossove reported in 1946 that his friends wondered why he, a businessman, was a collector. His response was that "a hobbyist is a man or a woman who wishes 'to get away from it all' and have something to make him or her so self-sufficient that hours of leisure never hang heavily." Self-sufficiency is a key element in the capitalist work ethic, and Kossove's picking it out as a rationale for collecting suggests an instinctive linking of work and leisure. Traveling salesmen, who were the first systematic collectors of souvenir spoons, felt the burdens of leisure more acutely than most because they were relegated in their time off to hotel lobbies or even less reputable gathering places of idle men. Collecting became for them a way to occupy their spare hours gainfully and take advantage of the fact that they could systematically search a much wider geographic area than the run-of-the-mill collector tied to a stationary job.[44]

To some extent, the willingness to privilege collecting over other leisure activities spilled over into a willingness to pass judgment on the type of collection as well. In the eighteenth century, Samuel Johnson had praised collecting in general but warned against "accumulating trifles" as a way of seeking distinction. Obviously Johnson thought the inherent virtue of the object transferred to the owner and an accumulation of trivial items endowed neither the items nor their owner with any prestige. William P. Brown, the editor of an early collector's journal took the same tack when he wrote in 1870: "Only those things which have a historical or scientific interest are worth preserving; some display their folly by gathering useless rubbish—the latest novelty we have heard of in this line, was the sale at auction in Paris of a valuable collection of warming pans." In the mid-1930s, a period when hobbies were enjoying almost universal approbation, the author of a general advice book on leisure dismissed people who collected "such enigmatical treasures as those composed of paper matches or different brands of pins or various other meaningless oddments." So obvious was the meaningless of such collections that the author gave no explanation as to why they were less worthy than stamps, although the implication was that they could never be worth much money.[45]

The desire to distinguish between good and bad collected objects mirrored the desire to separate good leisure from bad. Experts were always willing to provide neophytes with rules to assist them in self-improvement. Since so many self-styled leisure authorities promoted collecting as not only educational but also as a way to prolong life and make a man "a better husband, father, business man and citizen," it stood to reason that what was so beneficial to adults would apply even more importantly to children.[46]

Sometime in the late seventeenth century Cotton Mather's son Samuel went through his father's extensive library and cut out all the printers' emblems, which he pasted in a scrapbook. Cotton willed his collection to Samuel indicating either that he had eventually forgiven his son or that he wished to continue to punish him by making him live with the mutilated books for the rest of his life. If indeed Cotton forgave young Samuel's misbegotten excursion into childhood collecting, it may have been because he understood that between the ages of nine and twelve, most children go through a collecting phase. In fact, collecting behavior among children has been the object of more systematic study than any other form of hobbies.

In 1891 pioneer child psychologist G. Stanley Hall reported a survey of several hundred teenage boys that found all but a few had collections of stamps, coins, marbles, or a variety of other natural and manufactured detritus. With admittedly scant data, Hall concluded that girls were less apt than boys to engage in collecting. Hall's impressionistic conclusion was disproven a decade later by Caroline Frear Burk who examined the collecting behavior of more than twelve hundred California children between the ages of six and seventeen and found that more than 90 percent of them went through a collecting phase around the age of ten. Girls collected more, not less, than boys, but they preferred to collect items of sentiment and beauty like picture cards and seashells, while boys concentrated on stamps, cigar tags, and birds' eggs.[47]

Burk's conclusions about children's collecting behavior are dramatically illustrated by the early collecting career of A. S. W. Rosenbach whose uncle, a Philadelphia book dealer, introduced him to book collecting in 1885 when he was nine years old. Two years later he attended his first auction and bid twenty-four dollars for an illustrated edition of *Reynard the Fox*. The auctioneer extended Rosenbach credit and, noting the young collector's pleasure, commented that he knew bibliomania ran in families and could start at an early age but Rosenbach was the first baby bibliomaniac he had ever seen. The eleven-year-old Rosenbach combined the "instinctual" collecting of the preadolescent child with the competitive drive of male collecting to exhibit a childhood "mania" that was the mark of those who took their hobby too seriously.[48]

Burk's and subsequent investigations substantially confirmed William James's assertion that there is an "instinctive impulse . . . to collect property."[49] Intrigued by rodent and bird behavior, and eager to demonstrate which form of collecting was "a worthy use of leisure time," a spate of studies in the 1930s attempted to distinguish among hoarding (of necessities like food), accumulating (of items for sale or reuse), collecting information (such as bird-watching), and "scientific" collecting (acquiring objects to fill a defined series or set).[50] These and more recent studies suggest that the childhood collecting instinct might be a response to the realization that there is a finite supply of desirable goods, and those who suffer an acute sense of childhood deprivation are prone to neurotic adult collecting or hoarding.[51] For most people, however, the desire to collect declines rapidly after puberty.[52]

While the childhood propensity to collect may be developmental or instinctual, the adult support for the hobby has been purely cultural. Collecting fit the adult world's idea of what children should do in their spare time because it emulated adult conduct and seemed to develop skills and attitudes that were consonant with the prevailing ethos. In 1922 a cranky letter-writer to the *New York Times* acknowledged that childhood collecting might instill useful information, but said, "There is not a shadow of evidence to show that order or neatness transfers from a cabinet of insects to the care of the clothing, or from a stamp collection to the writing of letters, or from a coin collection to keeping one's room neat and orderly." He was, of course, correct; there was no such evidence, but that did not stop everybody else from asserting the global benefits of collecting—especially for boys.[53]

In 1940 *Popular Mechanics* published plans for "The Boy's Own Room and Museum" (see fig. 3.2). How such rooms promoted appropriate behavior was explained a couple of years later by an exasperated mother whose son's collections prevented his room from being properly cleaned. She suppressed her own instinct to throw out his seashells, miniature dogs, glass ornaments, stones, and Indian objects because she recognized "the boy has the beginnings of what it takes to get along in this world—interest in surrounding things and ability to sustain that interest." Instead she bought him a display bookcase, mounted a plaque over it that said "Denny Kelsey Museum," and satisfied both his need for collecting and hers for cleanliness.[54]

The idea that collecting nurtured positive attitudes shows up as early as 1830 when *Godey's Lady's Book* suggested that children be taught to build pasteboard trays "divided into compartments for the reception of the genera and species of shells." This activity, advised the writer, will "lead young persons to habits of order and arrangement." Catharine Beecher concurred. Writing in 1855, she recommended "the collecting of shells, plants, and specimens in geology and mineralogy, for the formation of cabinets." She said she had seen boys collecting and cleaning shells "with a delight bordering on ecstasy" and predicted that if parents would only set the course for their children, the youngsters would soon develop a taste for the collecting hobby. Antebellum advisers suggested collecting readily available natural objects, although they were not insensitive to the harm of collectors' depredations. In 1833 Lydia Child told girls that artificial eggs would look much prettier in Easter baskets than if "they had been real eggs stolen from a poor suffering bird." By the twentieth century, stamps, chromos, cigar tags, and other manufactured goods had become increasingly popular collectibles "in a world grown somewhat anxious about conserving wild flowers and wild bird life." Nevertheless, collecting birds' eggs apparently remained widespread among boys even after the practice was outlawed by the Migratory Bird Treaty of 1916. As late as 1933 a hobby writer was urging boys not to collect birds' eggs and nests (and tobacco tags) because they were worthless.[55]

Adults assumed that collecting aided children in three ways. First, collecting taught children organization skills. Second, it promoted knowledge about the collected objects. Third, collecting developed bargaining skills and a practical understanding of the marketplace. The qualities of organization and knowledge were self-evident; they were what distinguished collecting from accumulation. "One who simply accumulates odds and ends and

FIGURE 3.2 *Popular Mechanics* illustration of an ideal boy's room takes collecting and model building for granted as appropriate youth activities. (Reprinted from *The Boy Mechanic* [Chicago: Popular Mechanics Press, 1940], 10. Copyright the Hearst Corporation. All rights reserved.)

stows them away in a corner is not a collector," warned a 1941 textbook. "A real collector will take great pains to see that each specimen is carefully classified and understood." Learning itself was thought to be a form of collecting, so collecting objects was part of the process of collecting information. "When you are busy making, let us say, a collection of butterflies and moths, your mind too, is storing away a collection of its own," wrote Hildegarde Hawthorne in 1921. Stamp collecting in particular was seen as a painless way to acquire useful information since, as one expert explained in 1928, it "leads to excursions into geography, history, natural history, and art far more interesting than the dry study of these subjects." Natural objects, associated with recognized sciences, and stamps, because of their diverse geographic origins and historical iconography, were the collections most often recommended for children. There was, however, a broader sense that "once a child starts collecting stamps or toy banks or miniature porcelain animals, the very act of collecting becomes an education." Perhaps collecting was an education, but studies showed there was no positive correlation between collecting and success in school, and there may have been a negative one.[56]

The third presumed benefit of collecting was the cultivation of marketplace values and skills. "The kind of objects gathered count for nothing," claimed an educator in 1919; "it is the activity itself that is essential to the normal development of a child." He went on to explain that "the tot of two years when he starts to collect, has entered the first business enterprise of his life," and it has "the power to mark him a success or failure when he comes to his life work as man." Writing in 1883 Mary Blake told mothers that collecting provided them with "constant favorable opportunities for training children, morally as well as mentally." If her boy (all her examples concerned boys) took advantage of another child "by exchanging a worthless United States stamp for a valuable foreign one," the mother had a chance to "give him some forcible advice about common honesty." On the other hand, if her son were on the short end of such an exchange, she said it would teach him "to be more careful in his bargains and not to believe everything that is told him." Her general conclusion could not have been more specific: "Boys who have learned to be both honest and wary have made a good beginning in their business education." Not every Victorian advice-giver agreed that the game of business was worth the candle of marketplace morals. In her encyclopedic advice book *Queen of the Home*, Emma Churchman Hewitt warned against the dangers of collectors "swapping" because the practice fostered "two very undesirable characteristics—a desire for gain and a discontentment with the article possessed." Hewitt worried that swapping would teach boys to " 'drive a sharp bargain' with those younger or more innocent than themselves" and predicted that such dishonesty in childhood boded ill for the child's future.[57]

Both Blake and Hewitt agreed that collecting taught boys the techniques and values of business. They did not agree on the desirability of this consequence. Hewitt realized that her anticompetitive position might lead some fathers to complain, "You would have my son a 'molly-coddle'! I want him to be a man!" Her response was a classic statement of the contradictions involved in having "queens of the home" raising boys for the jungle of business: "The true man is the one who is taught from his earliest infancy to respect the right of the weak, be it in business or pleasure." She recognized the widespread feeling among men that driving a hard bargain was an act of manliness, and her response reflected a desire for a much gentler marketplace. In the 1930s, as had been the case in the past, girls were cautioned to avoid the market altogether: "Collect only what interests you. Do not buy simply because the books are first editions," explained "Book Collecting for Girls" in 1937, "or because you expect to sell them for a profit." By the 1950s, however, the gender distinction faded somewhat and parents were advised that "with a collecting hobby, the child has a good chance of learning about human nature and even economics, in the swapping and barter that adds spice and is part of a healthy competition."[58]

The collecting propensities of children and the subsequent trading activities, especially among boys, struck most observers of children's hobbies as commendable and less problematic than adult collecting. Children were never warned about the danger of compulsiveness, nor were there stories of boys and girls neglecting their other obligations in favor of their hobbies. While some observers saw a threat to morals in the temptations posed by marketplace trading, most applauded the lessons learned. For boys, collecting was practice for the life of business, and even for girls, it brought organizational skills and valuable knowledge.

Men, Women, and the Gendered Object

Collectors themselves acknowledged, and surveys confirmed, that no form of collecting among either adults or children was the exclusive territory of one gender, which is not to say there were no differences. Those differences, both real and perceived, are almost all artifacts of the way that collecting modeled the market economy. So pervasive was the conflation of men, market, and collecting that it has been difficult for most observers to even see that women were collecting, albeit in a style that was different from men. Most scholars consistently refer to collectors with the male pronoun. In part their gendered language reflects the convention of the generic male pronoun, but the rarity of references to women also stems from a more profound division in the structure of collecting.

Take, for example, the comparatively recent work of psychiatrist Frederick Baekeland who, in seeking to understand the preponderance of male art collectors, attributes the lack of women collectors to the contradictions of maleness in contemporary society. Not only are men biologically excluded from the creativity of reproduction, says Baekeland, but they are also discouraged from aesthetic expressions, such as adorning themselves with clothes, jewels, or other decorations. Collecting, he concludes, is one of the few socially permissible ways for men to do what is more widely available to women. The collection itself is both the symbolic child of the barren man and an aesthetic expression that allows the man's taste to invade the traditional female realm of the household. Finally, since art collecting involves items of value pursued and collected in an aggressive fashion, all these feminine qualities are expressed with a competitiveness that legitimates them as a male pastime. Baekeland's analysis would be considerably more convincing if he had addressed widespread collecting patterns of women, collecting behavior that he excludes because the collected objects are not art, are not aggressively collected, and are not objects of value. Therefore in some sense they do not exist.[59]

When scholars do mention women, it is usually to explain why they are not collectors. Sociologist A. D. Olmsted, for example, cites four modern studies that find 85 to 95 percent of collectors are men. Olmsted attributes this preponderance of males to female socialization, which privileges relationships over things. Olmsted does not mention, although it hardly seems irrelevant, that all the collected objects in the studies he cites (stamps, guns, and baseball cards) are traditionally associated with men. Had the investigators surveyed collectors of dolls, buttons, or Christmas plates, they would have undoubtedly discovered a very different gender mix. There have always been women collectors of "male" objects, and there have been, since at least the nineteenth century, female collectors of "female" objects such as chromolithographs and low-cost antiques. In the last twenty years the trend toward female collecting seems to have mushroomed with the manufacture of primary collectibles by companies like the Franklin Mint. The fact does remain, however, that until quite recently collecting of both handmade and manufactured objects was dominated by men.[60]

Students of childhood behavior have noted that while both girls and boys collected, boys were more likely to collect representations of the male world such as cigar bands and arrowheads or items that had been commodified like stamps and marbles. Girls on the other hand tended to collect representations of the female world such as dolls, flowers, and valentines. Birds' eggs were male-collected despite both their biological femaleness and their beauty, presumably because the collecting process was akin to hunting. Although books had become collectors' commodities among adult males, girls were much more likely to collect them than boys but apparently for their sentimental rather than their economic value.[61] The gender segregation of collectibles was by no means complete, for example, two-thirds of the boys Burk surveyed collected "cigar tags," but so did almost a quarter of the girls. On the other hand, a third of the girls collected "picture cards," but so did 9 percent of the boys. What Burk found at the turn of the century has been confirmed by modern studies that show men identify with objects symbolic of power, while women are attracted to aesthetic and emotionally meaningful things.[62]

Not only did boys and girls collect different things, they collected them in different ways. Burk discovered that boys were much more likely than girls to pursue the collected objects aggressively. They hunted, traded, bought, and sold, while girls were more often the passive recipients of gifts. Moreover, she found "boys show more sense of classification than girls, and girls exceed in decorative and miscellaneous arrangements." These gender-specific approaches to collecting may be why a 1918 study found an inverse correlation between girls' success in school and the number of their hobbies; only the boys' aggressive and systematic market-oriented collecting reproduced attitudes valuable for schoolwork. In 1928 Dorothy Sayers had her aristocrat-detective Lord Peter Wimsey tell his nephew that book collecting was "a perfectly manly pursuit. Girls, he said, practically never took it up, because it meant so much learning about dates and type-faces and other technicalities which called for a masculine brain." Whether or not Sayers was being sardonic, the sentiments reflected the widely held beliefs that men collected differently from women.[63]

Two qualities distinguish men's collections; they are valuable or they are explicit tokens of maleness—or both. Certainly, it has been easier for men's collectibles to become valuable because historically men control the wealth, and therefore the value of their collections may be as much a cause as a consequence of their desirability. We need not resolve this chicken-and-egg conundrum to recognize that men have almost always judged their collections in terms of monetary value and that they understood the ability to buy cheap and sell dear to be a sign of prowess. A 1928 study in Kansas found that at almost every age between nine and sixteen, boys were twice as likely as girls to collect things for sale. Girls' sentimental collecting passed with childhood, but "with boys the interest in collecting seems more genuine than with girls and tends to persist through the years," explained one female authority in 1933. Men recognized financial value and sought to develop it, but women lacked "this eager and exhilarating passion," wrote another woman collector. That was, she said, because "the natural impulse of a woman is to get rid of things. The natural impulse of a man is to hold on to them."[64]

Book collectors in particular have perceived women as the enemy, none more so than the poet Eugene Field who in 1896 described heaven as a place full of books but devoid of women. Women, he said, want food and love, but male collectors spend both their money and their emotions on books. Bibliophile Vincent Starrett conceded that book collecting was not a rational expenditure of funds and that "wives are eminently practical and they instinctively recognize the futility of the collecting habit, save as it has to do with such practical items as silk patches and bits of ribbon." Starrett was right insofar as most women stayed out of the self-aggrandizing cycle of male collecting: things are collected because they are valuable; things are valuable because they are collected. The only women collectors taken seriously by men were those who collected on men's terms. Those whose hobby was aesthetic or sentimental were stealth-collectors who simply disappeared from the historical radar. Pioneer autograph collector William Buell Sprague expressed typical ambivalence about dealing with women in the collectors' marketplace. Sprague did not like to buy or sell, but he was willing to trade items with other hobbyists including a few women who were among the finest of early autograph collectors. Writing in 1845 of one particularly complicated trade with a woman, Sprague confided, "I do not much fancy this sort of trading, especially with a lady, but I suppose the fact of having made one regular bargain need not stand in the way of being courteous & even generous afterward." To Sprague, courtesy and generosity were the norm for dealings with women and incompatible with business-like transactions. Even though they were among his most regular collecting companions, Sprague was not able to find a comfortable ideological place from which to deal with women.[65]

In 1921 the *New York Times* quoted a French publication to the effect that women could never be serious collectors even though some "assume the appearance of collectors." The French author said he had the same indulgent respect for them that one had for "children devoted to a hard game beyond their strength." Although the *Times* gallantly defended American women's collecting perspicacity, it gave no actual examples of collecting among women in the United States. In fact, other sources from the era indicate that women indeed avoided objects that had been commodified in markets dominated by men. While some women collected art, stamps, coins, and books, they were a small minority. In 1939, when the *Ladies' Home Journal* suggested that women could become more charming and beautiful by taking up hobbies, the magazine's beauty editor recommended they collect greeting cards, theater programs, bells, fans, buttons, maps, trays, historical dresses, dolls, earth from different places, "pictures of places you would like to go," spoons, and phonograph records. A similar article a decade later suggested the same sorts of items with only the faintest hint that any of these objects might appreciate in value. While there was an organized, if minor, market for buttons by the end of the depression, all the other objects mentioned by these two articles are classically female, that is, they were objects of beauty and sentiment not commodified collectibles with a full secondary market.[66]

The history of button collecting is a history of the ambivalence of female collecting. As decorative items buttons met the primary requirement of female collecting; they were pretty. The first U.S. button collectors were girls who, in the Civil War era, put together "charm strings" of 999 buttons. According to custom, the thousandth button would come from the man they would marry.[67] Charm strings of buttons were exemplary of women's collecting. The items were gathered for aesthetic and sentimental reasons and were displayed as expressions of beauty not wealth. There was, furthermore, no attempt to collect in a systematic, or what men liked to call a "scientific," way. Those women who did display their buttons in an organized fashion created their own categories. Some buttons were grouped according to materials (all glass buttons), others by subject (all buttons with a face), and some by even more whimsical categories such as filling a map of the U.S. with representations of the different states (corn in Nebraska, elk's horn in Wyoming).[68]

Except for a brief attempt in 1902 to organize a military button club, the hobby remained female, amorphous, and highly personal until 1939.[69] Then a book by Polly de Steiguer Crummett successfully started a move to bring business-like rationality to the hobby and, not coincidentally, to broaden its appeal to men. Otto Lightner, the publisher of *Hobbies*, "The Magazine for Collectors," which ran a large number of button advertisements, published Crummett's book and sponsored annual button shows in his home city of Chicago. The National Button Society was formed the same year, and while attempts to include large numbers of men in the hobby failed, Lightner and Crummett successfully imposed the postage stamp model of market-driven collecting on the hobby.[70] Crummett expressed the hope that her book would stimulate additional volumes "perhaps dealing with only one type of button, possibly only with a single button, even as the 1851 U.S. postage stamp had a substantial volume written about it, dealing with its numerous variations." The books that followed created enough of a market environment to remove buttons from the "feminine fad" category and give them the legitimacy of "antiques in miniature."[71] The foreword to a 1949 book on button collecting pleaded, "Don't dismiss button collecting, please, as a feminine vagary" and, in an attempt to purge buttons of their problematic association with female clothing, noted that prior to 1820 some of the fanciest buttons were made for men's clothes.[72]

The button boomlet sparked by Lightner in 1939 did alter the way women collected them. They increasingly accepted the market model for the hobby, although business-like references to value were always balanced by leisure-oriented justifications based on pleasure and aesthetics. For example, in 1948 Pat Norwood explained that she collected buttons because they let her meet with like-minded people and developed an appreciation of beauty, typically female qualities. At the same time she pointed out that rare buttons were escalating in price, some selling for as much as fifty dollars. The commodification of buttons in the World War II period marked a turning point in women's collecting in general. Postwar discussions of collecting were much more likely than prewar articles to characterize women as collectors rather than as enemies of collecting and to include at least some reference to the value of their collections.[73]

Parody as well as serious commentary reflected the new status of postwar women's collecting. The same kind of facetious exaggeration that had so long characterized descriptions of obsessed male collectors now began to appear with women as well as men as the butt of the humor. A 1954 piece told of a certain George Twiller who spanked his wife with a folded copy of *Happy Hobbies* when she augmented her collection of "pearl buttons, glass buttons, wooden buttons, [and] leather buttons," with the copper rivets from his fishing jeans. The divorce judge sided with the wife. The author concluded the piece by noting that his own wife had replaced most of their furniture with broken down antiques, including a four-poster bed complete with its original straw mattress, which she got in exchange for his "collection" of fishing rods. He hoped to find a more sympathetic divorce judge than George Twiller's.[74]

Despite a closing of the gap after 1939, the difference between men's and women's collecting remained. There is a rich body of psychological literature that suggests collecting fills anal-erotic, romantic, aesthetic, competitive, creative-procreative, aggressive, and obsessive-compulsive personality needs, most of which seem to have affected men more than women since men are always the objects of the studies. Whichever of these meanings collecting has had for any given collector, they have almost always been expressed in a manner consonant with the prevailing social-economic ideology. Male collecting has operated from its beginnings through a marketplace that involved almost all the elements contained in the buying and selling of nonhobby commodities. Even those scholars trying to tease out the nature of collecting's psychological attraction regularly couch their explanations either in market terms or in language easily reducible to market terms such as hunting, desire, possession, control, and order. Thus the collector who enters into the collectibles marketplace at any level is taking part in a specialized performance of capitalism. To the extent that the economy has been historically controlled by men, and to the extent that collecting mirrored the economy, collecting has been perceived as a male activity. It was not that women did not collect but that they did not collect in what were perceived as important ways. Just as female consumption was granted less importance than male production in the marketplace, sentimental collecting was subordinated to economic collecting in the leisure sphere. The specific patterns of collecting may have varied from fairly passive consumerism to extremely elaborate speculation, but however it was played out, collectors experienced their pleasure in a context that is both a product of and a producer of the ideology of market capitalism.

4   Constructing a Collector's Market

Anthropologist Arjun Appadurai has argued that modern society requires two separate kinds of knowledge, one for production and one for consumption, and it has been suggested that collecting is a model of consumption. This may have been the case historically for women, but for men in the past, and increasingly for both genders in the present, collecting seems to be more about the accumulation of wealth than the consumption of commodities. Since collectors do buy things, there is obviously a parallel with the general process of consumption, but unlike normally purchased items, collectibles are not consumed, and it is for this reason that the process is more akin to capital accumulation than to expenditure. Just as crafts are the ideological expression of the work ethic, collecting is the ideological expression of the free market. It replicates and confirms the legitimacy of risk-taking in a market milieu. English politician Augustine Birrell argued in 1905 that collectors were immune to the lures of communism because "no habits are more alien to the doctrine of the Communist than those of the collector." Early leaders of the Soviet Union recognized the truth in Birrell's comment as they struggled with the problem of stamp collecting. While the Soviet government wished to sell stamps abroad for their cash and propaganda value, it worried that stamp trading at home would promote speculation and other capitalist behaviors that would undermine proper socialist values.[1]

The Rules of Virtuous Collecting

The marketplace is both the mechanism of and a threat to the collecting hobby. Except for intangibles and purely sentimental items, objects are obtained through and disposed of in the market. Item for item trades take place within the symbolic economy of collecting, but buying and selling move the transaction from symbolic to real. Cash dealings are business, and for some collectors that alone makes them detrimental to the hobby. Only once, reported book collector Andrew Lang in 1910, did he ever "fall from virtue" by selling one of his precious books. To have done so regularly would have reduced his avocation to "a mere trade," and another collector of the same period said he strove to "keep his pleasure from sinking to a business."[2] In 1927, when an executive boasted that his stamp collection had risen in value, he was told by a coworker that he had the "wrong attitude" and that his financial orientation was "sordid." The collector defensively replied, "don't worry over my having the wrong attitude towards my hobby," and went on to assure his colleague that he would enjoy what he did just as much "if the market had gone off, and the collections were not worth a dollar."[3]

The value-laden phrase "wrong attitude" expressed a nearly universal ambivalence among collectors who were torn between measuring their collecting success in dollar terms and the fear that their hobbies might become another form of work. Yet measuring success in dollar terms was a major source of the hobby's pleasure because it was the way one kept score in the game of collecting. "My sport is book hunting," wrote A. Edward Newton in 1918, "I look upon it as a game." Newton knew he won the game when he saw a book he owned listed for more than he paid for it, even though he had no desire to sell. He loved his books more than money, but he used the money to track his standing. There was no desire to escape the calculus of the marketplace since there was no reason the price of pleasure could not also be an investment. In 1880 the editors of the *American Journal of Numismatics* reprinted, with cautious approval, a piece called "The Profit of Collecting." In essence, the article praises the collector who lives a frugal life and sacrifices personal amenities so that he can increase his collection, which in addition to bringing him pleasure, can be sold "at his death or before it . . . for such a sum as will materially add to the resources of his family."[4]

By the 1920s references to collecting as a form of capital appreciation had become almost reflexive. "Everybody collects something nowadays," proclaimed a 1924 guide to the hobby. "The difficulty is to find something that no one else is collecting and to gather up a collection that will not only give pleasure and be an enterprise," it continued, "but also will some day, if needs demand, fetch more than the modest sum already expended." The writer assumed that there would be a buyer for "something no one else is collecting," but even collectors who knew better could not resist boasting. In 1928 book collector A. Edward Newton called books a worse investment than stocks and suggested that book collectors laugh at sellers who tell them "such and such a book is a good investment." Go to a banker when you want to invest, he advised in that year before the great crash, go to a bookseller when you want to be extravagant, and "be satisfied when the game is called to get your money back." Yet this exposition of sobering realism about collecting was preceded by numerous examples of his own and others' economic triumphs in the book trade. He told of selling his early collection of first editions for enough to build a summer cottage, cited people who doubled their money in a year, described pieces bought for three pounds in England and sold for eight thousand dollars in the United States a few weeks later, and one that doubled its value literally in the wink of an eye at an auction.[5]

The depression appears to have done little to dampen the profit motive among collectors. On the contrary, hard times sharpened people's appetite for forms of investment that might do better than the falling financial markets. Book collector William Dana Orcutt cited ever-increasing prices for rare books "even during periods when the country is suffering from industrial depression and Wall Street prices are steadily declining." Traditional collectibles remained the favorite investments of those who wanted profit as well as pleasure from their hobby, and experts regularly assured the neophyte that "he is likely to have something that will retain much of its value even in bad times" and that "it may prove a safer investment than the more usual stocks and bonds." In a more adventuresome vein, the *New York Evening Post* suggested collectors consider Victorian antiques because, having exhausted the supply of antebellum antiques, collectors were bound to turn to the "erstwhile despised knickknacks and objects d'art" of the Victorian era. Anticipating the successful magazine of the 1950s with a similar name, a dealer in Los Angeles began publishing a newsletter, *Collecting for Profit*, in 1931. It offered lists and "money making information" on old books, autographs, and printed ephemera.[6]

On the eve of World War II, collecting and investment had become indivisible and spread well beyond the standard objects. British essayist Harold Child noted in 1939 that cigarette cards "are now coveted, collected, classified, catalogued, and commercialized by grown and serious men." Soon, he predicted with more prescience than his humorous tone intended, there would be Ph.D. dissertations on "cartophily" and tobacco stock would rise in value along with the cards "unless some dastard should start selling cigarette cards without cigarettes." The assumption of economic appreciation that had once been reserved for art, fine antiques, coins, stamps, and books was now applied almost unselectively to the residue of contemporary civilization. In 1943 book collector Jake Zeitlin recommended that people begin saving ephemera including war toys and comic books. Speaking of his ten-year-old son's reading habits, he noted astutely, "Whatever I may think of the comics, I know that a set of *Superman* may well bring this heir of mine a middling fortune by the time he is my age."[7]

Yet profit was still the serpent in the garden of collecting. Remembering his idealized youth, coin collector Conway Bolt claimed that in that golden age (around 1913) "no collector ever attempted to corner the market," but times had changed, and the generosity of the past had been replaced with people who were eager to "get rich quick." The pertinent word here is "quick." Most collectors welcomed the gradual gain in the value of their collections when it occurred as an incidental benefit of collecting. It confirmed both the collector's acumen and the legitimacy of capital appreciation in the real world. Windfalls were something else again. Collectors accepted and even dreamed about windfalls that came about naturally, which is to say accidentally, but decried those that were contrived by unscrupulous collectors or dealers.[8]

The first kind of windfall can be likened to buried treasure: nobody owns it because nobody knows its exists, and the collector finds it by accident. "In the breast of every collector there dwells the hope that some day he or she, as the case may be, will find something of great value in some unexplored hiding place," wrote one stamp collector in 1931. After World War II, as the market for paper ephemera and mass-produced consumer goods grew, the possibility of finding *Treasures in Truck and Trash*, as the title of a 1949 book put it, increased dramatically. Folklorists have suggested that American tales of buried treasure emphasize that it is still out there to be found, but if it is found it will bring bad luck because it is unearned. As modelers of the market, collectors were more willing than storytellers to accept unearned income. Nevertheless, even collectors distinguished between legitimate and illegitimate gain. If the treasure were found as a result of the collector's expertise, it was generally okay. Buying with the intention of selling quickly, however, was speculation and violated the spirit of the hobby; manipulating the market, of course, fell completely outside the pale of acceptable behavior.[9]

An 1866 tale by T. S. Arthur illustrates a number of these points. The protagonist, Mr. Henry, "a true lover of art," purchased a painting "from a real appreciation of its excellence; but, in doing so, he expended a larger sum than he could well afford." In the same sentence Arthur establishes that the collector's motives are pure but that the process of collecting has had negative economic consequences. Not only does the painting turn out to be too large for his parlor, but Henry discovers he needs the five thousand dollars for business. A friend suggests that Henry exhibit the painting and charge the public an admission fee. Unwilling to prostitute his picture Henry agrees to donate the proceeds to a charity but has second thoughts when the public proves willing to spend three hundred dollars a week to see the painting. Angry at having been caught in a moral dilemma of his own making, Henry consoles himself with the thought that the exhibit might produce a buyer because "when it becomes known how largely the exhibition has paid, its ownership will be regarded as a good speculation." Given a choice between gentlemanly scruples about the purity of collecting and practical considerations based on the cash nexus, the marketplace easily triumphs.[10]

Henry's attempts to manipulate the market, that is, drum up an interest in his painting, are all fairly straightforward and aboveboard. However, a couple of confidence men have a more elaborate plan. One of them plants a negative review of the painting in the local paper and uses it as the basis for a low-ball offer, knowing full well that "the Academy" is raising a special subscription to buy the painting. Once the swindlers get their painting, they plant a corrective article, but are stymied when the directors of the Academy become aware of the machinations and refuse to buy from the con artists. Stuck with the painting, they agree to sell it back to Henry at a loss, and Henry in turn sells it to the museum for enough to cover his costs.[11]

By buying beyond his means and coveting art too grand for his station, Henry had displayed a form of collecting hubris for which he paid through psychological discomfort with the art and a great deal of inconvenience. He was an honest businessman who, in essence, did not know his place. The crooks, of course, lost money for their marketplace dishonesty. The entire episode reflects Arthur's sense that collecting was a pastime fraught with danger because of the way it interfaced with the market. So long as a collector kept within his budget and bought out of love, not greed, it was a worthwhile pursuit, but when pride tempted the collector to reach beyond his means, or avarice tempted the speculator to manipulate the natural rule of the market, the consequences could be serious. The marketplace was the ultimate arbiter of things both economic and moral.

Arthur's moralistic assessment of the collecting pastime was widely shared by those who felt the collecting game, like business itself, was good because all participants played by the same rules. However, the desire to win tempted people to cheat and, morality tales not withstanding, collectors often felt that a tainted victory was preferable to none at all. Scottish scholar and poet Andrew Lang wrote a morally ambivalent parable in 1886 in which he told of a fictional fellow book collector, Thomas Blinton, whose passion for collecting corrupted him to his core. He loved books as commodities but not as literature. He coveted his neighbors' books, begrudged the good fortune of fellow collectors, and rejoiced in their failures. He took advantage of ignorant sellers and kept money from his wife so he could invest it in books. "Greedy, proud, envious, stingy, extravagant, and sharp in his dealings, Blinton was guilty of most of the sins which the Church recognizes as 'deadly,' " wrote Lang. Blinton then has a Dickensian dream in which he is carried away in bidding against the devil for rare books, cannot meet the bill, and watches his own collection go under the hammer to satisfy his debts. Blinton was no Scrooge, nor was Lang a Dickens. "If this were an ordinary tract," he writes,

"I should have to tell how Blinton's eyes were opened, how he gave up book-collecting, and took to gardening, or politics, or something of the sort. But truth compels me to admit that Blinton's repentance had vanished by the end of the week." A mere miser like Scrooge could be reformed, but a collector valued his volumes more than his immortal soul.[12]

The avaricious Blinton might as well have been a dealer, for dealers were often pictured as collectors gone bad. A gentleman, said book collector Barton Currie, could never become a dealer without acquiring "shabby, questionable habits." Since it was generally assumed that dealers were unscrupulous commodity mongers who loved profit more than beauty, they were often depicted as the legitimate butt of collectors' schemes to cheat them out of their wares. Unethical transactions that would have been condemned under any other circumstances were condoned when aimed at dealers. Charles Rowed, for example, gleefully told the tale of a buyer who complained to an immigrant dealer that a statuette of Admiral Nelson had only one arm, and the ignorant shopkeeper thinking it broken lowered the price by two-thirds.[13]

Book collector and dealer A. S. W. Rosenbach wrote a short story in 1917 in which a poor collector is about to spend his last dollar on a coveted volume. Before the sale is consummated, however, a much richer collector comes into the shop and offers the dealer ever-increasing amounts of money until the dealer reneges on his promise to sell to the first man and takes an extravagant sum from the second. The poor collector subsequently manages to join the rich one on a train trip to Chicago, fills his head with libelous stories about the dealer to make him think he had been cheated, and steals the book by switching it with a similarly wrapped tract, "A Sermon on Covetousness." Moreover, the poor collector apparently lives happily ever after with his ill-gotten gains, proud of having besmirched the reputation of the dealer and stolen a book that had been legitimately sold to another person. This is no ordinary cautionary tale; it is a fable without a moral, and since it was written by an active collector, at best the message is, "be careful about taking advantage of others lest you become the victim." At worst, it is a confirmation of the Darwinian world of the hobby marketplace where guile is pitted against money and the victors go home with the spoils.[14]

Douglas and Elizabeth Rigby noted fifty years ago, in what is still the finest overview of collecting, that "the collector bent upon his game of getting the best for as little as possible seldom feels bound to consider the ethics of the case" and that when "it comes to pitting his knowledge against a stranger's innocence he can put Machiavelli himself to shame and be proud of it." Baser instincts did not always prevail, but they were always there. In one of a series of popular short stories about collecting in the 1920s, Horace

Vachell had an elderly spinster ask a collector if a Ming vase she owned were worth twenty pounds. "A horrible temptation assailed him," wrote Vachell, because "no philosopher has yet ventured to set forth the ethics involved in buying and selling rare porcelain. Collectors themselves, with rarest exceptions, hold the opinion that it is lawful to buy in the cheapest market and to sell in the dearest." In this case, however, the collector, who was after all English and a gentleman, overcame the temptation and told the spinster the vase was probably worth two thousand pounds. Some real-life collectors extended the same courtesy to elderly widows but when dealing with less vulnerable owners had no compunctions about taking advantage of them. Wilmarth Lewis, on the other hand, remembered as "one of the great moments of my collecting life" paying a book collector's widow eight cents a volume for 250 selected books. "We all had twinges of conscience," he admitted, "but what collector can resist a bargain?"[15]

Taking advantage of supposedly informed dealers was less problematic since in that game the players were ostensibly more evenly matched. In 1927 antique collector C. R. Clifford recounted a rather elaborate story that illustrates the difference between taking advantage of the naive and the knowledgeable. Clifford's friend and fellow collector Bill Lovell had purchased a barrel of items from a farm auction for a dollar. Since Lovell did not know what he was buying, the transaction was more a lottery than anything else and Lovell could not be accused of taking advantage of the seller. To his delight he found a number of relatively valuable items, including an ironstone platter that he offered to sell to Clifford at fair market value. Clifford complained because the price was so much higher than Lovell had paid. Lovell responded that it had taken him twenty years of trading to gain the knowledge to recognize the difference between junk and antiques. "Ain't I entitled to cash in on my superior knowledge? What's the good of an education if you can't profit from it?" he asked. Clifford paid, took the platter home, and discovered that the old cloth in which it had been wrapped was a piece of printed chintz worth about five times what he paid for the platter. When Lovell complained that the cloth was not part of the deal, Clifford made him eat his own words: "Ain't I entitled to cash in on my superior knowledge?" In the marketplace of collecting, expertise is power and strategically exercised power produces a victory symbolized by the trophy of the acquired object—measured by the difference between its fair market value and the price paid. Beating a worthy foe was preferable to stealing from widows and orphans, but the ethos of collecting was the ethos of the market— both caveat emptor and caveat venditor.[16]

Susan Stewart has argued that in contrast to crafts, collecting "mimes the seriality and abstraction of postindustrial modes of production." In fact, collecting as a hobby embraces two forms, one that looks back to a preindustrial era and the other grounded solidly in the industrial world. Collectors of handmade objects, whether new or old, are imposing a rational business-like order on objects that represent an archaic mode of production; thus the preindustrial past is linked with the industrial present. Perhaps even more importantly, collecting of handmade objects creates serial structure and classificatory sets of items that originally were unique and probably distinct from other things in their class. On the other hand, those who collect manufactured products are combining the business-like hobby of collecting with the equally rational and efficient mode of mass production. They are, however, doing so in a way that creates uniqueness where there was a previously undifferentiated mass. Thus collectors of the past order the disordered while collectors of the present differentiate the undifferentiated. Both processes are vital to creating the specialized market economy in which collectors operate.[17]

Stamp Collecting: Commodifying the Ephemeral

Stamp collecting and industrial capitalism in the United States emerged simultaneously in the mid-nineteenth century. England issued the first government postage stamp in 1840 and other nations quickly adopted the idea. The United States printed its first official stamp in 1847, but it was preceded by "provisionals" issued by local postmasters. The collecting of these tokens would become not only the prototypical form of collecting but the prototype hobby as well. Stamp collectors were acutely self-conscious of the ways in which their activity mimicked real-world commerce. They appropriated the language of the commodity market and used it to both praise and criticize their leisure activity. As a form of disguised affirmation, stamp collecting was congruent with capitalism but in a way that provided a sense of relief from work. The author of a 1954 introduction to philately suggested that the hobby could boost "the lagging ego of the average American adult," who would "find compensation for a mediocre performance in his life's work in outstanding accomplishments in the charmed world of philately." But the author's idea of compensation consisted on the one hand of building monetary value in a collection and on the other of the possibility that "the common man" could "triumph over the exceptional man through sheer philatelic ability." In other words, the meaning of the so-called compensatory activity was drawn straight from the overarching ideology of competitive capitalism.[18]

The hobby's ideological meaning was not present at its creation; it took approximately twenty years for stamp collecting to become a male-dominat-

ed, market-oriented pastime. Women and children were the hobby's first participants and their interest was more aesthetic than economic. Stamp collecting initially attracted middle-class women because they had the most free
time and were always looking for light occupations to pursue at home. Less
than a year after England issued its first postage stamp, an English woman
was advertising for stamps with which to cover her dressing room walls.
Other women of the same era used stamps to decorate work boxes and
trunks. As late as 1880, well after stamps had become commodified by a secondary market, *Godey's* published a design for a "postage stamp table,"
explaining to its readers that, "rare postage stamps are gummed to the top."
By the turn of the century, however, the idea of using stamps as decorative
devices had become so absurd that philatelic journals made jokes about
stamp wallpaper.[19]

What may be thought of as the "aesthetic phase" of stamp collecting
came to an end around 1860 by which time the *Boston Daily Advertiser*
could note that stamps were developing differential values so that "amateur
stamp brokers" could get hundreds of common European and American
stamps for just half a dozen rarer Mauritius or Hawaiian stamps. Having recognized the transition from art object to marketplace commodity, the author
concluded that although "this elegant and curious 'mania' is now chiefly
indulged in by young ladies," it would not be too long before it would "take
possession of the more mature portion of mankind."[20] His prediction was
coming true even as he wrote, and once men displaced women as stamp collectors the very essence of the hobby changed. As additional countries adopted postage stamps, collecting spread until it reached fad proportions in
Europe during the early 1860s mirroring the market capitalism of the postbellum era.[21]

The transition from aesthetic to market collecting was reputed to have
received a boost from the unlikeliest of transactions. In 1871 a frequent writer
on collecting reported that "timbrophily" (an early alternative to "philately"
as a designation for "scientific" stamp collecting) had its origins in trading
canceled stamps to "heartless Hindoo parents" in return for "the little babes
they are accustomed to sacrifice before their idols." The writer explained
that the "barbarians" coveted these tokens either as offerings to their gods or
as decoration. The result, he said, was a "change in the economy of canceled
stamps," whereby counting houses saved stamps that they gave to poor boys
who used them as tuition for charity schools who in turn gave them to mis-
sionaries in India to rescue babies before they were set afloat on the Ganges.
This exchange of stamps for infants was doubtlessly a nineteenth-century
urban legend, but it embodies the change in meaning of stamps. Here it is
the heathen Hindus (not English ladies) who desire the stamps for aesthetic

purposes and the rational Europeans who use their value in the marketplace to rescue innocents from the crocodiles' jaws.[22]

There are no reliable historical figures or even good guesses about the number and composition of stamp collectors. Documentary evidence, however, indicates that boys continued to constitute an important segment of the stamp collecting population, but women and girls appear to have retreated from the hobby quite early. In 1871, when stamp collecting was contracting after the stamp "mania" of the 1860s, an American stamp paper defensively argued that the "fever" was not subsiding and that "not only boys are in our ranks, but prominent men and ladies of all classes are numbered with us." The reference to "ladies" may have been more a social convention than an indication of female participation ("boys" were not paired with "girls"), since almost all other sources from that period make it clear that males had come to dominate the hobby. Commenting on the rapid rise and fall of stamp clubs in the 1880s, for example, a Denver stamp paper said there were three kinds of associations: "those composed altogether of quite young boys; those composed of men and youngsters who have nearly reached manhood; and those composed of both the former."[23]

At first glance, the transition to male domination seems curious because philately was morphologically similar to collecting chromolithographed advertising trade cards, which was popular among girls. Like chromos, stamps were initially valued for their aesthetic qualities, but unlike commercially produced trade cards, the officially printed stamps came to be regarded as "important." Not only were they issued by governments, but they also had some intrinsic value (at least when uncirculated), and they depicted serious events, places, and people rather than the sentimental and humorous themes that appeared on the chromos. Most notably, however, stamps lent themselves to systematic collecting. It was easy to create conceptual sets but not too easy to complete them, and thus a market for desired stamps emerged. The markets in which they were traded were called *bourse*, like the French stock market, and it was men, of course, who could properly engage in the rough-and-tumble of commodity trading.[24]

While they were being excluded from the bourse, women were being given a central role in the emporium. This division of labor with men as producers and women as consumers is reflected in the distinction between collecting stamps and collecting trade cards. Stamps were commodities with market value that made them both symbolic and real capital; thus they were collected by men. Chromos, on the other hand, were commercially printed advertisements for commercial products given away for free to promote end-user consumption—printed tokens of women's roles to be collected by women. Ellen Gruber Garvey has argued that the mass-produced chromos not only stood for, but also embodied, the essence of postindustrial consumption. The girl collectors of these artifacts, says Garvey, were "apprentice shoppers, entering the discourse of consumption and learning to converse within it and respond to its conventions and imperatives." Not surprisingly, the girls tended to arrange their collections according to aesthetic or narrative principles, rather than the "scientific" classifications favored by the male stamp collectors. The girl's album or scrapbook symbolically reproduced her ideal world of the beautiful objects she could hope to buy.[25] The boy's stamp album, on the other hand, was less expressive and therefore less symbolic. The classificatory arrangement of stamps by country and year was an explicit acknowledgment of the existence of discrete sets with real market value. Unlike the chromo scrapbook, the stamp album was both a catalog and a repository of wealth. Thus even in their collecting hobbies, men produced and women consumed.

The commodification of stamps occurred early, but not completely. Even for men, stamps were not simply economic units. They assumed a commodity value because men desired to create collections of them, but men desired to create collections because the stamps had aesthetic, historical, or educational value and because their collections could be organized into a series of increasingly more difficult stages. Thus stamp collecting embodied an internal tension in which the stamps were simultaneously desired for their market value and for an intrinsic quality. By having both psychic and market worth, stamp collecting could function as a metaphor for the free market: a voluntary and pleasurable activity that trained boys in the techniques and values of commerce and that confirmed the legitimacy of the market economy for adult males.

The attractiveness of stamps was their most problematic quality, because the appreciation of beauty was thought to be a feminine attribute. In the 1890s, at about the time the chromo collecting craze was peaking, there was a brief flurry of activity by and about women stamp collectors. Although much of the attention appears to have been the doing of a small group of articulate female philatelists, their complaints of exclusion were sufficiently serious to cause at least one stamp paper to devote a special issue to them. The editor assured his readers that women were not relegated to gender-segregated auxiliaries in the association he represented but were given full voting and office-holding rights in the Philatelic Society of America. Be that as it may, the women collectors brought a very different set of assumptions to the hobby. Explained one male collector, "When to us, a stamp only represents so much money expended in its purchase, the philatelic female will weave a wondrous web of sentiment around it." It was simply assumed that "women love and enjoy bright colors and artistic pictures even more than men do" and would appreciate the opportunity to place their stamps in albums in "whatever novel and artistic designs they may devise."[26]

The question of how to arrange stamps in an album was in fact a visible symbol of the meaning of the collection. "To put a lot of stamps into an album, beginning with the smallest value and following it with the next higher value may do very well for a miserly collection," explained one woman collector, "but to arrange a collection of stamps to be attractive, as well as valuable, takes the fertile mind of a woman."[27] To women, the stamp collection, like the trade-card collection, was a medium through which they could express their creativity; it was not a compendium of economic value. "Collecting stamps for mercenary ends is not the true object of this science," wrote Mame A. Keene in 1894. The proper object was the "accumulation of such a collection as will satisfy his or her desire," and she reminded her readers "that it will be far more gratifying to arrange such a collection artistically." Maud Charlotte Bingham described in proud detail how she grouped some of her stamps in abstract designs and others in shapes appropriate to their categories: "The War departments were hinged on the pencil outline of a monster siege gun, the Agriculture departments on the outline of a plow, and the Justices on the tall outline of Justice standing on a foundation of her stamps."[28] Finally an unnamed woman collector in Chester, Pennsylvania, like the first woman collector who festooned her dressing room with stamps, used "rare stamps in fine condition" to decorate "articles of bric-a-brac in her boudoir."[29]

This careful gender distinction between monetary and artistic value was no Victorian anomaly. In the twentieth century women were pioneers in "topical" collecting, that is, collecting according to pictorial subject matter rather than according to chronological-geographical origins. Unwilling to conform to the standard "scientific" taxonomy, Fay Jordan, a collector in the 1940s, amassed forty albums of nothing but violet-colored stamps, including an example of the legendary "Post Office Mauritius."[30] In the 1930s Esther Schlosser, a professional stamp dealer, was encouraging other women to form stamp clubs while warning them not to turn the club meetings into "miniature Maxwell Streets" (an open-air market area in Chicago). The club members, she said, should "stress the classical beauty of stamp collecting and not commercialize the club so much as to make it distasteful to the genuine philatelist." Thus even a woman who was making a living buying and selling stamps rejected the market model as appropriate for women and instead emphasized the "romance" in stamps, "the long journeys they have taken, the messages they have carried [and] the pictures on the stamps themselves."[31]

The market model, which underlay stamp collecting from its earliest days, militated against female participation because both men and women perceived dealing as inappropriate feminine behavior. While the give-and-take of the marketplace provided stamp collecting with a masculine business-like aura, and the possibility of a real "find" gave it a speculative piquancy, something more was needed to justify philately as a hobby. Although men almost never commented on the aesthetic or romantic aspects of postage stamps, some of the qualities embodied in those two categories were included in the much-touted "educational" benefits ascribed to stamp collecting from its very earliest days.[32] Unlike aesthetic creativity, which was purely feminine, education was a positive good for both sexes. A female collector in the 1890s promised that collectors' "artistic tastes would be cultivated and developed by a study of the beautiful designs and colors" and that "their education would be broadened by a research into history, mythology, natural history, science and art." A male collector of the same era argued "that philately teaches history, geography and biography to a certain extent." How else, he asked, would one learn where Cundinamarca and Nowanugger were? How else indeed! By emphasizing the more rational virtue of education over the more feminine one of beauty, the men were able to fit the noneconomic benefits of the hobby into a grand scheme that was compatible with the mechanics of the free market.[33]

A study in the 1930s confirmed that adolescent and adult collectors did in fact know more about history and geography than noncollectors, but that was not enough for collectors; they wanted it be an antidote for dissipation as well. In 1871 a New Jersey stamp paper claimed that philately was not only a "pleasant pastime" but also a "useful labor." Stamp collecting kept young men at home and occupied minds that would otherwise have been idle, said the paper, going on to remind its readers that "an idle mind is the devil's workshop." While occupying the idle mind, stamp collecting also absorbed the idle dollar that might otherwise have been spent on social vices. The "few pennies" expended on stamps were better spent there "than at a billiard table, or at the bar" concluded the same writer. A contributor to an 1892 edition of the *Eastern Philatelist*, who candidly signed himself "Blue Nose," recounted the sad tale of his descent from his clean philatelic life style into drinking, smoking, and gambling after he left his small-town Nova Scotia home and fell under the evil tutelage of a big-city roommate. Fortunately he was saved from his life of debauchery when he discovered that two of his fellow clerks were collectors and began to spend his evenings working on stamps with them. In the company of these untainted young men he was "gradually weaned from any desire" to smoke, drink, or play cards.[34]

Some stamp collectors claimed that more than just fraternal alliances could come from pursuit of their hobby. Despite the fact that few women participated in the supposedly democratic fellowship of stamp collecting, there was still some sense—perhaps hope is a better word—among men that stamp collecting could improve their success with the opposite sex. If there were ever a poor pastime for meeting women, it had to be the male-dominated world of stamp collecting, yet the stamp press carried a surprising number of pieces in which stamps were the vehicle through which men came to know women more intimately. Such fantasies were augmented with true stories of meeting attractive young women by discussing stamps with them and with suggestions that single men invite their women friends to stamp activities.[35]

The calls from a few men and women to include more women in what was in fact the stamp *fraternity* highlight the male character of the pastime. Even sympathetic men characterized women collectors as "elderly maidens" who accumulated vast quantities of valueless stamps or as well-meaning but hopelessly ignorant mothers trying to understand the arcane philatelic references of their sons. Eva Earl, one of the most outspoken women collectors of the late nineteenth century, complained that the old established philatelic societies had a "taboo" on women and pleaded for the newer regional stamp groups to open their doors to women.[36] An optimistic woman collector had predicted in 1894 that there would be a "Ladies Philatelic Weekly Official Organ of the Ladies' Philatelic Circle of America" by the turn of the century. In fact, no exclusively women's stamp clubs developed until the great hobby boom of the 1930s, and even they were apparently short-lived.[37] (See fig. 4.1.)

Arguments for the social benefits of collecting could not completely obscure the recognition that philately could become a shameful disease. From its very beginnings in 1842 when *Punch* referred to stamp collectors as "Knights of the Spit-upon," satirists made fun of the single-minded pursuit of stamps.[38] A turn-of-the-century collector retold in rhyme how he "used to scoff and laugh and sneer, / At those who begged or borrowed or stole / The postage stamps they craved with all their soul," but who then himself "chanced to get one, then two, then three" and concluded, "It's catching, like measles, sir, you see."[39] Along with the joking tone that marked so much of the material about stamp "fiends" and stamp "mania," there are also indications that some, perhaps many, collectors were genuinely embarrassed by their pastime. In 1887 when a Colorado collector laid out some rules for assuring successful stamp clubs, prominent among them was the requirement that club officers be willing to admit that they were stamp collectors. "An officer, or for that matter a member of a society is of little account if he is ashamed of being a stamp collector, or of being known as one," he warned. Writing in 1893 of his youth, a southern philatelist told of how he would go off on a trip to collect, but he added, "I did not inform my employer what my object was on my vacation, as I had a dread of telling him I was a stamp collector, fearful lest I should lose my job."[40]

FIGURE 4.1 Portrait of the Minneapolis Women's Philatelic Society in 1939. (Reprinted from Charlotte Matson, "Minneapolis Women's Philatelic Society," *Hobbies* 44 [May 1939]: 67.)

To combat the negative implications of having a hobby, when that word still meant an unhealthy preoccupation, early male collectors attempted to transform stamp collecting into a "science." The neologism "philately" had been concocted in France in 1864 to give the hobby a scientific cachet, and it was used by those who stressed the technical elements of the activity.[41] Throughout the late 1860s and 1870s rationalized stamp collecting was known as the "French School," and the French approach was firmly established in the United States in the following decade.[42] True philatelists, wrote an American stamp paper editor in 1887, were "those who *scientifically* collect, classify, and arrange stamps."[43] Science was an adult, and a male, activity, and by extension, so was scientific leisure. Collectors in the nineteenth century referred to their hobby as a "science" so routinely that they began to use "science" as a synonym for stamp collecting.[44]

The aspects of stamp collecting that proponents deemed "scientific" included a variety of technical skills and knowledge having to do with water marks, perforations, engraving, and other physical properties of the stamps themselves. Certainly the prolific Eva Earl would have horrified scientific purists when she wrote of the pleasure she found in "cleaning the backs [of her stamps], the brightening up of their faces, mending little tears, adding here and there, a missing perforation." Scientific stamp collectors cared not about appearance but about two kinds of authenticity. First, the stamp had to be authentic in the sense that it was not a counterfeit, and second, its condition had to be authentic, that is not repaired or artificially enhanced. Authenticity was important because a genuine and undoctored stamp had more value in the marketplace than a copy or a repaired item. The idea of scientific stamp collecting was thus closely linked to the market—an aspect of the hobby that men took much more seriously than women like Eva Earl.[45]

The value created by systematically filling sets with authentic stamps sometimes erased the line between work and play for stamp collectors. Beginning stamp collectors could salvage stamps from envelopes, but once past the novice stage no collectors could realistically hope to build their collections from scavenging. They had to turn, enthusiastically or reluctantly, to the marketplace, which at first was actively opposed by postal authorities.[46] Government hostility to the informal curbside bourse initiated by French children in the late 1850s and English children in the early 1860s prompted police harassment of the traders:

> When sudden a gruff voice is heard,
> That all the thronging bevy stirred,
> I turned, and fix'd my eyes upon
> A bobby! crying—"Stamps, move on!"[47]

Government opposition was not limited to the street corners. Post office clerks resented the unorthodox use of their inventory and were, like the police, annoyed by the horseplay of the boys trading near their buildings. Until the 1890s postal authorities not only refused to cooperate with stamp collectors, several governments, including those of Canada and the United States, actually made it illegal to exchange or sell uncanceled stamps at more than their face value. This uncooperative attitude underwent a dramatic about-face after 1894, when Portugal realized that a collected unused stamp, especially one with a high face value, represented pure profit. Until the turn of the century, however, stamp collecting operated independently of governments through full-time dealers as well as casual street markets.[48]

When treating their stamps as commodities, collectors tended to adopt one of three models, each of which reflected a different perception of the marketplace. "Merchants" sold or traded their stamps either to fill their own collections or to make a modest profit on each transaction. "Investors" focused more on the increase in the value of their stamps over time than on the trading activity itself. Both the merchant and investor models assume that the collector was interested in enhancing his own collection and that profits, if any, were an incidental benefit. However, the "speculator" placed lucre before leisure. Unlike other collectors who "won" by completing their sets, the speculator won by striking it rich.[49]

The merchant model held particular fascination for the nineteenth century, especially as it operated among children. It seems that many boys, once they discovered that there were profits to be made in selling their own surplus stamps, recognized that they could make even more money by reselling stamps they had bought for that express purpose. Collector Dick Flint described how, as a boy, he visited the office of a stamp dealer and was shown stamp journal advertisements placed by private individuals. A rock collector, Flint was motivated to use an ad to sell his duplicate minerals, and then, intrigued by his success he traded a series of items that eventually got him about two thousand stamps. In order to save money on advertising Flint started his own stamp paper, which he used to trade for free ads with other stamp papers. Flint's story was more elaborate than most, but by no means unique. Disposal of duplicates, which were inevitable for boy collectors who regularly bought large unsorted lots by mail, was the beginning of active participation in the stamp market.[50]

Boy dealers were the bane of the hobby. Their limited capital and their propensity to ignore their commercial obligations prompted a good deal of criticism from adult dealers, many of whom published the stamp papers in which the small-time retailers ran their advertisements. Nevertheless, collector Guy Green had some kind words for boy dealers whom he characterized as "a unique and in some respects admirable feature of fin de siecle philately." Boy dealers, said Green, are just like adult brokers except that they deal "with the rise and fall of stocks writ small."[51] Observers instinctively used the stock exchange metaphor when describing this category of collectors, recognizing it for what it was, a nascent commodity market being born on the streets (as had the stock markets themselves).[52] A poem entitled "A Strange 'Change" that appeared in an English stamp journal sometime before 1869 portrayed a group of boys in Birchin Lane trading stamps with all the enthusiasm of stock brokers:

"Who'll give a Turkey for a Pole?
You see the envelope's quite whole."
"I'll take a Swedish for a Cape:"
"If I'm a monkey, you're an ape."
"A Pole's worth more than any Russian."
"One old Dane's worth a set of Prussian,"
"I want a Sandwich for a bear:"
"Why, that is not one-half as rare."[53]

Lest the analogy be lost on the reader, the scene was being observed by a broker who himself has just sold out his own shares on the " 'Change." "Philo.," a contributor to a number of western stamp papers in the 1880s was particularly enamored of the trader image. His short story entitled the "Bluffton Stamp Collectors' Society" opened with a scene of fourteen "bright boys" between the ages of ten and eighteen bartering stamps in a way that "resembled a miniature board of trade, only the articles bartered for were postage stamps instead of corn, and wheat, and pork."[54]

The stock exchange analogy is useful because it describes how the stamp collectors themselves used the investor and speculator categories. Investors were the more common and less controversial group since appreciation of value was incidental to their reasons for collecting. They bought for fun but took comfort in the knowledge that the money they spent could be recouped if necessary. "I collect stamps because I realize that some day I too will be an old man," wrote J. W. Longnecker in 1937. Collecting would provide him with something to do when he retired, and he expected that the stamps he was buying aggressively in 1937 could, if necessary, be traded for his "daily bread" when his income fell after retirement. Buy one of each kind, do not speculate in duplicates, counseled a writer in 1898, "I have seen too many booms collapse." Those who bought in anticipation of a continued run up in prices found that "the biter has been bitten," but buying carefully and holding on would prove to be "much more safe and a better investment than money in the bank." The implication here was that if one bought only for one's own collection and did not hoard duplicates against an increase in price then one was not speculating.[55]

By the hobby boom of the 1930s, speculating in duplicates had not only become routine, it was implicitly encouraged by the U.S. post office department, which churned out commemoratives at an unprecedented rate. Collector in Chief Franklin D. Roosevelt and Postmaster General James A. Farley worked together to encourage the hobby, and neither man exhibited an overly refined sense of ethics when it came to stamp collecting. Roosevelt, who was as much an accumulator as a scientific philatelist, would take stamps from any source willing to give them to him, and Farley was none too punctilious about distributing specially autographed unperforated sheets to friends. The New Deal speculative boom, however, was merely the culmination of a long, if not always glorious, tradition. More than thirty years earlier S. A. D. Cox had written, "I am not as a general thing in favor of speculation of any kind, but if one must speculate, let him speculate in as safe a thing as possible." He said, "if one exercises care in selecting and buying there is no danger at all of a loss." Stamps, crowed the article's title, were "Good as Wheat!"[56]

When Cox casually equated stamps with wheat he was explicitly acknowledging what most collectors took for granted: stamps were a commodity. Cox's insistence that they were safer than other commodities was a collector's, or perhaps a dealer's, self-serving hyperbole. Unlike other commodities, canceled stamps had no intrinsic value, and their price depended entirely on the continuing growth of stamp collecting as a hobby. Writing in the panic year of 1894 one collector optimistically insisted that "philately to-day rests upon a sound commercial basis" but then admitted that this was true only because of the "enormous accessions to our ranks in the near past." If collectors wanted to maintain the value of their stamps, he warned, they had better make sure their numbers continued to increase. Because they were useless, stamps were entirely artifacts of the market: collectors wanted stamps because they were valuable, and stamps were valuable because collectors wanted them. During the depression a business writer told a banker who had just sold a stamp for ten thousand dollars that he understood the supply but could not fathom the demand. "I do not understand that either," confessed the banker, but he added as though it were sufficient explanation, "youngsters start collecting stamps and multimillionaires pay for them."[57]

The speculator's dream was to discover the stamp the multimillionaire was willing to buy. It was a dream of finding buried treasure. All the collector needed was knowledge of which stamps were rare—and some luck. Stamp history is replete with accounts of great finds, many of which involve rescu-

ing stamps from the garbage.[58] Curiously there were almost no factual articles in stamp periodicals about people actually finding a rare stamp on an
old envelope in a trunk, but there was a lot of wishful thinking.[59] Philatelists
had less of a reputation for exaggeration than fishermen or golfers; nevertheless there was at least a minor tradition of telling tales of great finds:

> The philatelic liar sat
> Within his cheerless den,
> And told weird tales of startling finds
> To calm, attentive men.
> He told of trunks that he had found
> Just brimmed and running o'er
> With stamps that gaze of mortal eye
> Had ne'er beheld before.[60]

Rather than lie like the old codger in the poem, almost all the stories of
hidden philatelic treasure were admittedly just that, stories in stamp papers
and magazines that fed the dream without pretending they were anything
but fiction.

A fairly typical story in an 1893 edition of the *Southern Philatelist* com-
bines the investor and the buried treasure themes. The central character, a
twelve-year-old girl named Sarah, wins a stamp album for being the best
geography student at school. Although her gruff Aunt Sally would have preferred a crochet hook or silver thimble, Sarah explains that stamp collecting
will teach her geography, history, value, and neat habits. Despite Aunt Sally's
complaints about the waste of time and money, Sarah builds a large collection but is unaware of its value. When Aunt Sally loses her life savings in the
stock market and is about to lose the house, Sarah quits school to go to work.
Her first day on the job she sees an advertisement from a New York man who
will pay four hundred dollars for a "well filled stamp album." Sarah sells her
album, pays off the mortgage, returns to school, and gets an apology from
Aunt Sally. Sarah collected stamps because she enjoyed them, not because
she wanted to make money. Moreover, she rationalized the process to her
aunt by stressing the educational rather than the economic benefits of the
hobby. Sarah was neither a speculator nor a merchant but an accidental
investor untainted by the market who found treasure when she expected it
least, but needed it most.[61]

The impure hope that one might strike it rich was the guilty truth of affirmation that hid beneath the disguise of leisure for all but the most casual collectors. "Like some of my collector friends, I try to kid myself that the financial value of my stamps is not an animating motive," said a collector in the

1950s, but he admitted, "few things please me more than to find a marked increase in the catalog value of a stamp or set." Even writers who toed the official line could reveal the deeper economic truth. In 1925 Jack O'Donnell wrote that the only "real dyed-in-the-wool philatelists" were those who collected for "research" and the "rich memories of history and art." However, his entire *Saturday Evening Post* article concentrated on the risks and rewards of the stamp marketplace. The piece opened with the story of a high school student who used a gun to try to rob a dealer of stamps he could not afford to buy. It went on to talk of obsessed philatelists who would not sell their collections even though they were starving, of collectors who became dealers, and of people who found "buried treasure" stamps. Nowhere did the author write about education or aesthetics.[62]

The contradictory message of O'Donnell's article was, in fact, the contradictory message of stamp collecting as a hobby; it was leisure that was dependent on the market. The market of stamp collecting not only modeled the real world, it *was* the real world. Stamps were real commodities exchanged for real money. Therefore, the hobby not only taught the values of thrift and investment, it also held out the temptation of cheating and stealing. The young collector will "soon find that few pursuits present a wider field for willful fraud than philately," warned a turn-of-the-century writer, especially for mail orders. Collectors who ordered "approvals," that is stamps sent to potential buyers that they were supposed to purchase or return, could substitute inferior stamps for the ones removed from the approval sheets. For their part, purchasers frequently complained that they did not get fair value for money they sent to mail order advertisers.[63]

Because stamps were mass-produced items of historically recent vintage, having a large number of identical and equally valued stamps was quite possible. The problem for collectors was to determine what that value was. Stamp catalogs, which included retail prices for all known issues, were first produced in Europe and the United States in the early 1860s. Even with published prices, however, the value of a stamp varied with its condition, which was, to some extent, a subjective matter. More important, there were highly specialized areas of stamp collecting that were not normally covered by the catalogs, and the catalog prices themselves were only an approximation based on the previous year's sales. Thus the expert who attended sales and auctions, read some of the dozens of stamp papers that existed at any given time, and stayed abreast of the changing fashions in stamp collecting was in a position to recognize value in an item that would appear uninteresting to a neophyte or "layman."[64]

In 1898 a collector felt compelled to warn veterans not to take advantage of rookies they were introducing to the hobby. If the younger collectors "should happen to unearth some rare specimens," he wrote, "do not under any circumstances, 'exchange' with them, and thus secure for your own collection a few good specimens—at the cost, nine times out of ten, of a recruit to our ranks." Stamp collectors, unlike antique collectors who reveled in relieving ignorant rubes of their valuable possessions for a pittance, at least made a public show of not practicing theft by expertise. When an unrepentant rebel in a 1934 short story would not sell his Confederate stamps, a northern collector conspired with a southern collector to sweet-talk the owner. The old man was so flattered that he offered to give his fellow southerner any envelopes he wanted. While the two collectors had no compunctions about stroking the older man's ego, they were not willing to take advantage of him financially and insisted on paying him a fair price for the items.[65]

The stories and warnings about ethical conduct in stamp collecting embody the tensions inherent in the hobby. All transactions were exercises in the essence of capitalism. The participants had to weigh issues of individual knowledgeability and honesty, and of market value in both the short and long run. These issues in turn had to be balanced with the noneconomic elements of stamp collecting. The tensions existed both within the marketplace aspect of the hobby and between the marketplace and the psychological aspects. There was no way to resolve them. In fact, there was no need to resolve them, since it was those tensions that made stamp collecting so popular. The pleasurable elements legitimated stamp collecting as leisure. Yet the myriad ways in which the hobby paralleled real life gave it another kind of legitimacy. By mimicking the roles of the essential middlemen of capitalism, it recapitulated and affirmed the dominant ideology. Stamp collectors produced nothing of concrete value themselves, but their mutual demand for a finite supply of stamps made their hobby the perfect free market metaphor.

5 Deconstructing a Collector's Market

If, as the prototypical example of collecting, philately adhered to most of the commonly understood hobby and marketplace values, then antique collecting was the wild card that violated, even parodied, as many conventions as it followed. Antique collecting was a hobby, but one in which it was difficult to constitute sets, hard to store the objects; one in which women participated on a par with men, in which genuine aesthetics competed with mere rarity; and one where the ethical transgressions usually condemned by stamp collectors were raised to a piratical art.

As a subset of art collecting, antique collecting has deep European roots, and Americans have always sought fine European items to decorate their homes and display their wealth. Collecting American antiques on the other hand, is a relatively recent phenomenon and one that more neatly fits the definition of a hobby, both because its cost can be quite reasonable and because the collector can engage in the hunt for objects in the field as well as in the dealer's shop and auction house. There are scattered references to people collecting old American furniture in the eighteenth and early nineteenth centuries, but almost all those collectors were interested in the objects for their associational value. Thus an affidavit attesting to the purported fact that a particular wineglass had crossed the Atlantic in 1657 and had been used by George Washington guaranteed its importance independent of its aesthetic properties. A catalog of "arts, relics, and curiosities" displayed at the Brooklyn Sanitary Fair, which raised funds for the relief of Union soldiers during the Civil War, included objects that had been owned by William Bradford, Miles Standish, John Hancock, and George Washington.[1]

The objects displayed at the Brooklyn fair were part of a New England kitchen exhibit. Essentially a restaurant embellished with miscellaneous old objects and staffed by volunteers in period costumes, this, and other kitchens like it, raised both money for relief and awareness of the material past. There were at least seven such kitchens at sanitary fairs in 1864.[2] The interest in colonial kitchens disappeared at war's end but was revived ten years later at the Philadelphia Centennial Exhibition by Emma Southwick, who ran her

"New England Farmer's Home" (also referred to as the Old Log Cabin and the New England Kitchen) as a commercial enterprise. Like most nineteenth-century fairs, the Philadelphia Exhibition was much too involved in celebrating the industrial present to waste much time looking at the past. Southwick's kitchen not only served as a dining area but also as an instructive contrast to a modern kitchen next door. Its fireplace, candlesticks, spinning wheels, cradles, and other colonial objects served to show how far America had come in a hundred years. Other centennial celebrations in the Northeast also featured early American household furnishings in more historical and less commercial settings than Philadelphia. The exhibition in Salem divided its furniture display into three chronological categories; "period of discovery," "colonial period," and "revolutionary period," the first attempt to organize American antiques on other than associational grounds.[3]

Within two years of the centennial, a backlash against the excesses of Victorian design led to the country's first genuine antique boom. Although high Victorian style still had a good twenty years of life left, the early inroads of colonial-inspired simplification affected both the production of new furniture and the collecting of old. In 1878 Clarence Cook published *The House Beautiful*, an American exposition of the reformist design philosophy of Charles Locke Eastlake who, like John Ruskin and William Morris, advocated a return to simpler preindustrial styles. Cook railed against modernism in all its forms, attacking central heating, gas illumination, and indoor plumbing along with overstuffed Victorian upholstery. The book's illustrations of early American furnishings, coupled with the interest sparked by the centennial celebrations, prompted the manufacture of colonial-style "centennial furniture" in the 1880s.[4]

Collectors realized that if people were willing to buy facsimiles of old American pieces then the originals would be even more desirable, and the search for genuine American antiques began. The first antique store in the United States to carry American furniture appears to have been opened in New York City sometime in the 1870s.[5] The vast majority of collectors in those salad days of American antiques gathered their booty directly from the hedges and ditches where most of it had languished through several generations of Victorian mass production. In fact, it was considerably cheaper to buy a castoff from a farmer's yard then to pay a cabinetmaker to construct a reproduction. Cook notes that "a polite internecine warfare has for some time raged between rival searchers after 'old pieces,' and the back country is scoured by young couples in chaises on the trail of old sideboards and brass andirons."[6]

A composite illustration in an 1878 edition of *Harper's Weekly* showed that all the characteristics that would continue to mark American antique collecting were present at its birth (see fig. 5.1). Buyers are depicted as both men

FIGURE 5.1 An 1878 illustration from *Harper's Weekly* reflects the postcentennial interest in American antiques and the collectors' willingness to buy pieces of dubious quality. (Reprinted from A. B. Frost, "The Rage for Old Furniture," *Harper's Weekly* 22 [November 16, 1878]: 917.)

and women; most items are American-made; dealers are unscrupulous; and collectors are naive. The most prominent panel pictures a matron and her adult daughter in the shop of a dealer who is showing her an old grandfather clock. It is surrounded by smaller cuts in which the buyers are mostly men; a man carrying off a small spinning wheel from a country home, another man talking to a farm wife who is telling him that she has no old clocks to sell, and a doltish fellow looking at a smashed up chair and being assured by the owners "if you put new Legs, a Back, and Seat on that, it will make a lovely Chair." The acerbic commentary continues with a picture of a dilapidated cupboard with an auction lot number pinned to its side and with a scene in a shop were several workers are busy manufacturing "veritable antiques." It concludes with a huge crowd of more than a hundred well-dressed men and women clustered outside a rundown farm house and is captioned: "A Rumor having spread that an old Lady on Long Island has some old Chelsea China, a few Collectors go down to see it."[7]

The nascent American antique movement, generated by the Philadelphia exhibition, was given a substantial boost by the Chicago Columbian Exposition of 1893. Although the exposition is most famous for its beaux-arts White City center, many of the state buildings were built in colonial styles and prominently displayed a variety of American crafts. Even Emma Southwick and her Log Cabin Restaurant were back with another iteration of the colonial kitchen. These exhibits sparked an interest in craft production and drew attention to historic products. By the mid-1890s demand for American antiques had increased sufficiently to support what seems to be the country's first exclusively American antique dealer in Wethersfield, Connecticut.[8]

The practice of combing the New England countryside for quaint items had become common enough by 1895 to make it the subject for fiction. In her short story "A Righteous Bargain," Alice Brown tells of a slightly senile mother and her daughter who reject the offers of a slick Yankee trader for their coverlets and clocks. However, when the daughter leaves to sell butter in town, the dealer buys the items from the befuddled old lady who is subsequently mortified at having sold her prized possessions for nine dollars. When the daughter's offer to buy back the items is refused, she steals them from their storage place and vows to fight any attempt to retrieve them. Faced with such obstinacy, the dealer declines to press charges and leaves the women with their heirlooms. Besides being an acknowledgment of the popularity of antique collecting before the turn of the century, this story highlights several common themes in collecting Americana. First, collectors sought commonplace as well as fine items. Second, the desirable items did not have to be very old; the coverlets in the story had been made by the mother. Third, dealers were unprincipled, but country folk were not completely helpless. Finally, both sexes participated actively in the hobby. The dealer was male and the intended victims were female, but the women were quite capable of defending themselves, and the story seems to have been aimed at a female audience.[9]

Creating Provenance: Museums and Wealthy Collectors

American antiques were given the imprimatur of legitimacy by a series of museum directors who, around the turn of the century, began to mount serious displays of Americana as art. The pioneer of this movement was Charles Presby Wilcomb who operated yet another colonial kitchen, this time in the Golden Gate Park Museum in San Francisco in 1896. Wilcomb's kitchen, however, was not a theme restaurant but a serious attempt to re-create an authentic New England kitchen. Other curators mounted shows and published catalogues that inspired a new generation of collectors to appreciate the aesthetic and technical accomplishments of American artisans. The culmination of this trend was the 1909 Hudson-Fulton exhibit at New York's Metropolitan Museum of Art, which brought together silver and furniture from all over the Northeast. The Hudson-Fulton show was the first professionally curated exhibit of American antiques at a major American museum, and the Metropolitan purchased many of the objects in the show for its permanent collection. Guides to American antiques such as Esther Singleton's fully illustrated, two-volume *Furniture of Our Forefathers* contributed to the movement by showing vernacular styles along with the work of fine cabinetmakers such as Chippendale and Hepplewhite.[10]

The Metropolitan Museum of Art's decision to begin buying Americana prompted a dozen of the most serious collectors of American antiques to form the Walpole Society in 1910. Like the Hobby Club of New York, which was founded the following year, the Walpole Society was composed of wealthy amateurs, some of whom had become experts in the emerging field of old American household objects. Unlike the short-lived New York Hobby Club, the Walpole Society flourished, nurturing the careers of collectors who would go on to create the American Wing of the Metropolitan Museum of Art in 1924. The success of that project prompted the fine arts museums of Boston and Philadelphia to install permanent American displays of their own. The creation of the American Wing was one of a series of events that fed the great American antiques craze that continued through the depression. In addition to the museum exhibit, the boom in Americana was encouraged by the business career of Wallace Nutting, the collecting mania of Henry Ford, and the parallel activities of John D. Rockefeller Jr. At the same time, Henry Francis du Pont was bidding up prices of American antiques in order to furnish his family home in Delaware, but since Du Pont's activities were private until 1929, they did not contribute directly to the broader public interest in American antiques.[11]

In 1904 Wallace Nutting, a forty-two-year-old Congregational minister in Providence, Rhode Island, had a nervous breakdown and retired from the pulpit. He moved to Southbury, Connecticut, where he opened a studio that produced hand-tinted photographs of domestic landscapes and quaint interiors. What started as a hobby burgeoned into a minor industry that, at its height, employed two dozen colorists. In the years between 1905 and 1917 Nutting's studio turned out tens of thousands of hand-colored photographs, all ostensibly signed by the photographer and aggressively marketed as representations of good taste. Many of the interiors, complete with costumed models, were shot in his Southbury home, which he progressively restored to its pristine colonial form. Nutting estimated that by the end of his career in 1941 he had produced 10 million of these nostalgic photographs, causing one historian to claim, with as much truth as ridicule, that every middle-class couple married between 1904 and 1930 received at least one Nutting photograph as a wedding present. The mass distribution of these photographs and their widespread acceptance as emblems of culture and refinement did much to establish "early American" as one of the appropriate replacements for Victorian-style architecture and interior design.[12]

Because he shot so many of his photographs in his own home, which he tried to make as authentic as possible, Nutting gathered large numbers of antiques and developed a trained eye for colonial detail. Dismissive of modern design, Nutting asked, "has any shape been devised within a hundred years that cannot be surpassed by the shapes that went before?"[13] He answered that rhetorical question by opening a workshop in 1917 that turned out reproductions of classic American pieces for about a dozen years. "Copy and avoid bad taste," was his motto, and while he admitted that "not all the old is good," he firmly believed that "all the new is bad." Nutting's love of the American past, which expressed itself in the 1920s in a steady stream of books and articles on old homes and furniture, was fervently nationalistic. Sturdy American artisans of the colonial and early modern eras, unsullied by infusions of aristocratic continental taste, produced the perfect furniture for American homes. That purity, frozen in time, had to be preserved "because the only alternative is the making of mongrel shapes."[14] A character in a 1923 short story explained that he collected old furniture not because it was Americana, but because it was America. There was no Duncan Phyfe alive in the

1920s, he said, and nobody knew how to make a Windsor chair anymore. "And you think without Windsor chairs there can't be a country?" asked his friend. "Without the kind of work that went into 'em, there can't," he answered.[15]

Beginning in 1926 John D. Rockefeller tried to re-create a part of that lost land that knew how to make Windsor chairs by purchasing and restoring the entire town of Williamsburg, Virginia. The Reverend W. A. R. Goodwin, whose idea it was to transform his economically beleaguered village into a living museum of colonial life, had originally approached Henry Ford with his idea. Ford however was involved with a restoration project in Massachusetts and passed on the proposal. Rockefeller, who had recently given the French government a million dollars to restore Versailles, embraced the concept of re-creating the colonial capital of Virginia. Like Marie Antoinette's peasant village at Versailles, Williamsburg was to be a retreat "entirely free from alien and inharmonious surroundings" but with the added legitimacy of historical restoration. While the queen played shepherdess in the midst of aristocratic luxury, the costumed actors at Williamsburg would play aristocrats in the midst of the democratic squalor of the Great Depression.[16]

Critics have suggested that displays like those in the American Wing of the Metropolitan Museum of Art and Williamsburg promulgated a conservative political message consonant with the values of those who sponsored them.[17] No doubt, by idealizing preindustrial America, the exhibitions critiqued the depersonalization and class conflict of the postbellum world. They also celebrated a more ethnically homogenous America where the Protestant ethic had not yet been secularized to the work ethic. This was particularly true for Henry Ford who idealized the preindustrial past while he was busily generating the products that were wiping out its last small-town vestiges. His agrarian bias and his outspoken xenophobia were complementary to, if not actually the cause of, his intense interest in American history and its material culture. The ultimate expression of his collecting was the Henry Ford Museum and Greenfield Village, an idyllic conglomeration of associational and vernacular buildings that opened in October 1929. On the one hand, it was a paean to a world that he helped destroy. A mythical small town patched together from real buildings and filled with the commonplace objects of everyday life brought together from all over the country (see fig. 5.2). On the other, it was a museum of technology that celebrated the very engines of change that had wiped out small towns. Commentators loved the irony; Ford, and the thousands who followed his collecting lead, just loved the stuff. Writing in 1927, antique collector C. R. Clifford said Ford was "the greatest human factor in the country-wide canvass for antiques." Charles

FIGURE 5.2 A real stone churn and dasher were used to illustrate a 1929 novel that blended fiction with the interest in vernacular objects promoted by the collecting habits of Henry Ford. (From *Country Auction*, Marion Nicholl Rawson, 241. Copyright 1929 by E. P. Dutton, renewed 1957 by Jonathan N. Rawson. Used by permission of Dutton, a division of Penguin Putnam.)

Merz, an early biographer of Ford, noted that because of his collecting, "bean pots, glass castors, and china hens for holding breakfast eggs were brought home from auction sales in a whirl of triumph by the same ladies who had thrown them out of their houses thirty years before."[18]

Ford's collecting career had begun in 1914 when he started personally searching secondhand book shops for McGuffey readers like the ones he and his wife remembered from their own school days. By the mid-1930s he had purchased 468 of those repositories of Protestant virtue. In the meantime, however, his tastes broadened considerably. Four years later, in 1919, he undertook the restoration of his family home, in the course of which he attempted to replace all the original furniture and household articles. As in the search for McGuffey readers, Ford personally scoured the countryside looking for just the right carpet or stove. According to William Greenleaf, who has written the most complete survey of Ford's collecting career, once bitten by the collector's bug, Ford became an enthusiastic "frequenter of farmhouses, attics, barns, inns, and antique shops," for whom "the pursuit of the past, begun for reasons of family sentiment, was an immensely enjoyable hobby."[19]

It was a hobby, and although he pursued it on a scale commensurate with his vast wealth, he was always as much an accumulator as a connoisseur. His idea of antiques included the prosaic as well as the exotic. He said he wanted "a complete series of every article ever used or made in America from the days of the first settlers down to the present time." In addition to using professional antique dealers and personal agents, Ford employed his 35,000 car dealers and an empire of other underlings in the 1920s to comb the country for the ultimate collector's set, one of everything! The breadth of his interest was truly staggering. His collecting net was fine enough to capture the smallest object and strong enough to hold the largest. He gathered in clothespins, inkwells, and mouse traps, along with locomotives and steam engines. And while some of his objects had associational value, most were the everyday items of everyday people.[20]

Ford's aggressive buying bid up the price of American antiques, contributing significantly to a climate of speculation. Buyers are reported to have told greedy dealers, "You may be able to kid Henry Ford, but you can't kid me." When a character in a 1933 story balked at a piece of glassware priced at $250, the dealer showed her an offer from Ford for that amount. "Now I don't mind Ford buying antiques; I think it's awfully nice for a business man to have an outside interest," the buyer responded, "but if he isn't going to buy something I don't see why he has to go and put it out of sight for the rest of us." It is estimated that by the time he died in 1947 Ford had spent more than $10 million of his own money on the museums and in the process created a vast new market for the trade in old everyday items.[21]

In the 1920s, then, the combined influence of the commercial advocacy of Wallace Nutting, the provenance of the American Wing, and the high-profile collecting and restoration of both John D. Rockefeller Jr. and Henry Ford spurred Americans into a full frenzy of antique collecting and investing that would hardly pause even under the constraints of depression and war. For the upscale trade, the founding of the *Magazine Antiques* in 1922 marked the emergence of a body of experts, dealers, and connoisseur collectors large enough to support a journal full of technical articles and advertisements for rare and expensive pieces.[22] Where once fine European pieces had commanded a premium, now similar native items were preferred. In his caustic 1928 commentary on the trade, *Antiquamania*, Kenneth Roberts had a man trying to explain to his son why an American-made Chippendale chair was worth more than a similar chair made in England. The father, of course, can give no rational reason and is reduced to declaring, "it's a matter of spiritual feeling and sentimental association." Which, of course, it was. By the end of the 1920s all old American furniture had become associational collectibles. Association with a particular hero was no longer necessary; simple association with the country was enough.[23]

For those of modest means who could not afford Chippendale chairs, an authentic American ambiance could be achieved by salvaging old furniture from farmhouses. Unprincipled city slickers had been trying to take advantage of what they hoped were naive country bumpkins since the Gilded Age, but the rate of these cross-cultural encounters went up in the 1920s in direct proportion to the increase in the kinds of items city people were willing to collect. Back road canvassing by buyers could bring either opportunity or unwanted intrusion to the locals. Rustics who valued their privacy could get downright perverse when pestered by antique hunters. In 1925 a motorist who had spotted a desirable couch on the porch of a country cottage stopped and offered to purchase it. The owner demurred. The antiquer then visited the cottage day after day constantly upping his offer for the piece until the reclusive owner chopped it up and burned it to free himself of the daily intrusions.[24]

On the other hand, honest country folk quickly learned that dishonest city dealers could be forced to pay good money for old truck. Marion Rawson's 1929 novel *Country Auction* describes the predatory mood among American antique collectors in the late 1920s. Aunt Marthy Ann is liquidating her estate and dares hope that her old things might be worth as much as two hundred dollars. She is amazed when an honest auctioneer assures her a single chest could bring almost half that. Aunt Marthy Ann is not sure it would be fair to charge foolish city people so much for her old things, but she changes her mind when, during the days leading to the auction, she is besieged by one group of shady characters after another, all trying to bilk the old lady out of her goods before they are subjected to the open market of the auction. Taking advantage of her natural country friendliness, male dealers and female decorators invade her home offering to buy valuable items at ridiculously low prices, and when that fails, actually trying to steal them from off the shelves and tables.[25]

The hunger for American antiques was whetted by the government itself. At the end of the decade, the Bureau of Home Economics urged every family to incorporate at least one early American room into its home decorating scheme.[26] The ethnocentric fervor of collecting Americana combined with the get-rich-quick mentality promoted by the stock market boom of the 1920s to produce a hobby that confirmed traditional patriotic, aesthetic, and economic values all at the same time. The nationalism of the 1930s placed greater stress than that of the 1920s on folk traditions, but antiques were as fine a representation of the yeoman aesthetic as they were of the taste of patriot blue bloods. Praising the resurgence of folk handicrafts, historian Bernard DeVoto charged in 1938 that a decade earlier there had been "no trace of folk art"; there had been only "the vast American curiosity shop, the lumber room littered with ugly articles" bought by Americans "who had no love, no pleasure, no workmanship, no skill, and no toleration for these things." DeVoto's diatribe ignores the symbiotic relationship between antiques and native handicrafts that flourished through the 1920s but captures the element of liberal approbation that overlay the same relationship as it continued into the depression decade.[27]

Just as the chauvinism of the 1920s could become the folk-nationalism of the 1930s, so the economic speculation of the Jazz Age translated easily into the treasure hunting of the depression. Antique collecting was a hobby for all political and economic seasons. Antiques fit nicely into the patriotism of World War II and into the consumer sacrifices demanded by rationing. "Antiques require no needed labor, no material is consumed and there are no priorities in the industry," *Hobbies* magazine publisher O. C. Lightner reminded potential advertisers, and while driving through the countryside was definitely curtailed by gas and rubber rationing, department stores took up some of the slack by stocking antiques when they could not obtain new furniture.[28]

The Transubstantiation of Junk

The collecting of American antiques necessitated a redefinition of the term "antique." For most Victorians, antiques were items produced by highly skilled European craftsmen up to the end of the eighteenth century. They were, in other words, functional works of art, sometimes anonymous, but often from the hand, or at least the workshop, of a named artisan. American antiques were initially defined the same way, but the severe shortage of truly fine American objects meant that unless the definition were broadened, the hobby would remain out of the financial reach of most collectors. The colonial kitchen movement started the appreciation of the commonplace because, even in the finest homes, the kitchen was a place for functionality not conspicuous display. There simply was no tradition of aesthetic craftsmanship for the unseen tools of household production.

In the nineteenth century, even those collectors who prowled the back roads poking in hay lofts and chicken coops were usually hoping to find buried treasures that had once been major pieces in public rooms. There were, however, a few prescient Victorian collectors who anticipated the move toward collecting everyday objects. Alexander W. Drake, one of the book-collecting founders of the Grollier Club, also collected bottles, brasses, bandboxes, samovars, ship models, and bird cages.[29] While the brasses and samovars were probably foreign, the bottles were probably local. By the turn of the century, pioneer catalogers like Singleton and Nutting were following the lead of the colonial kitchen movement by including folk as well as high-style items in their books. Henry Ford's enthusiastic collecting of the ordinary and ephemeral in the 1920s prompted the full-scale acceptance of any old "junk" as antiques. In her wry *Mother Goose for Antique Collectors*, published in 1927, collector-writer Alice Van Leer Carrick commented on the phenomenon of infinite collectibility:

> Rummage in your woodsheds,
> Comb your attics clear;
> Bring all your rubbish out,
> The tourist season's here![30]

Taking note of the passion for junk-antiques, Ring Lardner wrote of a man whose new wife announced, "I hate this house and everything in it! It's too new! Everything shines! I loathe new things!" The husband proceeds to dirty and rumple himself, so he will not look too new, and then tells his wife he has "a pair of shears, a blow torch and an ax" with which he was going to antique the house, starting with the dining room table. "Junk snupper" was the self-deprecating title assumed by the collectors of the commonplace. First used by President Theodore Roosevelt's wife, Edith, junk snupping she said, "was the art of finding quaint and valuable things in junk heaps, and the ability to get them cheap." The term was popularized in the 1920s by collector-author, C. R. Clifford, who described how he would buy the wallpaper off the walls, the hinges off the doors, and indeed the wall and doors themselves, from appropriately old American buildings.[31]

So long as no one wanted it, an object was rubbish. When one, or particularly more than one person wanted it, it became a commodity, no matter what its condition, and if enough people wanted it, it was elevated to the status of an antique. "Here's a simple rule for collectors: if it isn't useless, it isn't a real antique," announced the headline of a 1926 article titled "Old Junk and New Bunk." Neither functionality nor provenance was needed. A fictional English butler said he was leaving his American employer because the man refused to furnish his house with real antiques and insisted on using "old chairs, bare and homely as a cheesebox," which he heard had come from a barn, and a dining table made of "old plain rickety pine" that he guessed had come from a stable. The employer used pewter rather than silver, substituted aged bottles for fine crystal, and enclosed his lights in cheap-looking tin sconces. The butler was convinced to stay, however, when the owner demonstrated that these broken down refugees from the farmstead were not cheap but commanded sky-high prices. The high price of old junk, explained the master, meant that only the very rich could afford to be truly democratic by emulating the appearance of their poor antecedents.[32]

Humorous references to the way that calling an object an antique could raise its status from trash to treasure, reflected an underlying discomfort with the concept of collectibility. Collectors needed something besides marketplace value to justify their hobby, which they got either from the aesthetic or the historical value of their collectibles. There was some disagreement between those who advanced an aesthetic reason for collecting antiques and those who saw an inherent value in historicity. The aesthetes rejected history for history's sake. Victorian objects, for example, were so ugly they were considered uncollectible. Writing in 1913, experts Robert and Elizabeth Shackleton observed, "If age alone were sufficient to constitute charm, the furniture disdainfully termed Victorian would now enjoy the beginning of a collecting vogue." It would never happen they said, because "they are based on bad taste and the absence of distinction and beauty." At the popular hobby level, however, the adage "age before beauty" ruled the day. Fewer than fifteen years after the Shackletons rejected Victoriana as uncollectible, people were collecting Victorian women's handicrafts, and by 1930 Victoriana had become an established category of American antique collecting. Walter Prichard Eaton also disdained Victoriana but admitted, "I too collect junk." It is not beautiful, he said, but "it actually hurts me to see any object once made and used by my ancestors go to oblivion, and because to save it and have it around reminds me constantly and pleasantly of the past."[33]

Once collectors agreed that age alone bestowed historical meaning, writers began to speculate about what current everyday items might be tomorrow's antiques. Such maunderings almost always turned out to be more prescient than parodic. In 1930 the president of the Collector's Club suggested that future collectors might seek out cigarette lighters, fountain pens, ink bottles, coffee percolators, alarm clocks, and even radios. In 1941 the New York Times published a remarkably similar list, musing that in a hundred years such mundane, and decidedly unaesthetic, items as auto horns, electric clocks, cameras, radio sets, cigarette lighters, cocktail shakers, bifocal glasses, and coffee percolators might be on the block at antique auctions.[34]

The privileging of history over style had its practical side. It meant that many more items and categories of items were available for collecting and more objective criteria such as age and rarity could replace subjective aesthetics as a basis for value. Factual information was obviously much easier for the amateur to master than the shifting subtleties of aesthetic connoisseurship. There was, moreover, a sense that the collected object created a direct connection to the past. Although an anonymous colonial bed might not have the same panache as one on which George Washington slept, at least someone of George Washington's generation had slept on it, and that historical nexus could never be present in a reproduction.[35]

The best of all possible collectors' worlds was achieved, of course, when age and beauty were combined. This was done most easily by equating the past with beauty and the present with ugliness. If the aesthetic could be absorbed into the temporal, then almost any old thing could be admired for its appearance and any new one disparaged. "We cannot become familiar with the furniture designs of the eighteenth century without having a better argument against the shortcomings of the furniture that is made and sold throughout the land today," wrote Charles Messer Stow in 1934, and the same held true for silver and glass. Like Wallace Nutting before him, Stow saw the preindustrial era as a golden age of design permanently destroyed by the coming of machines. The excesses of mass-produced Victorian furnishings left a legacy of respect for early American products that derived as much from how they were produced as from what they looked like. A 1927 collectors guide explained that the quest for American antiques was more than a craze because collectors had come to understand "the beauty of early American craftsmanship. It is a tried and sturdy beauty, beaten out of copper and lustrous silver by honest Colonial smiths, or stitched bit by bit by the skillful fingers of Colonial maids and matrons." Clearly the authors were concerned more with plain than fancy wares and were fabricating an argument that not only legitimated the commonplace as collectible but also linked age and craft with beauty.[36]

Economic Value and Ethical Values: The Price of Honesty in the Antique Market

Like stamps, coins, books, and fine art, antiques lent themselves to speculation because there was a formal market of dealers and auction houses that catered to collectors. The first American dealers in the late nineteenth century were unique less for their service than for their inventory, since wealthy Americans had collected and traded old European objects since the colonial era. As was the case with other collectibles, the antique object had both subjective and objective value. Subjectively it appealed to the collector's sense of taste or history. Objectively it was worth a specific amount of money determined by the marketplace, and even the noncollector could turn a lucky find into ready cash. Once the Americana excitement of the 1920s commodified everyday objects, a much larger number of people could be made part of the collecting culture, or more precisely, the collecting *economy*, even if they were not collecting themselves. Alice Van Leer Carrick held that "collecting is the one respectable form of gambling," an understanding that she expressed in her Mother Goose parodies:[37]

Old Mother Hubbard got up from the cupboard,
And lifted her voice in a paean,
Crying, "Ho, my good Rover, our lean days are over!
We'll sell this for pure Jacobean."[38]

By the same token, however, the collector could be hoist on her own petard.

Mary had a little lamp
When lamps were quite passé;
She gave a junkman twenty cents
To take the thing away.[39]

Mary then became a collector, realized she had given away a prize, tracked the junkman down to his "vast estate" and asked how she could get it back, "Go sell your house and summer camp! / the junkman quick replied." Old Mother Hubbard who got rich from her cupboard and Mary's junkman who got his estate from other people's discards were both creatures of the market who had no other interest in antiques than their price.[40]

Even though prices fell during the depression, the underlying dream of making a killing on some hand-me-down in the attic continued to pull non-collectors into the antique orbit. Although set in 1901, Thornton Wilder's *Our Town* was written in 1938 and expresses the continuing lure of antiques as a form of buried treasure. Julia Gibbs tells her friend Myrtle Webb that a dealer from Boston had come to their New Hampshire town and offered her $350 for her grandmother's highboy, which she had almost given away. Myrtle urges her to sell it and Julia says she would if she could use the money for a trip to Paris. Whatever aesthetic, historic, or sentimental attachments Julia may have felt for the furniture it was clearly secondary to the piece's cash value. Every-day items such as shaving mugs, mustache cups, porcelain knickknacks, and other forgotten bits of Victoriana were worth good money, advised a writer in 1930. His point was not that such items were beautiful, historical, or even old, but that other people wanted them, so collecting them was an investment.[41]

The value of antiques was fickle. Even before the crash, changing tastes or the discovery of a large number of fakes could undermine the price of once valuable items.[42] Wallace Nutting noted that antique prices fluctuated with "the condition of the stock market and the east wind and the goodness of dinner." Two-dollar items could sell for $15,000 and $27,000 items could sell for $270. Money made could also be money lost and, as with all specula-tive bubbles, the inflated prices of the 1920s burst in the 1930s. Nutting reported that in the mid-1930s some American antiques were selling for less than 10 percent of their precrash prices. Nevertheless, his advice was to buy currently unfashionable styles that were sure to appreciate in the years ahead. Other experts pointed out that antique prices had fallen less than stocks and since nobody was making any more antiques, people who could should buy since prices were sure to rebound.[43] Not always! As late as the mid-1950s, Duncan Phyfe furniture was still selling for a fraction of its 1920s prices.[44] Unmindful of the dangers, dealers and collectors in the 1950s were once more talking about antiques in market terms. Senator Margaret Chase Smith assured her readers that antique collecting was not only a relaxing hobby but also a good investment that serious collectors could look upon as a source of retirement income.[45]

Antiques could also be a job for the present since one could move easily from buying to selling. In 1900 the *New York Times* explained that most seri-ous collectors were men, because women only held items briefly before sell-ing them; they were really merchants, not true amateurs. The *Times* article points to one of the more unexpected aspects of the hobby: women were prominent and almost fully equal participants with men. The richest collectors and the upscale dealers were mostly men, but high-profile women experts like Esther Singleton appeared early and continued to play significant roles in antique collecting. Presumably because antiques were originally "female items" of interior furnishing, women were accepted without much fuss by male collectors. Women could move seamlessly from decorating their homes, to collecting, to dealing on a par with men.[46]

Like other collectors, antiquers were often conflicted by the opposing forces of leisure and investing. Mr. Cobb was a fictional expert collector who advised others about the value of their purchases. A banker by trade, Cobb found that his constant advising was fouling his leisure time, which "echoed the harsh sounds of business" with "the brisk patter of dollars and cents." Cobb concluded he could not fight reality and became a full-time dealer, but not a happy one. The innocent joy of admiring old objects had been irrevocably destroyed. Henry Pitt, on the other hand, the main character in a 1931 short story, parlayed the antique expertise he developed as a hobby to get a better job in an auction house. The authors disagree about the meaning of turning an avocation into a vocation, but they agree that it was not hard to do.[47]

It is particularly appropriate that the second character should find his hobby-related calling in an auction house, since auctions, like stock markets, epitomize capitalist performance. The seller and buyer come together in a formal arena where the outcome sets a benchmark for the true value of the antique. Collectors Robert and Elizabeth Shackleton felt that the auction's confirmation of their own valuation of an item was even more important than the "tingle of the contest and the thrill of triumph" in making the winning bid. When the Shackletons bid, both they and the seller knew what was at stake. High-priced antique auctions had an air of gentility and a presumption of honesty. The boom in commonplace items meant, however, that many collectors and most dealers obtained their antiques at small country auctions, which were neither genteel nor necessarily honest.[48]

The excitement of the bidding and the hope of finding an overlooked treasure made local auctions a particularly enticing combination of entertainment and speculation, especially during the 1920s. While the prices paid at Sotheby's might establish a benchmark for high-end antiques, prices at country auctions were more open to manipulation, which meant nobody could ever be quite sure of the real market value of an item. What was the true value of an item to the seller when the dealers who were bidding had conspired to keep their offers down and then to divide the ill-gotten spoils among themselves after the auction? What was the true value of an item to a buyer when the auctioneer implied that a piece of furniture was a colonial antique when it was really a Victorian copy?[49] Nobody knew, and despite the constant warnings, few seemed to care. It was true that the lure of the auction could be financially devastating, but if that occurred one could always follow the lead of the impecunious man in another of Van Leer Carrick's poems:

And when he found his purse was flat
With all his might and main
He had an auction of his own,
And filled it full again.[50]

The auction established a market price through a somewhat atypical three-way negotiation that occurred not only between the seller and the buyer but among the bidders as well. More commonly, price negotiations were bilateral, and in those situations there was even greater opportunity for one side to take advantage of the other. As is still the case, Americans were more reluctant than their European contemporaries to engage in bargaining on the retail level.[51] Rather than dickering over the value of an antique, Americans seem to have preferred misdirection, misrepresentation, and outright chicanery. At its most benign, such tactics could amount to no more than buyers feigning disinterest in what they really wanted or deprecating the quality of an item.[52] For their part, sellers could undertake relatively mild ruses, such as hiding good pieces in dark corners so their buyers would think that they had "discovered" something, or failing to enlighten buyers who thought a piece was something it was not.[53] Dealers, at least those who populated the literature of antique collecting, did not consider it their responsibility to educate the buying public, especially if the public thought it was pulling a fast one on the dealer.[54] It was in such doubly dishonest exchanges that the felonious heart of antique dealing lay. Out of the public spotlight of the auction floor, honesty sometimes appears to have been a commodity as rare as a genuine Paul Revere bowl, and the justice of the deceitful deceiving themselves was too rich an opportunity for writers of contemporary fiction to pass up.

How often life imitated art is unclear, but if there were any correlation between fiction and fact, antique collecting was a hobby replete with temptations to lie and cheat, if not actually steal. In the early part of the century Americans were regularly treated to tales of double-dealing on both sides of the Atlantic. Horace Annesley Vachell's fictitious English antique dealer, Joseph Quinney, who tried to maintain a semblance of honesty, was not above considering a scheme to turn six antique chairs into a dozen by pulling them apart and then combining them with new parts. He then compounded his dishonesty by buying his own semifakes at auction to create proof of their value. A canny farmer in a 1907 story casually mentioned that he had a closet full of plates similar to one that has just been auctioned at a high price. Antiquers rushed to his house and snapped up the dishes at bargain prices. Having second thoughts, one of the purchasers asked, "Didn't you say those dishes were old?" "I never said nothing, except that they were like the plate that feller had on the piazza," answered the seller. "You folks said they was old, and I thought you'd ought to know, so—"[55]

Both true and tall tales of antique fakes are notable for the glee with which they were told. While nobody actually condoned lying about the origins of antiques, there was a clear sense that the uneducated buyer was a sheep to be fleeced, and no sympathy would be lost on the naïf who took home a reproduction thinking it an original. The great antique boom of the 1920s brought with it an equally great boom in fakes. New pieces could be made to appear old, and poor-quality old pieces could be improved. All it took, said antique author Kenneth Roberts, was a few dollars worth of clear pine and a manure pile in which to bury the new piece for a couple of weeks. Creative counterfeiters lined drawers or wrapped items in old newspapers, or left dated letters in pieces to mislead the unwary. Clumsy items, explained another expert, could be made graceful with a little judicious turning and carving. "Hushabye, Baby, on the tree top," wrote Van Leer Carrick, "Daddy's below in Ye Chippendale Shoppe, / Gouging and sawing and patching with glue, / Making old furniture where there was new." The collapse of antique prices in the 1930s appears to have slowed the fake antique industry somewhat, but in 1931 *Hobbies* magazine could still print a joke in which the first furniture maker asks, "That bookcase isn't an antique is it?" and the second one replies, "No, but another day's work and it will be."[56]

In most commercial transactions each side assumes that the other is informed and that the item being sold is what it appears to be. While such a presumption held among better dealers and auction houses, there was a broad fringe of both buyers and sellers with larceny in their souls. Perhaps only the trade in horses and used cars has been more rife with dishonesty than the buying and selling of old household furnishings. It may be an overstatement to say that the antique trade operated on a presumption of dishonesty, but it does not seem too much to assert that fraud was more common in antique collecting than in any other major hobby.

The temptation to take advantage of a less knowledgeable seller or buyer was endemic in all forms of collecting. Neophytes either learned the field quickly or were soon relieved of their stock or their cash. Antique collecting was different because many of the collectibles were owned by untutored sellers. Dealers had the advantage with stamps, coins, books, and art (including fine antiques), since there was little likelihood of truly valuable pieces being owned by people unaware of their worth. Stories of great finds kept buyers ever hopeful, but the field had been raked for so many years that nobody really expected to discover an overlooked treasure. With American antiques, however, the field was new and self-renewing. Until World War II, collectors could realistically hope to find decent examples of preindustrial Americana owned by people who did not know their market value. Furthermore, after Henry Ford legitimated collecting industrially manufactured items, the age of collectibility was being constantly pushed forward so that almost anybody could fancy him- or herself a collecting pioneer and begin to collect almost any item that was no longer in production. For the first generation of any such collection, buyers thought they were getting great bargains from igno- rant sellers, and sellers thought they were getting great prices from addled buyers willing to pay for other people's junk.

Before 1945 the country was still sufficiently rural, communication still sufficiently incomplete, and a clear sense of American antiques still suffi- ciently vague that both buyers and sellers thought they could take advantage of each other. Unlike the stamp literature, which was full of admonitions and cautions about dishonest dealing, the literature of, and presumably the participants in, antique collecting delighted in stories of unfair marketplace dealings. Women and men alike, in fact and in fiction, boasted of taking advantage of others. "I myself am probably not a true collector," noted one antiquer, "for your true collector must be willing to thieve, lie, steal, flatter, cajole, and demean himself for the sake of an acquisition, whereas I can bring myself to do only some of these things." The Shackletons assured their readers in 1913 that there was no culpability in picking up a bargain from a person who did not appreciate the item and who "would far rather have a modern atrocity." They justified such trades as acts of artistic and historic preservation, since the owners would otherwise "break it or throw it away or dispose of it for a trifle to the next person who happens along." The Shackle- tons did, however, warn against trying to "beat down" prices, said that collec- tors should not "take advantage" of owners, and even extolled the "distinct delight" in overpaying for a prized piece of furniture when the seller needed the money for survival. They condemned the immoral exploitation of needy and unsophisticated owners even while they condoned paying low prices to ignorant sellers without ever suggesting how the buyer could distinguish between the two.[57]

C. R. Clifford, a collector whose "junk snupper" articles appeared regu- larly in the *Saturday Evening Post* through the 1920s, also advised collectors to exploit the seller's ignorance. He reasoned that buying a thousand-dollar piece of Staffordshire pottery from a Vermont farmwife for $5 was like scor- ing a round of golf under par, striking oil, or being dealt a royal flush. Yet he specifically warned against the common ploy of pretending to buy many items, paying for a few, then walking off never to return, because it angered sellers who then refused to deal with other collectors. At the same time, however, novelist and collector Booth Tarkington was explaining how one could offer to buy a calf for $350, then ask for the hooked rug hanging on the line to keep it warm. Paying the farmer an extra $2 one would announce, "Very well. I hereby purchase the rug; and upon second thoughts I find I have no definitely pressing need for the she-calf at this time."[58]

Tarkington also suggested substituting an inexpensive new item for a valuable old one. The idea that the natives could be bamboozled out of their valuable holdings with a few shiny modern trinkets had great appeal, and even serious advice-givers had no compunctions about recommending the technique.[59] Writing about the summer hunt for antiques in 1937, Margaret Jones Peterson suggested that motorists who spotted some desirable piece worm their way into the farm with a feigned need for a glass of water and only casually bring up the issue of "the little mahogany stand on the back porch" that "would be parted with merely for the price of a new oak one." Peterson justified taking advantage of the owners' ignorance by assuring her readers that in such a free exchange the morality of the marketplace meant that both parties were satisfied with the transaction, otherwise it would never have taken place. The fact that one of the parties had the advantage of special knowledge did not trouble her at all. Occasionally the farmers were depicted turning the tables on the antique hunters by salting their premises with new items that appeared old in the context.[60]

The issue of marketplace ethics became more complicated when the collector was trading with a professional dealer and expertise was assumed all around. Each of the complex variables that contributed to an item's value, such as age, provenance, condition, and so forth, presented an opportunity for one side to gain an advantage. Most of the literature focuses on dealer ploys, but collectors did not enter the fray unarmed. Kenneth Roberts reminded his readers in 1928 that dealers were often as unsure of their ground as collectors and that a strategically placed contemptuous laugh would remain with the dealer "for days on end, filling him with dreadful fear that his most cherished antique is not all that it should be." Roberts's suggestion was light-hearted, but his message was not. Antiques were not uniform commodities and nobody could ever be sure of their exact value, so both sides could play games in the marketplace. Fiction writers in particular were fascinated by the ethical conundrums inherent in the buying and selling of antiques. Very few of the stories allow dishonesty to triumph, but all suggest that both buyers and sellers had to be very careful because there could be no assumption of honesty on either side of the transaction.[61]

In a 1907 short story, "The Pickwick Ladle," two sophisticated American collectors, Peter and Edith Wyckoff, are traveling abroad when Edith discovers what may be a valuable silver ladle in a Dutch shop. The shopkeeper is unaware of the ladle's desirability and the wife wonders to herself: "Ought she to tell him? He was so punctiliously honest with her!" Honest dealing, however, could not be expected to beget honest dealing—certainly not from antique collectors. Both she and her husband withhold information from the shopkeeper. The story's author is torn. He does not want his characters to profit from misinformation, but as collectors he recognizes that they would delight in having used their expertise to obtain a bargain. He sets up a similar dilemma in a later story with the same characters when he has Edith inadvertently make a substantial profit selling a set of china whose cost she overestimated to a fast-talker who tells her they are part of his family's estate. Her feelings of guilt are assuaged when Peter reminds her that she acted in good faith and that the man was most assuredly a dealer who will be able to resell the dishes at a profit for himself. The protagonists emerge untainted, but the cautions about the corrupting influence of the marketplace are played off against the pleasures of turning a profit. "I don't know as you realize it," says an antique dealer in a 1931 short story, "but this bein' honest in my line of business is a darned complicated job."[62]

Collectors sometimes strayed from the straight and narrow, but the dealers described in collecting literature were almost always willing to misrepresent their wares or take advantage of less-knowledgeable sellers. In 1923 *The Lure of Amateur Collecting* recounted the story of a "Jew dealer" who attempted to buy some valuable chairs at an unfairly low price. He boasted of his prospective conquest to a chance acquaintance who bought the chairs at a fair price before the dealer could finalize the sale. Not incidentally he was able to sell them at a profit, proving that his honesty was both gentlemanly and good business. Other fictional buyers displayed somewhat more questionable values when they sought to bring errant dealers to justice. The protagonist in a 1907 short story, for example, discovered that he had bought a repaired piece of porcelain that had been represented as perfect. The buyer gave the dealer the choice of having his dishonesty exposed or buying back the piece. The dealer, of course, chose to buy it back only to discover that the new owner demanded twice what he had paid for it. Apparently blackmail in the pursuit of justice was no crime in the shadowy ethics of antique collecting.[63]

Writers recognized that women were prominent collectors but usually cast them as victims who were rescued from unscrupulous male dealers by other men. Joseph Hergesheimer, who wrote more than a dozen pieces about antique collecting during the 1920s, credited his female characters with a bit more guile. In his 1926 short story "Collector's Blues," he generally undermines gender stereotypes. The primary victim is a man who thought he knew more than he did about old glass and wasted his fortune on a large number of fakes and a handful of good pieces. After his death his destitute widow hatches a plot with the help of an honest dealer to sell back the bad glass to one of the most notorious of her husband's suppliers. By feigning disinterest in selling and letting him see a few of the genuine pieces, they lure him into buying the whole estate sight unseen for a very high price.[64]

The Hergesheimer story brings together many of the major themes in antique collecting, although it deliberately leaves out some others. Most notably missing are industrial-era antiques. As in all Hergesheimer's stories, the objects in "Collector's Blues" predated 1830 and were not part of the enthusiasm for manufactured Americana prompted by Henry Ford. Also absent was the widespread appreciation of unsophisticated pieces. Colonial vernacular pieces were as rare as manufactured goods in his short stories. Nevertheless, more than a dozen stories in the *Saturday Evening Post* that included long and fairly detailed descriptions of Chippendale, Hepple-white, and other high-end antiques were indicative of the widespread interest in antique collecting in the 1920s. These, however, were not stories of beautiful objects, nor were they stories of people who possessed beautiful objects. They were stories of people possessed by the objects or by the desire to possess them. Relationships with things competed with, and usually won out over, relationships with people. Lying, misrepresentation, market manipulation, and general moral turpitude motivated the characters. And even the heroes, as in the "Collector's Blues" story, engaged in subterfuge to right wrongs done to them.

If hobbies were a leisure expression of workplace values, then antique collecting brought men and women alike into the most ethically questionable arena of the business world. Unlike stamp, coin, and book collectors, antique collectors had no informal code of honor. Stamp collectors warned against exploiting the uninformed; antique collectors developed it into an art. Antique collectors carried their duplicity over into negotiations between ostensibly informed participants as well, with buyers and dealers constantly trying to mislead each other. This phenomenon is all the more noteworthy because antiquing was one of the few areas where women participated as the equals of men. The pattern was not due to the presence of women since it did not exist in the more exclusively female collecting hobbies, such as buttons or dolls. But neither did the presence of women appear to ameliorate the dishonesty.

The peculiar market dynamics of antique collecting probably stemmed less from the kinds of people who participated than from unique opportunities the field presented. From the latter part of the nineteenth century until World War II, there were probably more vulnerable naive participants in antique collecting than in any other hobby. As early interest in fine pieces was augmented by a newer desire for vernacular and manufactured items, the number of potential owner-victims grew proportionally. The first several generations of collectors who had the chance to steal candy from babies did so and generated a fairly elaborate discourse of justification for it. Even after the attics and basements of rural American had been emptied, antique collecting continued to offer numerous occasions for dubious dealings. The complexity of the items themselves meant they were more difficult to evaluate than most other kinds of collectibles and, by the same token, easier to misrepresent or counterfeit, both of which people believed were widely done.

Whether it was the highly organized stamp collectors with their albums and published price guides, or the wild and woolly antique collectors who played by the law of the jungle, collecting hobbyists made a business out of their leisure. Since it was a hobby, the business activity of collecting could be isolated from the economic tides of real life to perform its role as a metaphor and model. For most collectors the hobby illustrated the truths of the capitalist ideology without actually putting the hobbyist at risk. In this sense, collecting functioned effectively as disguised affirmation. The disguise, however was not only transparent enough to reveal the hidden truths, it could be ripped aside altogether. Because the dollars involved were real and the value of the objects could become substantial, the serious hobbyist ran the risk of the spillover leisure spilling back. Serious leisure could not get more serious than a hobby with uncontrollable real-world consequences.

Section 3

Handicrafts

6 Crafts, Tools, and Gender in the Nineteenth Century

Like collecting, handicrafts hide their affirmation of capitalist values in the disguise of leisure. Crafting, however, has been less likely
than collecting to shed its cloak of leisure and seriously impinge on the real-
world economic status of the hobbyist. Unlike collectors who celebrate the
financial aspects of their hobby, leisure crafters have been as likely to admit
that they lost money as they have been to claim that they saved money on
their pieces. Crafters, of course, end up with a product that could be sold,
and doing so sometimes has created a problem since it blurred the line
between hobby and business. Nevertheless, by its very nature crafting subordinates trade to production. A thing cannot be sold until it is made. Collectors let somebody else make it for them; crafters make it themselves. Where
collecting reproduces the ideology of the free market, crafting is an affirmation of the work ethic.

Affirming the work ethic is not the same thing as affirming work. In fact,
crafting often functions as an explicit critique of both the atomized factory
and the sterile office by re-creating the ideal artisanal environment. Hobbyist
workers choose their own projects, acquire their own materials and tools,
work at their own pace in their own space, and create a whole object from
start to finish. The freedom with which they operate, and the pride in the
product of their efforts distinguishes the hobby from work, but crafters are
making a commodity, and that makes their pastime consonant with the dominant ideology. Not only do crafters work in a socially prescribed way at their
leisure, the product of that leisure work is almost always a representation of a
similar object in the commercial world. Needlework, household decorations, models, do-it-yourself furniture — the crafter makes all these things to
be like similar items made by machines. Both the process and the product of
handicrafts carry a double message about the meaning of the modern workplace: production is good, but the circumstances in which it occurs are not.

Handicrafting, like collecting, has the charm of complete freedom. Working alone and out of love for the process, crafters create an object where
there was none before. Collectors' close ties to the marketplace may tempt

them to cheat, but crafters are not lured to violate broader social values. The handicrafter evokes the mythical purity of the preindustrial artisan, which is why partisans in the Progressive Era could use crafting to create the profession of occupational therapy to cure the ills of industrial society. Generations of handicrafters have followed the advice of occupational therapists and undertaken this work as a form of authentic leisure that carries none of collecting's implications of mental illness. Wooden chain carvers in the South, for example, uniformly saw their craft as a source of both physical and mental health. When asked if working two hours a day for more than year on a single chain was "a sickness, a malady?" one carver replied, no, it was a relief and a reaction against the tedium of his factory job.[1]

Despite the faith that both participants and mental health professionals have placed in the soothing effects of handwork, crafts have received nothing like the kind of close analysis that psychologists have given collecting. Although studies have shown that handicrafts are more popular than collecting, they do not present the same kind of ideological contradictions. Scholars are attracted to the paradoxical, the conflicted, the apparently inexplicable, and it would seem that the pleasures and rewards of handicrafts are too apparent to warrant much attention. Not only are there no psychological analyses of crafts, but there are precious few other kinds of scholarly investigations either. What empirical evidence we do have about crafts is, for the most part, incidental to broader investigations of leisure as a whole.

A variety of postwar studies have consistently shown that blue-collar workers replicate on-the-job skills and attitudes in their leisure time, a particularly straightforward example of spillover leisure.[2] Both the physical skills and the values necessary for success at work are carried over by these men into their leisure time, and their work experience makes them especially appreciative of the well-made object, on the job and off.[3] Despite its similarity to work, the craft leisure of skilled workers does, of course, have its compensatory elements; all leisure does. Assembly line workers interviewed for one study, for example, disliked their jobs, yet they ranked handicraft hobbies as one of their favorite pastimes (behind only television and sex—in that order), because crafts they said were "more stimulating than my job." Crafting appears to be no less popular among employed women than men, and studies show that female blue-collar workers prefer leisure that gives them control and a sense of completion, exactly the same kind of satisfaction that crafting affords blue-collar men. Male and female workers alike sought leisure that provided them with the meaning they felt was missing on the job, but they did so through activity that was a better job than their job.[4]

Both men and women employees perceive craft hobbies as a perfect job, freely started and freely stopped, controlled from beginning to end by the worker, and resulting in a product that reflects the skill and imagination of the hobbyist. For workers satisfied with their jobs, this perfect job is part of the integrated pattern of their lives and validates both the skills and the values that have made them successful at their vocations. For the dissatisfied worker the hobby is an escape into the job they wish they had. It is compensatory but compensatory in a way that affirms the dominant ideology: work is good.

Women and Crafts

For most of the nineteenth century, public leisure was a man's world. Women's leisure, like women's work, remained in the home, but the leisure grew as the work shrank. Women still had the ultimate responsibility to feed and clothe their families, but increasingly that was done by purchasing finished or semifinished products. Urban and suburban women grew neither food nor fiber at home, and for middle-class women, servants, commercial laundries, and an efficient school system took over jobs that had once been wifely duties. Relatively few working-class and almost no middle-class married women worked in the industrial economy.[5] Cut off from the new centers of economic productivity, women developed a distinctly female culture that gave them preeminence in home-oriented activities such as child rearing, running the household (including the purchasing of family goods like food, clothing, and housewares), and religion, even as the amount of time and effort needed for many of these tasks was shrinking.

The house was a "haven in a heartless world" not only for men escaping from the jungle of work but also for women. The larger world, complained Eliza Woodworth in 1865, was full of strangers who "incessantly misunderstand you" and "judge [you] in severe fashion." "Well you have a refuge — your home," she assured her readers; "there slander is not received against you. There no one thinks of laughing at you." Your family knew you and loved you unconditionally and provided sanctuary from competitors and critics. The new culture of domestic segregation produced its own set of values. While not anticapitalist or anti-industrial in any explicit sense, this female-dominated ideology opposed expressions of male aggressiveness that seemed necessary for success in a Darwinian business environment. The lack of synchrony between the ideology of the household and the ideology of the workplace was real, and nothing here is intended to deny the widespread attempts by Victorian women to quarantine the home from the harshness of work. The isolation, however, was not complete; there was leakage in both directions. Female secretaries began to bring familial values to the workplace, and concomitantly the ideology of business appeared in the household.[6]

"It is impossible to watch a number of women without being struck by their general indifference to rules and contempt for regulations," wrote an esteemed group of behavior experts in 1896, "unless they have been brought into contact with the laws of business life, which govern both sexes alike." Their point was illustrated by the profligate husband in an 1857 short story who rejected his wife's request that they rationalize their home by keeping track of their expenses, declaring, "I never had an 'expense book' as you call it, since I was born. Books are bothers enough at the office." Hobbies (and perhaps other home activities that remain to be explored) served to introduce women and children to those "laws of business life" without forcing them to leave the sanctuary of the home.[7]

There may have been good reason for middle-class Victorian women to apply business efficiency to the economic administration of their households, but there was very little incentive to rationalize their use of time, since for them time was not a scarce commodity. The eighteenth-century situation in which a wealthy young woman might dedicate five hours a day to accomplishments such as sewing and drawing remained unchanged well into the following century.[8] In 1876 a young bride from the "upper circles of society" was said to have had every care "scrupulously lifted from her shoulders by a doting and unwise husband, and beyond dressing for dinner, and attending to morning calls, she seemed not to have a duty in existence."[9] The widespread availability of servants to middle-class housewives created a need for ways to fill the hours of the day. Farm women, poorer women without servants, and those with very large families had no problem keeping busy, but for substantial numbers of middle-class women the temptation to do nothing was an everyday reality.

To avoid the sin of idleness, women, no less than men, were regularly urged to use their time productively. "Make it a rule, therefore, never to allow yourself to be idle," cautioned a Boston father to his daughter in 1834. "If you once form an industrious habit, you will never afterwards be able to content yourself in a state of inactivity."[10] Likewise, a poet in *Arthur's Home Magazine* advised her readers:

There's no enjoyment
In the employment
Of killing time;
Such hours of leisure
Are without pleasure,
And dull life's prime.[11]

Idleness was a snare, and having fun was suspect unless it prepared the participant for even greater productivity. Writers were particularly fond of Aesop's parable of the bow, which if left strung would lose its elasticity. Relaxation was necessary but only to increase efficiency. "The legitimate end of amusement is not answered in mere gratification," the same Boston father advised, "but in refreshing and invigorating the powers for the more successful discharge of duty." Unfortunately, it was not at all clear just what constituted a young lady's duty.[12]

For many of the wives and daughters of prosperous men, duty and leisure were hard to distinguish. Since before the Revolution, these women, who formed America's original leisure class, had been using handicrafts to fill time. An exasperated husband complained in 1758, "We have twice as many fire-screens as chimneys and three flourished quilts for every bed. Half the rooms are adorned with a kind of futile pictures which imitate tapestry." In addition he noted his wife had created boxes full of knit garters and was passing on these dubious skills to her daughters.[13] Artistically deficient eighteenth-century mothers unable to teach their daughters could send them to craft schools for instruction. In Boston, New York, Philadelphia, and Charleston men and women set up private academies to teach what would later be called hobbies to the daughters of the wealthy. Young ladies with time to fill could learn quill-work (making pictures out of rolled paper and small objects glued to a framed background), wax-work (making models of flowers and fruit out of wax), painting on glass, featherwork (making pictures by gluing feathers to a background), Japanning (lacquering small wood or papier-mâché objects), embroidery, and drawing.[14] Artistic crafts continued to be a standard part of the curriculum at female seminaries in the nineteenth century, and for those who lived too far from seminaries, itinerant teachers traveled the hinterlands bringing craft instruction to isolated ladies.[15]

Handicrafts created chores for girls who would otherwise have had none. They provided, explained one writer in 1834, a "method of occupying time, which may lead to practically industrious habits." Two books published in the 1830s at the very dawn of the American Industrial Revolution, recommended just such unnecessary chores. *The American Girl's Book* and *The Girl's Own Book* were filled with small craft projects that would provide middle-class girls with something to do when there was nothing to do. The projects in *The American Girl's Book*, reprinted in 1834 in *Godey's Lady's Book*, emphasized making reticules (handbags) but also included such classic craft items as pen-wipers, matchboxes, needle books, and pincushions. The second book reduced the stress on needle skills by introducing projects involving basket weaving, paper folding, and the preservation of natural objects such as leaves and butterflies.[16]

Crafts were used to train girls in work habits they could use to produce more crafts when they became women. The low cost of servants meant that even families that considered themselves poor, like the Marches of *Little Women*, often had a maid to do the heavy cooking and cleaning. "An hour or two, each morning," explained a housewife in an 1856 short story, was all that was necessary to keep the house in shape. The rest of the time she kept herself amused with her knitting, her music, her drawing, and her garden. In 1831 *Godey's* referred to women crafters as those "condemned to do what they please all morning" and recommended several craft projects to usefully fill the time. The alternative was to "lie on the lounge all day, en dishabille, with not a thought for anything but myself, that 'I would not, if I could, be gay.' "[17]

Frances Trollope was appalled by the idleness forced on urban wives when she traveled through the United States in the late 1820s. Those living in boarding houses who did not even have to do their own shopping or supervise the cooking were particularly at a loss for activities to keep them busy. Trollope described them as leaving the breakfast table to return to their rooms and admits, "as to what they do there it is not very easy to say; but I believe they clear-starch a little, and iron a little, and sit in a rocking-chair, and sew a great deal." So vital was craft work in keeping women busy that Trollope concluded, "the plough is hardly a more blessed instrument in America than the needle."[18]

Since they were unnecessary, women's crafts were not work, but because they simulated work they were clearly preferable to lounging around and complaining about the lack of a gay life. An idle mind, warned *Godey's*, "like the garden of the slothful, will be overgrown with briars and weeds."[19] "When God created Adam," explained "Aunt Sophronia" in an 1879 advice book, "he created also a business for Adam; he did not make him a gentleman of leisure." The same held true for Eve, and Aunt Sophronia suggested strongly that her two nieces take over some of the servants' jobs such as keeping their rooms clean and doing some serious sewing. The girls, who spent their time reading, napping, receiving gentleman callers, and doing fancywork, did not quite seem to have gotten the message since they responded, "Sometimes when we have been actually working for a fair, or festival, or preparing for a party, we have really enjoyed ourselves: possibly, it was because we were busy." Aunt Sophronia was fighting a losing battle. The most she could hope for was nieces who took their hobbies seriously. "We recognize how many hours there are in every day which, in ordinary lives, are not spent in the active pursuit either of business or amusement, and which must be filled up in some way," wrote Janet Ruutz-Rees, the author of *Home Occupations*, one of the first hobby books for women. Her solution was a series of "light occupations" such as handicrafts and collecting that, along with sewing, could keep Victorian women safe from idleness.[20]

All the "light occupations" in Ruutz-Rees's book were productive hobbies. She had sections on leather work, tissue paper ornaments, making wax flowers and fruit, painting and frame making, stringing beads, assembling scrapbooks, and collecting. They were, said the author, good things to do because they provided "valuable knowledge acquired in the pursuit of some favorite 'hobby.'" Ruutz-Rees put "hobby" in quotes, as though she were not quite sure that it was the right word to apply to these pastimes. In fact, she seems to have been the first author to use the word in its modern form. Written in 1882, her book is one of the earliest concrete expressions of the new Victorian leisure category of hobbies. All Ruutz-Rees's "home occupations" were handicrafts or collecting. People would continue to label other kinds of leisure "hobbies," but the appearance of this book confirms that productive leisure-time activities that one did alone and at home were being thought of as a discreet category called hobbies.[21]

Needle Crafts: Plain Sewing

Needlework was, of course, the craft most associated with women and the one most used to fill what might otherwise have been idle time. "There is no occupation so essentially feminine, at the same time so truly ladylike, as needle work in every branch, from the plain, useful sewing that keeps household and person neat and orderly, to the exquisite, dainty fancywork that adds beauty to every room," observed S. Annie Frost in 1881. As Frost indicates, there were two kinds of needlework: plain and fancy. Although embroidery was always considered fancywork, the distinction was based less on technique than on product. Practical needlework was called plain and was invariably praised, while artistic and decorative items were deemed fancy and often criticized as the fruits of idleness. In *Little Women*, Mrs. March tells her newly married daughter not to be ashamed of housework, remembering that she herself, as a wealthy young bride "used to long for my new clothes to wear out or get torn, so that I might have the pleasure of mending them; for I got heartily sick of doing fancy work and tending my pocket handkerchief." Comparing several marriageable young ladies, a man in an 1882 short story observed, "Cicely has more practical knowledge than the pair of them! True she can't sing airs from the last opera, nor do crewel work, nor paint high art cat-tails and sunflowers . . . but she can knit and darn, sew, cook, make cheese and butter, and all that sort of thing."[22]

Before 1850, which is to say before the widespread distribution of sewing machines, there was a constant supply of "white work" to keep middle-class women busy. The parlor workbasket, sitting next to a window chair where the light was good, held an endless stream of shirts, bed linens, underclothes, stockings, mittens, and other unembellished sewing waiting to be stitched when there was time to sit for a little while. Like the workbench, which was the home handyman's first undertaking, the workbasket was one of the most popular projects for needle women.[23] One could buy an elaborately compartmentalized worktable with a variety of pull-out and fold-down surfaces, but most women used a portable basket, which in itself was no minor affair. Catharine Beecher enumerated more than two dozen distinct categories of items that belonged in a well-supplied workbasket. These included a dozen different types of needles each with its own separately colored wax lubricants; coarse and fine scissors; an emery bag to clean pins and needles; and a lump of chalk for drying damp hands, before one even got to the thread, yarn, cloth, and buttons.[24]

As one of the few ways they could earn money on their own, there were always plenty of poor women willing to take in plain sewing, just as they took in wash.[25] Unlike washing, however, sewing was imbued with the mystique of femininity and all women were urged to do it themselves. Women who "hired out" their white work so they could have more time for activities they enjoyed more became objects of public criticism.[26] In these circumstances, even plain sewing took on hobbylike characteristics. The spread of the sewing machine after 1850 made the situation more complicated because sitting at a machine was incompatible with the traditional homey image of mother clicking her knitting needles in the twilight as she talked over the day with her family. In 1853 *Godey's* complained that the sewing machine had made plain work too efficient and that much of it had been banished from the parlor. However, the magazine assured its readers, there was still plenty of plain handwork that needed to be done, and women should disregard the tradition that prohibited them from sewing underwear in the presence of men. "No well-bred gentleman would scrutinize or inquire into the exact shape or purpose of any article a lady might be engaged upon," it said.[27]

Plain hand sewing (and knitting) posed no problem for women. It was something that had to be done, unequivocally a chore, but one that allowed women to sit and chat with friends, family, or even suitors, while not wasting time. Knitting in particular lent itself to simultaneous working and leisure. An expert knitter could knit "blind," that is without constantly looking at her hands, so she could work and talk, or even read, at the same time. Women who had mastered this trick could, in a Calvinist sense, have their cake and eat it too. E.B.D., who wrote regularly for *Arthur's Home Magazine*, recognized that women who took a few minutes out of their day to sit and read might feel guilty "that they are wasting time which might and ought to be otherwise employed." They could allay that guilt "if they could call in the aid of the knitting-needles to keep them company, and have a comfortable consciousness that, even as they amused and rested themselves" their work was progressing.[28]

Plain sewing could also justify socializing. In 1867 a group of young house guests confined by inclement weather gathered in the parlor to talk and sew. "Please wait," asked one, "until I get my work. The sight of eight other pairs of busy hands makes me fidgety while mine are idle." Having established her work ethic bona fides, she "tripped upstairs, returning in two minutes with a little papier-mâché 'Ladies' Companion,' furnished with a dainty set of implements of feminine industry with which she proceeded to hem a piece of linen." So powerful was the exculpatory effect of sewing that in the later nineteenth century sewing in groups became a standard way for women to get together without having to bear the social or psychological burden of idleness. Sewing circles met regularly in the afternoon to make clothes either to be given directly to the needy or to be sold to raise funds for some worthy charity. A couple of hours' sewing was followed by tea, which functioned as "a school for scandal and gossip." There the participants could snipe about the lack of preserves for the bread, or argue over whether their proceeds should go to "a school for the colored sect," "the Sons of Temperance," or in a dig at one of their number, to the "Old Maids' Consolation Society."[29]

Quilting parties were the most traditional form of socialized sewing, one to which men were sometimes invited (see fig. 6.1). Quilts were usually perceived as forms of fancywork, and quilting was recommended as the leisure one might indulge in "when all the new garments are made, and mending is an abomination." By the 1880s, in the era of the crazy quilt, patchwork had become an obsessional fad prompting some women to masquerade as dry goods dealers to get silk sample books from textile manufacturers as a way of adding to their store of patches, while others raided the jacket linings and handkerchiefs of their fathers and brothers. For the scavenging makers of silk crazy quilts, sewing had become a pure hobby, a game in which the search for scraps was as much a part of the fun as the construction of the quilt. The sewing machine had made mass-produced clothing readily available and transformed needlework from a source of work to a source of leisure.[30]

Needle Crafts: Fancywork

Until the invention of the sewing machine, "the drudgery of the kitchen was succeeded by that of the work-basket, whose pile of shirts and small gar-

THE QUILTING PARTY.

FIGURE 6.1 This drawing of a quilting party in 1849 shows crafting being used both to build bonds among women and as an opportunity to socialize with men. (Reprinted from T. S. Arthur, "The Quilting Party," *Godey's Lady's Book* 39 [September 1849]: frontispiece.)

ments seemed never to decrease," wrote Jenny June in 1866. Not a moment of time could be afforded for the gratification of any simple fancy, even in ornamental needlework," because women had to work "far into Saturday night" on "the necessities of the plainest work . . . and the inevitable weekly collection of family mending." Mechanization eliminated plain sewing and knitting as a core female experience, thereby transforming fancywork from a problematic time waster to a leisure-time expression of the womanly arts. As early as 1847 *Godey's* warned that a woman might feel "superannuated-like, and laid upon the shelf," when she first saw "a worsted stocking get up and knit itself." However, it assured its readers, real fancywork would never be taken over by machines. Some women who had shunned fancy needlework might be tempted to sew ruffles, tucks, and braids with their new machines, but most women abandoned plain sewing to machines and embraced fancywork not as a chore but as an art used "rather for the garnishment of homes than upon trappings for the person."[31]

Medieval and Renaissance aristocrats had done embroidery and other forms of artistic needlework as a way to keep busy, and that tradition continued into the early modern period in Europe and America.[32] A poem in 1830, for example, unfavorably compared women who spent their time drawing, painting, or playing music with the woman:

Who cheerfully warbles some rustical ditty,
While plying the needle with exquisite art.
The bright little needle—the swift flying needle,
The needle directed by beauty and art.[33]

The reference to "beauty and art" suggests that the poet was referring to fancywork like that described in an 1860 short story. "We had pretty transparent shades on the windows, and over them embroidered white curtains that fell in long, graceful folds to the floor," explained the bride of her new home. "I had embroidered the curtains in my leisure moments, and they were very pretty. The piano and table-covers were my work, too—crimson cloth, braided heavily. I had also knitted tidies for the rocking-chairs, and worked the covers for the piano-stool and two pretty ottomans."[34]

Except for the knitted tidies, most of the items in this list of accomplishments were probably embroidered. Ultimately there were very few surfaces, either household or human, that some hobbyist did not cover with decorated cloth. Tablecloths, lambrequins (hangings over doors and windows), floor rugs and mats, mats for bureau tops, chair backs, screens, panels, furniture pillows and cushions, pincushion covers, washstand backsplashes, and of course, women's and girl's clothing were all embellished with wool or silk patterns.[35] Not all fancywork was embroidery, but all embroidery was fancywork. Its aristocratic heritage made it attractive to haute bourgeois women for whom it was a sign that they had the time, taste, and skill to master nonfunctional pastimes. "Clad in a pure muslin wrapper," the protagonist in an 1866 story idled away an afternoon, "her plump hands, small, white, and firm, as only those of a healthy, youthful blonde can be; busied diligently, but not rapidly, with the alluring mazes of a large square of worsted embroidery, the favored daughter of nature and fortune leaned back in her sewing-chair and counted her stitches in satisfied patience, and thought such pleasant, unexciting thoughts as suited the hot day and her quiet mood."[36]

Just as machines made plain work less necessary, they made embroidery easier, so that by the mid-nineteenth century, needlework historian Rozsika Parker notes, "Embroidery and femininity were entirely fused, and the connection was deemed to be natural."[37] In 1804 a German printer began producing patterns on graph paper that could be easily transferred to the embroidery canvas. To make matters even more convenient, producers hand-colored these "Berlin patterns" so the embroiderer knew what color thread or yarn to buy, and the canvases were marked with a grid of colored threads to make it easier to count squares. After 1850 women could purchase canvases with the pattern and color applied directly on the cloth eliminating the need to transfer the picture from paper.[38] The lazy or unskilled embroiderer could buy "Berlinwork" or "needlepoint" with the patterns already completed, so that she only had to fill in the monochromatic background. The end result was that any woman who had mastered the basic embroidery stitches could produce a creditable piece of work.[39]

In the 1860s manufacturers introduced perforated cards that could be substituted for the canvas. Instead of cloth the hobbyist bought a piece of punched cardboard with the colored design printed directly on it, and then filled in the design by threading the yarn through the prepunched holes. Obviously, stitched cardboard could not be used for most of the traditional embroidery projects like clothes, furniture coverings, and pillows, which demanded a flexible matrix. Instead a whole new category of rigid projects emerged that provided women with some of the same constructional opportunities wood provided for men. Among the most popular were cards with religious, patriotic, and romantic mottoes on them, which after they were sewn, could be framed and hung on the wall. In addition, almost any of the projects described below, such as card boxes, bookmarks, baskets, wall pockets, and the like, could be made out of the perforated cardboard decorated with wool or silk.[40]

Embroidery, and its bastardized offshoots, were a microcosm of Victorian crafts. Technology transformed a traditional artisanal activity by making it faster, easier, and more accessible to a mass market with free time. There was no pretense that the hobbyist stitching a pious motto for the parlor was emulating a tradition of female artistry. She was doing something very much of the moment. She was playing a craft game that demanded no artistic ability and only a modicum of sewing skills. Like the paint-by-number pictures and precut furniture kits that would be popular in the next century, Berlinwork and perforated card projects depended on machines but created the illusion of skill so that the hobbyist had a sense of accomplishment, and something to do to fill idle hours.

Like all hobbies, fancywork exploited the discomfort that middle-class people felt when time lay heavy on their hands. Not everybody, however, was impressed, and advocates had to develop an argument to justify the activity. Because of its historical connection to aristocratic women, embroidery conveyed a sense of putting on airs. "There are many amongst the daughters and sisters of farmers and tradespeople whose minds never seem to expand beyond the narrow female routine of dress, gossip, fancy needle-work, novel-reading, and a smattering, it may be, of bad French and atrocious music," warned *Godey's*, which was itself a major purveyor of embroidery patterns. The article criticized women who whipped out "useless embroidery" at the first appearance of company while they carefully hid "the heap of undarned household stockings or family 'white work.'" When a certain Mrs. Foster, a farmer's wife, wished to raise her daughter's place in society she sought to teach the young woman how to play the piano, sing Italian songs, and do crewel-work, which her down-to-earth husband dismissed as "that foolish, useless crochet."[41]

Fancywork was decorative and therefore useless. It offended traditionalists who wanted women to attend to their (plain) knitting and activists who wanted them to attend to the cares of the world. An Oregon feminist complained that when women spent all their time on fancywork "men falsely imagine that the women of the land are content to do nothing else," while a church worker said of a piece she was shown, "To me, it is red with the blood of murdered time! It is criminal for any mortal being to waste so many of the hours the Lord hath given for His work in such folly as this."[42] "You know there is such a thing as busy idleness," a mother reminded her daughter when she refused to sew on a button for her brother because she was more interested in working on a "lamp mat."[43] Since fancywork was unnecessary, doing it was ipso facto an exercise in leisure, so both the process and the product became signs of frivolity, and their absence signs of application. Speaking favorably of his female bookkeeper, the shop owner in an 1868 story said, "no surreptitious novel, or equally contraband needlework ever nestled in her drawer or pocket, to be produced when the overlookers back was turned."[44]

Everybody agreed that fancywork was, in the words of Miss Leslie's 1831 *Girl's Book*, "occupation for play hours." One observer in 1875 warned women not to set a deadline for fancywork because to do so "is to make labor out of what should be recreation." It was, however, a special kind of recreation. Like all other hobbies, fancy needlework mitigated, even if it did not eliminate, the destructive impact of leisure. Lydia Marie Child, no lover of needlework, nevertheless allowed that it was better for girls "to tear up large pieces of cloth for the sake of sewing them together again" as patchwork "than to be standing round, wishing they had something to do." Forty years later "A Lady" writing in *Arthur's* used virtually the same language to defend fancy needlework, saying that it was "better to do that than sit the whole evening long with hands totally unoccupied," which was the charge leveled against men. Men "have no resource but striding up and down the room, like a bird that beats itself to pieces against the bars of its cage," wrote a defender of needlework in 1863. "While you are simply looking on and admiring, balancing the scissors in your unoccupied hands, or rifling and deranging the contents of your companion's work-basket," she charged, "the work is progressing." Fancywork may have been less commendable than real work, but it was certainly more meritorious than the devilry of idle hands.[45]

Female Crafts: The Origins of the Handicraft Hobby

While experiencing one of American literature's most famous deaths, Beth in *Little Women* spends her final weeks on Earth making mittens, needle-books, dolls, pen-wipers, and scrapbooks for neighborhood children. Beth's leisure was forced upon her by illness, but healthy women also claimed the right to spend spare time crafting, especially if they could, like Beth, unselfishly give the crafts away. "My conscience says that even I have a right to amuse myself for ten, fifteen, thirty minutes a day. I pick this up while I am waiting for my husband to come to supper—at no other time," explained a fictional wife, and besides which, she was making a gift for her husband.[46] "It need be only the idlest of idle hours that are given to fancy work," one writer assured women, "and yet a great deal that is charming and useful can be created." The writer listed the sorts of things she had in mind: "gay bunches of wax leaves and flowers," chair coverings and pillows, "cunningly contrived lamp screens," "warm lounge blankets," wall portfolios to keep household papers, and "small but tender gifts which no money could be spared to buy." As this list of worthwhile leisure projects makes clear, the term fancywork applied not only to ornamental needle projects but also to all marginally useful but highly decorative handicraft projects.[47]

The Ladies' Hand Book of Fancy and Ornamental Work, published in 1859, listed fifty-one categories of crafts. Forty-one of them involved needlework, including, among others, appliqué, bead work, braiding, lace work, tatting, and netting, in addition to the usual embroidery and knitting. However, it also included directions for projects that involved painting on glass and using tissue paper, wire, and pine cones. The book is fairly typical in its casual combination of needle and non–needle crafts. It was not the technique but the purpose that drew these activities together. The "work" sections that appeared regularly in women's magazines had little to do with work in the conventional sense. They were collections of projects that included needle arts and nontextile crafts. In 1830 and 1831, for example, *Godey's Lady's Book* published directions on how to make small boxes, workbaskets, flower stands, card receivers, and whatnots (decorative containers for odds and ends) from sheets of pasteboard; suggestions on making plaster casts of coins and small antiques; tips for painting on glass and on velvet; instruction on Poonah (making stencils to apply heavy color in an Indian style); and a rather improbable set of instructions on assembling a glass box with cloth ribbon. Forty-five years later, in just one typical issue, there were plans for a cane hot plate, a case for crochet materials with embroidered decorations, a stamped leather traveling case, a cardboard and silk cigar case in the shape of a Chinese pavilion, a footstool with an embroidered cushion, a knitted knee cap or warmer, a jet bead hair ornament, crochet wool boots, and an embroidered coin purse.[48]

Looking back from a late Victorian perspective on earlier craft hobbies, Lucy Maynard Salmon referred to them as "idle labor which is unproductive," necessary only because women could not work outside the home and most housework was done by servants. The same fastidiousness that kept women inside the home limited the kinds of crafts they could do. Commenting in 1854 on the seashell flowers that were sold as souvenirs at beach resorts, *Godey's* admitted they were pretty, but warned they were "scarcely adapted for ladies' work; the plaster, stiff wire, rough colors, and actual hard work, being matters by no means fitted for 'Delicate and dainty fingers!' " By the same token *Graham's Magazine* ruled out serious painting for women since bringing "all the paraphernalia of oil painting" into the house was not "advisable or convenient." Violating their own cautions against messiness, magazines did publish directions for making plaster and sulfur casts, and wax modeling, which was not much neater. For the most part, however, Victorian-era craft suggestions steered away from techniques that involved a lot of heating, mixing, smells, or spills, although a certain amount was inevitable since even the simplest glues and pastes had to be concocted at home.[49]

Craft publications occasionally suggested that women might carve in a variety of softer mediums that resembled wood, ivory, and metal, but did not require large cutting tools or hammers.[50] Because of the weight of the tools necessary to work it, wood itself was conspicuously absent from Victorian women's craft projects. Cardboard functioned as female wood, and the only real wood ever recommended for women's crafts was from salvaged cigar boxes, which could be cut with a sharp knife and pierced with a gimlet and awl, just like cardboard.[51] *Graham's Illustrated Magazine* tried to promote the "elegant and useful art" of making "papier-plastique" building models. Papier-plastique (not to be confused with the messier papier-mâché) was nothing more than gluing together model buildings from uncolored cardboard. The magazine praised this craft because it was clean. It was less messy than painting and leather modeling, and the crafter did not have to touch "the various pigments, balsams, plaster-of-Paris, moulds, &c., used in the manipulation of wax fruit [or] the powders, patterns, leaves, and other expensive adjuncts, required by those who work in wax flowers." Nor, it should be added, would the hobbyist expose herself to paralyzing toxins used in coloring wax models.[52]

The construction of papier-plastique building models never caught on, but the cardboard medium was literally the foundation of women's three-dimensional craft projects. Cheap and readily available, it could be cut with scissors or a small knife, punched with a light awl, joined with paste or yarn, and most of all, it could be covered with all the same items used to make pictures. The very first projects published in *Godey's* in the 1830s included cardboard boxes decorated with painted pictures and glued-on ribbons, and for the next seventy years, books and magazines described a myriad of cardboard objects. The majority were containers; they included boxes, baskets, whatnots, pouches, pockets, reticules, small cabinets, and little stands designed to hold visiting cards, playing cards, sewing items, hair, matches, flowers (including flowers made from paper, wax, and seashells), waste paper, clippings (from sewing), "poudre de riz" (rice powder used as a cosmetic), toilet articles, writing materials, jewelry, and unspecified household junk. Once they had made the cardboard framework, the hobbyists covered it with cloth, paint, alum, or most often, colored paper, which in turn was festooned with decorations composed from the usual menu of shells, pebbles, feathers, quills, leaves, and so forth. Noncontainers such as shrines, fire screens, and thermometer holders, were also constructed from cardboard and decorated with paint, stitchery, and, for those with limited artistic ability, with a variety of pasted-on pictures.[53] (See fig. 6.2.)

Women and girls had been gluing printed magazine pictures, postage stamps, and cigar bands on objects since they had become readily available before the Civil War. Women's spontaneous use of printed material sparked the commercial production of "potichomanie" pictures that were made to be cut out and glued to the inside of glass vases and jars. The spaces between the figures were filled in with oil colors and the result was supposed to resemble Chinese porcelain.[54] Cut and paste got even easier in 1864 with the invention of "decalcomanie," preprinted pictures and designs that could be

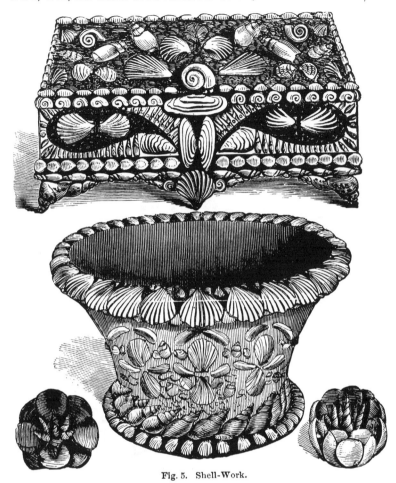

Fig. 5. Shell-Work.

FIGURE 6.2 Typical Victorian women's crafts projects decorated with embroidery and seashells. (Reprinted from C. S. Jones and Henry T. Williams, *Ladies' Fancy Work: Hints and Helps to Home Taste and Recreations* [New York: Henry T. Williams, 1876], 171, 237.)

transferred directly from paper onto a variety of surfaces including "crockery, china, porcelain, vases, glass, book-cases, folio, boxes, lap-desks, ribbons, dresses, etc." No surface was safe from this manufactured artwork that, like Berlinwork, prefigured the hobby kits that would become standard fare for twentieth-century crafters. It is not clear whether an 1855 cartoon in *Arthur's Home Magazine* is making fun of the daughter following the fad or the mother who does not understand it (see fig. 6.3).[55]

Fashion may have been sufficient justification for a cartoon character's craft work and probably all that could be mustered for activities devoid of any real skill, but crafting flourished because advocates believed it provided "graceful occupation, and opportunities for the display of good taste and dexterity in many interesting arts."[56] By the time of the Civil War, dexterity, if not good taste, was more or less taken for granted among middle-class women. The objects of their efforts remained fairly constant over the years, as did the materials and techniques used to make them. In fact, in 1860 *Godey's* reprinted verbatim plans for a pasteboard vase, a whatnot, and a card holder that it had first published almost thirty years earlier.[57] Crafters did not

MAMMA: Why, goodness gracious, Arabella, what on earth are you making that mess for?

ARABELLA: Mess, Mamma!—Why it's all the Fashion,—it's Potichimanie!

MAMMA [AGREEABLY SURPRISED]: Oh!—I see!

FIGURE 6.3 Pasting pictures on vases was a low-skill craft of the 1850s. (Reprinted from "Potichimanie," *Arthur's Home Magazine* 5 [February 1855]: 146.)

scorn novelty, and forms did vary in minor ways to reflect changing fashions in clothing, architectural, and home furnishing styles, but for sixty years, from around 1830 to about 1890, middle-class women enthusiastically participated in a fairly homogeneous set of handicraft hobbies. Women's magazines and specialized books produced a steady stream of instructions for a wide variety of "the beautiful and tasteful ornaments which afford much employment and amusement to the ladies."[58]

Victorian women approached their crafts from two directions. The first, and less common, stressed the function of the crafted object. Thus a book or article might feature plans for boxes, fire screens, or shrines, each one to be made out of a different material. Such a categorization emphasized object use, and assumed that the crafter needed, or at least wanted, a particular item. The second approach, which was more the norm, emphasized the process rather than the product.[59] The real purpose of crafting was not to make things—most of the craft pieces were only marginally useful; the real purpose was to occupy spare time, so hobbyists were expected to develop a craft "career." Starting as a novice whose products were hardly worth the cost of their raw materials, the serious crafter could become increasingly adept, proceeding through developmental stages that paralleled the apprentice-to-master career path of the traditional artisan. To do so meant to focus on the skills necessary to become an expert, concentrating on techniques peculiar to a specific medium, and thus the medium would inevitably be more important than the finished product. If the crafter became proficient enough for her products to compete in the marketplace, then she could, if she chose, cease to be a hobbyist and become a professional, and in doing so shift her concern back from process to product, but such moves were extremely rare.

The writers of Victorian craft plans took the progression from novice to expert more or less for granted and, unlike later craft authors, seldom divided their projects between easy beginners' plans and more difficult advanced projects—with the exception, of course, that children's crafts were always relatively simple. Hobbyists were given instructions about the basic tools necessary for the work and some directions about how to prepare the raw materials. Then, without missing a beat, the authors would introduce complex and difficult projects from the very beginning. This refusal to acknowledge a learning curve seems to reflect either a very high level of general craft skills among the readership of craft books and articles, or an extremely poor grasp by the authors of the process of skill development. Given the universal training that women received in the needle arts and the widespread instruction in the pictorial arts available to middle-class girls and women, it is probably reasonable to assume the former. Certainly many of the surviving examples of Victorian female craft show an extraordinarily high level of skill.[60] Those who had trouble mastering the intricacies of published designs received no sympathy from those who printed them. When a less-skilled woman complained that *Godey's* did not include sufficient detail in its craft instructions, the editor dismissed her by saying that the designs were sufficient for the "good workwoman" and that "bad ones would be no better off, no matter how long and particular the description."[61]

All women's crafts in the nineteenth century (and most in the twentieth) were characterized by their strong aesthetic component. The most common forms of purely artistic fancywork were pictures made out of something other than paint, such as feathers, seeds, beans, pinecone scales, porcupine quills, colored sand and pebbles, beads, seaweed, straw, seashells, moss, leather, paper (both cut and rolled), or of course, thread and yarn.[62] At the very end of the Victorian era, Emma Churchman Hewitt, a prolific advice-giver and author of *Queen of the Home*, defended fancywork because it could bring "an element of beauty" into otherwise ugly and barren lives and thus become the salvation of the aesthetically untutored. The recurrent adjectives used to describe craft projects emphasized refinement rather than control or authority. Craftswomen were the source of redeeming beauty, not the instruments of active change. For example, an 1876 advice book, *Ladies' Fancy Work*, referred to its own projects as charming, beautiful, tasteful, lovely, ornamental, exquisite, artistic, pretty, delicate, rich, rare, perfect, fine, and above all, elegant, but not skillful or useful. And only rarely did it comment on the possible cost savings of crafting.[63]

The flowery hyperbole that contemporaries used to describe the beauty of Victorian crafts was matched only by the scorn heaped on them by subsequent generations. Victorians were not unaware of their own design excesses, and craft supporters fought a losing battle against the ugly clutter of homemade decorations. Brought into the parlor of a genteel but modest family, a character in an 1870 story observed to herself, "Fancy work, too, leather and cone frames, embroidered ottomans—that is boxes covered with worsted [Berlin] work— and silk patch-work sofa pillow! It is not contemptible to be poor; it is to be tawdry." The opinion expressed by the visitor was shared by a significant number of Victorians, put off by women who had more time than either taste or talent. In 1888 a young woman asked an advice columnist if it was okay not to make "the little nothings, 'veritable trash' that one sees crowding many rooms [that] are to me simply time and material wasted." The answer was a masterpiece of equivocation. The editor, of course, agreed that there was no point in making "merely ornamental articles . . . that take a vast amount of time and can be bought for very little in the shops." However, she continued, things that were truly useful or beautiful were well worth making.[64]

Critics like Margaret Harvey recognized that much craft work was trifling, a foolish expense, an exercise in bad taste, and a waste of time that could be better spent learning real skills or saving souls. Yet she acknowledged that "the world ought to be thankful that [the crafter] has something to keep her out of mischief for awhile," and who could deny the hardworking housewife her "little bit of relaxation in the late afternoon or early evening?" It was true she said that not everything started was finished and not everything finished was beautiful; nevertheless, the process itself was beneficial because it developed aesthetic appreciation even if it failed to develop talent. In the final analysis then, fancywork could be defended even if it were neither very useful nor very attractive, since it was a harmless form of leisure that cultivated a woman's aesthetic sensibilities.[65]

The problem of what to do with the vast output of the Victorian crafts craze was solved in part by its synergistic relationship with Victorian clothing design and interior decoration. Despite regular cautions from decorators and fashion experts who warned women against the dangers of vulgar excess, most housewives seem to have equated beauty with the accumulation of highly decorated objects, on themselves and in their houses. In the home, figured carpets and wallpaper, highly carved and curved furniture, elaborate lighting fixtures, and similar machine-made items created a backdrop for the handmade crafts that were set on their surfaces and hung from their walls. Although they were made by hobbyists for their own use, the craft objects were not, strictly speaking, private. Many of them, such as reticules and embroidered clothing, were displayed on the maker in public. Others, such as pillows and containers, were displayed in the semipublic arena of the parlor or dining room. The women were proud of their handiwork and sought an appreciative audience, which led to the logical assumption that other people might also want to own the craft items they made.

The crafter might assume that the friends and family who were so lavish with their praise of her work might like to be the recipients of handmade gifts. "Not the most costly present bought with money would be so highly prized as the delicate trifle made by the fair hand that presents it," assured *Godey's* in 1847. Husbands and beaus in particular found themselves wearing slippers, smoking jackets, and caps; carrying cigar cases and shaving kits; putting their watches in watch cases and their feet on ottomans, all made by or enriched with the handiwork of their wives and sweethearts. Beth, of *Little Women*, embroidered such a pair of gift slippers for her next-door neighbor, who was so touched by the gesture that he gave her a piano.[66] One W.M.F., properly thankful for his gift of a watch case, and properly appreciative of the crafter's artistic skills, rhapsodized:

Time to me comes cased in beauty!
Perfect beauty—perfect art.
Ah, how more than simple duty
Is an offering of the heart![67]

Not everybody was so delighted with homemade gifts. A young bride sur-
veying her wedding presents in an 1882 short story turned to her husband in
despair: "But oh, Jack, I have tried them all: the tidies, and anti-macassars,
and sofa-pillows and foot-rests, and ottomans, and match-holders, and
scratch-my-backs, and all! and they do look too, too hideous." This was a dangerous admission indeed to be published in *Godey's*, where one had only to
turn the page to find directions for making more such objects, but the story
smoothed over the ugly truth by having the young couple put the items in a
single room where they could be appreciated for what they were, well-inten-
tioned gifts that lacked real artistic value. And old Aunt Hetty, at least, could
not understand why they had put all their prettiest things in one room.[68]

Selling Crafts: Fancywork and Fancy Fairs

Gifts of questionable quality might be relegated to a room by themselves,
but properly beautiful items were still required to fill the rest of the house.
"To-day the fad of the fashionable world is decorative fancy work," observed
N. H. Snyder in 1895; "it crops up everywhere, overruns cottage and mansion, and whatever fashion demands must be had." Housewives who could
not meet fashion's demands on their own could purchase some fancywork at
shops stocked with items made by poorer women. Snyder urged wealthy
women not to do their own embroidery because it took work out of "the
hands of the women who are forced to earn their daily bread by doing
needlework." Decorator Clarence Cook recommended that women, who
spent too much time embroidering slippers and smoking caps, turn their
skills instead to making curtains and furniture coverings for sale, using the
nascent English arts and crafts movement as a model.[69]

The references to semiprofessional women crafters that occurred with
some regularity after 1880 were prompted by a Centennial Exhibition display
of needlework from the British Kensington School, which provided an outlet
for the craft work of "decayed gentlewomen." The exhibit inspired American
artisan Candace Wheeler to establish the Society of Decorative Art to sell
the handiwork of women whose crafts met its strict standards. The response
was so great—and the quality of the work submitted so poor—that Wheeler
initiated a series of Women's Exchanges to sell unjuried fancywork. A hun-

dred such organizations were started after 1879. Wheeler herself would go on to work with Louis Comfort Tiffany and then start her own commercial art-embroidery firm. Most women, however, had neither her artistic skill nor her organizational ability, and if they wanted to test the quality of their work in the marketplace, they could either avail themselves of the exchanges, where they might make some money, or they could build their social prestige by donating their work to charity bazaars.[70]

Often called fancy fairs, for the fancywork was their main stock in trade, these ad hoc markets raised funds for worthy causes. Although by the 1880s some fairs had expanded to include "wheels of fortune, grab-bags, and sugar-coated lotteries," most avoided the appearance of gambling and, like their modern-day descendants, were flea markets that featured both handicrafts and donated goods. Traditional needlework for the poor, done either in sewing circles or alone, consisted of plain and useful pieces that could be donated directly to the needy; a fair or bazaar, however, created an intermediate step that permitted fancywork as well as plain sewing to be put to good use. Thus the charge that time spent at embroidery was time stolen from God's work could be turned on itself; in a charity bazaar the time spent on fancywork was time spent on God's work.[71]

Female abolitionists raised funds at Christmas fancy fairs beginning in 1834, and they were borrowing from an earlier tradition. As early as 1828, Frances Trollope described preparations for a fair in Philadelphia in which the wife of a professional man takes her carriage to the "Dorcas Society" (the biblical Dorcas made clothes for the poor) where she adds her contribution of "three ready-made pincushions, four ink-wipers, seven paper matches, and a paste-board watch-case" to the already well-stocked shelves. The seven women proceed to spend the afternoon sewing and talking of "priests, missions; of the profits of the last sale, of their hopes for the next, . . . of the very ugly bonnet seen at church on Sabbath morning, [and] of the very handsome preacher who performed on Sabbath afternoon."[72]

The items mentioned by Trollope were typical for fancy fairs in the nineteenth century. In 1855 *Godey's* reported that one of the most frequent questions it received was "how best to contribute to the numerous fairs that are constantly occurring in every part of the country for charitable purposes." The magazine said it did not have room to list all the things that could be made but reminded readers that "whilst people purchase articles at bazaars, in order to aid the charity, they like that their money should be spent for something not wholly useless either to themselves or others." In that spirit, it suggested glass boxes for thread and toilet articles, pen-wipers, and pincushions. The Sanitary Commission fairs during the Civil War, which sparked interest in American antiques, were a major outlet for women's crafts. Crafting for bazaars was so common that charitable intent was sometimes assumed. "Ah, my dear, I see you are making something for the Heathen Missionary Society Fair," an old lady comments to a young crafter in an 1872 story. "Yes, but this article is for a 'Home Mission,' for the benefit of an aged lady, one whom I know to be very worthy," replied the young woman, who was working on an afghan for her mother.[73]

Like cider pressing, corn husking, hog butchering, barn raising, and quilting, fancy fairs were an excuse for men and women to socialize under the cover of necessity. In this sense the bazaar was a mixed-gender extension of the sewing circles that created their inventory. Unlike their more rustic counterparts, fancy fairs could evolve into complexly nuanced social events that had more in common with high society parties than with hog butchering (except if one were given to sanguinary social analogies). "Mrs. Chester's fair was so very elegant and select that it was considered a great honor by the young ladies of the neighborhood to be invited to take a table," wrote Louisa May Alcott in 1868. Amy, the artist sister in *Little Women*, agreed to tend a table, not because of the social status but in order to help the freed slaves. Amy was, of course, slighted by the nasty May Chester but gained her revenge when her drawings, not May's painted vases, were all sold, and the local gallants showed their appreciation by buying the flowers at her table.[74]

The poet who wrote

Come, maids and youths, for here we sell
All wondrous things of earth and air;
Whatever wild romancers tell,
Or poets sing, or lovers swear,
You'll find at this our Fancy Fair,[75]

understood that fancy fairs were a marketplace for dreams as well as for fancywork, and romance was clearly the most important transaction for many fairgoers. A bachelor in an 1842 story suggested to his friend they spend an evening at a fancy fair. "You know that fancy-fairs are my aversion," the friend replied, "I don't know anything more disgusting than to see a room full of Misses, taking advantage of some either really or nominally worthy purpose, to exhibit themselves to the public, and to gratify a petty and an indelicate vanity, by flirting over their pincushions and doll-babies with any fellow who can afford an admittance shilling for the honor." The friend is at last persuaded to attend and naturally finds nothing but dignified and graceful women selling elegant and tasteful items that he is only too glad to buy, while being swept off his feet and into the multitalented hands of Miss Martha Grainger. In the 1880s Jenny June, *Godey's* social commentator, described how a woman who had been excluded from the local ladies' inner circle bought her way to favor by taking over full responsibility for supplying and staffing a stall at a major charity fair. Not only did she round up crafts to be sold but also recruited fashionable young women (including her major obstacle's daughter) to staff it and had special fair dresses made for the sales crew. The process, explained June, was exactly the same as buying large blocks of tickets to other charity events as an entrée into society.[76]

In theory, charity bazaars were marketplaces where value was established by supply and demand. In practice, the social subtext dramatically distorted the process. It is not clear, for example, whether the person who paid $150 in the 1880s for a quilt featuring a central figure of Oscar Wilde holding a lily and a sunflower was motivated by aesthetic appreciation (for the quilt or the man) or by a desire to impress fair organizers.[77] Certainly the "many rich Jews [who] paid large sums for articles, without regard to their actual value" in 1887 had nonmarket motivations.[78] If the buyers were friends, family, or swains, as they frequently were, the prices would likewise be distorted. When Mollie failed to notice Eustis, who offered a premium for several of the items on her table, he bought everything in sight to get her attention and declare his love.[79]

Unlike collectors' bourses, which were real marketplaces, charity bazaars were pseudomarkets whose prices were distorted by their charitable intent and sometimes by the personal relationship between the buyers and sellers. The mixed meaning of fancy fairs made people unsure how to conduct themselves on the sales floor. An 1869 etiquette book cautioned buyers against "cheapening the articles offered for sale" and warned sellers that it was unacceptable to "force articles on reluctant purchasers by appealing to their gallantry" or to refuse to give change just because the proceeds went to charity. Arriving at a just price thus became an exercise in compromise between the bourse and the parlor. Mrs. Daffodil, the ingenuous rustic grandmother in an 1866 magazine piece, was amazed at the outrageous prices assigned to the items at a fancy fair, and when a customer balked at the cost of a pen-wiper, the old lady told him, "Too high! why, it's for a charity; but 'tween you an' I, a dollar and a half is high for that little footey thing. Take it along for ten cents." A fictional Dr. Robbins took over sales duties from his wife at her booth and had a jolly time tweaking marketplace values and practices. When wealthy Mrs. Revere told him that the price of a beautiful afghan was too high, Dr. Bob promptly lowered the price tag from the top of the blanket half-way down. He teasingly increased the price on another item so that he could then knock it down to its original list price, and when challenged on his business practices, replied, "I am sorry to say the girls will do it, but for myself, I never cheat, I only financier."[80]

The literature's lighthearted treatment of the market aspects of the fairs, along with the recognition that their wares were often of inferior quality, located women's craft hobbies outside the serious world of real artisans and real finance, which is to say outside the world of men. It was important that women not lose sight of the distinction. The author of an 1856 story in *Graham's Magazine* made that clear when she wrote of Mary Oswald, who had a weakness for fancywork: "Not a new pattern of chair or slipper, not an ottoman or couvrette, appeared in the drawing-rooms of her numerous acquaintance, but she must begin one like it." When her friends organized a bazaar, Mrs. Oswald decided to finish all her half-done projects for the fair. Despite her husband's stern warnings about his precarious financial position, she bought materials on credit and pressed both friends and servants into helping her complete the items, which she then displayed at her stall with very high prices. She returned home to be confronted by her husband who informed her that his business, their house, and all its effects had been lost. "The beauty of the articles on your stall has been generally noticed, and their cost criticized," he told her; "this has certainly hastened the crisis." They recovered financially, but subsequently Mrs. Oswald adhered strictly to plain sewing.[81]

Gender and Tools

There was a reciprocal relationship between fancywork and the tools used to make it. Needles, their ancillary paraphernalia, and to a lesser extent, artist's tools were the craft instruments used by Victorian women and came to be identified with them. Professional tailors and upholsterers obviously used needles, and professional male artists used brushes; amateurs, however, adhered to a fairly strict gender division between heavy and light tools. Amateur women avoided heavier artisan's tools, and amateur men, such as there were, avoided the tools identified with women's work. The tools were, of course, intimately related to the materials, which were similarly gendered. Soft and light textiles in all their varieties were female, while hard, heavy wood and metal were predominantly male. Smaller house painting brushes occupied a degendered middle ground since household painting was one area in which men and women alike felt comfortable.

This gender distinction was universally accepted, and despite occasional efforts on the part of well-meaning reformers to break down such barriers, men understood that working with needles was feminizing, and women avoided heavier tools as inappropriately masculine. Thus an extremely self-sufficient spinster in an 1893 short story who dismissed men as "all thumbs and tongue" explained how she would use women's tools to do men's jobs: "While a man is calling to mind how his grandfather did things and is hunt-ing around for the proper tool, a woman'll take hold and put the thing through—like enough with a hairpin." The heavy tool rule was so funda-mental that those who suggested violating it offered more caution than encouragement. For example, in 1879 technical author Ellis Davidson turned his attention to women's crafts. He began by assuring readers that since "the sculptor's chisel and mallet have been wielded by the hands of Ladies," they could also use heavy tools for the projects in his book. Almost immediately, however, he warned his female audience that carving tools "will be found much too heavy to be satisfactorily wielded by the hands of ladies." The book continued this push and pull between telling women they could and could not use traditionally male tools. First he described where to find "neat little rosewood [tool] handles," but then wrote that wood on pro-jects should be "smoothened and its edges rounded by the cabinet maker." He suggested "there is no reason why ladies should not learn to use a small hand, or a tenon saw," but did not "wish to imply that we expect ladies to 'plane up timber,' " but then again, he did think they could learn to use a "miniature smoothing-plane to work the edges and corners of pieces they are making."[82]

Even though Davidson was an Englishman who usually wrote for men, he was not being overfastidious in his fears of the masculinizing effect of heavy tools. If anything, Americans were even more reluctant to recommend breaching the tool barrier. In her 1879 advice book, Julia McNair Wright somewhat vaguely described a chair made of a barrel "sawed into shape" and an "hour-glass stand" made of two wooden circles nailed to either end of a dowel. Were the women expected to do the sawing and nailing involved in these projects? Wright did not specify, but a raft of other home decorating suggestions from the same era left no doubt that professional craftsmen, not women, would wield the saws and hammers in even the simplest of jobs. Describing homemade furniture in her 1889 *Home Manual*, Mrs. John Logan assumed that the frames would be constructed by a cabinetmaker, and the woman would "paint white and varnish, then cover the seat with embroidered or plain plush, brocade, or any material that suits the fancy." Explaining why picture moldings were a good idea, Clarence Cook described the difficulties of having to call in a carpenter to hammer in the nail needed to hang a picture. To be fair, Cook was referring to the tricky task of finding a stud behind an easily cracked plaster wall. Nevertheless, the image of a housewife paying a professional carpenter to hammer in a single nail speaks volumes about the use of heavy tools by both women and their husbands in Victorian America. A husband took his wife to task for buying expensive new window boxes in an 1885 how-to article. She replied that she did not buy them but "had the carpenter make the boxes," which she then covered with Lincrusta (a stiff embossed fabric) and painted.[83]

The general rule that discouraged women from using any tool heavier than a paintbrush was, like any cultural norm, neither absolute nor immutable. Brass repousse, which involved hammering on metal, was added to the standard repertoire of female craft work in the latter part of the century, and isolated reformers regularly, if unsuccessfully, called for greater female competence with hand tools. For example, both Beecher sisters regularly urged women to become more useful around the house. Harriet observed: "We think it would be an advantage for women to learn to use the more ordinary tools of a carpenter—the plane, the gimlet, the screw, and the screw-driver," because as Catharine added, they never knew when they might move west, where there were no mechanics for hire. In a highly unusual expression of confidence in women's ability to use heavy tools, *Godey's* suggested that women could also use a miter box, saw, hammer, and nails to make wood picture frames. And Janet Ruutz-Rees thought women could master rasps, files, mallets, gouges, and chisels to carve fancywork decorations in their picture frames.[84]

Homemade furniture presented women with an opportunity to break the heavy tool rule, but few seemed interested. In her history of the Victorian parlor, Katherine Grier concludes that box and barrel furniture was common among poorer families who sought a middle-class appearance on less than a middle-class income. They were not made in factories, but it is not clear from Grier's account whether wives, husbands, or local carpenters were making these pieces. When "Mertie" gave directions for making a barrel chair in 1870, she said that even though most women thought such a project could only be made by a man, her plans could in fact "be done by any lady who can manage a hammer and nails, and the little rough work that is needed is within the power of any school-boy or man-servant." While the tone of the article was generally one of empowerment, it did assume that structural work would be done by the "fair amateur carpenter or the village professional," either of whom would obviously have been a man.[85]

While they avoided anything heavier than a paintbrush, Victorian women were willing to use brushes in practical as well as artistic projects. *Arthur's Home Magazine* assured its readers that there was "no reason why women should not be able to be independent of the house painter" for little jobs like painting furniture, doors, or window frames. The magazine went on to provide quite detailed instructions for "graining," the popular but complex procedure in which combs and stiff brushes were used to scratch a false grain into layers of wet paint. While not common, painting large surfaces and even entire rooms was not entirely outside the purview of Victorian women. If they could not afford real carpet, women were urged to make a floor covering out of layers of painted, decorated, and then varnished brown paper. And one writer described a man and his wife working together refinishing a wood floor.[86] Nevertheless, experts usually limited their advice to choosing colors and assumed the householder's job was to put up with the chaos that ensued "when the painter with his pots, the paper-hanger with his paste, and the carpenter with his tools, revel unrebuked amid the scattered household gods."[87]

Craft Work for Men and Boys

Nineteenth-century women had their needles and paint brushes and a culture of creativity that justified their use. No equivalent existed for men, but none was needed since middle-class men generally avoided craft activities. Men were not discouraged so much as they were not encouraged to be handy. Nevertheless, the tradition of male tool use was an ever-present assumption in the discussions of craft activities.

The gender division in tools showed up clearly in the pastimes recommended for boys. A few women suggested that, along with their sisters, boys should be taught needle skills, but even advocates recognized that any boy who did ran the risk of "being made a girl of." If their sons were understandably reluctant to take up needlework, mothers were told to encourage the more masculine alternative of woodwork. "A Lady" writing in *Arthur's* thought it was worth the mess and noise that boys made "with knife, hammer and saw" so long as they remained "contentedly within doors." "A boy who is not learning to use his hands is learning highway robbery," warned a high school principal in 1885. Catharine Beecher concurred, telling fathers that when they provided tools and instruction for their sons to make "wheelbarrows, carts, sleds, and various other articles," they were contributing "both to the physical, moral, and social, improvement of their children." In addition to keeping their hands from Satan's work, there was a real sense that the tool-using youth was acquiring practical skills. Facility with tools could always "be made a means of support in case of adversity," explained the same principal, which is what several of Jo March's students in *Little*

Men did when they used their skills at carpentry and mechanics to raise pocket money.[88]

In 1859 *Godey's* recommended that boys be given tools just as soon as they could be trusted not to destroy the house or themselves, and if possible, be given a workshop as well. The workshop would ideally be supplied with "a work-bench, and vice, and perhaps a small foot-lathe, one or two planes, augers of several sizes, one or two chisels, saw, and hammer." Not only would this shop provide "an escape from the temptation of evil associates," it would be the source of useful objects such as ladders and boxes. *Arthur's* recognized the affinity of boys and tools when it offered a nice selection of fifteen tools in a tool box as a premium for soliciting ten subscriptions to Timothy S. Arthur's children's magazine (see fig. 6.4). Clearly, boys were expected to continue the tradition of male mastery of tools in a form roughly analogous to their sisters learning sewing.[89]

The differences, however, were significant. Girls learned both the practical and the decorative, while boy's work was always practical. Moreover, since fewer fathers knew or used manual skills, and since real woodwork required a dedicated space and a variety of relatively expensive tools, boy's woodcraft was not even remotely as popular as girl's needle craft. It did, however, contain the germ that would allow it to flourish even as women's fancy-work fell into decline; it was useful in a way that was not vulnerable to usurpation by manufactured goods. Explaining why it was good for boys to learn to use tools, an 1893 book described how a boy could save his family money by taking apart a frozen lock that only needed cleaning and oiling to be put right.[90]

If boys could be genuinely useful about the house, why couldn't men? There were certainly those who tried to convince Victorian husbands that they should develop skills with tools, but they did so in a way that illustrates how far men had drifted from their traditional roles as household conservators. Writing in 1869, Harriet Beecher Stowe urged the home-owning husband to become a "handy man [who] knows how to use every sort of tool that keeps his house in order." She suggested the handyman could replace a broken window pane, solder a leaking pipe joint, attach a piece of peeling furniture veneer, tighten a loose hinge screw, and patch a leaky roof. In what may be the earliest use of the do-it-yourself phrase as specifically applied to home maintenance, the author of an 1876 article in the English magazine *Leisure Hour* advised, "If you want a thing done, do it yourself." The author described the tools needed to complete the same sorts of repairs Stowe mentioned and concluded "there is always a satisfaction in feeling that things about us, and especially things belonging to us, are right and tight, in a sound and serviceable condition." For Stowe, however, household repair and

FIGURE 6.4 Boys are shown playing with woodworking tools, which were offered as a premium for soliciting subscriptions to a children's magazine. (Reprinted from "Boys! Boys!" *Arthur's Home Magazine* 40 [1872] n.p. [advertising section].)

maintenance was not a source of pride but an entirely practical affair that would save the homeowner time, money, and the general household disruption caused by professionals taking to the shop items the homeowner could have repaired by himself.[91]

Perhaps because household maintenance was promoted as practical rather than pleasurable, men avoided it as a chore. Thus just as their wives paid servants to do their housework, middle-class men paid craftsmen to do theirs. Historian Faye Dudden, for example, describes a Brookline, Massachusetts, housewife who regularly spoke about herself and her husband as "working" about the house when in fact they were simply supervising hired help. In the 1860s when Harriet Robinson annually set aside a full month for the spring cleaning of her Malden, Massachusetts, home she had the occasional assistance of hired help, but her husband, William, followed the standard male pattern and decamped for the duration. Over the years, as the Robinsons improved their house by installing weather stripping, repapering rooms, refinishing furniture, and putting in a new mantle (among other things), according to her biographer Claudia Bushman, neither Harriet nor William ever "lifted a finger toward household maintenance."[92]

It is possible that middle-class men only a generation or two removed from the farm may have feared a loss of status if they did manual work around the house. Certainly having servants rather than wives do cooking and cleaning was an important mark of respectability, yet there is no evidence in the record that home maintenance was held in disdain by middle-class Victorian husbands. It is as though the skills necessary to do day-to-day household chores simply atrophied as men increasingly earned their livings at white-collar jobs away from their families. Tools were not needed in offices; sons no longer saw their fathers tending the homestead; and the tradition of manual competence faded away. The occasional adult male who took up tools around the house was in no danger of being thought odd or unmanly, although he was certainly unusual.

Nineteenth-century males did so little work around the home that it is hard to draw any general conclusions about their motivation and attitudes other than the simple fact that work with heavy tools was an admired but seldom practiced activity among middle-class men. The scattered references to male handicrafts that do exist paint a basically familiar picture. Victorian men, like their twentieth-century counterparts, did some light carpentry and helped decorate their homes either to save money or to gain the satisfaction of having created their own environment. Historian Joan Seidl has shown that men who cooperated in decorating their Minnesota houses usually helped decide what a hired professional would do, but a few of the more adventuresome undertook heavier jobs such as hanging the wallpaper. In 1881 a brother and sister with "slender purses" described how they and another couple spruced up an inherited house. The men did all the jobs requiring heavy tools, the women all the jobs with light tools. The men oiled the wood floor; the women papered the parlor. The men nailed up wainscoting and cut brass stencils; the women pasted up pressed plants and stenciled the walls. The men "turned blacksmiths and altered the [fireplace] grate"; the women sewed new cushions and decorated pasteboard wall "placques." The men sawed the legs of a table into new shapes; the women painted it a new color. The men made the frame for a fireplace screen, while the women sewed and decorated its cover. The men and women worked cooperatively, but with a strict sense of gender division based on the nature of the tools.[93]

Each of the jobs done by the men in the previous example (except perhaps for cutting out the brass stencil) was typical of what men might do in an interior decoration project—if they did anything at all. The Beecher sisters, for example, did assume that some men would be willing and able "to use plane and saw" to build the elaborate sliding wall screen they described in their 1869 advice book, *The American Woman's Home*; at the same time they factored the cost of a carpenter into the project, recognizing that woodworking skills were probably more the exception than the rule among middle-class men. "If your husband or brother, or someone else's brother, cannot be coaxed to help you," advised an 1888 article on making a music stand, "go to a carpenter and get him to make you a saw-buck." Almost every writer who suggested that an amateur make a project appended the professional alternative, but the contrary was almost never the case. Victorian men could do small jobs around the house, but hiring professionals was the norm.[94]

There are scattered indications that a few middle-class men retained the woodworking skills that had once been widespread and that they used these skills in hobbylike ways. In a rare example of cabinetmaking as recreational activity, a Philadelphia physician was reported to have made an elaborately carved trestle table in 1851 "as a pleasant recreation during his leisure moments." The magazine said that the workmanship "could hardly be exceeded by the most skillful artist in ornamental woodwork," and the accompanying picture confirms that it was indeed an accomplished, if aesthetically dubious, piece of work. A more well-known nineteenth-century doctor, Oliver Wendell Holmes, boasted to his friend and patient Edward Bok, "Do you know that I am a full-fledged carpenter? No? Well, I am." Holmes then advised his friend to get a hobby that was different from his work because "it is not good for a man to work all the time at one thing. We doctors call it a safety valve, and it is.[95]

Both doctors in the previous example engaged in woodworking purely as a relief from work, which is to say as a hobby, where the practical result was less important than the enjoyment of the process. Thus they were an exception to the general rule that most male household work was practical rather than recreational. Somewhat more typical was the widespread practice of people modernizing interiors on their own when they could not afford professional decorators (a term that encompassed a variety of craftsmen who worked on the interior of houses). For example, around the time of the Civil War, marble mantelpieces, which had been an obligatory symbol of middle-class status, began to fall from fashion, and both tenants and home-owners took it upon themselves to update their parlors.[96] Such was the case in 1883 when a young man, faced with an unprepossessing room, fixed it up in a way that epitomized male affinity for big tools and avoidance of small ones. He did no sewing at all; all cloth accouterments were simply draped over furniture. However, he refinished the floor and did some interior painting, but his greatest achievement was to remove the "common-place marble mantel" and replace it with a home-built pine shelf and mantle combination.[97]

Men's and women's craft hobbies in the nineteenth century were divided primarily by tools and secondarily by medium. Men almost never used textiles and needles, while women avoided wood, saws, and hammers; the gender segregation was not total. Small projects such as light painting that were not identified with a particular sex were sometimes done by both men and women. Similarly, both men and women were targeted by manufacturers of wood engraving kits. This close work, which involved carving printed designs in wood blocks, straddled the line between traditionally male woodwork and traditionally female craft fancywork. No hobby, however, was more important in breaking down the wall between men and women than the new craft of fret sawing, which combined female aesthetics with male tools and materials.[98]

Fret Sawing: A Hobby for Both Genders

After the turn of the century, as electric power was introduced into home workshops, woodworking tools got larger, heavier, and even more masculine in character. Power confirmed the dominance of men. Curiously, however, in the Gilded Age, both a conformation and a major exception occurred in the general rule that women stayed away from wood and the big tools used to shape it. The conformation was the lathe, and the exception was the fret saw.

As early as the sixteenth century, lathe work moved out of the cabinetmaker's workshop and into the gentleman's craft shop. A small number of wealthy hobbyists continued the tradition of upper-class turning in Europe through the nineteenth century. Americans do not appear to have been widespread practitioners of this aristocrat's hobby, although in the 1780s and 1790s the administration of Cokesbury College in Maryland set aside time in the evening for student recreation that included "the carpenters', joiners', cabinetmakers', and turners' business." The rarity of the hobby is confirmed by an 1856 article in *Arthur's* in which neighbors mistake a clerk's hobby lathe for an ironing mangle and a lens grinder, forcing the clerk to lead an otherwise exemplary life so as not to raise suspicions with his atypical behavior. Amateur turning may have become more common after the Civil War when readily available treadle-driven fret saws could also be used to drive small lathes. Most of the literature, however, suggests that fret saws were used mainly for sawing.[99]

The foot-powered fret saw (also called a scroll saw or jigsaw) was an American invention that used the same propulsion mechanism as the sewing machine, a flywheel driven by a treadle. The setup could also drive a lathe, a small circular saw, and, most importantly, a drill, which was used to make the holes necessary to start the dozens of interior cuts in a typical fret saw design.[100] The first treadle-driven fret saw was patented in 1865 and within ten years had become something of a fad. One contemporary source claimed more than thirty thousand foot-powered saws had been sold by 1877, and another that in the four years after 1874, fourteen thousand treadle saws were sold, about half with iron frames and half made from wood.[101] By the end of the 1870s, an iron saw with lathe and drill attachments could be had for only $8.00, and in the mid-1880s full-size iron-frame saws sold for as little as $3.50, or as much as $22.50 (see fig. 6.5). At the lower end, the cost of a treadle saw was surprisingly close to the $1.50 price of a handheld spring-steel saw frame.[102]

Unlike sewing machines—which cost about twice as much but for which there was an immediate use in the home—fret saws made nothing essential. Thus they can lay claim to being the first leisure "power" tool. Handheld jigsaws had been used by jewelers and dentists, who did particularly delicate work, and in the mid-1870s Italian artisans popularized fret-sawn openwork that was sometimes called Sorrento-work. Aside from the music rests on pianos and organs, there was no established use for open scrollwork, and thus the fret saw craze of the 1870s and 1880s was very much a problem invented to meet an existing solution; scroll saws begat scrollwork. Contemporaries gave credit to demonstrations at the Philadelphia Centennial Exhibition and other fairs in the East for popularizing the fret saw. "Nothing in the exhibition of mechanical processes in [Centennial] Machinery Hall had such a constant crowd of observers as one of these sawing-machines," reported *Harper's*. More than three thousand inlaid vases made by fret saws were sold as souvenirs.[103]

Unlike any other woodworking tool before or since, using the fret saw crossed gender lines. Illustrations from the time show women working both with handheld jigsaws and with a "velocipede scroll saw" run by a wheel with bicycle-type pedals. Advertising for some of the larger treadle saws included references to their use by both "boys and girls," and the first how-to book of fret sawing noted that "numbers of ladies practice this beautiful art, and are really most skillful at it." The full extent of each gender's involvement is unclear, but circumstantial evidence points toward substantial female participation. The materials used, the objects made, and the light weight of the most popular handsaws were all compatible with a woman's hobby. The wood was rarely thicker than a quarter inch and often as thin as the cardboard that women used in other crafts. The popular decorative wall hangings and pious mottoes were sawn-wood versions of standard embroidered fancywork (see fig. 6.6). The most popular saws were not the large iron and wood treadle-driven machines but the much smaller and cheaper handheld steel U-frame saws. In 1878 a writer estimated as many as 75,000 of these

TEN EYCK N.Y.

THE FLEETWOOD.

FIGURE 6.5 A high-end version of the treadle-driven scroll saw with an attached drill and blower. (Reprinted from Edward H. Moody, *Catalogue and Price List of Scroll Saws and Scroll Saw Material* [Hartford, Conn.: Star Job Printing, 1884], 5.)

small saws had been sold in the previous four years, along with 24 million of their easily broken blades.[104]

While large numbers of women may have crossed onto male turf by sawing wood, men still dominated, although they did not monopolize the hobby, as claimed by one scrollwork collector.[105] In both England and the United States projects were targeted at boys, and most manufacturers of large treadle machines directed their advertising toward males.[106] An 1885 pattern catalog guaranteed "that a fret sawyer working industriously two hours for fifteen evenings will have ample time to make the article complete."[107] By setting the production time in the evening, the catalog assumes male use; women did most of their crafts during the day when the light was better and their husbands and children were not at home. Men, but not women, were

FIGURE 6.6 Scroll saw pattern of the Lord's Prayer. A virtuoso project that combined technical skill and traditional feminine subject matter. (Reprinted from Raymond Francis Yates and Marguerite W. Yates, *Early American Crafts and Hobbies* [New York: Funk, 1954], 133.)

told they could use the saws to make money: "One young man we know of, who found it impossible to obtain employment at any mercantile pursuit, became possessed of a foot-power scroll-saw, and by its aid, produced brackets, card-baskets, match-boxes, frames and other articles, to give him, when sold, a clear profit of five dollars per day."[108]

Yet this hobby in both its large and small saw versions broke down established gender barriers in odd ways. It introduced significant numbers of women to a form of woodworking and at the same time was the original male craft hobby. The first American instruction book, *Fret-Sawing for Pleasure and Profit* by Henry Williams, was written for men but resembled a typical woman's fancywork manual. It was not a book about making manly practical things but about ornamentation that "elevates and teaches, and all such emotions smooth the rough places of life, rendering a tribute to the light of the home." With its stress on home, aesthetics, piety, and genteel education, the language of Williams's rationale is traditionally feminine. However, instructions for constructing machinery and references to selling products in the market make it clear that, at the very least, men were as much an audience as women, and that fret sawing broke down gender barriers in both directions. Women used men's tools on men's materials, and men did women's decorative fancywork for traditionally feminine reasons.[109]

For twenty-five years, during the last quarter of the nineteenth century, the general patterns of craft activity, other than in fret sawing, remained fairly rigid: women worked with light materials and tools; men, when they worked at all, used heavier tools on wood and metal. After the turn of the century, however, fret saw exceptionalism became the norm. That is to say, many more women engaged in crafts that used heavier tools, and many more men used tools around the house. The fundamental gender division between light and heavy work would remain, indeed remains to this day, but a discernible, if slow, trend took hold that would reach its climax in the great do-it-yourself movement after World War II.

7 Expanding the Boundaries of Crafts

Victorian handicrafts fell into disrepute around the turn of the century, but the disdain was more for the style than the process. In 1908 Agnes Repplier, a collector and leisure essayist, wrote a droll critique of her great-grandmother's fancywork hobbies. Great-grandma made "filigree baskets that would not hold anything, Ionic temples of Bristol-board, shell flowers, and paper landscapes," Repplier reported. She messed "with strange, mysterious compounds called diaphanie and potichomanie, by means of which a harmless glass tumbler or a respectable window-pane could be turned into an object of desolation." Expressing her amazement that the ability to create these "ornamental arts" could have been considered an "accomplishment," Repplier noted that a central principle of Victorian craft work had been "the reproduction of an object—of any object—in an alien material. The less adapted this material was to its purpose, the greater the difficulties it presented to the artist, the more precious became the monstrous masterpiece." Yet at the same time, the 1895 book *Fancy Work for Pleasure and Profit* was reissued, full of instructions on how to beautify houses with homemade "mantel drapes, screens, wall-pockets, toilet sets, dainty table linen, cushions, photograph holders, and all the numberless odds and ends that go to make up the pretty home comfort of a room."[1]

The criticism of the first author and the praise of the second were not as antithetical as they seem. What became unfashionable was not fancywork per se but the Victorian love of excess. Reined-in and redirected, crafts actually experienced a renaissance in the first decades of the new century. Women continued to be mainstays of hobby crafts, but the term "fancywork" with its feminine needlework origins faded away to be replaced by the designation "crafts," which alluded both to the arts and crafts movement and to the masculine "craftsman." As crafts, not fancywork, handwork was reborn as a pastime for both men and women in a stylistic environment that rejected the feminine and embraced the masculine.

The Arts and Crafts Movement and Leisure Crafts

At its least innovative, the new crafts movement did little more than modify methods, materials, or design on items that would have been instantly recognizable to any Victorian craftswoman. Pyrography, for example, was all the rage for the first dozen years of the century. This was a new craft for women insofar as it used a different technique (a burning pen) to draw pictures on different materials (wood and leather). The objects themselves, however, were the usual mix of boxes, whatnot shelves, bookends, wall plaques, match safes, picture frames, taborets, and so forth, all factory-made with the pictures already stamped on them. Some of the items reflected the new era by being simpler in design than their Victorian antecedents and featuring romantic scenes of Gibson girls and their beaus. Others, however, were less contemporary, with illustrations of landscapes, animals, and fraternal crests that were virtually indistinguishable from high Victorian styles. The wood and leather backgrounds and a burned-in picture gave pyrography a rough outdoorsy feel that seemed to fit the new arts and crafts aesthetic, but the hobby itself was neither art nor craft—simply another in the line of hobby kits that started with Berlinwork and would culminate with plastic airplane models.[2]

Much of the appeal of scorched wood and leather lay in its contrast with the fussy, overstuffed, and richly textured designs of Victorian taste and its compatibility with newer masculine styles. As one contemporary noted, these new looks promoted interiors in which everything was "simple, plain, strong, and vigorous, rich and harmonious in coloring, and absolutely uncrowded." There were, in fact, two new looks. The first, with its emphasis on straight lines, exposed joints, and natural materials, was generically referred to as "arts and crafts," but the architecture was often called "craftsman" or "bungalow," and the furniture labeled "mission." The second new look was the self-consciously preindustrial "colonial" style, also called "early-American" that accompanied the discovery of domestic antiques. Pre-Revolutionary styles such as Queen Anne and Chippendale were well beyond the skills of most home crafters to reproduce. There were, however, more chaste forms that ranged from pristine Shaker to rustic vernacular, which lent themselves to amateur construction and would, along with the mission style, provide a stylistic resource for hobby crafters. Even though mission and colonial styles evoked different historical epochs, many decorators in the 1910s were willing to combine the styles since they shared an austerity of design. The new styles marked the reemergence of the home as a location of masculine identity and activity, not merely as a retreat from the jungle of business.[3]

Masculinized styles were part of the backlash against industrially produced simulacrums of finely crafted furniture. These ostentatiously handmade objects were part of the arts and crafts movement, which originated in
England in the last quarter of the nineteenth century from the aesthetic and
political theories of John Ruskin and William Morris. In the United States,
Morris's ideas were promoted by Gustav Stickley, designer, furniture maker,
and publisher of the *Craftsman*, the de facto organ of the American wing of
the movement. Both the English and American branches promoted artisanal
manufacturing as an alternative to industrialism. The problem, wrote Caroline Hunt in 1903, was that the village cabinetmaker had deserted his shop
and "moved up to town and become an employee in a great manufacturing
establishment, and the housewife, having ceased entirely from producing,
has learned to content herself with buying and using." The solution, she
said, was spreading the new arts and crafts aesthetic so that the housewife
consumer would demand, and professional artisans would make, authentic
handmade items.[4]

Hand manufacturing was never going to replace factory production, and
in that sense the arts and crafts movement was a quixotic crusade. However,
because craftsman-style objects revealed their structure and acknowledged
minor variations and imperfections, they were inviting to amateurs. Not
everybody was happy with the trend; contemporary critics decried the forgiv-
ing nature of the style. "We have long made a virtue of the 'little irregulari-
ties,' the 'artistic accidents' of hand work," complained one in 1909. "Such
things may very readily become an affectation, a convenient excuse for
unskilled technique, at the hands of a worker of immature practice and experience." Social reformer Mary Simkhovitch thought the crudities of the style
meant it had only two possible uses. The first would be to train "the deaf, the
deformed, and all those who are shut out by physical defects from the common occupations of industry." The second was to amuse amateurs who were
also, to use Simkhovitch's unsympathetic, but probably accurate words,
"industrially defective." Like the handicapped, amateurs did not compete in
the labor market, and again like the handicapped the experience of handwork could be instructive without having to justify itself economically. For
these reasons, crafting as a hobby was able to grow while the revival of a professional artisan class remained a utopian vision.[5]

Although Stickley's primary interest was in manufacturing and social
reform, he recognized the amateur interest in the arts and crafts movement
and suggested that a "workroom" could replace the library or den in the average suburban home. The *Craftsman* praised homemade objects because
they brought the needs and skills of the crafter together in a product that was
"fitting, suitable, comfortable, restful, convenient, made of good materials

with proper tools and a certain amount of technical skill," and thus "not only an admirable sample of workmanship, but a real bit of art." Those who achieved the skill level described by Stickley might try to sell their output, and as early as 1907 there are references to "The Pleasure and the Profit of Making Beautiful Things." Most amateur crafters, however, did not seek financial justification for their hobby but understood it as a healthful and productive relief from regular work. "Hundreds of business and professional people are learning that while the day's toil fags brain and nerves, the evening passed in using the hands as pleasing labor soothes the wearied body and calms the distracted mind," explained an article in *World's Work*. Then it evoked the charming domestic picture of "the tired lawyer or the exasperated editor" recuperating from work by making book bindings or carving ivory "while his wife reads aloud to him."[6]

The image of a wife reading to her husband who is engaged in manual leisure is an extraordinary one for the history of hobbies. Until the arts and crafts movement, only women had used their hands during free time. Now, in the first years of the twentieth century, men were being encouraged to join their wives at the worktable as a way of undoing the ills of industrialized labor. Any worker who was half a man, said one author in 1907, would chafe at a system that "kept him making day after day the same parts of the same objects." What such a man needed was an opportunity to make something unique from start to finish. Then he could hold it up and say, "That's my work, every inch of it, from original design to finishing touches. It represents my taste, my individuality, my patience, my skill, my industry. I had a jolly time making it and I'm proud of it!" There is no assumption in this imagined boast that the craft object is a piece of fine craftsmanship that would find a buyer in one of the sales rooms run by local arts and crafts societies. Its value was psychological not economic, a fact more explicitly recognized by Madge Jenison, another advocate of amateur crafts, who noted that " 'the clear joy of creation' is about as near to heaven as we get in this world and a man experiences it when he makes a shaky table." By acknowledging that the amateur's table is likely to be shaky, Jenison was one of the very first people to stress that the value of the arts and crafts movement was not in the artful product but in the crafting process.[7]

The masculine presence in the arts and crafts movement was new, but women still dominated home crafting, continuing to use it as a buffer against idleness. There are women, cautioned a crafts writer in 1910, whose lives are so empty that "when the daily household duties have been attended to they are entirely without resource." These occupationless women were reduced to frequenting "the waiting rooms of railway stations and large stores merely to kill time and to watch those around them." Like their male counterparts who hung around pool halls and barrooms, there was a simple solution; "if a love for making useful things could be brought to such people their entire outlook would be changed, and life would become more full of meaning."[8]

Indications from the early part of the period are that women continued to do rather traditional forms of household crafts, most of which involved needlework. The products of this work were used for personal and household decoration or, in an economic pinch, sold to raise pin money. For example, a 1904 compilation of "100 New Money Making Plans for Untrained Women" cited about a dozen instances of women making and selling classic Victorian craft pieces including lamp shades, shell decorations, feather muffs, and hair ornaments. By 1910, however, fewer than half the crafts suggested in a book for women were textile-based, and most, such as pottery, repousse, and block printing, had a definite arts and crafts flavor. The new female hobbyist, like the metal worker pictured on the August 1915 cover of the *Modern Priscilla*, was more willing to use heavier tools on nontraditional materials (see fig. 7.1).[9]

Crafts in the Marketplace

As women branched out into a greater variety of crafts, they sought to take advantage of sophisticated consumers who they hoped would "be willing to pay a fair price for good handwork."[10] Rather than working for charity, they could work for themselves. The most famous of the professional artisans, people like William Stickley who made furniture or Maria Nichols Storer who made art pottery, were indeed able to ride the new aesthetic to fame, if not fortune. There were also appreciable numbers of people, especially women, who never received public recognition but capitalized on the demand for handcrafted items by operating small businesses in homemade crafts. Some were poor women looking for a way to earn a living by working at home, while others were middle-class women who were anxious to experiment with new artistic and business opportunities. In either case, selling arts and crafts had strong backing from Progressive Era clubwomen who supported a variety of such ventures as an appropriate artistic response to women's roles in the new century.[11]

The tradition of selling poor women's crafts, started by the New York Exchange for Woman's Work in 1879, continued into the early twentieth century. In 1904, for example, the New York Exchange occupied two stores and did a business of eighty thousand dollars per year. Women who sent their crafts to the New York store and scores of similar exchanges throughout the

FIGURE 7.1 Idealized woman crafter of the arts and crafts era doing light metal work. (Reprinted from "The Craft Worker," *The Modern Priscilla* 29 [August 1915]: cover.)

country were not part of the new arts and crafts movement. They were traditional women with traditional women's skills who submitted mostly needlework. But even poor women could not compete with factories, and in 1910 a social worker who opened a "Home Industries Association" on the lower east side of Manhattan as an outlet for immigrant handicrafts said she hoped that American women would "rouse themselves to the patronage of hand-made work instead of the cheap machine-made stuff that is sold in the cheaper stores."[12]

Middle-class crafters tried very hard to avoid the stigma of poverty attached to the exchanges. "Who is eligible to do craft work?" asked a 1916 article on "how to organize and conduct a home industry" in the *Ladies' Home Journal*: "Any needy woman who has failed to support herself by common Labor? . . . A woman left suddenly a widow with children, who must earn money at once to feed them? . . . Any woman who has a little knack or skill with her hands and wants some new thing to amuse her?" No, no, and no! These kinds of women, said the magazine, would lack either the talent or the time to develop the level of skill necessary to become a serious artisan. To the extent that they did become artisans, the arts and crafts movement breached the wall between amateur and professional and created a small but influential class of crafters who sold their wares in stores and thus brought the economic legitimacy of the marketplace to the previously genteel hobby of fancywork.[13]

By dissolving the rigid divide between amateur ladies and professional craftsmen, the arts and crafts movement opened the door wider for professional female crafters on the one side and for amateur male hobbyists on the other. In 1897, for example, two women in Deerfield, Massachusetts, organized a club for practitioners of colonial embroidery. Within a few years women and men who were interested in other forms of colonial craftsmanship had joined the group, which called itself the Deerfield Arts and Crafts Society. By 1905 the society was sponsoring an annual crafts fair that drew buyers from all over New England. In addition to traditional needlework, the fair featured weaving, handmade rugs, artistic ironwork, baskets, and hand-carved furniture. None of the crafters was a full-time artisan; rather, they were local townspeople who pursued their crafts as hobbies but enjoyed the confirmation, and presumably the money, brought by selling their products to the public. The Deerfield crafters thus crossed the traditional lines in both directions; women sold their goods and men did hobby crafts.[14]

Although the number of professional crafters was small, and most of their careers short-lived, their leisurelike work legitimated the worklike leisure of hobbyists. In 1902 a contemporary noted the rise of a new group of "master-hands," each of whom "is his own designer, skilled worker and dealer—in brief, his own employer. There are women also who are designers and workers and are their own saleswomen." In the New York City area, women ran workshops where they made vases, carved chests, hammered copper, and worked leather. There were probably several hundred such self-employed crafters of both sexes earning their livelihoods by making "furniture, iron-work, copper and brass, lace, rugs, carpets, violins, tiles, pottery, fine chinaware, leather work, chests, jewelry, silverware, buckles, clasps and other enameled ornaments, baskets, woodenware, terra-cotta vases and architectural ornaments."[15]

The emergence of a small but articulate group of professional crafters marked a sea change in the way the public perceived handicrafts. What had been a spare time activity for idle ladies, and the occasional gentleman, became a widely admired profession with its own styles, firms, spokesmen, and publications. Handicrafters, whether operating independently or as part of cooperatives or companies, could never satisfy the public's demand for cheap products. Nor did many of them realistically hope to do so. They did create a new appreciation for handwork and shifted the dominant aesthetic from complex machine-produced forms to simpler designs that could be made by a crafter, even if most of them were mass-produced in Grand Rapids and mass marketed in the Sears and Roebuck catalog.

Social Benefits

Since it kept participants busy, and because idleness was always assumed to be a prerequisite for trouble, crafting, like so many other hobbies, seemed to be both a restorative and a preventative. As a restorative, supporters said it had the power to reestablish mental harmony to those who lost their emotional way. "The results of experiments made as to the effect of handicrafts on the feeble-minded or for nervous cases have been most encouraging," wrote a hobbyist in 1910, and her position was confirmed by professional mental health workers. The director of a New York mental hospital described the benefits of "Diversional Occupation" in 1916, explaining that it not only took patients' minds off their troubles but gave many of them a sense of accomplishment and even the skills necessary to reenter the world of work. Crafts took their place alongside collecting as a prophylactic for the ills of leisure. "The first two steps towards delinquency and crime are generally truancy and idleness," cautioned a writer in the *Craftsman* in 1905. He invoked the standard warning of Satan's intentions for idle hands and then described in some detail how boys "of our better classes" who had no household chores could be kept busy with handicrafts.[16]

If crafts were a cure for mental illness and an antidote for delinquency, then they warranted being taught in school to everyone, not only to those who planned to use them professionally. There were some scattered precedents for teaching crafts to boys. Around 1800 John I. Hawkins, an English immigrant engineer, opened what appears to have been America's first non-vocational craft school in Bristol, Pennsylvania. Hawkins offered "to instruct any students a few hours each day in the practical use of tools employed in various kinds of manufacture," because he believed in the "practicability of uniting study with as much useful manual labor as would keep the body in health." Twenty-five years later in New York City, John Griscom started a high school that taught "the easier parts of carpentry, joinery, casting, turning, etc." along with traditional academic subjects.[17] And in the early 1870s, boys in Boston could attend the Boston Whittling School, an informal after-school workshop where they used jigsaws, lathes, and "a few simple tools" to make "brackets, matchboxes, small chests, checker boards, and such trifling things."[18] All these institutions were isolated pioneers in what would become the manual training movement, a pedagogical reform that sought to integrate crafts skills into the standard school curriculum.

Manual training was introduced to Americans by a Russian demonstration at the Philadelphia Centennial Exhibition in 1876. The Russian system used a series of progressive exercises to teach students a set of standard manual skills that could then be applied to a variety of trades. Thus at its inception, manual training was an academic substitute for apprenticeship with a specific vocational intention. About a decade later, in 1888, John Ordway, one of the pioneers of the Russian system learned of the Swedish sloyd system and significantly modified his approach to manual training. Although fundamentally similar to the Russian model, the sloyd system emphasized the broad developmental benefits of learning manual skills and was thus complimentary to progressive educational theories of reformers like Maria Montessori and John Dewey. Together, these two schools of manual training made widespread inroads into American education. Initially, most of the programs they inspired were vocational in nature, but the broad educational goals of the sloyd system and an increasing interest in teaching children arts and crafts skills created a school context in which manual training could spread to the whole curriculum.[19]

As vocational training, craft classes were self-justifying. Manual training teachers, however, wanted to integrate their discipline into the general curriculum, and to do so they developed several rationales for hobbies as a socially beneficial form of leisure. On a purely practical level educators rejected the arts and crafts movement's vision of a neo-Gothic world of artisans, but they did believe that having students reproduce the phylogeny of craftsmanship would help them understand "emotionally as well as intellectually the relation of man to production." The sloyd system, noted one educator, "puts blood and bone and energy and ambition into the most flaccid-looking boy."[20] They argued that the muscular coordination and digital dexterity learned in manual training would aid in general mental development.[21] "It is the law of all human development," explained a California educator, that lessons transferred "from the outward to the inward, from the physical to the spiritual."[22]

Finally, many supporters of manual education saw it as a vehicle for teaching aesthetics. "Drawing and manual training are rapidly finding their way into all public schools," observed the president of a midwestern art association in 1903; "if it could be made plain that they belong together we would then teach arts and crafts." Thus arts as well as crafts could help move manual training from a form of education exclusively for troublesome, academically inferior students to an integral part of the education of all children, including those from the middle class.[23] "The purpose of this form of training is not to make carpenters, mechanics, etc., of the pupils," explained one shop teacher, "but to give the child an all-around development."[24] Using these arguments, supporters were able to increase the number of manual training programs in U.S. schools in the first decade of the century from about four hundred to the point where, according to a contemporary source, "some form of handwork is to be found nearly everywhere, even in small towns and little country schools."[25]

It was an easy step from the schoolroom to the home hobby. Ira Griffith, a shop teacher and frequent contributor to *Suburban Life* magazine, promoted the "plain, square Mission type of furniture" as both suitable for woodworking beginners and as compatible with the aesthetic dictum that form should follow function. "The rapid introduction of manual training into the schools of the country is having its effect upon the home," he wrote in 1910, "more boys and men than ever are engaged in handicraft work at home." He recounted how he had learned the rudiments of woodworking at home, holding the lamp for his father as he worked into the night, and looked forward to a new generation of men passing skills onto their own sons.[26]

Vernacular Crafts for Boys

A distinction needs to be made between the growth of home crafts for boys in the decades after 1900 and the arts and crafts style—if not the arts and crafts movement. There is no doubt that the movement was one of a series of streams that converged to encourage craft instruction in the schools, but as a stylistic influence it had to share the stage with both "Indian-pioneer" projects and useful household objects whose style could generously be called "vernacular." Many advocates of craft hobbies for males found aesthetics irrelevant. As a pastime traditionally associated with females, they felt that handicrafts for men and boys had to appear as manly as possible, which meant shunning even the masculine arts and crafts style.

This pattern was set in 1882 when Daniel Beard, founder of the Boy Scouts of America, published the first edition of *The American Boys' Handy Book*. As a major evangelist for the redemptive effects of outdoor activities, Beard's book combined nature and handicrafts. In addition to tips on making gear for camping, hunting, and fishing, the book contained a series of projects for toys such as kites, boats, guns, traps, sleds, and miscellaneous small wooden items. Beard made no attempt to encourage aesthetic sensitivity; indeed, most of the chapter entitled "Every Boy a Decorative Artist" was about the technical aspects of shadow pictures and photography. Beard's books inspired a host of imitations. In a 1919 review of how-to-do-it books for boys, Henry Lanier suggested that "if a boy were to be confronted with all the manuals of carpentry and mechanics aimed at him since the day of Dan Beard's pioneer 'American Boys' Handy Book', he'd certainly decide that life didn't offer enough time to read and use tools both," which would have been fine for Lanier, who had little use for the purely practical nature of boys crafts books.[27]

Lanier criticized most of the how-to craft books not only for their technical shortcomings but also for their refusal to promote style, concluding that poor instructions may have been a blessing if they prevented more spool projects: "Better, much better, that all the old spools in the world should be burned or lie and rot rather than that a boy should feel proud of having turned them into such aggressive stupidities as 'spool pen-racks' and 'spool candlesticks.' " In the true spirit of the arts and crafts movement, Lanier declares, "after all, there is such a thing as taste and fitness even in the simplest articles of every day." Lanier was particularly critical of A. Neely Hall, whose children's craft books dominated the field into the 1920s. Unlike Beard, Hall's idea of camping was sleeping out in the backyard, and almost all his projects were home-based as well as homemade, but like Beard, all his projects were oblivious to style. As Hall noted in the introduction to a 1911 book, his plans used "old boards, grocery boxes, cigar boxes, barrels, tin cans, worn-out pans and tins, pails, broomhandles, spools, discarded clocks, broken chairs and other furniture, old hats and clothing, stovepipe, clothes-line, screen wire, and other things too numerous to mention." These are hardly the raw materials of artistic creativity; they are, however, the raw materials of household practicality and thus mark the children's version of the nascent do-it-yourself movement.[28]

Although Hall provided instructions for making the usual sports equipment, games, and toys, most of his designs were for practical household items, and one book includes plans for turning the attic into a boy's room, a project that was just beginning to become a do-it-yourself standard. Hall's projects, most of which first appeared as articles in boys magazines, were quite consciously designed to reintroduce suburban boys to mechanical skills: "The man of today who excuses his inability to do this or that by admitting that he is not handy, was one of the boys of yesterday who did not bother about making kites, constructing conveniences for the house, and building boats, wagons, tree-huts, and the like." Unlike the Beechers fifty years earlier, Hall did not preach the necessity of becoming a handyman; he assumed it and made it clear that the handy boy was the father of the handyman.[29]

Crafts were a social good not only because they helped develop the whole person and re-created lost mechanical skills but also because they had dollar value. "The great majority of schoolboys have had to realize the fact that pocket-money is not inexhaustible, and that the purchase of cabinets, book-shelves and so forth makes sad havoc with the weekly or monthly allowance," observed a hobby proponent in 1912. "Now all of this can be remedied with a little practical knowledge of sawing and planing." In 1911 Hall wrote about a group of six boys in Dayton, Ohio, who had set up their own firm to manu-facture mission-style furniture, and for those who did not have the skills to make furniture, he had a chapter on simple household "contrivances" that could be sold door-to-door.[30]

Manual training had its major impact on boys who were introduced to preindustrial craft skills that had fallen out of fashion. Girls, on the other hand, who had maintained a handicraft tradition through the nineteenth century found more of the same in most school programs. With few excep-tions, manual arts training for girls emphasized needle crafts and excluded woodworking or any other activity involving the use of heavy tools. Throop University in Pasadena, the arts and crafts antecedent of the California Insti-tute of Technology, along with its allied elementary and high schools, did extend full craft equality to girls, but it was an exception. Even well-inten-tioned advocates of women's crafts like Hall, found it hard to imagine that girls could really do the same sorts of projects as boys. In *Handicrafts for Handy Girls*, he pointed out that "girls are competing with boys in some of our manual-training schools [which] is proof enough that . . . any girl can become efficient in wood-working," but he undermined his support by sug-gesting wooden construction be done with help from brothers and fathers. And he always advised "a neatly put on covering of cretonne" to hide what he implicitly assumed would be botched female woodworking.[31]

The Emergence of Domestic Masculinity

Left by their fathers to be raised by their mothers, Victorian boys had little exposure to masculine values, including those necessary for success in a business world where many of them would be working for somebody else. Historians of the postbellum era have suggested that male gender anxieties induced by industrialization were resolved away from the female-dominated home. In separate studies, Mary Ann Clawson and Mark Carnes show how these men escaped from women into the all-male world of fraternal orders. According to Carnes, their ritual-filled meetings provided men with psychological permission to break from the inhibiting bonds that tied them to their mothers. Clawson goes even further, claiming that fraternalism "was an alternative to domesticity, one that worked to preserve rather than deny the primacy of masculine social organization." Men's worlds of both work and leisure lay beyond the white picket fence. The rise of muscular Christianity and athletics, the continuation of fraternal orders, and the emergence of the Boy Scouts after 1900 are all indications that male groups remained an important source of masculine self-identity into the new century.[32]

Along with this continuation of homosocial bonding, however, an antithetical trend emerged in which men found companionship and masculine identity inside the home. Beginning very tentatively in the nineteenth century, this new identity took on a recognizably modern form at the start of the twentieth with the assistance of the arts and crafts movement, the growth of manual training in schools, and the boys vernacular crafts movement. These trends figuratively and literally opened a door through which men could enter their own homes to reassume the masculine role of artisan, if only in a leisure-time environment. Long before "do-it-yourself" became a common term in the 1950s, male householders began to take on the obligation of repairing and improving their houses as part of the rise of "masculine domesticity." Moving from the position of a somewhat remote pater familias, the new suburban husband was, according to Margaret Marsh, willing "to take on increased responsibility for some of the day-to-day tasks of bringing up children" and make "his wife, rather than his male cronies, his regular companion on evenings out." Men also began to stake out areas of activity at home that became their particular domains. By doing so they created spheres of "domestic masculinity." Unlike masculine domesticity, which had men doing jobs that had once been women's, domestic masculinity was practiced in areas that had been the purview of professional craftsmen, and therefore retained the aura of preindustrial vocational masculinity. The two concepts are complimentary, but domestic masculinity acknowledges the creation of a male realm inside the house.[33]

Octave Thanet accepted both masculine roles in his Arkansas country home. When he was in the city he preferred to be "urban and civilized," but in the country he was willing "to be rural and natural and primitive, and live close to the grass." Primitive living, in Thanet's view, included taking on some traditionally female tasks, such as helping out with the cooking, and some of the new male jobs, which included household painting, hanging wallpaper, putting down carpets, repairing tinware, running the lawn mower, and laying bricks—using his wife's pancake spatula for a trowel. He, however, drew the line at building a chicken coop for the couple's excursion into the chicken and egg business. For that, he called in a carpenter.[34] Thanet felt comfortable taking on some of the physical obligations of home ownership only when he was in the country and could play the role of a farmer. With somewhat less justification, but no less enthusiasm, suburban husbands adopted the same attitudes on their quarter-acre homesteads.

It was perhaps only a fortuitous historical accident that these new masculinized homes were built in the "craftsman" style, but the image of the craftsman, an artisan in his leather apron surrounded by the tools of his trade and the products of his own hand was the perfect one for the new domestic masculinity. "Any fool can write a book but it takes a man to dovetail a door," declared Charles F. Lummis, a romantic primitivist who, with the help of local Indians, built his own Pasadena Arroyo home. The masculine-artisan equivalency is central to the meaning of home-based manual skills. Historian Michael Kimmel has observed that the "heroic artisan," one of the traditional tropes for defining masculinity, needed to be recast for the industrial age, and Mary Ann Clawson points to the artisanal imagery of the Masons as doing just that.[35] Fraternal orders, however, took men away from their homes and allowed them to become only symbolic artisans. In the twentieth century basement workshops kept the husband in his home and allowed him to become, or at least try to become, an actual craftsman. Home improvement articles in arts and crafts magazines were addressed to "the handicraftsman" and "the amateur craftsman," confirming the artisanal image.[36] "Six months before this book shelf was made Mr. Hartog had never handled a carpenter's tool," explained the caption to a photograph of chairs and shelves in the *Craftsman*, reassuring white-collar workers that their lack of workshop experience was not an insurmountable obstacle.[37]

The plain styles of the early twentieth century lent themselves admirably to home construction. At the same time, however, the steady growth in indoor plumbing, central heating, and electricity meant there were many more household systems that needed maintenance and repair. The tradition of hiring professional carpenters for rather simple tasks had not disappeared, but a new group of householders was willing to do anything, including building the house itself. Companies that manufactured prefabricated bungalows before World War I gave buyers the options of having professionals build the houses, assembling the houses themselves, or having the shells constructed by others and doing the finish-work themselves. More than forty thousand such house kits were sold in Los Angeles alone.[38]

Do-it-yourself has always been a movement of homeowners. While low-income people are largely excluded from owner-occupied housing today, that was not always the case. As Olivier Zunz, Richard Harris, and others have demonstrated, throughout the nineteenth and early twentieth centuries urban blue-collar workers (especially immigrants) often owned homes at close to the same rate as white-collar workers, and an extraordinarily high percentage of these were owner-built. Harris attributes this often ignored phenomenon of working-class home ownership to a fortuitous convergence of need, skill, and opportunity. In particular, cheap land on the unimproved fringes of cities gave workers the chance to own modest cottages, especially if they were willing to provide "sweat equity" by building some or all of the houses themselves.[39]

Few middle-class men had the skills to build their own houses, but increasing numbers of them took a hand in shaping their home environment, and in those salad days of do-it-yourself, it was easy for home maintenance and improvement to be leisure since it was not expected. As a form of relief, household work soothed troubled minds by providing men with a masculine alternative to effete office work. Typically, a 1910 article entitled "Recreation with Tools" explained that every person needed some interest aside from daily work in order to "maintain that balance and poise—physical and mental—which is so essential to right living."[40]

Although they tended to be smaller than their Victorian predecessors, there was a strong sense that the craftsman style bungalows so popular after the turn of century should make room somewhere for a man's workshop. This "factory in miniature," as one writer called it, would serve the practical purpose of storing the tools necessary to do the "numerous small repairs" that would otherwise be left undone since they were "hardly of sufficient importance for the calling in of a carpenter or a plumber." In addition, the shop would be the place where men could pursue messy craft hobbies without bothering their wives.[41] Men wanted their own space, and household repair and improvement offered an excellent rationale for setting aside some territory for themselves. The kitchen was the woman's bailiwick; the bedroom was shared but, according to decorators writing in 1919, still considered "the one room in the house above all others where the woman's taste reigns supreme." The living room was family space, and smaller homes had fewer libraries and dens. Where could a man turn for a physical place in the home that was his alone?[42]

The problem of gendering limited domestic space faced A. L. Hall when he moved into his moderate-size house in 1908. Hall "was given" a rear room on the second floor as a den. At the same time, however, he encroached on his wife's territory by storing his household tools in the kitchen. When Hall found that he had little use for the den, he followed his wife's suggestion and converted it into a workshop for his new woodworking hobby. He equipped the unelectrified workshop with four treadle-driven machines—a circular saw, lathe, scroll saw, and grindstone—and proceeded to build furniture of his own design. Hall's wife seems to have accepted the noise and dust from the shop, and a surprising number of other writers at the time also found no problem in suggesting that workshops share space with living quarters. In the long run, however, shops and bedrooms could not function peacefully side by side, and men deserted the spare upstairs room for the newly invented basement.[43]

Until the 1890s a house's foundations enclosed an earthen-floor cellar, a dark, damp place with access through a short exterior stairway covered with heavy wood trapdoors. With the coming of central heating, the cellar became the basement, a place to locate the furnace and to store the coal to feed it. Floors were paved; more attention was paid to making the walls watertight; and an interior staircase gave direct access from the kitchen. By 1915 water heaters, washing machines, and other household equipment had taken up residence in the basement. This was part of a pattern in which people chose to spend money on technology rather than floor space. With libraries, dens, and parlors being sacrificed to water heaters and flush toilets, the first generation of do-it-yourselfers staked a subterranean claim next to the furnace, which was already men's territory because of the labor necessary to shovel coal and ashes. The concrete walls and unfinished ceiling of the basement defined a new male space (see fig. 7.2). From there, generations of men would produce a steady flow of household objects and regularly emerge with hammer and Stillson wrench to keep their homes in tip-top order.[44]

"To go down to that little corner, after a day's aggravating mental drains, and make something for the house, a magazine rack, or something even simpler" was just the tonic needed to rejuvenate the tired businessman, explained a 1908 article in the *Craftsman*. He might also, the author added, do "gardening, plumbing and paperhanging, and other things." Thus even Gustav Stickley's own magazine folded craftsmanship and home maintenance into a new form of "fun" that had previously been the work of "a duly accredited mechanic." In this spirit of fun, *Popular Mechanics*, a professional engineering review, transformed itself into an advice magazine for home-owning amateurs. Filled with equal parts of hobby crafts and home maintenance, *Popular Mechanics* became the model for men's magazines that substituted saws for sex. Firms began to offer boxed tool kits that would enable

FIGURE 7.2 An unusually candid picture of the less than ideal conditions in an early basement workshop in 1910. (Reprinted from Ira S. Griffith, "Cabinet Making as a Handicraft," *American Homes and Gardens* 7 [September 1910]: 345.)

any man to realize his crafting fantasies (see fig. 7.3). These were not necessities; they were objects of desire like Hammacher, Schlemmer's beautiful eighty-five-dollar combination bench and cabinet that came with ninety-five tools.[45]

The home craftsman who supplied himself with a collection of tools could think about undertaking some of the furniture plans published in a variety of shelter magazines, but despite the simplified mission style published projects still assumed a sophisticated command of woodworking skills. In fact, one author felt constrained to assure his readers that it was no violation of the craftsman's code for them to have their stock cut to size at a planing mill since "there will be plenty of work remaining, so that you will have a perfect right to claim the finished piece as of your own handicraft." He was certainly right about that since almost all furniture plans of the period called for mortise and tenon joints, which the writers never bothered to describe, taking it for granted that their readers knew how to execute one with a hammer and chisel.[46]

For those less skilled, companies were already offering "Home Built Arts and Crafts Furniture" kits that needed only assembly and finishing. For $3.90 in 1907, a homeowner could buy presawn oak pieces and finishing materials for a mission-style porch swing that, the advertisement said, would

FIGURE 7.3 Two advertisements for home tool kits from a 1908 edition of *Suburban Life*. (Reprinted from *Suburban Life* 7 [November 1908]: 239, 257.)

save 75 percent over an assembled piece. Given its location in a middle-class magazine next to the "Amateur Craftsman" column, the advertisement was also meant to appeal to the homeowner who wanted to participate in the arts and crafts movement but did not have the skills or tools to do so. The knocked-down (as they were already called) kits could have been a joint project for husbands and wives to build together, since women continued to specialize in paint brush activities.[47]

The overall role of women in defining the home environment was reduced a bit by the shift away from the Victorian interior cluttered with its homemade knickknacks, but what women lost in traditional fancywork they gained in nontraditional "masculine" tasks. Thirty-five years of female scroll sawing was finally paying some dividends. As the advice author Helen Campbell noted in 1912, "the jig-saw has done much to convince people that girls can handle tools," and moreover, there was no reason why every girl could not "learn how to drive a nail properly, how to plane and joint and all the more delicate operations of carpentry." Such skills, she said, would allow girls to become the person who was "handy about the house" and do what otherwise would be contracted out to the village carpenter. In a similar vein, Mary Edith Griswold suggested to the readers of *American Homes and Gardens* that "beautiful furniture for summer use can be made by a handy man or woman with a kit of tools which will cost under a dollar, the only really essential ones being a T square, a saw and a hammer." She did add that "in the most enlightened homes a regular work-bench is found" but clearly did not assume it to be the sole property of the house's males (see fig. 7.4). Griswold suggested projects for both girls and boys, and illustrated her article with two photographs of young women doing woodwork at a fully equipped cabinetmaker's bench. Griswold and Campbell's enthusiastic endorsement of female woodworking clearly drew inspiration from women's roles in the arts and crafts movement, but even then, Campbell advised her reader against physical stress, suggesting that the reader "employ a carpenter to do any really laborious work that you may require."[48]

There is only scant evidence that either women or girls took the advice to become more active in household construction, even in the construction of a new form of box furniture invented and promoted by a woman. Just as the rectilinear design of mission furniture made it easier for men to take up cabinetmaking, it also lent itself to the even less demanding manufacture of furniture out of discarded packing crates. Victorian box and barrel furniture had a very bad reputation. Barrel chairs in particular would not hold their shape once they were cut, and the utilitarian shape of boxes had to be disguised by a thick padding of upholstery. That was changed by the arts and crafts aesthetic and

Louise Brigham. Brigham had become adept with heavy tools during her New England girlhood and pursued an arts education at the Pratt Institute in Brooklyn. After graduating, she entered the growing field of social work, opening a settlement house in Cleveland where she constructed her first piece of box furniture to demonstrate methods of low-cost living to her immigrant clients.[49]

Making a frame for a screen

FIGURE 7.4 Woman in home workshop making a wooden screen frame. (Reprinted from M. E. Griswold, "Home Made Summer Furniture," *American Homes and Gardens* 8 [August 1911]: 291.)

Intrigued by immigrant folk arts, Brigham visited nineteen European countries and studied at Sweden's Sloyd Institute to better understand traditional crafts. She encouraged handwork among her clients and founded an association in New York City to sell their products. Her greatest impact, however, was not in the area of traditional folk crafts but in a new technique that she invented. During an extended visit to a coal mine in northern Finland, she was housed in a poorly appointed cottage and took advantage of discarded packing crates to furnish her eight rooms with box furniture. Her experience, she said, made her feel "anew the truth, so familiar to all, that work to be of real value must be honest, useful, and beautiful, and Ruskin and Morris spoke as clearly in the arctic regions as in the settlements or studio in New York."[50]

When Brigham returned to the United States, she settled in a four-room apartment on New York's upper east side, which she furnished entirely with packing crate furniture made from wood that cost a total of $4.20; this in an era when a single piece of factory-made furniture could cost a week's wages. She constructed tables and chairs, desks and sofas, bookcases and plant stands, all from salvaged wood. Brigham made no explicit claims to the mission style, but she was favorably received in the *Craftsman*, and her pieces, with their right angles and uncovered wood, were clearly at home in the age of Stickley. Her furniture looked better than traditional crate and barrel pieces because she did not try to retain the crate's original structure. Instead of padding or combining already existing shapes, Brigham disassembled the boxes, sorted the wood by size, straightened the nails, and then reassembled the pieces in entirely new forms. The wood was still cheap, thin pine, but the finished piece looked nothing like the original crate.[51]

Louise Brigham promoted her idea locally by organizing neighborhood boys into a club to scavenge boxes and bring them back to a workshop housed in Gracie Mansion (later to become the official mayor's residence). There the 115 boys produced furniture for their homes and toys for themselves (see fig. 7.5). The concept of box furniture received national publicity from hobby writer A. Neely Hall, who included chapters on the process in two of his books (although he neglected to credit the technique to Brigham). Brigham published a how-to-do-it book on box furniture in 1909, and an illustrated article entitled "How I Furnished My Entire Flat from Boxes" appeared in the *Ladies' Home Journal* the following year. The *Journal* article seems to imply that box furniture could be and should be made by middle-class women, but the flimsiness of the pieces, the poor quality of the wood, and the limited design possibilities would have been an obstacle to any but the poorest women or to boys furnishing their own rooms.[52]

FIGURE 7.5 Boys organized by Louise Brigham collecting boxes with which to make household furniture of her design in 1915. (Reprinted from Louise Brigham, "How Boys Make Furniture from Boxes," *St. Nicholas* 42 [January 1915]: 241–42.)

Louise Brigham's experiments in box furniture represent something of a breakthrough for women, not only because the technique was conceived and promoted by a woman but also because it received publicity in a national woman's magazine. Brigham understood that her designs would not make any inroads among middle-class women, but in a parallel development, middle-class women did alter their role in household decorating, shifting away from the solo production of knickknacks and focusing a bit more on major projects, which were often undertaken in conjunction with their husbands. This was the case with W. L. Hicks, who designed and supervised the building of his house in Glen Cove, Long Island, in 1910. To furnish the house Hicks recycled a number of old pieces of furniture, turning a bedstead into chairs and resectioning an old table. Acting as an artistic assistant, his wife decorated the finished pieces with ornamental carving.[53]

Mrs. Hicks's decorative carving replicated the activities of a small number of professional woman artisans, but it was atypical for housewife hobbyists who appear to have been much more comfortable with a brush than with a gouge. After the turn of the century women began to expand their painting domain beyond artistic decoration to more substantial tasks. In 1917 Marion Pitcher described how a group of women got together to scrape the old finish from secondhand furniture (there was no pretense that these were antiques), after which they would refinish the pieces. The willingness to undertake heavy painting began to extend to the house itself, although here women continued to defer to men on those jobs that required working in high places. "Women Do Not Paint" insisted a 1912 Dutch Boy paint advertisement that showed a woman directing a professional painter working on a ladder outside her home. Because they feared alienating their professional customers, manufacturers of building and maintenance materials would not advertise for direct sale to the public until the do-it-yourself boom of the 1950s, so the focus of the ad on professional painters was not unusual.[54]

Despite the lack of commercial encouragement, both wives and husbands began to paint the inside of their houses. Garrett Winslow, whose 1912 article may be the first to self-consciously use the phrase "Do-It-Yourself" (capitals, hyphens, and quotation marks in the original), called on men not to hand over the repainting of their interiors to professional decorators. Just a month later in the same magazine, an article entitled "What a Woman Can Do with a Paint Brush" assured readers that "any woman, indeed, possessed of average energy and the ability to read and follow directions on a can of paint or varnish can be her own decorator," although it did caution that "painting a whole house or barn may possibly be tried by the ambitious father, but his wife, who classes ladders and scaffolds among the implements of a dangerous trade, is undoubtedly glad to have professional labor called in."[55] (See fig. 7.6).

By 1912, then, suburban homeowners were participating in two novel forms of do-it-yourself. The first was done by husbands and wives together and was an element in masculine domesticity. The other was done only by men and was part of what I call domestic masculinity. When men and

FIGURE 7.6 Housewife showing "what a woman can do with a paintbrush" in 1912. (Reprinted from Agnes Athol, "What a Woman Can Do with a Paint Brush," *Suburban Life* 15 [November 1912]: 268.)

women undertook household chores like interior painting with rough equality, they were contributing to the degendering of the home. It seems only appropriate that the new gender-inclusive living room be painted by either men or women—or perhaps by both together. However, when husbands alone took over household jobs that had been previously done by professionals, like exterior painting or household building projects, then they were doing something different from masculine domesticity; they were carving out a gender-specific role within the house—domestic masculinity. Such activities were exclusively male, and doing them gave men a sense of special ability that may well have compensated for some lack of masculine affirmation at work. Since women were also expanding their participation in home maintenance and repair, there was some overlap in the home improvement sphere. Nevertheless, a sense of uniquely male household competence that paralleled the traditional skills of the farmer and artisan would continue to expand in the twentieth century until it blossomed into the great do-it-yourself boom of the 1950s.

Women's Crafts in the 1920s

The gradual diminution of fancywork crafts as a form of female leisure continued through the 1920s. As growing numbers of young middle-class women joined the workforce in various clerical positions, they had less need for genteel pastimes that would involve them in productive activity. By the end of the 1920s, 4.75 million women held white-collar positions; this was five times the number of white-collar women in 1900. Married middle-class women still did not work outside the home in appreciative numbers, but as the availability of full-time servants decreased, the demands on women's time in the household increased. Electrical appliances that the housewife ran herself were hardly a substitute for a live-in maid, and rising expectations of cleanliness and child care further eroded free time. While these changes did not eliminate the need for productive leisure among middle-class women, they certainly made it less central to these women's lives. Women who wanted to could take advantage of the degendered legacy of handwork left by the arts and crafts movement to work on household furnishings, but as Jean-Christophe Agnew has argued, modern interiors created a world "in which the power of purchase held sway over the older authority of personal mementos and personal craft alike." The pride of consumption competed with the pride of production, making the function of women's hobbies increasingly similar to men's.[56]

Traditionalists fought a rear guard action against the demise of fancy needlework, hoping that women who were used to buying factory-made clothing and linen could be lured back to the beauty of the hand-stitched article. The Needle and Bobbin Club of New York City, formed just after World War I "for the purpose of stimulating and maintaining an interest in handsome fabrics, lace embroidery, weaving and tapestry," sought to help immigrants sell their needlework in America.[57]

Middle-class publications also held out the possibility that hobby crafts could be converted into sources of income. *Needlecraft Magazine* regularly ran articles and advertisements telling its readers how they could use their skills to earn a living sewing for others. The Dennison Manufacturing Company, which made art supplies, sponsored courses in stores that taught women how to craft crepe paper flowers and explained that "one whole section of the course is devoted to the money-making possibilities of this delightful craft." Similarly, another hobby supply catalog asked "Why not make money on your porch?" It assured its customers that "if, in your spare moments you make these attractive things for others, you will find that there is a ready demand for them." When Ray Schmidt, the kept woman in Fannie Hurst's novel *Back Street*, found that she had too much time and not enough money, she turned to "fashionable, lucrative, and genteel" china painting to augment the undependable income from her lover.[58]

In addition to craft pastimes like china painting that had remained unchanged for eighty years, women of the 1920s could also undertake much more ambitious projects, moving with their husbands into household maintenance and improvement. Active female participation in household repair and improvement was still considered a bit of a novelty in the 1920s, but one for which little apology or rationalization was needed. Describing some basic electrical repairs that could be handled by the homeowner, Arthur Wakeling's book *Fix It Yourself* said it would "give the man (or woman, in these modern times) of the household such information as will allow him to go ahead and do some of the [electrical] jobs." And *Popular Mechanics* included a picture of a woman soldering a pan in an article entitled "Soldering for the Home Mechanic." When women could be included in the rubric "home mechanic," the landscape of household do-it-yourself was clearly shifting.[59]

The *Modern Priscilla*, a popular magazine for young women, struck a somewhat more ambivalent note in its advice book on do-it-yourself decorating. In a section describing how a "girl made for herself the furniture for an attractive bedroom," the book was vague about just who was doing what. Thus the girl "had attached" bedposts to a box spring, but "she made from packing cases a seat with bookcases at both ends." The use of different verb forms when applied to typical and atypical activities seems calculated not to place inappropriate expectations on the reader, who could interpret the language in the way she felt most comfortable. When, however, the authors talked about painting, they took no refuge in syntax. "Do all your work in a room that is as free from dust as possible," they ordered, when explaining how to strip finish with lye, and the accompanying illustrations showed a young woman in a long smock and head kerchief going through all the steps in refinishing a desk (see fig. 7.7). The popularity of painted furniture in the 1920s prompted a

Applying lye solution.

First coat of flat color.

Sandpapering it down.

Follow the grain.

Final pumice rubdown.

Applying the decoration.

FIGURE 7.7 Steps in refinishing a desk as illustrated in a how-to-do-it book for women in 1925. (Reprinted from *Modern Priscilla Home Furnishing Book* [Boston: Priscilla Publishing, 1925], 215–20.)

spate of articles on how to make the natural wood finishes of the arts and crafts era disappear under coats of maize, apple green, and pale peach. Men were still called on for structural alterations, but women undertook the arduous task of taking old pieces down to bare wood and applying the new color.[60]

As it had for three generations, decorative painting continued to be the most popular woman's handicraft, and the tradition of coming up with novel mediums and original applications continued. Manufacturers of paint, wax, celluloid, and wicker supplies all provided catalogs, instruction books, and direct sales to the consumer to keep women productively busy in their spare time. A wax crayon firm tried to convince women that by dissolving their product in alcohol (a product admittedly in short supply during Prohibition), they would produce a wax paint that could be applied to porcelain, glass, metal, wood, and cloth. From waste baskets and sewing baskets to cuff links and garters there were few things that could not be painted with dissolved wax. "The fact that one is unable to draw is no hindrance," said the company, because women could produce "scissors painting" with its printed crepe paper, an updated version of decalcomanie, now called decalos.[60]

While technical skills were not dismissed, companies made sure that the mere lack of ability would not keep a woman from crafting. With only the faintest hint of dismay, a 1923 catalog asked home crafters "who of us is there who does not cherish some woven thing—perhaps a braided or a knotted rug—that some great grandparent made from a thrifty collection of patches and trimmings in long tedious hours of hard work?" The contemporary housewife, however, could not be faulted for not doing the same, since "the modern rush of life has smitten the old custom and art of rug making a cruel blow." The company solved the problem by supplying the would-be rug-maker with a color-printed canvas and a special rug needle that would allow her to "easily reproduce the old masterpieces in her leisure." Women could produce rugs with almost the same efficiency and creativity as workers on Ford's assembly line. In fact, if she wanted to make the household equivalent of the tin lizzie, she could buy a baby carriage kit: "The carriage frame is so made that nothing is left to the imagination of the person, but to finish it in a style and weave to suit the individual taste." The preliminary manufacturing had be done by workers further down the line (in a real factory), and all she had to do was complete her step in the process to produce a finished product.[62]

The House as a Form of Leisure

In her book of parodic Mother Goose rhymes, Alice Van Leer Carrick, who reserved most of her barbs for antique collectors, did take one swipe at crafters, and in doing so captured not only the superficiality of many handicrafts but also the fundamental difference between the activities of men and women. The culminating verse of "The Attic That Jack Built" lists the wife's hobbies, some of which like pyrography and hammered brass, were clearly carryovers from the arts and crafts era, but locates them in a space made by her husband:

This is the space all cozy and snug
Reserved for the antique-style hooked rug
That will follow the book ends hammered from brass
That followed the burnt-leather pillow cover
With Gibson girl and her heavy lover,
That followed the burnt-wood ping-pong set
The followed the hand-painted taboret
That was made by wife who went plumb daft
Over each All-America art and craft
And filled up the attic that Jack built.[63]

It was no mere literary conceit that had the crafts filling up the attic that Jack built. Judging from the dramatic increase in do-it-yourself literature, the role of men in caring for their homes grew so palpably during the interwar years that the house was transformed from a place *in* which to do things to a place *on* which to do things. Home improvement magazines in the 1920s simply ignored changes in styles and continued to publish plans for straight-lined mission-style furniture that made up in simplicity of construction what it lacked in current fashion. Furthermore, the great antique craze of the 1920s helped by popularizing colonial styles including easy-to-replicate early-American vernacular. A character in a 1926 short story was impressed by the furniture produced at a southern industrial training school: "With its new-ness lost, its edges softened, it would be a perfect example of the earliest Colonial furniture. . . . Here he realized, primitive furniture was being fash-ioned by primitive minds, for a primitive use." What a "primitive Negro" could make, so might a self-taught homeowner.[64]

The passing of the arts and crafts style may have slightly reduced the num-ber of do-it-yourself furniture projects published in advice magazines, but the shortage was more than balanced by an increase in home maintenance and improvement suggestions. Between 1890 and 1930 the number of pri-vately owned homes more than tripled, while mass distribution of automo-biles in the 1920s encouraged the growth of new housing developments beyond the confines of streetcar and rail lines. The percentage of these homes owned by skilled workers was actually higher than that owned by pro-fessionals, and Richard Harris suggests "that the families of male blue-collar workers did more work within and upon the home than did those of other groups." Trumpeting the benefits of his forty-hour work week in 1926, Henry Ford explained that his men "have been building houses for themselves, and to meet their demand for good and cheap lumber we have established a lum-ber yard where they can buy wood from our own forests." When Rose Feld investigated the leisure activities of steel workers who had just gotten an eight-hour day in 1924 she discovered that a high percentage of them were constructing garages for the cars that the Ford workers were making.[65]

The smaller suburban house was becoming an arena not only of masculine competence but also of masculine play. Plans for homemade laborsavers like bicycle-driven lawn mowers, battery-run hedge trimmers, chicken-operated hen house doors, and remote ignition switches for water heaters filled the pages of *Popular Mechanics* and other do-it-yourself magazines. While these implements may in fact have saved some time and effort if they ever worked, they contained an element of exuberance that made them as much playful as labor saving. When a later author titled his book *Make Your Home Your Hobby*, he was drawing on a tradition that began in the 1920s when the house itself was becoming a hobby, both the location and the object of leisure time activity, and a source of masculine pride. Combining spillover and compensatory elements into the overarching category of masculine skill, *Popular Mechanics* said that "hobbies requiring work with hands are not confined solely to those who practice callings of totally opposite character. Toilers in shops and mills derive much enjoyment in doing on their little home workbenches the same kind of things at which they are employed."[66]

With this new conception of the house as a pastime came the growing belief that maintenance and repair work could be satisfying in the same way as more obviously creative constructive projects. The hobby label that had first been applied to furniture-building projects in the arts and crafts era continued, of course. A wealthy businessmen could talk about "maintaining healthful equilibrium" by working in a "small, well-appointed carpenter shop in the rear of his house," and a minister who said "mere idleness brought me no rest" found relief in cabinetwork. But home maintenance could bring the same mental health benefits. "Do It Yourself" urged the title of the first chapter in a 1924 home repair book, since the best form of rest was taking up a "work hobby" that would provide a sense of accomplishment and ward off nervous collapse. Saving money and avoiding inconvenience would remain an important reason for do-it-yourself household repair, but writers increasingly recognized the psychological satisfaction that made household care a satisfying hobby and not a chore.[67]

The shifting balance between necessity and pleasure meant that, for the first time, how-to writers could begin to acknowledge what most home owners had discovered for themselves: do-it-yourself did not necessarily save either money or aggravation but could be pleasurable nevertheless. In a general how-to article on setting up a home workshop, James Tate advised "Mr. Amateur Mechanic" to be sure he had the tools necessary to fix a loose coffeepot handle, put up a few shelves, make the screen door fit, and repair the cord on the toaster. Tate was not advocating do-it-yourself repairs because they would save the homeowner money. On the contrary, he said he was addressing "the man who gets more fun out of twenty dollar's worth of time spent in tinkering with tools than in paying out five to have the job done." In other words, Tate turned the traditional rationale for home repair on its head. It was neither the cost saving nor the convenience of bypassing professionals that mattered, it was the satisfaction of doing it yourself—even if you lost money in the process.[68]

Home improvement became a major new rationale for craft instruction in school. In 1918 the National Education Association had issued seven goals for education, including "worthy home membership" and "worthy use of leisure time."[69] Advocates of craft instruction combined the practical and the pleasurable, explaining how learning to use tools prepared a boy, or "a girl, for that matter," with the skills to "make necessary repairs about the house" and with a hobby.[70] Experts took it for granted that boys would transfer the skills they learned in school to useful home-based hobby projects. A. Neely Hall prefaced the 1929 version of his endless stream of hobby books with a quote from a Northwestern University psychologist: "A good scholastic record is important, but a new way of carrying out ashes without getting dust on the family washing, is just as important." Thus the advocates of manual training continued to see it not only as vocational training for some but as life training for all, and an important part of that life would be the role of the father in keeping his own home in shipshape order.[71]

8   Home Crafts in Hard Times

Leisure, which had seemed so desirable during prosperity, became a distinct liability in the 1930s. The average manufacturing work week fell almost 25 percent between 1929 and 1934, with more than a 20 percent drop in average hourly earnings. That meant typical employed manufacturing workers were making 40 percent less in 1934 than they were before the depression. Even for employed middle-class workers, there was a great deal of additional leisure time and much less money to spend on it. "What do you do if you've given up your membership at the country club and you can't afford a trip South and you're too jittery over business — or the lack of it — to sit down quietly with a book," asked an article in a publishing trade journal. "If you're in fashion," it answered, you take up a hobby such as arts and crafts. "The whiskered old alibi, 'If I had the time' went out when the New Deal came in," explained *Better Homes and Gardens*. A book entitled *How to Spend Your Husband's Leisure* commiserated with the plight of the wife of an unemployed man who had previously been at home only on Sundays or when he was sick, now he had "come back to the home [and] invaded woman's sphere." The book suggested the wife help her husband start a craft hobby, which was far better for men then "simply sitting and mulling over their hard luck." Many men did, creating a new class of crafters who had more time and less money. According to the advertising journal *Printers' Ink*, manufacturers were "operating their plants days and some nights and holidays to supply the demand of businesses and professional men, as well as boys, who have rigged up a workshop at home."[1]

Men and boys with home workshops could make jigsaw puzzles, which enjoyed fad popularity in the early 1930s and were selling at a rate of 10 million per week in 1933. Die-cut cardboard puzzles captured the low end of the market, but amateur puzzle sawyers took advantage of high commercial prices for wooden puzzles and the newly introduced electric scroll saws to help fill the demand for better quality puzzles. Home crafting magazines published jigsawing instructions and patterns, ran contests for new patterns, and provided advice on how to sell or rent the products. According to puzzle historian Anne Williams, hundreds of unemployed craftsmen and technical professionals began home businesses using their design and woodworking skills to produce puzzles for the craze. A group of unemployed men in Reading, Pennsylvania, started their own puzzle company under the auspices of the municipal recreation department, and in the spring of 1933 received an order for a hundred thousand puzzles. While some of these puzzle sawyers may have started as hobbyists, most of them were in it for the money; it was a way to make ends meet until they could return to their chosen professions, which all but the most successful puzzle makers did when the economy improved.[2]

Making jigsaw puzzles for money transformed a hobby into a job. This transition was usually less problematic for crafters than collectors. Unlike collectors who risked disapproval from fellow hobbyists if they placed undue emphasis on profit, crafters had to deal only with their own sense of appropriate leisure behavior, which means they had to decide whether their hobby was worklike relief from work or leisurelike supplement to it. The craft literature does not dwell on the issue, but the conflict did not go wholly unnoticed. An amateur luthier, for example, charged his friends only the cost of materials for his high-quality violins, saying that if he did otherwise "he could not think of this avocation as a hobby, consequently it would lose much of its appeal." Similarly, John Ray, a New Orleans bird carver always gave away his carvings because he did not want to undermine the hobby nature of this activity and because he felt that a bird carved for "gain and not for pleasure is bound to lack the essential quality of spontaneity." Nevertheless, the temptation to confirm the worth of one's products in the marketplace and to earn a little extra cash, particularly in hard times, was strong.[3]

Most hobby proponents in the depression perceived the transition from full-time amateur to part-time professional to full-time professional as a relatively seamless one, but at least one expert acknowledged that there was a real distinction between a craft hobby and a craft business: the amateur "makes what he likes; he makes it as he likes; and he spends on it as much time as he likes," while the professional "must remember, all the time he is working, that time is money." This caution was relevant to crafters who were weighing the relative value of regular work time and hobby–work time, but for the unemployed or underemployed spare time had little monetary value, so most craft sales advice in the depression did not have to draw too fine a distinction between the relative values of work and leisure time. It did, however, have to distinguish between those people whose hobbies were still mostly leisure and those who thought they could use hobby skills to develop an alternative income.[4]

The alternative income advocates tended to be neo-Jeffersonians who disliked the city, its people, and its machines. A South Carolina agricultural engineer who had no problem with inefficient farmers being squeezed off the land, nevertheless claimed they could make a living by producing artistic handicrafts, such as those made by European peasants. Those actually familiar with the working conditions of European artisans argued that most handmade goods were inferior and made under such "frightful conditions" that "there can be but little joy in their creative work." Such nay-saying did not find much sympathy among craft advocates who were much more likely to agree with the Appalachian crafts promoter who predicted that "the time will come when every kind of work will be judged by two measurements: one by the product itself, as is now done, the other by the effect of the work on the producer."[5]

The depression interest in professional handicrafting had a distinctly rural bias, derived from the popular notion that country folk were purer and more natural in their use of hand tools. In a 1935 essay entitled "The Arts of Leisure," Marjorie Greenbie described how an urban Jew, "Ikky Ikstein," used an electric light and a small aquarium to make an ugly lamp that he was able to sell for five dollars. Ikstein thought he was on the road to riches, but "the cold truth," said Greenbie, "is that not one in ten thousand, making things by hand in his leisure hours, can hit on a product which can be marketed in sufficient quantities, at popular prices, to make even a minimum living." Greenbie, however, made an exception for sturdy Protestant yeomen motivated by pleasure, not profit. As a supplement to agrarian self-sufficiency, crafting made sense. "If you are a rural New Englander in winter, and have a tight roof over your head, and a house banked with fir from the forest against the winds, and a roaring fire of wood from the wood-lot, with plenty more wood in the shed, and vegetables in the cellar, not to mention maple syrup, milk from the cow, eggs from the hens, pork put away from the fall killing, and apples in the barrel, and if you have an untold number of quilts and hot stove lid to go to bed with," then you would appreciate the value of an extra dollar or two brought in through the sale of crafts.[6]

Greenbie pointed to the state-sponsored League of New Hampshire Arts and Crafts as a model of what could be done by people with the appropriate cultural background. The league taught "country people how to make things which will be interesting and distinctive enough to attract buyers among the summer people." The New Hampshire League, with a paid director and working in conjunction with the state board of education, used federal and state money to send teachers throughout the state to instruct people in pottery, rug making, weaving, jewelry, silversmithing, needlework, woodworking, and enameling. The handiwork of these newly minted crafters was sold through twenty league stores and at an annual craft fair. By 1939 the league had seventeen hundred members, some of whom earned as much as two thousand dollars a year from their crafts. In fact, the project was so successful in generating additional income for part-time crafters and retired people that it continued well into the postwar era. In 1934 there was an attempt to create a federation of such craft guilds that would coordinate "a back to the land movement through [craft] industry." It failed, but was part of a broader interest in folk arts and crafts that were linked to the colonial style and American antiques.[7]

The folk-craft revival of the Great Depression had roots in the arts and crafts movement but differed from it in significant ways. Unlike the earlier movement, it was sponsored by a variety of "official" institutions that, according to a contemporary, included "folk schools and settlement houses; Agricultural Extension, Works Progress Administration and other government agencies; educators in many places and physicians" who sought to teach people lost indigenous crafts. Almost all the projects focused on rural residents, mostly in the northeast and Appalachia, who had no alternative sources of income. Thus the rural craft revival was more a relief effort than an attempt to reform industrial capitalism. Consequently it focused on traditional forms and created no equivalent of the craftsman or mission style.[8]

By the same token, the rural handicraft movement carried considerably less ideological baggage than the arts and crafts movement. Both liberals and conservatives could find support for their positions in the traditional American values expressed by folk crafts. The Daughters of the American Revolution and Pi Beta Phi Fraternity, for example, joined Mrs. Calvin Coolidge and Mrs. Herbert Hoover in 1934 to sponsor a national tour of crafts produced by members of the Southern Highland Handicraft Guild. A complex federation of professional and part-time crafters, the guild tried to preserve Appalachian crafts and the way of life that produced them while helping poor mountain folk develop skills, styles, and rational business practices that would provide a meaningful cash flow. At the same time, New Deal agencies including the Tennessee Valley Authority, the Works Progress Administration, the Farm Security Administration, and the National Youth Authority worked closely with the guild, and Eleanor Roosevelt joined the two Republican former first ladies as a tour sponsor. In fact, Mrs. Roosevelt personally financed the New York State Education Department's Rural Homecraft Project, which was her home state's version of folk craft development.[9]

Urban and suburban crafters got virtually no support from official agencies, and only how-to-do-it magazines encouraged the roadside sale of suburban handicrafts. In the final analysis, except for those promoting the rural handicraft revival, most depression-era craft advocates seemed to accept that few if any people were going to be able to replace their lost pay with income from the sale of home crafts. Crafts for most people were still a hobby, but the financial strains of the depression forced a greater awareness of the economic elements of the hobby, emphasizing the businesslike ideology that lay at the heart of this form of serious leisure. *Popular Science Monthly*, for example, provided a log book in one of its publications because, it said, "an orderly system for keeping track of how much time and money is spent on each home workshop project is just as important as a neat method of storing tools and materials." Crafting was so serious that the magazine suggested that one of its projects was amusing, easy, inexpensive, and would provide "a pleasant relief from more serious home workshop tasks." When one form of the hobby was promoted as relief from another form, then the first form was serious indeed. Thus, while crafting was not a substitute for a real job, its job-like characteristics were widely recognized.[10]

Lifting Depression

Most publicly sponsored urban craft programs were designed to teach people specific leisure skills so they could use their free time productively, if not remuneratively. It was at this level that crafting and collecting merged under the hobby rubric. When the San Diego Recreation Department decided to hold a hobby fair in 1939, it took what recreation professionals considered the bold move of showing crafts and collections together. Each group had previously had its own show, but a contemporary recreation journal pointed out, "it was left to San Diego to discover how closely related the recreation efforts of craftsmen and hobbyists [i.e., collectors] really are, and how well the products of those efforts can be exhibited in a common fair." Although they involved very different kinds of physical activity, collecting and crafting were both forms of serious leisure that embodied the same set of values that endeared them to teachers and recreation directors. Why can't we, asked a recreation director, "train our children to use [leisure] in a constructive way instead of a destructive one? In other words, beat Satan to it!" Because municipal craft programs taught children and adults of both genders, they provided light hand tools and heavy power tools. In areas as diverse as Cleveland, Detroit, and Westchester, New York, recreation centers ran programs that taught leather craft, marionette making, basket making, embroidery, knitting, weaving, and textile printing, in addition to woodwork. A survey taken at the end of the decade revealed that handicraft classes were offered by the municipal recreation programs of 364 cities and that well over a hundred thousand people participated in them.[11]

Teachers and writers emphasized the sense of independence and self-discipline that crafting promoted, and the manual skills, as one shop teacher pointed out, were useful not only in carpentry but also in surgery. Marjorie Greenbie, the ethnocentric supporter of New England folk crafts, argued that manual training, like Latin and algebra, was a source of "intellectual discipline" and was even more important because it also promoted "moral discipline." Crafting, she said "brings an immediate retribution for shoddy, insincere work. If you don't put on a roof honestly, it leaks. If you don't sew honestly, the garment comes apart." There was, in other words, an honesty in the performance that gave the performer a sense of self-worth, a sense of agency in a world wracked with uncertainty.[12]

More so than in any other period, craft advocates in the 1930s stressed the psychological benefits of the hobby. A private school principal explained that because teenagers were prohibited from using "the creative power developing within us to produce the ultimate miracle, a new individual, [they] must use it to create something else—that being the only safe outlet for it." Unlike sports and physical exercise, which lacked an element of creativity, she advocated shop work to protect youths from "morbid and degenerate practices." Rather than expelling an offending boy it would be better, she said, to "turn him into a workshop (and every other boy with him), and let him hammer or pound or chisel the pent-up feelings out of his system, and eventually satisfy his emotions by the sight and feel of the beautiful thing he has made." Explicit approval of sexual sublimation such as this was rare, but creative and procreative imagery was common. The introduction to the 1930 *Home Workshop Manual* ran through a series of anecdotes in which a man fixes a clock his wife is about to throw away, a doctor repairs a washtub the maid had punctured, and a father makes a two-story dollhouse for his little girl. What tied these acts together was not any money they may have saved but the pride of accomplishment they provoked. Bored by their regular work, unable to "bring forth babies," men needed something to make them feel good about themselves. "Making things with the hands is one of the most soul-satisfying experiences of the human race because it helps the individual to put into concrete form his own feelings," wrote the author of *Crafts for Fun*.[13]

The male crafter, explained Professor Edward Thorndike of Columbia University, could compensate for the fragmented nature of modern work by recapturing the lost craftsman's satisfaction of starting and completing work on a particular project. Hobby experts assured men that all sorts of psychological dissatisfactions produced at work could be remedied in the craft workshop. A staff member of the National Recreation Association visiting the Westchester County Recreation Center in 1932 noted that a "man was finding relief in the Workshop from the incessant financial worries of the past two years. You can't really think of stock markets and bank balances," she explained, when you are doing creative projects. An unhappy lawyer turned to amateur cabinetmaking and, as the piece emerged in his hands, he said, "I felt a more complete, lasting satisfaction . . . than I felt after winning my first big case in court."[14] The literature of the 1930s is full of testimonials to the palliative effect of crafting on the woes of stress, from work-generated nervous breakdowns to marital breakups, diagnoses of terminal illness, and retirement.[15]

Whereas men were psychologically threatened by work, women were seen to need relief from mental pressures brought on by family and biology. "If you are sick of housework, and making the same old clothes last another season, and no chance to call your soul your own—what with having the children under foot instead of away at boarding school? When the depression has got you down, what do you do about it?" asked *Publisher's Weekly*. "You don a smock and paint, or you seize a chisel and learn the delightful fragrance of freshly gouged wood, or seated before a loom you watch the pattern grow as you rhythmically toss the shuttle back and forth, while boredom and restlessness fade away and financial worries gradually spell challenge, not disaster." Traditional advocates of women's crafts continued to promote the hobby as a balm for the unique vicissitudes of female life. The National Women's Relief Society of Salt Lake City, which recommended crafts for "women who, having reared their family, find themselves with little to do in their homes," warned that "this type of woman is particularly prone to a 'nervous breakdown,' especially during the time of menopause."[16]

A Model Hobby

If mental health required a form of compensatory relief that came from the pride in a job well done, model making was a particularly popular way to achieve that feeling. H. J. Hobbs, a frequent writer on the benefits of hobbies, told *Parents' Magazine* readers that, for fathers, "work-a-day strain at the office is increasing with shorter working hours." He recommended model building as a way to relieve the strain because it had "the power of a sedative in calming his nerves and diverting his attention from business worries." Hobbs then seemingly regretting his sedative metaphor, rushes to assure his readers that it also "enlivens, refreshes, because it affords a vital interest." Continuing his paradoxical imagery, Hobbs points out that for the businessman's son, model building "is less a means of diversion than it is a disciplinary training and an everlasting game." Hobbs pronounces the apparent paradox of disguised affirmation without a word of explanation because he takes the dual nature of hobbies for granted; they are training in the form of diversion.[17]

According to the Leisure League of America, which promoted depression-era hobbies, adult model makers, who were almost exclusively men, preferred boats and trains, while boys favored airplanes. The league's support for model building was part of a pattern of institutional encouragement that ranged from schools and municipalities to large corporations. General Motors, for example, began its Fisher Body Craftsman's Guild in 1930; the guild awarded scholarships for the best model of the firm's corporate symbol, a Napoleonic coach.[18] At a more popular level, historian Joseph Corn has noted that almost every issue of *Popular Mechanics* in the 1930s had "a major article on building miniature locomotives, ships, sailboats, doll houses, or some other kind of model."[19] When rival *Popular Science* published plans for boys to build a "simplified" racing schooner, the hull alone required more than fifty complex hand-cut pieces, indicating a high level of skill among boy modelers.[20]

Advocates of model boat building emphasized its inherent maleness. Builders of display models could decorate their dens and stand by proudly while their friends, like those in a Gaar Williams cartoon, admired their work—although one of the cartoon characters had the temerity to ask, "What's it good for, Frank?" Building decorative models demonstrated prowess with tools, but building sailing models demonstrated skill plus an ability to make something that worked, perhaps better than anybody else's. In many cities, model yacht building and racing was a school-sanctioned activity that combined shop class construction and extracurricular clubs to race the end products. Shop teachers explained that it was "great sport" for fathers and sons to race their school-built model sailboats, and *Parents' Magazine* reminded readers that father-son model building was leisure with a lesson: "While they are working at a boat they are learning how to work." The stress on intergenerational male bonding must have had some success, since the *New York Times* reported that quite a few of the two thousand models of the French passenger liner *Normandie* entered in an international contest in 1936 were submitted by father-and-son teams.[21]

American men seem to have preferred sailing ship models, although European hobbyists also built power-driven craft. The English in particular had almost a century of experience with what they called "model engineering," that is, working models of powered boats, trains, and farm machinery. The advent of airplanes, however, provided a great stimulus to both representational and functional model making in the United States. As early as 1911, there was a model flying club for Chicago high school students, but the use of airplanes in World War I and Lindbergh's 1927 trans-Atlantic flight fueled a veritable craze for model planes. At the dawn of the Great Depression, model airplanes had become a multimillion-dollar business with about two thousand manufacturers.[22] In 1930 one magazine claimed that "airplane model building unquestionably exceeds in importance and popularity all other avocations of American youth." Many of these planes were "tinplate" models and kits, that is, prestamped parts that could be assembled in the form of famous airships like the *Spirit of St. Louis* and the *Graf Zeppelin*. The Metalcraft Corporation alone sold $140,000 a month worth of stamped model plane parts in 1929.[23]

For the most part, however, nonflying display kits took a back seat to flying models. By the mid-1930s 2 million flying model airplanes were being built each year, about a quarter of them powered by tiny internal combustion engines pioneered in the United States. Throughout the 1930s model builders joined clubs and competed in contests under the auspices of a variety of private and public sponsors. The competitive nature of the hobby and the functional rather than artistic principles that underlay it effectively kept female participation to a minimum. The interest in flying models had taken on an international flavor in 1927 when an English aristocrat had established a cash prize and trophy for sustained flight. In the years that followed, the Playground and Recreation Association of America ran regional flying competitions culminating in a national meet in Memphis.[24] The tournament committee featured aeronautic luminaries like Orville Wright and Charles Lindbergh, who assured model builders that they were developing practical skills. In 1949 one "hobby consultant" claimed that innovations made by hobbyists in the 1920s and 1930s "saved months of experimentation and thousands of lives" in World War II.[25] The claim seems unlikely, since the rubber-powered, paper-covered, balsa wood models had much more in common with the previous war than the subsequent one. Although an American rubber-powered plane set a world duration record of forty-three minutes in 1939, easily defeating gasoline-powered models, engine-driven airplanes were the wave of the future. By the beginning of World War II, rubber band models had disappeared from the pages of hobby magazines in favor of plans not only for constructing the planes but also for making the engines themselves.[26]

Both model ships and model airplanes were characteristic male craft hobbies. The constructed model was a testament to the skill of the builder, and the functional versions could stand in for their makers in head-to-head contests to determine dominance. Furthermore, model airplane building provided the sense that hobbyists were participating on the cutting edge of scientific advancement. Model trains, on the other hand, could claim few of these advantages. Trains were old technology, and there was almost no practical way to run them competitively, although there is one report of races on parallel sets of tracks. Trains were also much more complicated machines than either ships or planes; a really good model train required machined metal parts that were far beyond the skills and budget of most hobbyists. Nevertheless, model trains carved out a hobby niche of their own, which included elements of pure consumption, consumption modified by craft creativity and pure craft. The model train hobby, in other words, was defined by the acquired object more than the process of acquiring it and at one end of the spectrum was closer to collecting than crafting.[27]

The first model trains in the early nineteenth century were prototypes used to attract potential investors for real railroads. Crude tinplate or cast-iron push trains appeared in the 1830s, but actual model railroading began in the mid 1850s with clockwork and miniature steam locomotives. Very few hobbyists attempted to build their own locomotives, and only a few more tackled other cars. Thus model railroaders were, for the most part, consumers of somebody else's creativity. The advent of electric trains at the end of the century merely added another factory-made form to clockwork and steam-driven trains. Model railroading participated in the dominant capitalist ideology not by reproducing its values either speculatively like collectors or productively like crafters, but as consumers. Illustrations from the nineteenth and twentieth centuries feature not only factory-made trains and tracks but also manufactured accouterments such as signal lights, stations, and trestles. William Weeden, the publisher of the *Youth's Companion*, tried to subvert this consumerist bias by giving away steam-powered locomotives as an incentive for gathering subscriptions; he explained that "America is the land of the great railway kings and managers. Now every boy, owning one of these engines can become President of his own railroad."[28]

The Lionel company, which absorbed a number of earlier train makers in the 1920s, dominated the ready-made American market in the depression with its self-proclaimed "standard gauge." Buying Lionel trains was the most popular, but least impressive, way to be a railroad hobbyist. There was, in fact, a status hierarchy within the train fraternity. At the top were the comparatively few men (perhaps a hundred in 1939) who built "live steamers" from scratch. These were meticulously detailed replicas of both contemporary and historical trains pulled by steam locomotives that varied in size from a few inches to monsters that cost thousands of dollars and could haul passengers around elaborate garden setups. Of course, some of these hobbyists, like Vincent Astor who had an eighteen-hundred-foot layout on his Rhinebeck, New York, estate, hired professional model makers rather than doing any work themselves. Twenty years later, Walt Disney followed in Astor's footsteps, first in his backyard and then in the world's most elaborate model train setup, Disneyland. Somewhat less exalted than the live steamers were the modelers who replicated the external appearance of the trains, but for the sake of safety and cost substituted electric motors for steam engines. Finally, at the bottom of the pyramid were the toy modelers who bought their trains and most of their scenery ready-made and contented themselves with setting up and running their manufactured playthings.[29]

Wealthy celebrities joined common people in assembling elaborate electric train sets, and truly devoted hobbyists participated in a style that took on a collector-like compulsiveness. A San Antonio railroader is reported to have spent eighty thousand dollars on his layout, which was housed in its own one-hundred-by-two-hundred-foot shed, and a less affluent, but just as obsessive, Los Angeles railroader filled his house with tracks, spent the food budget on rolling stock, and told his wife if she did not like it she could leave. She did. Men not blessed with fortunes, and unwilling to sacrifice their marriages, could enjoy elaborate model layouts by pooling their resources and labor. Model railroad clubs involved a greater than average degree of craft activity to make the model environment, if not the models themselves. In 1937 there were at least one hundred such clubs throughout the United States, a number that would grow to more than a thousand by 1951. Model clubs provided men (women and children were permitted only on visitor days) with a place to fraternize and play with elaborate multiline systems such as the one in Milwaukee, which had more than a thousand feet of rails and two hundred cars.[30]

While Lionel and American Flyer were selling manufactured trains to millions of children and adults, slightly more ambitious crafters could assemble their railroads from kits, which had been around for twenty years. The most elaborate locomotives could take as long as three thousand hours to put together. Because observers tended to lump together everybody from the most dedicated crafter of live steam locomotives to the most passive tinplate operator, it is hard to gauge the extent of model railroading in the 1930s. One 1936 article estimated there were a quarter of a million model railroaders, but another the same year put the number at only a hundred thousand. In any case, model railroading had an element of the fad about it. Most participants bought the components ready-made and did little more than assemble them. But for the dedicated minority, model railroads provided an opportunity to exercise craft skills and find satisfaction in making their own toys.[31]

Structuring the Craft Experience

Because model railroading involved more consumption than production, schools did not sponsor the same kinds of clubs for model railroaders that they did for plane and boat builders. Schools wanted their clubs to encourage participation in pastimes that used free time productively and taught specific skills, values, or both. Crafts obviously met these requirements, and manual training programs (variously referred to as manual arts or education; industrial arts, education, or science; and sometimes simply as vocational education) were the logical source of advisers for school hobby clubs. Manual arts journals increasingly carried articles on craft hobbies, and a survey of industrial educators in Washington State found that they consistently ranked the recreational benefits of shop instruction as more important than its vocational training benefits.[32] A staff member of the Philadelphia Board of Education concluded that handicrafts offered a solution to the surplus leisure created by the depression. He advocated a highly structured program of school craft instruction, not only to keep children "out of mischief" but also to build "skills and attitudes" for the rest of their lives.[33] A junior high school shop teacher wrote, "the commandment of old may eventually be rewritten to read: 'One day shalt thou labor and do all thy work, but the rest of the week thou shalt use for thine own growth and development.' "[34]

In order to ensure that leisure time was used for "growth and development," manual training instructors extended their expertise into the general school population and from there into the students' homes. Recognizing that home workshops were an effective way to promote craft skills and reinforce values of work and creativity, manual arts teachers encouraged students and parents to set up their own shops. "Assuming an idle brain is the devil's workshop," wrote one shop teacher (once again relocating the site of Satan's mischief from the hands to the head), "we can alleviate the situation to some extent at least, by keeping the boys out of pool-rooms, taverns and other undesirable places by encouraging such a worth-while activity as provided by the home-workshop setup." Hobby writer A. Neely Hall described how an eight-year-old, overstimulated from listening to the radio, was able to recover from his nervous malady by working on models in a basement shop built by his father. The dangers of ignoring a boy's desire for a home workshop could hardly be overstated; radio addiction was the least of their problems. A junior high school instructor from Kansas warned that the parent who waited to install a home workshop until "his or her son has been shot down for highway robbery, or some similar crime, has waited too long."[35]

The shops proposed for boys could be as simple as a board clamped to a chair seat or as elaborate as a four-hundred-dollar layout of power tools that included a "drill, lathe, jig-saw, band-saw, circular saw, joiner, mortise machine, sander attachments, metal saws, files and a router," all of which was improbably described as "a small cost" shop that could be "placed in one side of the boy's room, on a back enclosed porch or in a corner of the basement." Vast arrays of power tools were rare, but drill presses, such as that on the cover of a 1933 *Home Craftsman* magazine, were not uncommon. On a different magazine cover, a boy is shown putting the final touches on a doll's bed, while his father smiles proudly around the corner. As with model building, the theme of father and son working together on shop projects was a frequent one. Fathers become interested in boys craft hobbies, explained a college professor, "and the result is a father-and-son team, which makes the shop a co-operative enterprise between the two." Although fathers pictured in do-it-yourself magazines give the impression of being middle class, there is some evidence that blue-collar sons were more likely to have home workshops than those from white-collar households.[36]

Crafts were more popular among boys than collecting, but hobbies of all kinds remained far down on boys' lists of favorite activities. Crafting's popularity was probably not helped by its ties to school classes, to potential adult vocations, and to household chores. Explaining why crafts education was necessary for schoolchildren, one supporter noted that "a handiness with tools and materials . . . can often be used to good advantage in the maintenance of the home." In fact, in 1937 a couple of industrial arts instructors published a textbook that dispensed with all the usual creative wood and metal work activities usually taught to junior high school boys and focused exclusively on "household mechanics." By teaching about plumbing, electric appliances, household masonry, maintaining windows and doors, and applied wood and metal work, the book was training handymen, not artisans or hobbyists. Teaching home maintenance to boys was not common, but it does show how the creative and practical aspects of crafts were combined in school as well as at home. Crafting a chair and stopping a faucet leak were seen as part of a continuum of male practice drawn together by their common use of heavy tools.[37]

This collapsing of the creative and the practical into a single category provided a basis for the proliferation of adult home workshops during the 1930s and for the concomitant expansion of home maintenance and improvement literature. A variety of specialized magazines catered to home handymen headed by the perennial leaders in the field, *Popular Mechanics* and *Popular Science Monthly*. *Popular Mechanics* pioneered the category before World War I and remained one of the most successful magazines for householders well into the 1950s.[38] Arch rival *Popular Science* was able to carve out a place for itself by promoting the "National Homeworkshop [*sic*] Guild." Founded in 1932 in Rockford, Illinois, as an independent voluntary association, local clubs held regular meetings for members to share ideas and discuss projects. The magazine elevated the guild to national status in 1933, claiming that it was "the best solution yet offered for the intelligent and enjoyable use of the increased leisure insured to everyone by the NRA [National Recovery Administration]." Within two years the guild had 156 clubs in forty-four states, a number that doubled by the end of the decade.[39]

The National Homeworkshop Guild represented a halfway point between the Victorian period, when a relatively few men participated in household projects as a convenient but unnecessary activity, and the 1950s, when it would become a virtual obligation for the suburban homeowner. As a formal institutionalization of workshop hobbies, the guild was evidence that work around the house was neither unexpected nor commonplace. That which is never done cannot be institutionalized and that which is ubiquitous does not have to be. In other words, by the Great Depression significant numbers of householders were working in and on their houses, but they still felt a sufficient sense of distinctiveness to join an organization of like-minded men.[40]

Class and Gender in Depression Crafts

While the economic concerns generated by the depression seem to have prompted an uptick in male craft activity, the picture for women is somewhat less clear. A number of sources mention an increased interest in sewing, but the evidence for that is mixed. On the one hand, manufacturers of paper sewing patterns added low-cost lines to their catalogs and flourished during the 1930s, an indication that women were making their own clothes to save money. On the other hand, in her magisterial history of knitting, Anne Macdonald devotes an entire chapter to "the thirties knitting craze," detailing how 10 million women took up the craft so that public conveyances, movie theaters, and college classrooms were filled with the soft click of knitting needles. Macdonald, however, makes it clear that these women were participating in a hobby fad, not substituting home production for purchased knitwear. Similarly, in an article titled "Needlework Is Definitely BACK!" *American Home* magazine claimed that an increased emphasis on the "fruitful use of leisure" and "the general trend toward more gracious ways of living" had led women to rediscover the " 'pickup' work of grandmother's workbag." The article described a variety of fancywork activities including embroidery, needlepoint, crocheting, rug hooking, and quilting, all of which were decorative and none of which could be considered money-saving.[41]

College women throughout the country may have been knitting argyle socks for their boyfriends, but they were not sewing their own clothes in any appreciable numbers. The National Retail Dry Goods Association was so concerned with the drop in yard goods and notions sales that it launched a pilot program in 1938 to revive interest in sewing among schoolgirls in San Francisco. Despite the depression, it was still apparently cheaper to buy manufactured clothes than to make them at home. A 1933 YWCA survey of one thousand "business girls" found that only 18 percent of them sewed, ranking it thirteenth on a long list of leisure activities. More women played cards, played tennis, and went dancing than sewed. And from the sewing industry's point of view, things were worse than they seemed because in terms of interest (as opposed to participation) sewing ranked even lower. A sampling of high school girls in Washington confirmed this disinclination to sew, finding that only about a quarter of them sewed in their spare time.[42]

In 1933 Needlecraft Magazine hopefully announced that women were giving up the "gay lights of some great city" and returning to "cook and sew as their mothers and grandmothers did." "Making, and oftentimes designing their wardrobes," the magazine said that these women were finding sewing " 'just loads of fun,' and a real relief from the days spent at bridge and such diversions." Except for knitting, there is, in fact, no evidence of any such trend among women who played bridge in the glow of big city lights. It is, however, true that rural women continued to sew at a much higher rate than their urban sisters. Nearly half of a survey of rural Midwestern homemakers listed sewing as a leisure activity. The actual percentage of sewing wives was probably much higher since the author of the survey noted that "it was evident that some of them were uncertain as to whether or not it should be classified in this [leisure] category," but as one respondent noted, "I am putting here because I love to sew." Purely recreational fancywork did not fare as well. The author of the survey expressed amazement that fewer than a third of the respondents did the traditional leisure needle crafts of "knitting, crocheting, hemstitching, embroidering [or] needlepoint." She suggested that "thirty years ago a study of leisure activities of farm women probably would have indicated that 'fancy work' was a hobby with practically everyone who had any leisure." Thus even among a group of women who were both poorer and more used to doing craft activities in their everyday lives, needle craft hobbies had fallen prey to passive leisure such as the radio.[43]

As they had for a hundred years, women continued to engage in traditional female handicrafts, but their numbers may have been declining, especially among working women. A small 1934 survey of eighty-seven Cincinnati teachers, three-quarters of whom were women, found that many of them collected in their spare time, but none listed crafts as a hobby. Similarly in much larger surveys, less than 6 percent of female office workers and only 10 percent of elementary school teachers engaged in arts and crafts (collecting was not included in the latter survey). When asked why they did not engage in crafting, the elementary school teachers said it was because they had never learned how to. It would seem that by the 1930s, the female tradition of passing on craft skills from mother to daughter had largely disappeared. Even among farm women only 21 percent of a Midwestern sample listed handicrafts as a hobby. This was, to be sure, a rate at least twice that of female white-collar workers but still a very modest minority of all the women surveyed.[44]

Crafts, other than textiles for women and woodworking for men, were losing their gender identity. Advocates who were trying to overcome the feminine image of crafting took pains to degender even those books whose projects were clearly aimed at women. For example, two books, the gendered *Handicraft for Girls* and the neutral *Handicrafts as a Hobby* contained almost identical chapters on stenciling, papier-mâché, party decorations, textile crafts, small metal crafts, basket making, and leather working, but none on needle fancywork. Books increasingly used gender-neutral language and pictures so as not to alienate potential readers of either sex. By the same token, some general craft books aimed primarily at males also avoided gender-specific language.[45] The greater willingness of men and women to undertake crafts traditionally identified with the opposite sex was picked up by *Popular Science*, which ran articles showing men making metal, resin, and celluloid plastic jewelry, doing leather work, and macramé, although it drew the line at anything involving sewing. It illustrated stories on woodcarving with women, and showed both men and women carving linoleum printing blocks. Craft supply houses and popular magazines were also evenhanded in their presentation of projects. While textile weaving remained a feminine pastime, basket weaving and light wood projects were either shown without models or with models of both sexes, and fifty years after it started, fret sawing remained a hobby for both men and women.[46]

The eroding division between men's and women's crafts, along with falling wages and unemployment, contributed to increased female participation in household improvement. While a housewife might not have thought twice about bringing a broken appliance to the repair shop or calling the plumber to fix a leak a decade earlier, the financial exigencies of the depression prompted a rash of how-to-fix-it articles for women. Yet the very language of female participation was an explicit acknowledgment that home maintenance and repair was a male world. Women who did their own repairs continuously emphasized that their skills freed them from dependence on men. In 1936, when Martha Wirt Davis instructed women how to hammer a nail—and how *not* to hammer a screw, she stressed convenience and pride, not cost savings. Her husband did not have time to fix a burned out iron cord and the electrician she called could not make it until much later in the day, so she decided to learn how to do repairs herself. She discovered that "there is quite a bit of satisfaction in being able to fix one's own cords, open stubborn windows, unstop stopped-up sinks, put new washers in leaky faucets or replace burned-out fuses without calling for male assistance."[47]

A smattering of schools picked up the theme of female independence and began to offer exclusively girls shop classes in the mid-1930s. In 1938 J. C. Woodin published what appears to be the first textbook on home mechanics for girls. He explained that he hoped to "allow housewives to deal with minor, everyday problems without having to call professional repairmen or wait for their husbands to come home." He wanted to instill them with "that feeling of accomplishment, which comes with work well done, and of pride in the ability to do the things which most women have to depend on men to do for them." The vocabulary of empowerment and the promise of independence from men confirms the andric nature of home repair. Empowerment and freedom were not exclusively male feelings, but experiencing them was part of feeling free from males and by implication feeling male-like.[48]

"If You Make It, She'll Paint It," proclaimed a headline in the *Home Craftsman*. Since "the shadow of a woman influences every man in his workshop," said the article somewhat ominously, why not bring her as well as her ideas into the workshop (see fig. 8.1). To the extent that workshops had become an exclusively male sanctum, inviting women into the shop would undermine the masculine meaning of the work. As the headline indicated, however, wives were not being invited to participate in the actual construction of projects, simply to select and apply color—a job especially suited for them since "women come equipped that way."[49]

For the workshop to retain its gender-enhancing mystique it had to remain not only a male realm but a voluntary one as well. In good times craftsmanship was a sign of manly self reliance, but in bad times it could be a sign of economic impotence. Thus workshop advocates went out of their way to describe wealthy do-it-yourselfers who were motivated by pleasure not necessity. The *New York Times* made a point of commenting on doctors, lawyers, and bankers who rolled up their sleeves in workshops that sometimes took up large portions of their homes. Similarly, the Leisure League of America explained that "tucked away in a closet of one of the swankiest of New York's apartment hotels there happens to be a woodworker's bench, a power lathe and an amazing assortment of hand tools ready, at a moment's notice, to make the sawdust fly!"[50] (See fig. 8.2.)

Hard data on home handicrafts are scarce, but scattered surveys and anecdotal evidence present a consistent, if incomplete, picture of a moderately popular hobby that indeed drew from all classes but had a special attraction for workers who already possessed manual skills. When more

If You Make It
She'll Paint It!

IT'S probably true that the shadow of a man influences every purchase a woman makes, and it is just as likely that the shadow of a woman influences every man in his workshop. If so, why not bring this "shadow" into the shop occasionally and let her paint the projects you make? You can trust her to select suitable color combinations—women come equipped that way. She'll enjoy the work because it gives her a chance to vent her artistic impulses; she'll share your work with enthusiasm and free you to make other projects. And the best reason of all is that she, too, needs the relaxation she'll find in her new hobby. It'll do you good to share your hobby and share The Home Craftsman.

FIGURE 8.1 Women in the depression were invited into the man's workshop to exercise their special skills with paints and brushes. (Reprinted from "If You Make It She'll Paint It!" *Home Craftsman* 2 [March–April 1933]: inside back cover.)

than two hundred adults in Greeley, Colorado, were asked what they did in their leisure time, gardening was listed first, but "home workshop" came in second. Whereas gardening was more-or-less equally divided by gender and class, all of the home crafters were men, and blue-collar workers outnumbered white-collar workers by four to one. Blue-collar workers were more likely to have manual skills, but certain white-collar jobs also predisposed workers toward craft hobbies. A description of America's first all-male hobby show stressed that "whether the exhibitor was a surgeon or a pipe-fitter, a contractor or a silk-hose maker, a beer baron or a minister, each had a long-concealed desire to rise from the rank of the 'handy man

FIGURE 8.2 Men without a basement or garage were told they could shoehorn a
shop into an apartment closet. (Reprinted from *Giant Home Workshop Manual*
[New York: Popular Science Publishing, 1941]: 124.)

around the house' to a publicly acknowledged creator of beauty." While
probably rhetorical rather than factual, the author's choice of white-collar
professions was telling. She listed surgeons, contractors, textile manufacturers, beer barons, and ministers; all but the minister would have likely
been familiar with tools and their application. In addition to whatever ideological reinforcement these crafters may have obtained from their hobby,
they were also participating in a more conventional form of leisure

spillover; they were practicing the same physical skills off the job that they had developed on it.[51]

An engineer at the General Electric research laboratory argued, in a classically compensatory vein, that "the average engineer turns to something other than engineering to occupy his spare time." Indeed, most of the engineers who answered his questionnaire listed sports as their favorite pastimes, but said the researcher, when he was not doing sports, the average engineer was down in his cellar "in a pitch-dark cubby-hole over in a corner, developing pictures; or, just as likely, he is in front of a whirling lathe, drillpress, or buzz saw . . . creating a piece of furniture that will call for real craftsmanship, or perfecting a gadget for putting out the cat and answering inconsequential telephone calls after he has retired." In fact, more than half of those responding to his questionnaire had active home workshops. In other words, the author's own evidence belied his conclusion. Although he instinctively believed that engineers would not do engineering in their spare time, he demonstrated that more than half of them did precisely that.[52]

Three other surveys from the depression era confirm this pattern of skills spillover into home workshops. One found that, regardless of income, men who participated in "constructional" work were twice as likely as those men who did nonconstructional work to have a craft hobby. A second, rather haphazard, survey of Iowans with home workshops again found that almost half used white-collar or blue-collar manual skills at their regular jobs. Finally, a survey of the members of the National Home-workshop Guild found that at least 56 percent of the 631 men (and 2 women) who replied had jobs in which they worked with their hands. This figure is conservative since it does not include a large number of men who listed themselves as "teachers" many of whom were probably industrial education instructors. Thus it seems reasonable to conclude that home crafts during the depression favored manual skill over class as a predictor of participation. The people most likely to be home crafters were men who used tools on the job, from white-collar engineers and doctors to blue-collar craftsmen.[53]

Preserving and Improving the Home

Rural home dwellers, whether they were farmers or service workers, operated in a culture where tool use was taken for granted as, by extension, was work around the house. A survey in rural Colorado found that families spent very little money on home improvement and upkeep since most of such work was done by the husbands. "The father of the family is able to plaster, paint, calsomine, put in shelves, electric outlets, and build additional rooms as finances permit," noted the author. Then, indicating that do-it-yourself had much of the same meaning for rural dwellers as it did for suburbanites, he concluded, "this constitutes a summer leisure activity." Except for the chapters dealing specifically with agricultural matters, how-to books for farmers were remarkably similar to those for suburban homeowners. Even many of the homemade furniture and gadgets suggested by rural life advisers were interchangeable with those that appeared in popular home mechanics magazines.[54]

The similarity between rural and suburban do-it-yourself reflected a common desire for cost savings and a sense of satisfaction. "I am sitting on a home-made chair," wrote one author, and "the greatest reward coming out of this piece of work was the fun of making it with my own hands." However, he went on to point out that there was also "a dollar-and-cents moral to be drawn" since it cost him less than a commercially produced chair.[55] Underlying the claims of pride and practicality was a poignant sense of self-reliance; if a man could take care of his own home and build his own furniture, he had special resources with which to face the vicissitudes of life. Although the depression drove down the price of craftsmen, making professional home improvement cheap, insecurity made even employed people more cost conscious. "Work cannot be left to a mechanic without risk of having a small job develop into a large one, or of being overcharged," wrote the author of a do-it-yourself manual in 1934. You pay a handyman a $1.50 to install a $3.00 flower box and then pay another $2.00 six months later to correct the work of the first one, when you could have done it yourself for a dollar's worth of wood, explained another.[56]

The same feelings that led homeowners to believe hired help was too expensive, even when it was cheaper, prompted a growing stress on the corruptibility of the physical environment; everything, jobs and homes alike, was more precarious. "Contrary to popular belief," warned *House and Garden*, "houses don't stand still. They either march forward or they slip back." Houses, like cars, needed to be maintained; the work could be done professionally if necessary but would be much more satisfying if done by the owner himself. The quirky household hints and oddball projects that had established the home as a hobby in the 1920s kept appearing in how-to magazines—where else could one learn how to dig a planting hole with dynamite or make a door-closer from an automobile water pump?[57] The 1930s, however, subordinated novelty to a more conservative sense of the household workshop as a redoubt where the beleaguered homeowner could exercise those masculine skills that enabled him to keep a very dangerous world at bay. In times of economic instability, money and position were transient, but practical skills gave one a sense of survivability. "If you can cook a meal, sew on a button and use a saw and hammer, you can face almost any situation," observed one atypically androgynous do-it-yourselfer; "if you can't do these things, you may be a railroad president, but you are not a completely self-reliant human being."[58]

The sense of protectiveness that depression-era householders developed toward their homes gave rise to a new book genre that signaled the maturation of household repair and maintenance as a distinct subset of home-based shop work. The pioneer book in this field was C. T. Schaefer's *Handy Man's Handbook*, published in 1931 by Harper and Brothers, which proclaimed itself to be "the first attempt to present all of the fundamental [repair and maintenance] information in a single volume, carefully arranged for instant reference." Schaefer's book differed from the usual hybrid of creative furnishing projects and household maintenance hints by focusing almost exclusively on home care. It explained how to maintain woodwork, hinges and locks, ceilings, walls, floors, plumbing and wiring, and some household appliances. The book's popularity spawned a clone from rival publisher Little, Brown, and by the beginning of World War II, home repair books and home craft books had become entirely distinct categories.[59]

The division of do-it-yourself books into separate maintenance and craft genres was not an indication of an equivalent distinction in the minds of men. Most do-it-yourselfers continued to collapse both kinds of activities into a single category. The National Homeworkshop Guild did not distinguish between small projects and large, between work in the house or on it, or between the creative and the routine. The home projects it promoted shared only the use of heavy tools. When asked what they did in their workshops, 94 percent of the guild respondents said they used it for "recreation." At the same time, however, 73 percent said they used it for "home repairs." The survey did not ask, and there is no way to know, whether the respondents perceived recreation activities and repair activities as separate, but given the way household repair, maintenance, and improvement suggestions appeared side by side with constructive projects in the literature, there is no reason to assume that the householders themselves made much of a distinction. The two types of activity were connected by the kind of tools used to do them and by the similarity they held to paid labor. "The features incorporated into this book," promised the author of the very first home-care manual in 1931, "should prove particularly valuable to the man who has his own workshop and makes a hobby of woodworking and home maintenance." Not only did the author link woodworking and home maintenance to the workshop, but he also labeled them parts of the same hobby. Working at home with heavy tools could be either leisure or a chore. In fact, keeping that distinction a bit blurry meant that men could scrape and paint peeling exteriors with at least some of the same sense of satisfaction as building a coffee table.[60]

Men and boys alike resonated to the siren song of heavy tools. Magazines and books that gave instructions on what tools to buy, how to use them, and what to make with them proliferated during the depression. Even though surveys indicated a relatively low participation rate, reading about craft technology appears to have surpassed athletics, sex, and violence in its attractiveness to young men. Two separate surveys found that *Popular Science* and *Popular Mechanics* were the favorite reading material of adolescent boys, exceeding both sports and pulp fiction magazines. These magazines set the agenda for 1930s craft activity. They carried a variety of articles on crafts projects, many of which were regularly anthologized in books called "manuals" and "cyclopedias." Like the magazines from which they were excerpted, these books contained an eclectic cross-section of articles ranging from instructions on homemade tools and house maintenance tips to plans for both simple and elaborate workshop projects.[61] On the simple side, for example, *Popular Science* published plans for rough shelves for canned goods and crude bins for potatoes to go in the basement. On the elaborate side, it also printed plans for homemade venetian blinds, which required cutting slats, sewing tapes, and constructing pulley mechanisms.[62]

Less ambitious homeowners could assemble furniture kits, modernize furniture by stripping it of decorations, or make box and barrel furniture, which was experiencing something of a renaissance (see fig. 8.3).[63] Slightly more adventuresome crafters could turn to a second category of depression-era do-it-yourself publications, the woodworking manual, which focused on the male hobby of furniture making, although the books emphasized relatively simple projects.[64] These easy-to-make project books and articles targeted men with shops, the most dedicated segment of the craft fraternity. Although the projects may not have been fine cabinetmaking, they were exercises that produced minor trophies that attested to a certain mastery of tools. Separate surveys of both boys and men with shops, found that they made small household items such as shelves, bowls, and stools most often, followed in popularity by models. Male shop owners had no interest in designing the items they built; for them the pleasure was in the construction. They said they wanted better plans, tools, and materials so they could exercise their manual skills, and they rejected labor-saving items such as precut furniture kits.[65] In response to this demand for plans they could execute at home, a shop teacher from New Jersey started the first syndicated newspaper column of woodworking plans in the mid-1930s.[66]

BUILDING A

Barrel Chair

a quaint, useful, and very inexpensive piece of furniture

FIGURE 8.3 Barrel chairs, popular homemade furniture since the Victorian period, were still being promoted on the eve of World War II. (Reprinted from *Giant Home Workshop Manual* [New York: Popular Science Publishing, 1941]: 67.)

The more serious, but nonexpert, craft hobbyist found popular style coming to his rescue once more. Except for outdoor furniture, such as the Adirondack chair, arts and crafts style furniture disappeared completely in the depression. Colonial furniture, however, remained popular. When the price of good furniture rose beyond his budget, H. Clay Tate decided he could make it himself (see fig. 8.4). He explained that he and his wife "selected Early American as our choice because of its beauty and simplicity, and also because it lends itself well to the home craftsman's equipment and ability." Tate did not even own any tools when he made this decision, but he had taken manual training in high school and that was enough to give him the confidence that he could build his own colonial furniture.[67] Tate's task (or perhaps his craftsman's conscience) may have been eased somewhat as manual training teachers reluctantly began to give hobbyists permission to use

I made my own furniture

FIGURE 8.4 Illustration of simple homemade colonial-style furniture perennially popular among craft hobbyists. (Reprinted from Clay H. Tate, "I Made My Own Furniture," *American Home* 17 [May 1937]: 58.)

substitutes for traditional joinery. "Although the construction shown on the working-drawings is to be strongly recommended," conceded one teacher-author, "it is possible for the beginner to do a good job by using wood-screws and nails, with a good glued joint in place of the mortise-and-tenon or dowel type of joining." However, many of the early American plans published during the 1930s still assumed that the crafter could in fact execute a mortise and tenon joint and could turn spindles and legs on a lathe as well.[68]

When a self-declared book of "Simple Colonial Furniture" required a lathe for almost every piece, the situation was clearly ripe for some other style, which could be made without heavy power tools but would be more acceptable than disguised crates and kegs. The need was met by the arrival of "modern" furniture, a new style that, like arts and crafts furniture, had the advantage of using simple forms and simple joints, but was neither stylistically passé like mission nor historically old-fashioned like early American (see fig. 8.5). No one was quite sure what to call modern furniture; "modern," "modernistic," "modernage," "modern manner," and "skyscraper" (although, not

FIGURE 8.5 "Skyscraper-style" modern furniture featured in a home workshop plan book could be made with simple joints that were nailed together. (Reprinted from Arthur Wakeling, *Home Workshop Manual* [New York: Popular Science Publishing, 1930], 46.)

"deco") were all used by designers of do-it-yourself plans. No matter what its name, its benefits for the home crafter were obvious. "Above all, modernistic furniture is simple in construction," promised *Popular Science* editor Arthur Wakeling in 1930, "Every home worker, if he has good designs to follow, can build decorative modern pieces quickly, easily, and inexpensively."[69] Like mission furniture, modern furniture had no ornate decoration or curves, but unlike mission furniture, which required mortise and tenon joints, modern furniture used case work construction. Its joints could be butted and held together with glue and screws or even nails. By the end of the depression, modern furniture designs had become a mainstay of popular do-it-yourself magazines often appearing side by side with simpler colonial pieces.[70]

Shops and Tools

Whether they were fixing household appliances, storing tools for home maintenance, or making furniture, men in the 1930s took it for granted that they would operate out of a home workshop that was their special space. "The next time you have a few spare minutes that need not be spent in your garden," suggested *Better Homes and Gardens* in 1931, "step into your home workshop and make a number of corn handles and bonfire forks so you will be prepared for the next picnic." The projects described would have not have taken much time, much skill, or many tools. Nevertheless, the author matter-of-factly assumed that the homeowner could step into his home workshop to carry them out. By 1935 writers and hobbyists regularly referred to "workshop fever" and "shopmania," using the same sorts of disease metaphors previously reserved for collecting.[71]

Plans for workshops ranged from grandiose to modest workbench-cabinets that could be tucked away into a corner of the garage or basement. The Leisure League of America suggested that basements were probably the most practical location, but the attic was a possible alternative, if one did not mind carrying a ten-foot plank through the house and up the stairs. The garage could be used, although most garages were rather modest affairs recently constructed to hold the 1920s generation of low-cost cars. Several surveys indicate that two-thirds or more of all shops were located in basements, with garages coming in a very distant second.[72] The basement's popularity grew as heating systems changed. Basements had been ceded to men in the teens because they were filled with dust from the coal bin and ashes from the coal furnace, which it was the husband's job to tend. With the advent of gas and oil furnaces in the 1930s, "the dingy, dirty cellars of former times are passing," noted *The Householder's Complete Handbook*, and women as well as men began to have plans for the basement. "If a man has the slightest inclination toward a hammer and saw," warned Julian Starr, "he should resist all dulcet-toned suggestions that he surrender his basement or any considerable portion of it to a 'rumpus room.' " More than 600,000 people in six cities visited "Castles Underground—The Cellar Reborn," a furnace company exhibit that showed how basements could be transformed into playrooms, dens, studios, and of course, workshops.[73]

Basement workshops were tokens of the husband's new role as handyman. What had been convenient but voluntary householder incursions into the realm of professional craftsmen were becoming expected, if not yet required, exercises in manual competence. What was once a hobby of small creative projects was now also a hobby of maintenance and repair. The financial exigencies of the 1930s cemented the trends brought about by the suburban expansion of the 1920s and made do-it-yourself a common component of middle-class male activity. *Homo faber* had returned to the cave. It was now in his basement and contained a workbench that allowed the middle-class homeowner to reintegrate the meaning of work. While he might be limited to more routine or intellectual production on the job, now, like his forefathers, he could produce with his hands at home at a *work*bench in a *work*shop. These terms were not mere anachronisms; they continued to express the sense that using tools to make and repair things was man's work even while it was his leisure. Men and tools were bound in a definitional loop; to be a man one used the tools, and using the tools made one a man.

Romantics could wax rhapsodic about old saws and planes that retained a "residue of the merit" of their artisan owners, but traditional tools were giving ground to power tools as emblems of manliness. As early as 1929 *Popular Science* home workshop editor Arthur Wakeling assumed that in addition to lathes, one could find "electric drills and complete motorized home workshop outfits . . . in any amateur shop that pretends to be up-to-date and complete." Wakeling was premature, but power was coming. A "tremendous amount of light-power equipment has been sold to the layman for the home work-shop," noted one writer, and another said that power tools for home use were "a depression baby."[74] If so, it was a small baby whose cost was high. A medium-price motor-driven jigsaw, drill press, or lathe, designed and built for hobbyists and sold in department stores, cost about twenty dollars. This was 2 to 3 percent of the average gross income, a substantial investment by any reckoning. Nevertheless, the Delta company, which had produced the very first home power tool in 1924, increased its sales every year through the depression. In 1933 Delta published a thirty-two-page magazine of testimonials from hobbyists almost all of whom "licked 'Old Man Depression' " by gaining health, happiness, and income with the firm's power tools.[75]

By the beginning of World War II, shop teachers had begun to encourage boys to acquire their own power tools, including "lathes and lathe tools; band, jig, and circular saws; . . . drill presses; bench grinders; shapers, and the like" (see fig. 8.6). Boys and men unable to afford the high tariff for commer-

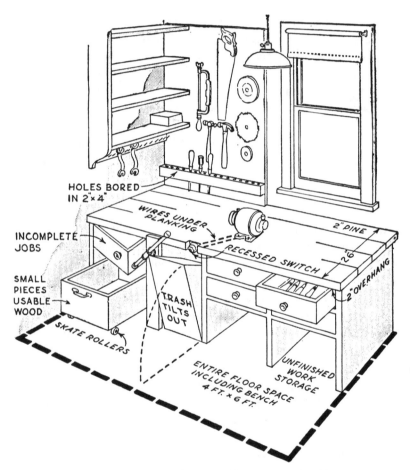

Bench with space for small motorized home workshop outfit in which the separate units are driven by one motor and a countershaft

FIGURE 8.6 Depression-era plans for a home workshop include built-in electric motor that could be used to drive a circular saw, a lathe, a jointer, and a grinder. (Reprinted from *Amateur Craftsman's Cyclopedia* [New York: Popular Science Publishing, 1937], 247.)

cial power tools could make their own from plans in the popular technology magazines. *Popular Mechanics*, for example, published make-it-yourself plans for bandsaws, table saws, lathes, shapers, grinders, and drill presses, which could be assembled, in the case of a bandsaw, from "standard iron-pipe fittings, two discarded model-T Ford front wheels, a single piston from the same car, and a few other pieces of scrap materials," plus a motor that had to be purchased.[76]

Data on the extent of power tool use by amateurs are contradictory. One survey of home workshops in Lima, Ohio, in 1935 found that significantly fewer than half had any power equipment at all—and much of that was homemade. On the other hand, a poll the same year of the more serious craftsmen who had joined the National Homeworkshop Guild determined that almost two-thirds of them had some sort of electrically driven tool, most commonly a lathe and circular saw. Finally, a small survey in Ohio at the end of the decade found that about a third of home workshops had a circular saw or a wood lathe and about a quarter had a jigsaw or drill press. It was unusual, then as now, to find a home workshop with a full spectrum of power tools, but it seems fair to say that a fully equipped electric workshop was the dream of serious amateurs. When one magazine printed an illustration of what it called a "typical" power-driven basement workshop in 1937, it showed the shop of Milwaukee industrialist Louis Allis. Like the average-Joe, Allis's workshop retreat was in his basement. He is pictured working at his drill press while his son uses an electric scroll saw (see fig. 8.7). While he might have been a millionaire manufacturer of electric motors, Allis was also a craftsman participating in the democratic fraternity of home-based artisans, along with "bank and industrial executives, opera and movie stars, salesmen, professional men, mechanics and laborers," all of whom were numbered "among the ranks of the home shop operators."[77]

The depression did not radically change the nature of home crafts, but it did focus attention on the economic implications of craft activity. For the most part, the fact that crafts could be substituted for purchased objects or could themselves be sold to others emphasized the close connection between a handicraft hobby and a craft business. At the same time, however, there was an undercurrent of disquiet with the explicit economic benefits of home craft work, especially in the area of household repair and improvement. It was all very well and good to do things around the house that had market value, but if those activities were the result of economic problems, then they were not voluntary, and if they were not voluntary then they were not leisure.

The increased ambivalence in the meaning of crafts did not deter participation during the 1930s. On the contrary, public and private agencies pro-

TYPICAL is this basement workshop of Louis Allis, Milwaukee electric motor manufacturer, equipped with small lathes, drill presses, saws, and other power and hand tools. Photo courtesy Delta Mfg. Co., Milwaukee

FIGURE 8.7 Milwaukee industrialist Louis Allis shares his "typical" basement workshop with his son in 1937. (From "Millions in Power Tools for Craftsman Hobbies," *Steel* 100 [May 17, 1937]: 28. Photo courtesy Delta International Machinery Corporation.)

moted crafts, along with other hobbies, as the perfect way to occupy surplus leisure time. The net effect of the boom in jigsawing, model building, and increased home improvement was to blur the line between work and hobbies and thus acknowledge even more prominently the special role of hobbies in preserving work values during times when work itself was at risk.

9   Kits: Assembly as Craft

Hobbies lost their high profile with the end of the depression. The danger of idleness that came with forced leisure disappeared in the high-employment economy of World War II. With jobs so widely available, the work ethic seemed safer and authorities were less concerned with promoting productive leisure. The war did, however, erode gender distinctions in the area of household repair and maintenance when it forced large numbers of women to take up those heavy tools they had always avoided. Although that change was, for the most part, temporary, it gave women a new appreciation of the role of home handyman and helped set the stage for a more cooperative postwar approach to household maintenance. It also further reduced gender distinctions in home hobby crafts in part by expanding the use of kits that took even less skill to complete than their prewar antecedents. Wartime kits, used for both recreation and therapy, were more gender neutral than earlier craft kits, and their continued production in the late forties and fifties provided opportunities for both sexes and all ages to experience the sense of accomplishment that had previously been reserved for people who had mastered fairly technical skills.

The cost-saving rationale for do-it-yourself repair and maintenance disappeared with the end of the depression, but the war brought shortages of products and professional craftsmen that once more threw homeowners back onto their own resources. The "possibility of being able to take up the telephone and call in a service man to do minor repairs dwindled to the vanishing point," observed the *New York Times* in 1943. In a pictorial feature on how to choose and use basic hand tools, *Better Homes and Gardens* explained that "the average family (which, before the war, called in the plumber or carpenter to make small repairs) is up against the same manpower shortages that have the Boeings and the Henry Kaisers in a fret." The article concluded with calculated evenhandedness, "it's up to the most dexterous member of the household to be Mr. or Mrs. Fix-it." As long as there was a man in the house, both he and his wife took it for granted that she would set the agenda but that he would do the heavier work. Thus the illustrator for a

1942 article in *Parents' Magazine* showed the wife directing her husband's use of heavy tools in four pictures, but doing light work herself in only one. "No matter how punk a carpenter you are, you can build anything . . . if your WIFE wants it badly enough," observed a reluctant household carpenter in 1942.[1]

The theory of male dominance over home maintenance and improvement remained unchallenged through the war years, but the absence of men forced acknowledgment that women too could use tools around the house, if only in an emergency capacity. "Womenfolk," noted a female author in 1945, "are the temporary guardians of the menfolk's precious supply of tools." Engineer S. S. Pheiffer confirmed the continuation of male hegemony over tools when he complained in 1944 that his wife thought he should be able to fix anything around the house, which he could not. He warned his readers, "Don't let an appealing, helpless look throw you. . . . Remember that a woman can repair almost anything—given time and a hairpin." Pheiffer's jocular remarks about female mechanical competence were not meant to be taken too seriously, but hobby writer and handyman Earnest Elmo Calkins was quite sincere in 1943 when he urged homeowners to undertake their own electrical and plumbing repairs. Although Calkins's prose and the accompanying illustrations appear to be aimed at men, he is careful to point out that "half the ills plumbing and electric wiring are heir to can be cured with not much more skill than it takes to darn a sock." His use of a sewing analogy was meant as encouragement to his female readers who, he noted, were being taught how to make such repairs in classes "sponsored by the very concerns that once preached the doctrine of consumptionism and obsolescence: the plumbing manufacturers and the power companies."[2]

Since doing it yourself was often the only way to get anything done during the war, women took on a greater share of household maintenance, both in conjunction with their husbands and by themselves. Examples of them doing heavy work such as putting in a parking area and refinishing a basement began to appear, although there was still a certain amount of ambivalence in the idea of women doing men's work. When Rachel McKinley Bushong wrote an inspirational (as opposed to an instructional) article in the *American Home* that described how she painted walls and made furniture, the cartoon illustrations showed a woman hammering and sawing with much less competence than the determined self-taught do-it-yourselfer of the text. The *Woman's Home Companion* described the frustration of "Betty Grey," a homemaker whose vacuum cleaner stopped. Unable to get competent repairs or replacement parts, she reverted to hand cleaning and announced, "Every time I take a lick at a carpet with my broom, I'll think, 'This is for Hitler,' and, 'That is for Tojo.' "[3]

Most advisers, however, had little use for female impuissance and urged women to fix it themselves. Sabina Ormsby Dean remembered being embarrassed as a girl by her mother who made her own window screens and installed her own plumbing. But when the war came and women every-where were forced to learn the skills she had grown up with, she could boast in the title of a 1943 article, "It Didn't Take a War to Make a Carpenter Out of Mother." A variety of organizations set up adult education classes for women during the war so they could nurse their ailing homes and appli-ances for the duration. The YWCA, the U.S. Extension Service, and espe-cially the American Women's Voluntary Services (a private wartime support organization) held classes to teach women to change fuses, splice wires, trou-bleshoot appliances, paint, plumb, and do simple wood repairs. "Every woman her own handyman!" proclaimed one instructional article. Only rarely did one find a traditional reference to the woman as instigator but not participant in household improvement—and even then she might be vul-nerable to her husband's uniquely wartime response: "How can you say such things when you are a riveter?"[4]

Hobby crafts retreated in the face of high employment and reduced leisure time but continued to be recommended as relief for harried wartime desk workers. "Nature intended that man should live by the use of his hands," declared Chicago's superintendent of schools, but "civilization dic-tates that many men and women must live by the use of their brains." Invok-ing the classic assumption that leisure should balance work and be produc-tive at the same time, he explained that "psychologist and psychiatrist fre-quently prescribe that office workers and professional people devote some of their time to craftwork in order to relieve nervous tension."[5]

The psychological benefits of handicrafts received their biggest wartime boost not from high-strung office workers but from occupational therapy for wounded servicemen. Occupational therapy had been successfully used in the rehabilitation of soldiers from World War I, first in England and Canada and then in the United States. In early 1943 the Arts and Skills Project of the American Red Cross Hospital Recreation Corps changed from a way to occupy long hospital days to a coordinated program with doctors and profes-sional therapists seeking to rehabilitate specific physical and psychological abilities. Wounded servicemen were instructed in various forms of art, wood-working, leather craft, metal craft, basket weaving, ceramics, and also in what had been the essentially female crafts of weaving and macramé. In the postwar period, Hadassah, the women's Zionist organization, adopted craft rehabilitation for its hospitals in Palestine, and sanitariums in the United States embraced the technique for both physical and mental rehabilitation. Therapists for academically retarded students and teachers of emotionally disturbed adults praised crafting as a way to rehabilitate people who were "uninterested in life and not able to come to grips with their daily problems."[6]

It stood to reason that if the worklike elements of crafts could be used to heal the infirm, then the hobby could also be used prophylactically to forestall the onset of unwanted attitudes and behavior. So just a month after the war ended, the navy launched a servicewide campaign to encourage hobbies among sailors. Shore bases and ships created craft centers where sailors could partake in thirty-seven official craft hobbies, which read like a catalog of traditional handicrafts. Needle crafts were missing, but weaving, knotting, and braiding were included, as were all forms of woodworking, model building, metal work, and decorative crafts such as pottery, leather craft, and plastics. Naval officers who supported the craft initiative claimed that handicrafts would lead to happier sailors because "the navy believes that an individual must be busy before he can be happy." The naval chief of personnel fell back on his own version of the classic bromide: "An idle man's brain is the devil's workshop," and he agreed with other officers who said, "Every sailor whose interest is snared by hobby crafts should be one less problem for the navy."[7]

Whether as rehabilitation or as recreation, handicrafts in the armed forces contributed to a growing degendering of the hobby. World War II servicemen and women regularly made handicrafts that crossed gender boundaries. Women had always made items for men as gifts, as had men for women. Now, however, each sex seemed willing to use "other-gender" tools especially on new materials that were gender-free. When the army held an exhibition of GI crafts at New York's Metropolitan Museum of Art in 1945, entries came both from wounded soldiers doing occupational therapy and from those awaiting deactivation. One of the winners was a member of the Women's Army Corps who carved a wooden chess set. Four of the other winners, three men and a woman, made projects out of plastic. Bakelite blanks, a form of cast resin, were widely distributed in occupational therapy kits that also included plans and tools. When the military market dried up, the kit manufacturer switched to the civilian market adding Lucite and Plexiglas (both forms of transparent thermoplastic) to his line. Salvaged Plexiglas bubble-windows from warplanes had been used by both men and women to make jewelry, candlesticks, cigarette cases, and letter openers toward the end of the war. Even though the plastics were shaped with woodworking tools, they had a large following among servicewomen and service wives, apparently because the newness of the medium neutered it and because its shiny transparent nature made it a natural for decorative craft items.[8]

The Decline of Fancywork

When the war ended Rosie the riveter returned to her home and so did her GI husband and, from the perspective of household handicrafts, both of them had been transformed by their experiences. Historians of the family often characterize gender roles in the 1950s as "neo-Victorian," and for good reason. The crises of the 1930s and 1940s made a husband at work and a wife at home with their children an extremely attractive prospect. Three million women left the labor force in the year after the war, and gave birth at a rate 20 percent greater than during the war years. The baby boom and suburbanization of the GI generation created an environment that would, at first blush, seem conducive to a surge in craft activity. Typical suburban wives did not work, and "the vacuum cleaner, the dryer, the dishwasher and dispose-all made a mockery of Mary's housework," wrote John Keats in his 1956 exposé of suburban life, *The Crack in the Picture Window*. The appliances "left her with at least two more hours each day to enjoy the benefits of life in Rolling Knolls." Keats wondered, "what the hell do they do with this time?" Mary sought the advice of a psychiatrist who asked, "have you considered a hobby? How would you like to do some ceramics?" The neo-Victorian housewife was guided to the classic Victorian solution to the ennui brought on by excess leisure. In the words of a home economics professor, "we garden away our troubles, paint the answers to our problems, or stitch out the perplexities of life."[9]

However, women who had persevered through the depression and war were not about to take up fancywork as a solution to their problems. Data indicate that decorative handicrafts, which had been in decline since 1900, continued their downward slide after the war. Although a survey of retired women teachers found more than 80 percent of them sewed for a hobby, less than 10 percent did other forms of crafts. At the other end of the age spectrum, three surveys found both low interest and low participation in handicraft activities among high school students. Fewer schools, municipalities, and businesses sponsored hobby shows and classes. Men and boys, however, continued to engage in woodworking, because it was directly connected to home improvement, and home improvement became the new focus of crafts for both sexes. In her cultural history of Levittown, Barbara Kelly notes a similarity between the handwork plans in the 1950s and those in the Victorian period. Kelly's recognition of the importance of craft hobbies in postwar suburbia is well taken, although she questions the need for make-work to fill spare time. Many of the crafts she cites, however, were not make-work at all; they were home environment projects, such as refinishing the basement, that had little in common with nineteenth-century decorative handicrafts. While the housewife's preoccupation with artistic crafting was a shadow of its former self, she was moving out into more substantial kinds of craft activity.[10]

The general decline in decorative crafts did not daunt handicraft advocates, who continued to promote them as a way to earn extra money. It was an uphill battle. People may have been receptive to homemade items during the financial crunch of the depression and the material shortages of the war, but not in the materialist suburban culture of the 1950s. The only sure way to earn money from hobby crafts after the war was to sell supplies to other crafters. Hobby shops, a virtually unknown category before the war, became quite common, even in relatively small towns. Hobby shops sold craft materials such as plastic lace, unpainted china, candle wax, and small sheets of metal, often in the form of kits, but crafts made from kits were even less desirable than traditional fancywork. Charitable groups, like the children in a Wisconsin Sunday school, could still sell cutting boards, bird houses, and other simple items at craft fairs, but even these outlets were disappearing. *Profitable Hobbies* magazine, which obviously had a vested interest in promoting craft fairs, was nevertheless reduced to advising churches to charge admission to fairs where hobbies were displayed but no crafts were sold. How many people, after all, would want to buy somebody else's plastic model?[11]

Simpler modern styles and readily available power tools meant that more-serious crafters could dream of literally turning their workshops into miniature factories, if they could find customers. *Profitable Hobbies* magazine, which published between 1946 and 1957, was a major proponent of erasing the line between avocation and vocation. There are no data on how many hobbyists tried to sell their crafts or how successful they may have been, but a flurry of books and articles claimed, on the basis of anecdotal evidence, that money could be made. Encouraged in some cases by state programs, rural and small town residents who made salable items in their spare time had some success marketing them through local outlets. For example, local crafters in Pass Christian, Mississippi, turned their annual Christmas bazaar into a year-round shop in 1956, and a similar store in Hamilton, Ohio, sold foodstuffs and crafts made by more than 150 people. These programs, like the women's exchanges of the 1880s and 1890s, allowed housebound women (and some men) to market homemade items for profit. While some of the participants may have been hobbyists, most seem to have participated in order to make extra money, and they had to account for the costs of production in the price of their crafts.[12]

Despite sobering advice about the difficulty of earning money from selling crafts, *Profitable Hobbies* and *Popular Science* both promoted the idea that hobbyists might be able to opt out of the rat race by professionalizing their hobbies. Their pages were replete with tales of people who opened roadside stands where they successfully sold crafts and souvenirs that could be produced cheaply and in quantity. The magazines offered plans that featured simple wooden lawn ornaments and novelties, plastic household items, holiday decorations, costume jewelry, and unapologetically kitsch souvenirs such as thermometers embedded in ears of corn. Like Victorian crafts, these projects aimed at a low common denominator by stressing novelty over form. However, unlike Victorian fancyworkers, postwar crafters displayed precious little concern for mastering an exacting manual skill. That would have slowed down the process and made them economically unfeasible. These commercialized crafters were even further removed from arts and crafts—era amateurs whose work was both more substantial and more grounded in a philosophical aesthetic.[13]

The simple nature of crafts made for sale reflected the debased state of handicrafts in general. Even those hobbyists who had no intention of making money from their handiwork shied away from the highly demanding projects common before the war. Fine amateur crafting did not disappear, but it certainly became less visible, shouldered aside by mass-produced kits and other quick and easy projects that had a one-size-fits-all quality. Distinctions between men and women, or young and old, faded in postwar hobby projects. The new simpler crafts for everybody were the amazing, do-everything slicer and dicer of productive leisure that retained the positive reputation of prewar crafts, bestowing positive moral and economic values while they enriched, relaxed, and rejuvenated the hobbyist. They provided constructive leisure for both young mothers and older women, explained a San Francisco teacher, while the proprietor of a New York craft school claimed crafting forestalled heart attacks and nervous breakdowns. Handicrafts, said another educator in 1953, "offer opportunities for the training of work habits and for the development of muscular skills, initiative, creativeness, and self-expression."[14]

Working on the Line at Home

The continuing erosion of gender-specific fancywork crafts was significantly encouraged by the growing popularity of kits. The term "kit" was used rather loosely but usually referred to a group of craft items designed to produce a specific end product that were sold as a package. Kits almost always included precut or preformed pieces and often contained glue, paint, sandpaper, small shaping tools, and other parts necessary to complete the job. A 1949 catalog for American Handicrafts, the country's biggest supplier of hobby craft materials to schools, camps, and similar institutions, offered a wide variety of kits for things like woven rush stools, Indian beads, mari-

onettes, pottery, "shell creations," pot holders, and wood carving. The kit
package severely limited hobbyists' creativity but greatly facilitated their productivity. Thus plastic glue-together kit models, which would appear in 1950,
were not an innovation so much as a continuation of a trend that dated back
to the printed Berlinwork canvases of the 1850s. Printed and precut pyrography blanks in the 1910s and knocked-down furniture from the 1910s on were
also precursors. The kit boom of the 1950s was different because it was not a
product fad, but a conceptual fad.[15]

There was nothing in kits that prevented people from moving on to
more autonomous creativity, and manufacturers disingenuously billed their
kits as introductions to crafting. A kit could become the first step in a lifetime journey of crafting, but the proliferation of different kinds of kits suggests that rather than moving vertically to more skilled or creative expressions of the same craft, hobbyists moved laterally to an equally elementary
kit in another medium or simply to another object in the same medium.
The qualitative difference in postwar kits was not their lack of creativity;
amateur handicrafters always used plans drawn up by professionals. Nor was
it solely the lack of skill they demanded; Victorian publications often
included introductory plans that required only minimal skills. The difference was in the packaging. The package meant that the hobbyist did not
have to engage the hobby at a higher level of abstraction. Nonkit crafters
needed to think about what sort of craft they wanted to do, what projects
they should pursue, what materials they needed to do it, and what tools
were called for. Kit assemblers needed only to buy the box. There were no
preliminary steps, no planning or organizing, no thinking about the
process. In other words, the hobbyists did not have to engage the craft intellectually. Everything came to them; they did not have to go to it, so when
they finished with one thing they could go on to another. They were not
painters, leather workers, or model makers; they were kit assemblers. "In
many of the kit projects the hard jobs are already done," explained a hobby
tool manufacturer, "leaving you free to concentrate on the enjoyable
assembling and finishing operations."[16]

In the popular imagination, crafts came to mean the superficial assembling of preformed pieces. The kit was the ultimate victory of the assembly
line. Whereas craft amateurs had previously sought to preserve an appreciation for hand craftsmanship in the face of industrialization, kit hobbyists
conceded production to the machine. They became the leisure-time equiva-
lents of the apocryphal Ford worker who, as his last wish before retiring,
requested permission to finish tightening the bolt he had been starting for
thirty years. Kit assemblers did not dream of designing the product or form-
ing its parts. It was enough that they could surpass the Ford worker's wish and

actually assemble the whole thing. Forty years of assembly line mentality had transformed the public's understanding of personal agency from that of the artisan to that of a glorified factory worker. "Assembly liners," read the caption to a *New York Times* picture of two boys putting together a plastic model, "as in Detroit, it is necessary to refer to blueprints to make sure the hard-top convertible comes off right."[17]

Paint-by-numbers kits allowed would-be artists to use factory methods to assemble paintings at home. "Was it art or just a hobby?" asks cultural historian Karal Ann Marling. It was, of course, no more art than gluing together a plastic model was a craft. The hobby industry itself avoided invidious distinctions by embracing all the categories equally; its trade journal was called *Craft, Model, and Hobby Industry*. By eliminating both art and craft from manual hobbies, kit manufacturers provided postwar consumers with a work-like pastime that not only precluded creativity (as published plans always had) but also minimized skill. In her perceptive critique of the leather-craft industry, Deborah Nelles concludes that kits were an attempt by business to create a world in which "the work activity of the industrial laborer and the kit hobbyist was the same." It was advertising, she says, that gave the kit assembler the illusion of creativity, but in reality kit hobbies were a reinforcement of industrial production. Nelles sees kits as an attempt by industry to deprive hobbyists of an opportunity "to develop their own creativity and skill," and then to protect themselves from the anger of the deprived workers by making it appear as though kit assembly were actually a craft.[18]

Nelles illustrates her point by describing the dramatic growth of the Tandy Leather Company, a producer of leather-craft kits for the burgeoning hobby market. Originally a supplier of leather to the shoe repair industry, the company was brought into the hobby business by the founder's son who had experienced the popularity of leather craft both for rehabilitation and recreation in the navy. The company began producing leather kits in 1950, which it sold by mail and through small shops. The consumer received cut, punched, and in many cases, tooled and colored pieces of leather; in addition, difficult pieces were already glued up. The hobbyists' job was to stitch the pieces together to make wallets, purses, belts, and moccasins. Along with leather and lace, the kits contained all necessary needles, buckles, and snaps. Even though the crafter had almost no control over the appearance of the finished product, Tandy's advertising used all the traditional craft terms to describe its kits. It said the hobbyist would learn craft skills, called the projects "unique," and promised that the crafter would save money. Nelles charges Tandy with creating not only "a mass alternative for creative expression" but "an alternative which reinforces the work habits and patterns of industrial labor" by rationalizing leisure.[19]

Hobbyists could find kits to make objects of almost every imaginable material. In addition to leather, plaster, and wood, there were kits that used mosaic tiles, string, paper, linoleum blocks, yarn loops, and sheet metal. The material, however, that came to be most identified with the kit craze of the 1950s was plastic. Its ability to be injection-molded into intricate shapes at low cost made it the perfect medium for reproducing replicas of just about anything. Prior to the introduction of plastic, model kits for planes and boats had demanded a fairly high degree of technical skill from the assembler, which, said the man who invented plastic kits, discouraged hobbyists. His models were designed to be assembled in half an hour or less. Some of the old wood kits came with die-cut pieces, but most expected the builder to know enough technical terminology to read complex instructions and be able to cut intricate parts from blocks of wood. "When the kit arrived," wrote Nathaniel Benchley, "I thought at first that they'd forgotten to pack most of the materials. There were a few slabs of balsa in assorted lengths, some envelopes containing what looked like ants, and a sheet of instructions about the size of a newspaper." Benchley's model-building saga was a classic novice's tale of ineptitude compounded by ignorance, precipitating house-hold disarray and spousal conflict, and resulting in a model so invested with time and pain that he would not give it to the son for whom it was ostensibly made.[20]

Stripped of its comedic facade, Benchley's rendition of his excursion into model making incorporated many of the elements that made crafting so pop-ular with the guardians of the public weal. He stayed at home and out of "air-conditioned bars"; he developed manual skills in a worklike environment; he produced an object of beauty and value; he worked with and for his son; and he built a sense of pride along with his model schooner. Writing more seri-ously in *Today's Health* in 1958, Barbara Humphrey advocated model build-ing as the perfect man's hobby for almost all the same reasons Benchley made fun of. She acknowledged that women could build models but did not want to. "The men and boys think this is good," she noted, "because it leaves them a masculine realm yet uninvaded by females." Models gave fathers and sons a psychological space of their own in the house where the father could relive his boyhood and the son could dream of his future. Furthermore, Humphrey said bankers liked model building because it gave them a chance to use their hands for a change and factory workers because it gave them a chance to use their hands to do "more delicate handwork than that required on the assembly line." Both of them, she noted, "gain satisfaction from being able to see a project through from beginning to end and from being in com-plete control." Humphrey ends her piece with the advice, "don't be embar-rassed if a model kit falls out of your briefcase."[21]

Nowhere in her article does Humphrey say what kind of model or what kind of kits she is talking about. While she may have had in mind the intricate kind of balsa wood model that gave Benchley such trouble, most Americans in 1958 would have assumed she was writing about plastic kits. The Gresham's Law of crafts had condemned traditional modeling, if not to extinction, then at least to obscurity, and only the most generous commentator could have imagined that plastic kits provided the benefits Humphrey described. Generous commentators, however, were not in short supply. An executive with the Hobby Industry Association explained that it favored "creative type" hobbies over collecting. He cited as examples painting by the numbers, ceramics, copper enameling, and "putting together plastic models of planes, trains, cars, and boats. Dollar-wise," he explained, "more money is being spent on plastic models than on any other hobby."[22]

Kits were far and away the fastest growing segment of the hobby industry, with sales increasing from 44 million dollars in 1945 to over 300 million dollars in 1953. Industry figures on kits lumped together ten-cent gliders and hundred-dollar models of cabin cruisers that came with their own engines. Nevertheless, the literature makes it clear that plastic model kits were the dominant form (see fig. 9.1). Lewis Glaser, the president of Revell of Venice, California, is generally credited with starting the plastic kit boom. In 1950 he began making plastic models of the Maxwell automobile that played a prominent role in comedian Jack Benny's routine. This, and other scale models did not sell well as toys, but then Glaser hit on the idea of selling them as unassembled kits. Apparently the process of gluing together the pieces of the car gave people a sense of accomplishment, since half the people who bought them were adults. Revell quickly added ships, planes, wagons, stagecoaches, and firearms to its line, and other firms produced models of virtually every vehicle that ever carried a person in war or peace. There were even, ironically, mass-produced models of custom-made racing and show cars. Some models (including models of human beings) came with transparent panels so that interior engines (and organs) were made visible.[23]

Although the end product of a plastic kit resembled a craft, the process of making it was more akin to assembling a jigsaw puzzle (although puzzles took longer to complete). Like a puzzle, the plastic model was a relatively inexpensive method of whiling away half an hour, and when it was done, the builder needed another one. However, unlike jigsaw puzzles, which could be recycled, the completed model was a permanent symbol of time profitably spent. Not only could plastic models be assembled physically, but they could also be assembled into sets. Manufacturers and retailers promoted series, although given their ready availability there was no secondary market for plastic models. Thus making plastic models was a pseudocraft that pro-

FIGURE 9.1 Hobby shop owner displays one of the many plastic models available to kit assemblers in the mid-1950s. (Reprinted from "From Toys to Hobbies: Way to Men's Hearts," *Business Week* [January 28, 1956]: 56.)

duced a pseudocollectible that ended up cluttering rooms in the 1950s the way fancywork had seventy-five years earlier.

Plastic vehicles were the icons of the 1950s kit craze, but they had to compete with other forms of kits, some of which could move the hobbyist into a much more serious realm of assembly. While most kits were designed for the production of small personal or decorative items, there was also a market for much larger kits that, depending on the buyer's motivation, could be seen either as an extension of the kit hobby craze or as a money-saving option for the handy homeowner. As they had since the 1910s, manufacturers sold unfinished, knocked-down furniture kits by mail and through department stores. Many of the kits required no more than screwing on legs and applying a coat of stain and varnish. The concept was not new, but the scale certainly was. In 1953 Cohasset Colonials shipped twenty thousand knocked-down versions of cobbler's benches, Windsor chairs, trestle tables, and other perennial favorites of the early American style. Kits expanded into newer areas as well. High fidelity audio equipment kits were sold by at least three different manufacturers. Air conditioning for cars and homes was available in kit form, and the really ambitious kit assembler could spend thousands of dollars, and as many hours, putting together a thirty-foot inboard cruiser.[24]

From plastic models to cabin cruisers, kit hobbies shared the same basic elements: the design of each was set by the manufacturer who used machines to form the component parts. The job of the hobbyist was to assemble those parts in the prescribed order. The result was a product identical to similar products also produced and assembled in factories. The hobbyists' pleasure came neither from creativity nor skill but from a sense of satisfaction with having put something together with their own hands. From another perspective, however, there were major differences between a home-assembled trestle table, an audio amplifier, and a plastic model. The model was as likely to have been made by a child as an adult, who would have no practical use for a ship that would not float or a plane that would not fly. Useful items such as the table and the amplifier were most likely assembled by adults who were saving money as well as passing the time. By doing the assembly themselves, adults who built practical kits were engaging in a form of do-it-yourself, an indisputably productive hobby.

10   Do-It-Yourself: Expected Leisure

More serious crafters avoided kits, but the things they made covered the same spectrum of applications from the purely decorative to the eminently practical. In two 1957 issues, for example, *Workbench* magazine carried a variety of projects that reflected the multiple divisions within the world of craft hobbies. Coconut shell planters, fabric lamp shades, and homemade handbags were essentially similar to women's crafts that had appeared a hundred years earlier in *Godey's Lady's Book*. Somewhat more male-oriented were plans for a shadow box, wooden lawn figures, and a "novelty wheelbarrow planter." None of these projects required any advanced woodworking skills, but all assumed a level of manual competence that would have been unusual in a suburban man until after World War I. Finally, the magazine ran plans for practical home improvement projects that were clearly within the male purview, and while not unique to the 1950s (similar articles could have been found throughout the 1920s and 1930s) were becoming more typical. Articles about creative uses for masking tape, dealing with oversized screw holes, and preparation for house painting had little to do with traditional craft skills or products, but everything to do with the new expected role of the suburban husband as handyman.[1]

Whatever other similarities there may have been between the Victorian family and the GI generation, there were significant differences in how they viewed manual labor around the house. Middle-class men and women in the 1950s did more with their own hands and did more together than their Victorian great-grandparents could ever have imagined. Writing in 1957, anthropologist Margaret Mead commented approvingly on the trend toward men once more working around the house with their wives. "The do-it-yourself movement," she said, "is not just a hobby. It is often a pleasant and meaningful contribution to family life." By working together in the home the husband and wife were building family bonds while they were improving their surroundings. Men were expected to be there for their wives, for their children, and for themselves, but at the same time, popular images of feminized suburban men seemed to warn of dangers in the role of suburban dad. The increased calls for paternal presence clashed with the continuing assumptions of traditional gender models, catching men in a no-win position. Home crafts and do-it-yourself projects provided at least part of the solution. Along with car care, lawn care, barbecuing, supervising boys' sports, and taking out the garbage, household maintenance and repair permitted the suburban father to stay at home without feeling emasculated or being subsumed into an undifferentiated entity with his wife.[2]

In 1950 Harry Zarchy published a pastiche of pastimes called *Here's Your Hobby*. Tossed in among chapters on raising tropical fish, archery, and butterfly collecting was one entitled "Home Repair." However else they differed, all the other activities involved were obviously leisure pastimes. Yet here in their midst were twenty-four pages of instructions on how to unstick doors, replace window panes, stop a faucet from leaking, and otherwise attend to the chores of home ownership. In Zarchy's mind, however, these were not chores; they were hobbies. Maintenance, repair, and improvement; routine and creative, they were all lumped together into a new leisure category soon to be called do-it-yourself. Certainly it could be difficult, frustrating, and even expensive, but that was true for most hobbies. Like all productive leisure, do-it-yourself was worklike, but it was not work. People did it because they wanted to, not because they had to.[3]

Still, as cultural theorist Kevin Melchionne has recently observed, do-it-yourself is structurally different from most other hobbies because it is often less creative and almost always more practical. Recognizing that the home maintenance and repair aspects of the new hobby made "handicrafts" an inaccurate label, several publications in 1950 called the activity "how-to-do-it." Commenting on the fact that the government included pamphlets on household upkeep in its catalog of hobby publications, *Science News Letter* called the new phenomenon the "how-to-do-it" hobby. In the same vein, Robert Kingery published *How-to-Do-It Books: A Selected Guide*, a bibliography of hundreds of instructional publications on everything from acrobatics to yacht racing. Both the government's and Kingery's scope were too broad, and their how-to-do-it nomenclature never caught on, but each had grasped the new principle; doing it yourself was not a chore but a hobby. By 1954 the government had released a whole new package, or "kit," of pamphlets on home repair, and handyman books had become national best-sellers.[4]

Do-it-yourself (including crafts and maintenance) satisfied all the standard expectations for a hobby. It could be done alone in spare time; it replicated and reinforced work values, which gave the hobbyist a sense of psychological fulfillment, and had the added benefit of being useful. From a compensatory perspective working at home rejuvenated the hobbyist. "It has afforded me mental and physical recreation, which has enabled me to do my daily professional work with far more efficiency," explained a physician. "Give me a man with a hobby of working with his hands and I'll show you one who enjoys life, has a clear mind for business problems, who will live longer," wrote do-it-yourselfer Walt Durbahn in 1954. It also had a strong element of atavistic congruence; relearning manual skills confirmed the real meaning of labor. "Man is a creator," wrote a hobby author; "to conceive an idea and watch it grow in your hands . . . is a soul-satisfying process." "America Rediscovers Its Hands" was the title of a piece in *American Magazine* that sang the praises of laying tile, hanging wallpaper, and converting the basement to a recreation room. By using its hands, America was "reaping all kinds of benefits—material, mental, and spiritual."[5]

A 1958 survey of about two hundred do-it-yourselfers in the greater Little Rock area confirmed the psychological benefits provided by the hobby. Eighty percent said they engaged in the activity because they "enjoyed working with [their] hands and creating something new," and 60 percent said they "found in it a sense of creative self-fulfillment." The language of the questionnaire stressed the creative elements of do-it-yourself, and it is possible that if the routine maintenance and repair activities had been separated out the answers might have been different. Yet neither the author of the study nor most other commentators on do-it-yourself thought to distinguish between the two kinds of activities since homeowners appear to have obtained about the same satisfaction from being creative as they did from doing maintenance. Household repair and maintenance clearly embodied two distinct but complementary qualities; it was both practical and psychologically satisfying. It was, in other words, the perfect embodiment of the work ethic. To be productive was to be fulfilled; relief from one kind of work could be found through another kind of work, not through idleness or passive leisure.[6]

The Suburban Homestead

In 1944 the trade journal *Modern Plastics* had predicted there would be a craft boom in the postwar world. "World War II is a mechanized war in which every man has acquired some skill with his hands," it suggested, and they, their factory-trained wives, and the "thousands of others who will be urged to take up crafts work by their doctors as a treatment for nervous and mental ailments" would make things out of plastic. Rather than make plastic doodads (except perhaps in the form of kits), the veterans came home, got married, had children, and moved to the suburbs where they exercised their new skills on their new homes. During their service years millions of Americans had "learned for the first time how to repair radios, engines and dozens of other machines," and "housewives who had been punch-press operators, welders and electronics technicians found that it was no trick to fix a leaky faucet or paper a room," noted *Time* in a cover story on do-it-yourself. "The once indispensable handyman who could fix a chair, hang a door or patch a concrete walk has been replaced by millions of amateur hobbyists who do all his work—and much more—in their spare time and find it wonderful fun," concluded the magazine.[7]

Business Week, which continued to urge its upscale readers to use their "well-equipped home workshops," christened the new movement in 1952 when it proclaimed the 1950s "the age of do-it-yourself" and said that by taking on maintenance and repair chores themselves, the 7 million suburbanites who had moved into new homes were turning their houses into a hobby. Although the phrase "do-it-yourself" had been used from time to time at least as far back as 1912, this was the earliest prominent use of the term in the 1950s, and the one that gave it widespread currency. Within the year, the phrase had become commonplace, spread in part by a series of regional "do-it-yourself" expositions that featured tools and materials for use in what was frequently claimed to be 12 million suburban workshops. This figure, which originated with the U.S. Department of Commerce, seems unlikely since it means that fully half of all owner-occupied houses in 1950 would have had to have workshops.[8] However many there actually were, their number was obviously growing even in houses that provided almost no room to work. These included tiny so-called efficiency houses and a surprisingly large number of houses, built by some of the most prominent developers of the time, that had neither garages nor basements in which to set up a workshop.[9]

In the thousands of northern California houses constructed by Joseph Eichler, for example, there was literally no place to put a workbench. Eichler's modern-style homes, like all houses built in California after 1945, completely abandoned what had been only rudimentary basements even before the war. Their shallow roofs offered no attic for expansion or work space, and most models substituted an open carport for a garage. Eichler's Frank Lloyd Wright–inspired houses did have the advantage of providing a perfect backdrop for postwar modern furniture that relied heavily on plywood and used simple case work construction details for everything from cabinets to couches. Postwar modern had a strong family resemblance to 1930s moderne both in its emphasis on planar design elements and its chaste surfaces. Fifties modern, however, avoided the repetitive geometry of moderne and used tapers and angles that gave it a "futuristic" look. Like moderne (and like early American and mission as well), postwar modern was a "mascu-

line" style, eschewing decoration in favor of openly expressed structural elements that made the furniture easy to build (see fig. 10.1). "There are no
tricky joints to fit; no fancy carving, inlay work, or wood turning that would
require either power tools or broad woodworking experience," assured the
author of a *Better Homes and Gardens* article that promised in its title "You
Can Be Your Own Cabinetmaker." The author explained, "My husband,
Paul, designed and made all five of these units without previous woodworking experience."[10]

Easy to build did not have to mean unsophisticated. *American Home*, for
example, printed pictures of furniture built for motion picture sets and
glamorous West Coast homes as examples for do-it-yourselfers, and Bill
Baker, a Hollywood set designer who had also made furniture for movie
stars, published designs that home crafters could build. *Better Homes and
Gardens* offered do-it-yourself patterns for a series of pieces designed by
young Los Angeles artisan Sam Maloof, who would go on to be the most
celebrated fine furniture designer-builder of his generation. The plywood
industry, which by 1953 was selling 10 percent of its output directly to homeowners, was a major promoter of do-it-yourself modern furniture projects.
Modern furniture, with its strong California influence, was less at home in
the traditionally styled suburban tracts that were being built in the East.
Nevertheless, 1950s modern did share one thing with more traditional early
American furniture; they could both be made with the same basic woodworking skills, and it was, therefore, common to find plans for modern
pieces and early American pieces sharing space in the same do-it-yourself
books and articles. Californians could build modern pieces for their Eichlers, and easterners could make colonial furniture for the Cape Cod houses
being built by developer William Levitt.[11]

Levitt, who built more than seventeen thousand houses in Long Island's
Levittown alone in the decade after the war, made them only slightly more
conducive to do-it-yourself than the West Coast Eichlers. Like the Eichlers,
Levitt's first two-bedroom houses lacked both basements and garages, but
they did provide an unfinished attic where the handy homeowners could add
a couple of extra bedrooms to hold growing families. Without a place to put
a workshop, do-it-yourselfers had to take the suggestion of the Armstrong
linoleum company and build a kitchen-workshop, which, according to
Levittown historian Barbara Kelly, is what Levittown husbands did, no doubt
to their own and their wives' discomfort. Workshop or not, the attics were
remodeled, a step that was taken for granted by both the builder and residents.[12] In a comment that seems directed at the cookie-cutter Levitt houses,
one contemporary commentator attributed the whole do-it-yourself movement to a combination of attic expansion and the fact that "some of the less

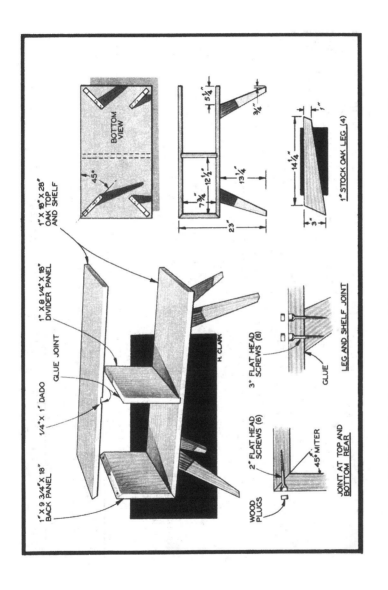

FIGURE 10.1 End table plans in 1950s plan book feature straight cuts and simple joinery. (Reprinted from "Modern End Table," *Build It* [Greenwich, Conn.: Fawcett Publications, 1950], 124.)

expensive new houses are so uniform in appearance that their owners go in for craftsmanship in order to give them a bit of individuality."[13]

The Cape Cod and later ranch style of the Levittown houses prompted more than half of those who moved into them to abandon their preference for modern furniture in favor of something more traditional, and 70 percent of those chose early American (see fig. 10.2). Sitting in a colonial chair to watch television was probably no more anachronistic than the Cape Cod house itself, built with mass-production methods and materials, but somehow the unexpected juxtaposition of past and present seemed more stark in the furniture. At Levittown's first community crafts fair in 1954, one resident proudly displayed his colonial high fidelity cabinets that housed the electronic parts in a "grain bin." In addition to fitting the Cape Cod style, colonial furniture was easy to build. An article on "all-thumbs craftwork" that coincided with the first wave of Levittown houses, featured early American pieces the author said he built with few tools, no plans, and in one afternoon without a workshop; "Since I possess just about enough manual dexterity to

House plants now grow in a miniature cradle that I cut out and assembled in a few hours.

FIGURE 10.2 Colonial-style "all-thumbs craftwork" continued to attract do-it-yourselfers in the 1950s as it had for more than fifty years. (Reprinted from Jerome Parker, "I'm Proud of My All-Thumbs Craftwork," *Popular Science* 152 [March 1948]: 194.)

tie my shoelaces, no one has been more pleasantly surprised at this success than myself."[14]

Even if they had to scramble a bit to find space for a workshop, members of the GI generation worked around the house in unprecedented numbers, if only because there were unprecedented numbers of families with new houses. These do-it-yourself families were universally described as middle class. Blue-collar families were essentially invisible. Subsequent studies have shown that working-class men are just as likely as white-collar men to work around the house, although they are somewhat less liable to perceive it as a leisure activity. Since tools are a natural part of their lives, do-it-yourself is the most basic sort of spillover leisure for manual workers. Journalist Pete Hamill calls tools the "nouns of work," and remembers his working-class father spreading out his tools on the kitchen table of their Brooklyn apartment in preparation for making minor repairs. The lack of a workshop or even of his own home did not stop the elder Hamill from relishing the sense of masculine power he got from using his tools at home.[15]

Their confidence buoyed by all the publicity, homeowners made ever bolder inroads into new areas of home improvement—sometimes to the point of overextending themselves. As a result, in the mid-1950s experts began to urge do-it-yourselfers to recognize their limitations and not take on jobs such as fixing roofs or foundations. Major structural repairs, they warned, were beyond the capacity of the weekend worker and might result in damage to both the home and the homeowner. The vast majority of do-it-yourselfers heeded this advice and limited themselves to small repairs, cosmetic improvements, and light construction projects that, for the first time, were being promoted by the manufacturers of building and maintenance products.[16]

Before World War II manufacturers had been afraid of alienating their professional customers by advertising for public consumption. That policy changed during the wartime labor shortage. Kentile, the maker of glue-down floor tiles, claims to have pioneered direct sale to do-it-yourselfers in 1942 when it began to show customers how to lay their own floors. Whereas prewar advertisements featured professional craftsmen, a 1945 advertisement showed a woman painting the interior of a child's bedroom, and the professional painters working on the exterior were relegated to a small secondary cut. It took a few years for advertisers to realize the full extent of the new market, but by mid-decade, the sensitivities of professional artisans were forgotten, as manufacturers of tools, paint, wallpaper, floor coverings, wood, and a host of new materials such as plastic laminates, fiberglass panels, and aluminum (which could be cut with woodworking tools) began peddling their products directly to homeowners. Newspapers and magazines introduced special do-it-yourself sections that ran features on what to do yourself and advertisements for what products to use.[17]

Home improvement projects got a particular boost from new materials and tools. Pretrimmed wallpaper, and washable, water-based latex paint applied with a roller were especially popular. Eight million three-dollar rollers were sold to homeowners in 1954, along with 150 million gallons of paint. Novel forms of floor tiles made from asphalt, cork, rubber, and plastic made it easier to install new floors, and fully half of all floor tiles were bought directly by homeowners. Painting and papering were the most common do-it-yourself projects, more than twice as popular as either electrical work or woodwork, which followed in rank order. Before the war fewer than a third of homeowners had done their own painting, but that figure rose to 80 percent during the 1950s, with roughly similar numbers for wallpapering. Instructions for these projects could be found in new monster manuals like Emanuele Stieri's sixteen-hundred-page *Complete Home Repair Handbook*. Despite its name, the book was a bit of a throwback, containing plans for small projects like the ever-popular cobbler's bench and major undertakings such as remodeling the attic and basement. It also showed the homeowner how to maintain and repair every part of the house and its contents from the gutters to the septic tank.[18]

If remodeling an attic or basement were insufficient challenge, do-it-yourselfers could tackle a whole house. Despite one recommendation that potential house builders take a professional aptitude test to assure that they possessed the requisite mechanical abilities, most do-it-yourselfers assumed that their enthusiasm and willingness to learn from their mistakes would carry them through. The fictional Mr. Blandings, who "built" his dream house in 1946, hired professionals to do every job, but the trophy of building your own house was "the greatest hobby of them all." When a writer of the same period said that his brother-in-law, a college professor, was building his own three-bedroom house, he hastened to add, "when I say he is building it, I mean just that. . . . His is the hand that holds the hammer as well as signs the checks."[19] The media had ignored blue-collar workers who built their own homes before World War II, but when middle-class families began to tackle the ultimate do-it-yourself challenge, they captured much more attention. Estimates of owner-built houses ranged from 10 to 40 percent of all new construction.[20] Home-built homes ranged in size from modest five-hundred-square-foot cottages to large houses, such as the one that took George and Anne Swan seven years to build in a Minneapolis suburb.[21] In a job as big as a house, the couple tended to work together (see fig. 10.3). "Brushing cement dust out of her hair," one such wife announced, "I've had to start wearing long-sleeve dresses to hide the muscles in my arms."[22]

FIGURE 10.3 The most ambitious do-it-yourselfers built their own homes from the ground up, with wives and children pitching in. (Reprinted from David Dempsey, "Home, Sweet [Homemade] Home," *New York Times Magazine* [March 31, 1957]: 26; illustration by Carl Rose.)

Power Tools

By mid-decade only reading and watching television were more popular forms of recreation than do-it-yourself among married men. By some estimates, do-it-yourselfers were spending $4 to $6 billion a year on supplies and tools such as the newly developed handheld quarter-inch drill. Ruth Schwartz Cowan has shown that the introduction of household machinery often relieved the burdens of men much more than those of women, but the portable drill may have been a small step toward redressing the balance. Just as the vacuum cleaner increased work for women by raising expectations of cleanliness, the portable drill upped the ante for male work around the house by bringing power to the casual handyman. "It makes every man his own building boss, his own carpenter, his own cabinetmaker," promised Collier's in 1954, and enables him to make "everything from a closet shelf to a basement playroom."[23]

Before World War II, creative do-it-yourselfers had jury-rigged portable drills by mounting drill bits on small jigsaw motors, but the result was both awkward and weak (see fig. 10.4). Black and Decker, a manufacturer of industrial equipment, had tried to sell its heavy-duty portable electric drills to farmers in the 1930s, but high-priced drills found little market in a depressed agricultural sector, much of which still was not electrified. In 1946 the company decided to try again. This time it produced a smaller, cheaper tool, and targeted home owners as well as farm owners (see fig. 10.5). It was the right tool at the right time and became the emblem of the do-it-yourself movement. Suburbanites bought an estimated 15 million drills from Black and Decker, and a variety of other manufacturers, in the next eight years.[24]

At twenty to twenty-five dollars apiece, the portable electric drill brought power equipment down to a price that fit the young family's budget and to a size that fit in a toolbox as well as a workshop. Whereas in the 1930s drills (in fact, drill presses) had lagged far behind lathes, saws, and grinders in popularity, in 1958 one survey found that almost three-quarters of handymen owned a portable electric drill, twice as many as the next most popular power tool, a table saw. The survey numbers are substantiated by government statistics that show of the $95 million worth of portable power tools sold in 1953 (up from a mere $6 million in 1946), do-it-yourselfers bought five times as many drills as saws. Since portable drills were often the only electric tools many do-it-yourselfers owned, manufacturers offered attachments that used the drill to power other devices. These included, most successfully, polishers, sanders, and grinders, and, less successfully, saws, lathes, hedge trimmers, and pumps.[25]

By 1953 all four of the major portable electric tools were available to the home handyman. In addition to a drill, do-it-yourselfers could buy portable

FIGURE 10.4 Home crafter jury-rigs a portable drill by attaching a bit to a jigsaw motor in 1930. The resulting tool was both unwieldy and weak. (Reprinted from Arthur Wakeling, *Home Workshop Manual* [New York: Popular Science Publishing, 1930], 65.)

sanders, routers, and jigsaws. In all, there were about one hundred different types of power tools made for the home market in 1952; just ten years earlier there had been only twenty-five. Crafters who wanted more than handheld tools, but did not have the money or the space for a full set of stationary tools, could buy a combination device for about $225. Shopsmith marketed the first

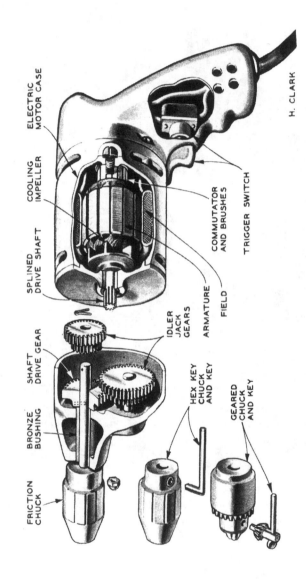

ELECTRIC
MOTOR CASE

COOLING
IMPELLER

SPLINED
DRIVE SHAFT

COMMUTATOR
AND BRUSHES

TRIGGER SWITCH

FIELD

ARMATURE

IDLER
JACK
GEARS

SHAFT
DRIVE GEAR

BRONZE
BUSHING

FRICTION
CHUCK

HEX KEY
CHUCK AND KEY

GEARED
CHUCK AND KEY

H. CLARK

GENERAL CONSTRUCTION AND FUNCTION OF THE AVERAGE 1/4" PORTABLE ELECTRIC DRILL

FIGURE 10.5 Exploded view of first-generation portable quarter-inch drill that became the home handyman's standard in the 1950s. (Reprinted from "The Quarter Inch Drill," *How to Use Power Tools* [Greenwich, Conn.: Fawcett Publications, 1953], 117.)

one in 1947, and sold more than a hundred thousand units in its first six years. The Shopsmith combined a lathe, table saw, and horizontal drill press on a single bench (see fig. 10.8). In 1953 Shopsmith and its imitators were selling $24 million a year worth of these multipurpose tools, often through low-cost classes that gave men a chance to try them out. The most serious crafters continued to buy separate saws, lathes, planers, jointers, and other large stationary equipment necessary to do fine woodwork, or in fewer cases, metal work.[26]

Big stationary power tools, like fast horses and cars, were an extension of their owners, as important for what they represented as for what they could do. Soon after the war, the editor of the English hobby magazine *Model Engineer* told of being invited to the home of a new acquaintance to see his shop, which occupied one of the best rooms in the house. "It was replete with fine lathes, milling and drilling machines, and work benches. Around the wall were elaborate cabinets, shelves and drawers which were filled with chucks, milling cutters, screwing tackle, drills, reamers, micrometers, and almost every conceivable kind of small engineering tool." Suitably impressed, the editor asked to see the output of this imposing arsenal of hardware. Somewhat sheepishly the shop owner showed him one half-finished model engine. It would, of course, have been better to have crafted something elaborate with all this expensive equipment, nevertheless, the hobbyist was proud enough of the tools themselves to invite one of the country's leading experts on modeling to admire the means if not the ends.[27]

Recognizing the iconic role of power tools in the do-it-yourself movement, the government drafted them to serve in the cold war. Government-sponsored exhibitions in Paris and Stockholm in 1956 featured demonstrators in model home workshops. The *New York Times* zeroed-in on the contrast between the U.S. display in Paris, with its emphasis on the productive use of leisure time, and the exhibit of the People's Republic of China that featured the heavy industrial production of the current five-year plan, with the headline, "U.S. 'Do-It-Yourself' a Contrast to Red China Plan in Paris Fair." In Stockholm, the entire U.S. exhibit was built around the do-it-yourself theme, celebrating the way American crafters could make bowls and chairs in their basement workshops. The audacity of taking American tools and crafts to the country that gave the world the sloyd system of craft education and that retained its reputation for producing exceptionally fine handicrafts does not seem to have bothered either the Americans or the Swedes, who were reported to be impressed with American know-how.[28]

The postwar proliferation of power tools gave amateur craftsmen the capacity to cut and drill quickly and accurately with much less training than required for the effective use of hand tools. The enthusiasm with which they embraced power tools confirmed the eclectic definition of hobby crafting.

William Morris, the English founder of the arts and crafts movement had envisioned a world where "all work which would be irksome to do by hand is done by immensely improved machinery; and in all work which it is a pleasure to do by hand, machinery is done without." American amateurs grasped this principle more quickly than Morris's own countrymen. When a group of English experts toured U.S. industrial education programs in 1950 they were disturbed by the large number of power tools they found in school shops. "What do your pupils do later if they wish to take up woodwork as a hobby, since they have been accustomed in school to do everything with power tools?" the visitors asked. The answer was obvious: "They would, in taking up any hobby, first acquire the necessary machine tools." For the English, woodcraft was a hobby that involved traditional methods of hand construction. For the Americans, it was a useful way to occupy free time, and the instruments of that usefulness did not define the legitimacy of the enterprise.[29]

The widespread use of power tools raised new concerns about personal safety. A misused hammer could result in a black-and-blue finger; a misused power saw could result in no finger at all. John Keats accused the media of misleading would-be handymen by telling them that they could fix up their houses with "simple plans [and] simple kits," when in fact they ended up spending $785 for tools to build a dollhouse, fell off their roofs while putting up gutters, and cut through their arms while constructing fences. At a 1955 American Public Health Association convention session devoted to the dangers of power tools and chemicals in the home environment, a physician warned that "poisons and machinery considered too dangerous for use in industry were used freely in attics, garages, basements, kitchens and workrooms."[30] The manufacturers of the Shopsmith worried that their combination lathe, table saw, and drill press was capable of inflicting digital mayhem in three distinctly different modes, so they redesigned it in 1954 to "make the new model attractive to women." This did not mean making it easier for women to use but allaying the concern of the average woman who was "likely to discount [her husband's] ability to keep his fingers away from a saw."[31]

The Necessary Hobby

Influenced perhaps by female participation in the war effort, a conscious attempt was made to incorporate women in the 1950s do-it-yourself movement. In March 1953 New Yorkers turned out at a rate of more than six thousand a day to visit the first of its kind do-it-yourself trade exposition in Manhattan. The organizers of the show included demonstrations of hair preparations, cosmetics, slenderizing, and beauty aids, alongside electric drills and home welding kits. By defining do-it-yourself quite literally as anything that people did for themselves, early do-it-yourself shows included women both by suggesting they could participate in household repair and, more characteristically, by trying to sell them personal-care products. "While men are trying out power tools or investigating a plastic car that comes in a kit," the *New York Times* said, women could find plenty to interest them in displays of decorative mirrors, artistic enameling, bookbinding, and textile glues that eliminated the need to sew. Commenting on another of the early do-it-yourself shows, the *Times* said, "the wife of the house, with her sewing machine and home-permanent curlers, seems as much of an addict as her husband even when he orders her out of the home workshop."[32]

The *Times* was anachronistically harsh in its reference to women being ordered out of the workshop. The public discourse generally admitted them, although in a limited capacity. Marianne Shay, for example, was pictured in a New York newspaper as "Miss Do-It-Yourself" (see fig. 10.6). Shay was not *Miss* anything. She was married, had recently moved with her husband from Iowa to New York, and was looking for work. Shay realized that she had done many of the projects that would be featured in the New York do-it-yourself show and asked for a job at the exposition. The show's organizers found Shay photogenic and sufficiently knowledgeable about tools to hire her as a symbol of the new do-it-yourself woman who could demonstrate everything from wallpaper to welding. Wielding heavy tools and dressed in her blue jeans and plaid shirt, Shay was far removed from her Victorian predecessors who would hardly have lifted anything heavier than an artist's brush. Nevertheless, she was still sufficiently unusual to be the object of publicity, and it is clear that many of the tools she posed with were not ones she used in her own home.[33]

The do-it-yourself shows stressed painting and sewing for women, which continued to be female territory. A magazine feature entitled "Hobbies That Hold Your Family Together" explained that "the husband and a 12-year-old son did most of the carpentry work" on new furniture the family was building, while "a ten-year-old daughter helped with the staining and varnishing, the wife did the upholstering." Washable water-based latex paints, applied with the newly invented roller, made women more willing to undertake larger painting projects that could cut the cost of repainting a house by two-thirds.[34] Nevertheless, Emanuele Stieri pictured women on only two of the sixteen hundred pages in his home repair handbook—those dealing with upholstery. In fact, there appears to have been something of a resurgence in sewing among women after the war. In 1953 paper sewing patterns were selling at twice the rate of the prewar years, and almost 2 million sewing machines were sold for domestic use. A survey conducted by New York Uni-

Women showed quite as much interest as men in the modern time-saving tools
demonstrated by Marianne Shay at the Do-It-Yourself show in New York City
—and just about as much skill in operating them as the average male amateur

FIGURE 10.6 Marianne Shay demonstrating that women could use heavy "men's" tools at the first do-it-yourself show in New York City. (Reprinted from Lenore Hailparn, "She Did It Herself," *Independent Woman* 32 [June 1953]: 202.)

versity found that more than 40 percent of the customers at a New York department store had made their own draperies.[35]

Outside of painting and sewing, women were still limited participants in the do-it-yourself movement. Almost half the men in one survey said they *sometimes* got help from their wives in performing do-it-yourself jobs. However, *most of the time* more than two-thirds of the men did these chores alone. The do-it-yourself experience was one of tentative togetherness. Men did not want to give up their claim to the workshop, but there was always the danger of exclusivity getting out of hand. Historian Elaine Tyler May reports the story of an unfaithful wife who explained, "my husband expends all his energies on carpentry hobbies or such and never seems to need me more than to have a hot meal ready." Doing work together kept couples busy and out of temptation's way. A few writers urged women to undertake heavy work on their own, but most assumed that wives would assist and men would do the arduous labor. For example, a woman's hands are shown holding a board that a man's hands are sawing in one 1953 article, and a photo illustration for *American Magazine* the same year depicts a woman carrying both the rear of a long board and a how-to-do-it book, with the man holding the front end of the board and a box of tools.[36]

The new do-it-yourself togetherness extended to the hardware stores and lumberyards where couples purchased their home improvement supplies. As early as 1948 the all-male lumberyard took its first steps toward becoming the degendered home improvement center, welcoming "the appearance of the little woman in the yard."[37] This was no small concession; before the war lumberyards did not sell to the public and did not want women on the premises. "We felt that a lumberyard was no place for ladies," remembered an executive, "and if any had called on us they might have scared off some of our contractor customers."[38] As the do-it-yourself movement gained momentum, manufacturers began to market their products through point-of-sale displays in lumberyards and hardware stores. Phil Creden, an executive with a lumberyard chain in the Chicago area, described how the old spittoon atmosphere of his company's yards gave way to "enlarged, streamlined, and redecorated" stores that made consumers feel as comfortable as contractors.[39] In 1952 Atlanta businessman Dillard Munford, opened what appears to have been America's first do-it-yourself store designed to provide "the householder with all — or with as many as possible — of the goods and tools to repair, maintain, enlarge, and improve his property."[40] A year and a half later Munford had nine stores and reached two conclusions about success: first, the bigger the store the better because people no longer wanted to do business in "shops," and second, "concentrate on women customers (because a man figures 'if a woman can do it, I can do it')."[41]

The problem was that most women could not, or at least did not "do it." Women's traditional aversion to jobs involving heavy tools and heavy labor remained an impediment to full participation that do-it-yourself supporters struggled against. "It has long been a popular conception that women know little or nothing about handling craft tools," wrote an author describing how women could work with an electric jigsaw. It seems that by 1955, even the once nongendered jigsaw had drifted into the male realm. There was certainly no conspiracy to keep women away from electric tools. Conceding that "power tools are usually thought of as a man's playthings," a book on how to use them insisted, "they can be just as useful and time saving in the hands of a woman. Any intelligent female can be taught to cut wood on a saw and drill holes with a drill press," because using woodworking tools was "simpler than threading, adjusting and running a sewing machine."[42]

The power tool book showed a woman using a ten-pound belt sander on a vertical surface. Others suggested that if a woman learned to use heavy tools, she could then use a welding torch to brown baked Alaska or boast "to her bridge club about how she repapered Junior's room or mended a leak in the kitchen with nothing except an acetylene torch and a set of plumbing tools."[43] This swelling, but mostly futile, rhetorical chorus of female competence was encouraged by schools that sought to teach girls and women how to use heavy tools. In a variation of the fathers-and-sons-in-the-shop motif, one expert advised, "Give Sister tools too. She will enjoy working with Dad's supervision and may be a more meticulous workman than her brother." A junior high school in Santa Monica, California, integrated girls into its woodworking classes in 1955 in order to create "a generation of housewives who're capable of driving a nail to hang a picture."[44] The New York Home Bureau ran a women's home carpentry class so they could "install an extra shelf, put up a curtain rod or build a bookcase." Adult education programs in the 1950s made it a point to open up their woodworking shops to women who participated on an equal footing with and, at least in one instance, in equal numbers with men.[45]

William Orkin, the producer of the first do-it-yourself exhibitions in the mid-1950s observed a sharp increase in the number of women attending his shows over the first three years. Orkin thought the women were the do-it-yourselfers because they had "husbands who are firm believers in the *don't-do-it-yourself* theory." Perhaps, but more likely, they were attending to get ideas for projects they expected their husbands to do. From a gender perspective the changes in do-it-yourself during the 1950s enlarged the roles of both men and women, yet men cemented their position as home handyman more than women expanded their role as assistant handyman. Women were now free to help with home improvements if they wanted to, but men were expected to. In an adult version of the tomboy pattern, the wife who did a man's work around the house was admired for her competence, but the husband who did not was less than a man. By the 1950s being handy had become, like sobriety and fidelity, an expected quality in a good husband.[46]

Wives, like those portrayed by John Keats in *The Crack in the Picture Window*, felt contempt for men who could not perform the marital act of home repair. One woman complained that her husband did nothing but examine the cracked plaster she brought to his attention, and she had to call in a professional to repair it. A second was even more dismissive of her husband. "I wanted Buster to put up a towel rack for the children," she reported. "I went out and bought it for him, screws and all, and gave it to him and told him where I wanted it," but he did nothing but read his paper. "I guess I'll have to put the rack up myself," she concluded. Keats was not sympathetic to the domineering and emasculating wife who made all the decisions, but his satire reflected social expectations about who initiated and who executed household projects. By one estimate wives bought 80 percent of do-it-yourself patterns for their husbands. Handling heavy tools was man's work; the woman's job was to tell him what to do. Your wife "wants to know why you can't save a lot of money and maybe build a whole set of living room furniture," wrote a correspondent in 1954, who had "recently returned from five years abroad to find America under a cloud of home-workshop dust." "It would be," wives said, "relaxing and would give you something to do weekends instead of sitting around drinking beer in your bare feet and listening to the ball game."[47]

A survey of male homeowners in the Little Rock area found that a significant number of them attributed their household activities to the "insistence of the wife," leading the interviewer to conclude that women were "the boss in the homes of Pulaski County, Arkansas." "Honey, you're going to make a chair," Judge Edward Fisher's wife told him one day in 1950. Fisher agreed only after he realized this would be the excuse to buy the table saw he had "long been worshipping at the hardware store," but then his wife withdrew her request when she learned the saw would cost more than buying a chair. He promised to make a set of chairs, and she raised the ante by adding sofas, bunk beds, cabinets, and window screens to the list. He agreed, and the "honeydew syndrome" (honey do this, honey do that) claimed another victim. Humorous complaints of henpecked husbands were a traditional form of male self-pity, but they had previously hinged on wives telling their spouses what they should not do (drink, gamble, stay out late) not on what they should do (fix the faucet, put up a shelf, paint the kitchen).[48]

The bossed-around do-it-yourselfer was being told do something is wife expected him to do and that she did not expect to do herself, even if she could. In other words, the image of the oppressed handyman was actually an image of continuing male dominance over the world of heavy tools. "He loves to putter around the house / To the great enjoyment of his spouse," ran the opening lines of an advertising ditty in 1945, and it ended by noting the admiration of the community: "Neighbors marvel; you'll hear them utter: / 'Wise little handyman, Peter Putter.' "[49] Such references imply that the male role of handyman was passing from voluntary to mandatory and confirm the social value placed on work around the house. The kinds of household repair, maintenance, and construction projects done by men did not change significantly during the 1950s, but the very doing of those projects became a requirement of masculinity.[50] In 1947 Sprague Holden coined the term "house-husband," not to describe a man who did traditional women's work at home but as a label for a man who had undertaken the role of keeping the house in good shape, in other words, the man who shouldered his responsibilities for household upkeep, just as a housewife did for hers.[51]

While the home workshop was no substitute for the fraternal lodge or neighborhood saloon as a venue for male bonding, it would do in a pinch. In a 1954 advertisement for Corby's whiskey the casually dressed men have obviously stepped out of the house, and away from their wives, to admire a half-finished Windsor rocking chair, while helping themselves to more whiskey from a homemade serving cart (see fig. 10.7). Their collective retreat to the garage workshop to smoke, drink, and admire the artisanal prowess of the householder all bespeak male camaraderie built on a shared appreciation of the masculine role of suburban handyman. A *Look* magazine feature on oxymoronic "White-collar work clothes" explained that the new "unhired man" was a "brainworker," who needed something appropri-

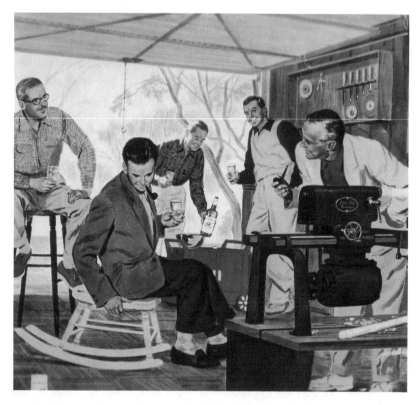

FIGURE 10.7 Corby's whiskey advertisement shows men bonding with the aid of alcohol, tobacco, and big tools. (Reprinted from "Do-It-Yourself Project That Always Wins Praise," [advertisement] *Colliers* 134 [October 1, 1954]: 2.)

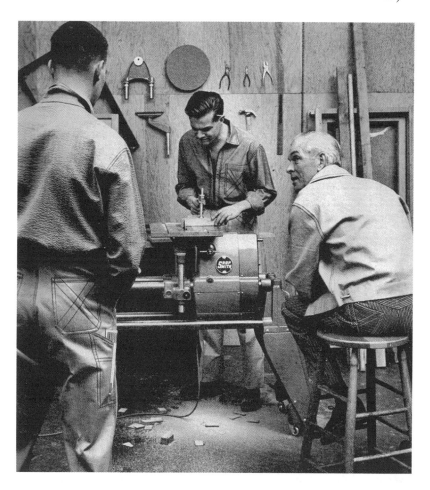

FIGURE 10.8   *Look* magazine featured an article on fashions for do-it-yourselfers. Models are shown with a Shopsmith multipurpose power tool. (Reprinted from "Do-It-Yourself Man," *Look* 17 [September 22, 1953]: 114.)

ate to wear "when he stops to boast with neighbors at cocktail time" (see fig. 10.8).[52]

In many communities the men had little choice but to congregate in each other's workshops. Postwar subdivisions like Levittown did not provide traditional male gathering places. There were no bars, pool halls, or clubs in the new communities, and houses themselves lacked not only dens and libraries but often basements and garages too. Eventually, Levitt acknowledged the role of automobiles in suburbia by adding carports to his houses, thereby creating space for do-it-yourselfers as well. Thus by the time of the great do-it-yourself boom of the mid-1950s, Levittown husbands could convert their carports into garages and their garages into workshops that would provide them with a sanctuary of their own. A 1955 *Popular Mechanics* cover showed a couple in a model home tugging each other toward their respective rooms, she toward the kitchen, he toward the workshop.[53]

Do-it-yourself was for adult males what sports were for youths, a virtual badge of manhood. Just as boys took pride in their athletic ability, grown men boasted about their craft skills: "A man makes a chair, a desk, a house, puts a washer in a leaky faucet, builds a kayak, paints a crib, and he spends the rest of his life and yours telling you about it." So far as business analyst Roger Babson was concerned, do-it-yourself won easily in the competition between crafts and sports as the more appropriate expression of masculinity, and did so because household improvement was a pastime that acted like work. Referring to do-it-yourself as a "practical hobby," Babson said the industry helped "parents set a fine example for their children" because "it not only is better for the kids to see their Dad working—instead of playing golf—but it enables the father and boy to work together and become better acquainted."[54]

The father-and-son-in-a-workshop picture had been a staple illustration since the 1930s, and its popularity continued apace in the 1950s (see fig. 10.9). Fatherhood, as historian Elaine Tyler May points out, "became a new badge of masculinity" after the war. Father could no longer fulfill his duties by merely being a good provider, he also needed to act as a gender role model for his sons, who were in danger of being mollycoddled by their mothers into sissyhood if not outright homosexuality. Sharing hobbies, especially ones that involved traditionally masculine activities like using heavy tools, gave fathers a structured environment in which to interact with their sons. Even a "family workshop" in a woman's publication typically shows a father painting a chair while his son uses an electric jigsaw. The female part of the family is nowhere in sight.[55] While they might be shown doing work around the house, women rarely, and daughters almost never, appeared in illustrations of home workshops. So important was the workshop in creating gender identity, that in 1952 the Museum of Modern Art in New York set up a woodworking shop so that apartment-dwelling fathers and sons could experience the same intergenerational male bonding as their suburban counterparts. "Most people think of sports as the main recreational activity for sons and dads to enjoy together," said one father working with his eleven-year-old boy, but he noted that crafts like woodworking not only gave them an opportunity to work together, but also allowed them to use their "hands and heads and share a practical learning experience."[56]

By using their hands, do-it-yourselfers evoked the image of the independent artisan who produced an object by himself from start to finish. It was an

FIGURE 10.9 Cowboy star Roy Rogers shown in his workshop with his two sons. (Reprinted from *Popular Mechanics* 112 [August 1959]: 125. Copyright the Hearst Corporation. All rights reserved.)

implicit critique of the segmentation of contemporary employment that a few made explicit. "Effective use of time in leisure can compensate for the lack of satisfaction in daily work," wrote a psychologist in 1957, who argued that "the do-it-yourself movement is a good beginning" to finding the personal creativity missing from the job. Likewise, the generally conservative *Senior Scholastic* magazine explained to its student audience that "many workers feel like cogs in a big machine. They have routine jobs and never see the results of their work so they turn to their homes for that opportunity." The article cited an expert who claimed that white-collar workers felt "guilty" about using their brains instead of their hands and relieved that guilt by working on do-it-yourself projects.[57] Do-it-yourself apologists, in an unselfconscious confirmation of Marx's core critique of industrialism, condemned the fragmentation of work and the alienation of workers. "The average American worker has often lost sight of the end product he is helping to build; his feeling of accomplishment has been whittled away as his job has become only a tiny part of the whole production process," claimed ideologically conservative *Time* magazine. "But when we build a kid's sandbox or an outdoor fireplace in our spare time, or paint a kitchen or raise a little garden," said *American Magazine*, "we satisfy an old, old hunger which lies deep within us."[58]

Writing in 1958 Albert Roland, the only academic analyst of do-it-yourself in the 1950s, said household projects were "real" because they confirmed masculine competence and reflected Thoreau's observation: "Drive a nail home and clinch it so faithfully that you can wake up in the night and think of your work with satisfaction." Working on their own homes, as Thoreau did on his cabin, gave do-it-yourselfers "the satisfying feeling of individual identity and measurable accomplishment" that they failed to get from their everyday jobs. Roland concluded that "millions have taken to heart Thoreau's example, withdrawing to their basement and garage workshops to find there a temporary Walden." *Harpers* reassured its readers that they were not losing the work ethic and that "the grim forebodings about American 'non-participation,' the fear that we were turning into a nation of passive consumers of amusements, were largely unjustified" because they were taking to their workshops in their leisure time.[59]

A self-generating cycle had been created. As more people did their own household chores, the number of professionals willing to work on small projects shrank. In 1958 Francis Coughlin of Chicago rued the passing of the "good $5-handyman (former cost about a dollar)." Coughlin needed some light soldering done, had to fix a couple of broken slats in his bed, wanted to replace a burned out wall switch and rewire a lamp, and he could not find a competent person to do so—at any price. Coughlin's complaint about the cost of craftsmen was a common explanation for the popularity of do-it-your-self. Contemporary observers, including the federal government, claimed that skilled workers were harder to find and more expensive than before the war.[60] While it is true that skilled labor was more expensive than it been in the depression, it is also true that it was much cheaper than it had been dur-ing the war.[61] Cheaper or not, homeowners did factor the cost of construc-tion labor into their decisions to do house maintenance work themselves. In his 1958 survey of Arkansas homeowners, for example, Viron Hukill found that three of the top four reasons cited for do-it-yourself work were economic. However, the dollar amounts saved were relatively small, and Hukill con-cluded do-it-yourself activity did not appreciably improve the economic situ-ation of the homeowners.[62]

Far from saving money, doing it yourself could be a distinct economic lia-bility, which is why one article on "what *not* to do yourself," proffered the unlikely advice that the do-it-yourselfer undertaking a major project hire a professional supervisor. Since the lack of supervision was what made do-it-yourself a respite from work, the suggestion was inappropriate, but not unwarranted. Mordant commentators regularly told of do-it-yourselfers who spent more on projects than the store-bought price and alienated their fami-lies in the process.[63] Stories and cartoons of do-it-yourself disasters acknowl-edged that home-built was not necessarily better-built. In sharp contrast to earlier periods, in the 1950s almost nobody complained about poor profes-sional work. It was, after all, unlikely that a professional would forget to install a staircase in the house he was building, wall up his wife in the attic bedroom he was constructing, or build a boat on the third floor of a New York City building so that it had to be lowered to the sidewalk by piano movers.[64] "Make a professional feel better by viewing an amateur's botch," said one not-too-handy man, "and you've scattered a little sunshine."[65]

Something more important than saving money was going on. The con-stant, often indulgently humorous, references to handyman disasters make it clear that for do-it-yourselfers there was pleasure in the pain. Cartoonist Morris Brickman drew a do-it-yourselfer sitting on his tool box staring at a misbegotten table and weeping as he repeated over and over, "It's only a hobby—a hobby—just a hobby—only a hobby—" The quintessentially male pastime of reveling in self-inflicted discomfort had moved indoors. One no longer had to play football, climb mountains, or sail outside the har-bor to experience the perverse joy of suffering. Now even the unathletic man could participate in the community of manly perseverance by wasting money, bruising his fingers, and making six return trips to the hardware store; one guide to remodeling cautioned men not to begin projects on a Sunday when building supply stores were closed. The ham-handed homeowner might make a mess, but at least it was his own mess, and he could take pride confronting, if not always overcoming, obstacles.[66]

Just before World War II, a newspaper columnist and do-it-yourself author named Julian Starr praised leisure woodworking by describing the compensatory benefits of creativity. The cure for the boredom of repetitive jobs, he said, was to find recreation "as far removed from daily occupation as a man can achieve." Starr claimed that sports could not fill that role since their competitiveness made them too worklike, but he went on to promote shop work for white-collar employees because of its ideological congruence. He celebrated the fact that "skill takes the place of thought, because 12 inches today is 12 inches tomorrow. A good joint, once learned is a good joint forever" and noted that "fixed values of this sort are a tremendous consolation in a world where the most fundamental concepts are subject to change without notice." Do-it-yourself might not be work, yet much of it had to be done, if not by the homeowner then by a paid professional; it might not be work, yet it was the exercise of creativity and productivity; it might not be work, yet it required planning, organization, knowledge, and skill, the same values necessary for success on the job; it might not be work as it was—it was work as it might be.[67]

Starr's contradictory analysis of do-it-yourself derived from the culturally marginal location of the activity; it was leisure and yet it was work. By embracing two oppositional categories, do-it-yourself was able to become an instrument of domestic masculinity. As leisure it could be done voluntarily, distinct from the arena of alienation that was the modern workplace; this was its disguise. As manual work it could confirm the dominant ideology and the homeowner's ties to his yeoman-artisan forefathers, creating a new stereotype of masculinity and an affirmation of the work ethic. By ceding men space for a workshop and proprietary interest in the house, women helped perpetuate a male domestic sphere. The hammer, saw, and quarter-inch electric drill became the emblems of the new masculinity, and men who refused to master them did so at some risk to their standing in the eyes of spouse and community.

Conclusion

Hobbies became a widely promoted form of leisure for children and adults because they are different from everyday work, yet confirm its importance. As leisure, hobbies are voluntarily undertaken pleasurable activities. Participants work without supervision, at their own pace, on projects of their own choosing from beginning to end. As with all leisure, the unconstrained elements of hobbies contrast with the mandatory nature of work. These contrasting aspects of hobbies both distinguish them from work and emphasize the ways in which work is unpleasant. Yet as a peculiarly productive form of leisure, hobbies also confirm the underlying legitimacy of work. For a leisure activity to be a hobby, it must, above all, be productive. Like work itself, hobbies generate a product and therefore hobbyists have something to show for their time; it has not been wasted. Even if they never even think of selling the products of their leisure, hobbyists know they have economic value, and that knowledge ties their free time to the ideals of the market economy. Furthermore, the process of creating the hobby product generates an intrinsically rewarding sense of accomplishment that is analogous to the feeling of satisfaction that comes from putting in a good day's work and thereby reinforces the work ethic. Thus even while hobbyists are enjoying the ways in which their pastimes are different from work, they are reproducing the underlying ideology of the system in which that work takes place.

The ability of hobbies to simultaneously critique and confirm daily work demonstrates how the conflicting concepts of compensatory and spillover leisure can be reconciled. Rather than understanding leisure either as compensating for desirable elements missing in work or reflecting fundamental patterns found in work, hobbies show us how leisure can do both. By analyzing leisure from a variety of perspectives, we see that the psychological freedom of doing what one wants to, how and when one wants to is not necessarily incompatible with the fundamental values of market capitalism. Indeed, hobbies arose as a recognized and socially sanctioned leisure category in the wake of industrialism because they were a way for people to engage in leisure, which was now separated physically from work, without abandoning the values that had been so essential to the rise of capitalism. If capitalism is culturally hegemonic then productive leisure is surely one of the instruments of its continuing domination. Yet the voluntary nature of the activity gives hobbyists a sense of freedom that dissipates the pall of oppression that would otherwise make hobby activities indistinguishable from work itself.

As a popularly derived category, there can be no hard and fast definition of which activities are "legitimate" hobbies, but collecting and handicrafts are generally acknowledged as particularly good examples. The very meaning of the term changed in the late nineteenth century as collecting and crafts came to be used synonymously with "hobbies." Whereas a hobby had once been understood as an eccentric preoccupation with a particular issue, cause, or activity, it was transformed to mean the benignly productive use of leisure time. People might poke fun at hobbyists who took their leisure too seriously and did not know how to relax, but the kidding was based on a deep respect for the pastimes that banished idleness. From the Progressive Era to World War II, educators and other guardians of the public weal promoted collecting and crafts as "worthy uses of leisure time," consolidating the idea that both children and adults should have hobbies to ward off the detrimental effects of either too much work or too much leisure. During times of prosperity advocates promoted hobbies as a morally safe haven from work, and during the depression they became a way to affirm the importance of productivity in a period of enforced idleness.

Collecting has always been the more problematic of the two main branches of hobbies. While crafting involves the straightforward use of manual skills to produce an object of beauty and value, success in collecting depends on the often suspect functioning of market forces. Some people, especially women, could collect for purely aesthetic reasons and remained aloof from the value of their collections, but the vast majority of male collectors, and many women as well, have approached their hobby in the spirit of the marketplace. The associational or artistic qualities of collectibles might have some legitimacy in their own right, but those qualities were most important to the extent that they contributed to the item's rarity and consequently to its desirability to other collectors. In order to know the present and predict the future value of objects, collectors have had to develop expert knowledge, making collecting "educational." Expertise, however, is often just an incidental consequence of the desire to be on the winning end of a commercial transaction. The leisure world of collecting has, in other words, echoed the real world of business.

The advent of industrialism changed the previously elite world of collecting by creating a new set of objects to be collected. Unlike traditional collectibles, which were created to be unique and valuable, the new industrial collectible was made to be discarded. The ephemeral nature of even expensive manufactured objects had the unintended consequence of creating a new category of rare objects—things that had not been thrown away. Postage stamps were the first manufactured collectibles and philatelists became the exemplars of industrial collecting. They created a rational "scientific" pastime whose rules of conduct became a model for subsequent collectors of everything from buttons to beer cans.

Unlike stamp collectors, who tried to maintain a hobby culture of honesty, antique collectors practiced a form of capitalism that was red in tooth and claw. Neither men nor women displayed much concern about the niceties of commercial intercourse as they misrepresented their wares and misled each other, hoping to take advantage of marketplace ignorance to score a coup that would confirm their superiority in the rough-and-tumble game of antique collecting. As the definition of collectible antiques broadened from finely handcrafted pieces to more crudely made vernacular objects, and finally to include manufactured goods, the opportunities for success and failure expanded accordingly. By the 1930s almost any object that was no longer made could be bought and sold as part of a hobby that simultaneously celebrated both the material and the ideological heritage of the United States. Collecting had become a form of "deep play" that mirrored fundamental cultural values, from the self-conscious rational honesty of stamp collecting to the devil-take-the-hindmost free-for-all of the antique trade.

In contrast to collecting, which has had to overcome various negative associations, handicrafts do not lend themselves to commercial chicanery and therefore have received unreserved support as a healthy pastime. Untainted by the marketplace, hobby crafting began as an appropriate leisure activity for Victorian ladies with a surfeit of free time. Barred from the productive arena and relieved of household duties by servants, nineteenth-century middle-class women took up crafting as a way to pass the time productively. Even though Victorian women's craft had only marginal economic value, the pastime was widely praised as superior to such alternatives as reading novels or visiting. Embroidering watch cases and pasting pictures inside glass jars may not have produced items that could compete in the commercial market, but they did provide participants with a sense of purpose, and they could be sold at the pseudomarkets provided by fancy fairs. Yet precisely because the charity fairs were not real marketplaces, Victorian women could sell their wares there without violating cultural mores. Their participation in this parallel economy made the world of their husbands less alien.

Until the turn of the century, the husbands avoided craft work at home. While many enthusiastically pursued the "white-collar" hobby of collecting, there was no cultural context that would make the "blue-collar" pastime of crafting attractive to middle-class males. That context was provided after 1900 by American adoption of the English arts and crafts movement. The movement's celebration of craftsman masculinity dovetailed nicely with the broader masculinization movement of the Progressive Era. The new masculinity made it acceptable for middle-class men to imitate the working class as long as it was done nostalgically. Thus they could act like vanished pioneers, cowboys, Indians, or craftsmen and recapture for themselves some of the lost individuality that had characterized preindustrial men. Taking up tools at home, like taking up athletic equipment on the ball field, was an expression of a more vigorous way to be a man; there was a muscular domesticity that paralleled muscular Christianity.

In the sixty years that followed, men became increasingly more comfortable working around their own homes. What started out as a somewhat romantic attempt to recapture the artisanal past evolved into a sphere of masculine competence inside the household. This domestic masculinity began as a voluntary excursion into making furniture in home workshops and grew into ever-widening circles of home maintenance and repair. By the post–World War II suburban boom, in fact, the voluntary nature of domestic masculinity had shrunk considerably, being a home handyman became one of the obligatory aspects of suburban home ownership.

While men were carving out a sphere for themselves inside the house, more traditional forms of handicrafts were becoming degendered. In the 1920s and 1930s craft books and kits made a deliberate effort to appeal to both men and women. There were, of course, exceptions. Sewing remained a female realm, albeit a shrinking one, and making models of ships, planes, and trains was a strictly male pastime. Nevertheless, as the hobby industry grew, manufacturers of supplies sought to maximize their customer base by aiming their products at all genders and ages. The universality of handicrafts had been given a considerable boost when the new profession of occupational therapy turned crafts into "medicine" before the First World War. World War II enhanced this acceptance when veterans hospitals used both traditionally men's and women's crafts to assist the rehabilitation of wounded soldiers. Hospitals introduced new kits and new plastic materials that were quickly turned into civilian products in the postwar period.

The kit craze of the 1950s may have marked a low point in hobby crafting by reducing the productive process to the assembly of preformed parts. Yet together with the do-it-yourself movement of the same period, kit assembly brought hobbies to an extremely wide audience. Just as do-it-yourselfers could quickly glue precut tiles to their floors and paste precut and prepasted paper to their walls, they and their children could stick together plastic models or sew together precut and punched leather kits to gain the satisfaction of having done something productive with their hands without having to go through the laborious process of learning a craft skill. However far removed such activities may have been from the skills needed for the best of Victorian women's crafts or mission-style furniture building for men, they functioned in intrinsically similar ways. The crafters were using their free time productively and by doing so were endorsing the importance of the work ethic.

Both crafts and collecting experienced a sharp increase in commercialization after World War II, but the intrusion of businesses hoping to make money from hobbyists was part of a tradition that stretched back almost 150 years. Critics have taken the commercial exploiters of hobbies to task for debasing genuine skills, and there can be no question that craft kits and made-to-be-collected figurines diluted the need for technical knowledge and know-how. The resurgence of high quality handicrafting that accompanied the cultural upheaval of the 1960s was a return to the romantic notions of the arts and crafts era and an explicit rejection of the overly commercialized hobby activities of the 1950s. Nevertheless, it does not seem historically honest to judge the role of commerce in hobbies too harshly since this entire category of leisure was itself a product of industrialism. Hobbies were not a recognized pastime until industrialism and commercialism separated production from the household and made the family a unit of consumption. Hobbies domesticated the ideology of capitalist industrialism by providing a way to safely bring the practice of finance (collecting) and production (crafts) into the household and thereby helped bridge the gap between home and workplace that had been opened by the Industrial Revolution.

Notes

Introduction: Context and Theory

1. John F. Kasson, *Amusing the Million: Coney Island at the Turn of the Century* (New York: Hill and Wang, 1978), 108–9.
2. Two recent historical examples are Lawrence W. Levine, *The Unpredictable Past: Explorations in American Cultural History* (New York: Oxford University Press, 1993); Robin D. G. Kelley, *Race Rebels: Culture, Politics, and the Black Working Class* (New York: Free Press, 1994); for mostly sociological examples see, *Cultural Studies*, ed. Lawrence Grossberg, Cary Nelson, and Paula Treichler (New York: Routledge, 1991).
3. John R. Kelly, "Situational and Social Factors in Leisure Distribution," *Pacific Sociological Review* 21 (July 1978): 327; Rhona Rappoport and Robert N. Rappoport, "Four Themes in the Sociology of Leisure," *British Journal of Sociology* 25 (1974): 215–16; Peter Witt and Gary Ellis, "Conceptualizing Leisure: Making the Abstract Concrete," in *Recreation and Leisure: Issues in an Era of Change*, ed. Thomas L. Goodale and Peter Witt (State Collage, Pa.: Venture Publishing, 1985), 105–6; Stanley Parker, *Leisure and Work* (London: George Allen and Unwin, 1983), 8–9; Mihaly Csikszentmihayli and Judith LeFevre, "Optimal Experience in Work and Leisure," *Journal of Personality and Social Psychology* 56 (1989): 815; John Clarke and Chas Critcher, *The Devil Makes Work: Leisure in Capitalist Britain* (Urbana: University of Illinois Press, 1985), 3; Hyam I. Day, "One Psychologist's Contribution to a Discipline of Leisurology," in *Perspectives on the Nature of Leisure Research*, ed. David Ng and Stephen L. J. Smith (Waterloo, Ontario: University of Waterloo Press, 1982), 107; John Neulinger, "Value Implications of Denotations of Leisure," in *Values and Leisure and Trends in Leisure Services* (State College, Pa.: Venture Publishing, 1983); Philip Ennis, "The Definition and Measure of Leisure," in *Indicators of Social Change*, ed. Eleanor Bernert Sheldon and Wilbert E. Moore (New York: Harper and Row, 1968), 526–31; Sheila Mullett, "Leisure and Consumption: Incompatible Concepts?" *Leisure Studies* 7 (1988): 241–53.
4. Parker, *Leisure and Work*, 39, 62–71; Mark Twain, *The Adventures of Tom Sawyer* (New York: Harper and Brothers, 1875), 33.

5. Hyam I. Day, "Leisure Satisfactions: Playfulness and Workfulness," *Proceedings of the Third Canadian Congress on Leisure Research* (Edmonton: University of Alberta, Canadian Association for Leisure Studies, 1983), 381–82, 395.

6. Seppo Iso-Ahola, *The Social Psychology of Leisure and Recreation* (Dubuque, Iowa: W. C. Brown, 1980); Gary Ellis, "The Measurement of Perceived Freedom in Leisure," *Journal of Leisure Research* 16 (1984): 110–23; Manuel London, Rick Crandall, and Gary W. Seals, "The Contribution of Job and Leisure Satisfaction to the Quality of Life," *Journal of Applied Psychology* 62 (1977): 328–34; John R. Robinson, *How Americans Use Their Time: A Social-Psychological Analysis of Everyday Behavior* (New York: Praeger, 1977); David J. Duncan, "Leisure Types: Factor Analysis of Leisure Profiles," *Journal of Leisure Research* 10 (1978): 113–25; Parker, *Leisure and Work*, 9; Janet E. Stockdale, *What Is Leisure? An Empirical Analysis of the Concept of the Role of Leisure* (London: Sports Council and Social Research Council, 1985), 71–77.

7. Alan Roadburg, "Freedom and Enjoyment: Disentangling Perceived Leisure," *Journal of Leisure Research* 15 (1983): 15–26.

8. Day, "One Psychologist's Contribution," 110; Roger Caillois, *Man, Play, and Games* (New York: Free Press of Glencoe, 1961), 5–25.

9. For example, see Colin Lindsay, "Social Indicators and Leisure: Problems and Potential," *Proceedings of the Second Canadian Congress on Leisure Research* (Toronto: Ontario Research Council on Leisure, 1979), 65–66.

10. John R. Kelly, "Work and Leisure: A Simplified Paradigm," *Journal of Leisure Research* 4 (1972): 50–62; John R. Kelly, *Leisure Identities and Interactions* (London: George Allen and Unwin, 1983), 9–10; John Neulinger, "The Need for and the Implications of a Psychological Conception of Leisure," *Ontario Psychologist* 8 (June 1976): 13; John Neulinger, "Key Questions Evoked by a State of Mind Conceptualization of Leisure," *Loisir et Société/Society and Leisure* 7 (spring 1984): 25–36; Mihaly Csikszentmihayli, *Beyond Boredom and Anxiety: The Experience of Play in Games* (San Francisco: Josey-Bass, 1975), 29; Howard E. Tinsley and Thomas L. Johnson, "A Preliminary Taxonomy of Leisure Activities," *Journal of Leisure Research* 16 (1984): 236; Ronald Cosper, "Occupation and Leisure Participation: A Multi-Dimensional Analysis," *Proceedings of the Third Canadian Congress on Leisure* (Edmonton: University of Alberta, Canadian Association for Leisure Studies, 1983), 425.

11. Csikszentmihayli, *Beyond Boredom*, 8–9.

12. For examples, see Boris Kabanoff "Validation of a Task Attributes Description of Leisure," *Australian Journal of Psychology* 33 (1981): 260–69; Douglas A. Kleiber and Guy R. Dirkin, "Intrapersonal Constraints to Leisure," in *Constraints on Leisure*, ed. Michael G. Wade (Springfield, Illinois: Charles C. Thomas, 1985), 17–42; Robert A. Stebbins, "Amateur and Hobbyist as Concepts for the Study of Leisure Problems," *Social Problems* 27 (April 1980): 413

13. Csikszentmihayli, *Beyond Boredom*, 22–23, 45–46; Mihaly Csikszentmihayli, "The Concept of Flow," in *Play and Learning*, ed. Brian Sutton-Smith (New York: Gardner Press, 1979), 260; Richard G. Mitchell, *Mountain Experience:*

The Psychology and Sociology of Adventure (Chicago: University of Chicago Press, 1983), 153–69; Helen B. Schwartzman, *Play and Culture* (West Point, N.Y.: Leisure Press, 1980), 322.

14. Csikszentmihayli and LaFevere, "Optimal Experience," 818; for an analysis of the particular problems of defining women's leisure see Leslie Bella, "Women and Leisure: Beyond Androcentrism," in *Understanding Leisure and Recreation: Mapping the Past, Charting the Future,* ed. Edgar L. Jackson and Thomas L. Burton (State College, Pa.: Venture Publishing, 1989), 151–79; Joseph Levy, *Play Behavior* (New York: John Wiley and Sons, 1978), 136–53; Mitchell, *Mountain Experience,* 156, 159, 171; Csikszentmihayli, *Beyond Boredom,* 139, 181; John M. Roberts and Garry E. Chick, "Quitting the Game: Covert Disengagement from Butler County Eight Ball," *American Anthropologist* 86 (1984): 549–67; Dale Dannefer, "Rationality and Passion in Private Experience: Modern Consciousness and the Social World of Old-Car Collectors," *Social Problems* 27 (April 1980): 396–99.

15. For example, see Mike Cormack, *Ideology* (Ann Arbor: University of Michigan Press, 1992), 12–13; for a definition of values, see Geert Hofstede, *Culture's Consequences: International Differences in Work Related Values* (Beverly Hills, Calif.: Sage, 1980), 19–22.

16. Nicholas Abercrombie, Stephen Hill, and Bryan S. Turner, *The Dominant Ideology Thesis* (London: George Allen and Unwin, 1980), 29; Daniel Miller, "Modernism and Suburbia as Material Ideology," in *Ideology, Power, and Prehistory,* ed. Daniel Miller and Christopher Tilley (Cambridge: Cambridge University Press, 1984), 38; John Clarke, "Pessimism versus Populism: The Problematic Politics of Popular Culture," in *For Fun and Profit: The Transformation of Leisure into Consumption,* ed. Richard Butsch (Philadelphia: Temple University Press, 1989), 31; Chris Rojek, *Capitalism and Leisure Theory* (London: Tavistock Publications, 1985), 106–32; Dorothy C. Holland and Margaret A. Eisenhart, *Educated in Romance: Women, Achievement, and College Culture* (Chicago: University of Chicago Press, 1990), 29–32; Hans-Erik Olson, "Leisure and Ideological Control: The Swedish Case," in *Elra Workshop: Meeting on Leisure Research,* ed. Lars-Magnus Engstrom and Hans-Erik Olson (Växjö, Sweden: University of Upsala, Department of Government, 1983), 429–30.

17. Clarke, "Pessimism versus Populism," 34–38; N. Parry and F. Coalter, "Sociology and Leisure: A Question of Root and Branch," *Sociology* 16 (1982): 220–31; Don Dawson, "Leisure and Social Class: Some Neglected Theoretical Considerations," *Leisure Sciences* 8 (1986): 47–61.

18. Max Weber, *The Protestant Ethic and the Spirit of Capitalism* (New York: Charles Scribner's Sons, 1958), 47–78; A. W. Bacon, "The Embarrassed Self: Some Reflections upon Attitudes to Work and Idleness in a Prosperous Industrial Society," *Loisir et Société/Society and Leisure* 4 (1972): 23–39; Daniel T. Rodgers, *The Work Ethic in Industrial America* (Chicago: University of Chicago Press, 1974), 1–29; A. Thio, "American Success Ideology and Coerced Conformity: Toward Clarifying a Theoretical Controversy," *International Journal of*

Contemporary Sociology 11 (1974): 12–22; R. Buchholz, "Measurements of Beliefs," *Human Relations* 29 (1978): 1180; Stockdale, *What Is Leisure*, 23–24; Adrian Furnham and Maria Rose, "Alternative Ethics: The Relationship between the Wealth, Welfare, Work, and Leisure Ethics," *Human Relations* 40 (September 1987): 561–73.

19. Clarke and Critcher, *The Devil Makes Work*, 5; Douglas A. Kleiber, "Fate Control and Leisure Attitudes," *Leisure Sciences* 2 (1979): 239–48; Roger Ingham, "Psychological Contributions to the Study of Leisure—Part Two," *Leisure Studies* 6 (1987): 8–9; Boas Shamir, "Unemployment and Free Time, the Role of the Protestant Work Ethic," *Leisure Studies* 4 (1985): 333–45; T. Kay, "Active Unemployment—A Leisure Pattern for the Future?" *Loisir et Société/Society and Leisure* 12 (1989): 413–30; Lionel S. Lewis, "Working at Leisure," *Society* 19 (1982): 27–32; Robert A. Stebbins, "Serious Leisure: A Conceptual Statement," *Pacific Sociological Review* 25 (April 1982): 256–57; Robert A. Stebbins, *Amateurs, Professionals, and Serious Leisure* (Montreal: McGill-Queen's University Press, 1992).

20. Paul A. Breer and Edwin A. Locke, *Task Experience as a Source of Attitudes* (Homewood, Illinois: Dorsey Press, 1965), 19–21.

21. Robert Dubin, "Industrial Workers' Worlds: A Study in the 'Central Life Interests' of Industrial Workers," in *Work and Leisure: A Contemporary Social Problem*, ed. Erwin Smigel (New Haven, Conn.: College and University Press, 1963), 54–68; Nels Anderson, "The Work Leisure Dichotomy," in *Work and Leisure*, 29; Louis H. Orzack, "Work as a 'Central Life Interest' of Professionals," in *Work and Leisure*; John R. Kelly, *Leisure Identities and Interactions* (London: George Allen and Unwin, 1983), 105–8; David K. Banner, "The Nature of the Work-Leisure Relationship," *Omega* 2 (1974): 186; Elmer A. Spreitzer, "Work Orientation, Meaning of Leisure, and Mental Health," *Journal of Leisure Research* 6 (1974): 207–19; Robert C. Atchley, "Retirement and Leisure Participation: Continuity or Crisis?" *Gerontologist* 2 (spring 1971, part 1): 13–17; S. J. Miller, "The Social Dilemma of the Aging Leisure Participant," in *Older People and Their Social World*, ed. A. M. Rose and W. A. Peterson (Philadelphia: F. A. Davis, 1965); Theodore Caplow, *The Sociology of Work* (Minneapolis: University of Minnesota Press, 1954), 124–25; Harold L. Wilensky, "Work Careers and Social Integration," *International Social Sciences Journal* 12 (1960): 543–60; Harold L. Wilensky, "Orderly Careers and Social Participation: The Impact of Work History on Social Integration in the Middle Class," *American Sociological Review* 26 (1961): 521–39.

22. Breer and Locke, *Task Experience*, 6–19.

23. Menahem Rosner, "Changes in Leisure Culture in the Kibbutz,," *Loisir et Société/Society and Leisure* 2 (1979): 471; Breer and Locke, *Task Experience*, 6–7; Melvin Kohn, *Class and Conformity: A Study in Values* (Homewood, Ill.: Dorsey Press, 1969), 166–67; Kohn, "Occupational Experience and Psychological Functioning: An Assessment of Reciprocal Effects," *American Sociological Review* 38 (1973): 97–118.

24.   John R. Kelly, "Three Measures of Leisure Activity: A Note on the Continued
      Incommensurability of Oranges, Apples, and Artichokes," *Journal of Leisure
      Research* 5 (1973): 56–65; Clifford Geertz, *The Interpretation of Cultures* (New
      York: Basic Books, 1973), 443; Neil H. Cheek Jr. and William R. Burch Jr., *The
      Social Organization of Leisure in Human Society* (New York: Harper and Row,
      1976), 207.

25.   Erik H. Erikson, *Childhood and Society* (New York: W. W. Norton, 1950),
      211–21; John M. Roberts, Brian Sutton-Smith, and Adam Kendon, "Strategy in
      Games and Folk Tales," *Journal of Social Psychology* 61 (1963): 185; the best
      overall description of their theory can be found in Brian Sutton-Smith and John
      M. Roberts, "The Cross-Cultural and Psychological Study of Games," in *The
      Cross-Cultural Analysis of Sports and Games* (Champaign, Ill.: Stipes, 1970);
      apparently unaware of Roberts and Sutton-Smith's work, much of the theory
      was replicated in Omar Khayyam Moore and Alan Ross Anderson, "Some Prin-
      ciples for the Design of Clarifying Educational Environments," in *Handbook of
      Socialization Theory and Research*, ed. David A. Goslin (Chicago: Rand
      McNally, 1969), 571–79.

26.   Brian Sutton-Smith, John M. Roberts, and Robert M. Kozelka, "Game Involve-
      ment in Adults," *Journal of Social Psychology* 60 (1963): 27.

27.   John M. Roberts and Brian Sutton-Smith, "Cross-Cultural Correlates of Games
      of Chance," *Behavior Sciences Notes* 1 (1966): 143; John M. Roberts and Gary E.
      Chick, "Human Views of Machines: Expression and Machine Shop Syn-
      cretism," in *Technology and Social Change*, ed. Russell Bernard and Pertti J.
      Pelto (Prospects Heights, Ill.: Waveland Press, 1987); Francis P. Noe, "A Com-
      parative Typology of Leisure in Nonindustrialized Society," *Journal of Leisure
      Research* 2 (1970): 35; Harry Eckstein, *Division and Cohesion in Democracy*
      (Princeton: Princeton University Press, 1966), 92–94; Gary B. Jackson, "The
      Conveyance of Social Beliefs and Values through Aesthetic Sport: The Case of
      Kendo," in *Play: Anthropological Perspectives* (West Point, N.Y.: Leisure Press,
      1977), 82–93.

28.   Jay Mechling, "Patois and Paradox in a Boy Scout Treasure Hunt," *Journal of
      American Folklore* 97 (1984): 35–37; for an imaginative but much less successful
      effort, see Hugh Gardner, "Bureaucracy at the Bridge Table," in *Side Saddle on
      the Golden Calf*, ed. George H. Lewis (Pacific Palisades, Calif.: Goodyear,
      1972), 138–53.

29.   For a good summary of the debate, see Jiri Zuzanek and Roger Mannell,
      "Work-Leisure Relationships from a Sociological and Social Psychological Per-
      spective," *Leisure Studies* 2 (1983): 327–44.

30.   Clarence E. Rainwater, "Socialized Leisure," *Journal of Applied Sociology* 7
      (May 1923): 258–59; Donald E. Super, *Avocational Patterns: A Study in the Psy-
      chology of Avocations* (Stanford, Calif.: Stanford University Press, 1940), 2, 6–9,
      105–9.

31.   Wilensky, "Work, Careers, and Social Integration," 544; see Barry D. McPher-
      son, "Influence of Infra-Organizational Parameters on the Leisure Pursuits of

Adult Men," *Canadian Congress on Leisure Research* (Canadian Congress on Leisure Research, 1975), 35–36.

32. Stanley Parker, "Work and Nonwork in Three Occupations," *Sociological Review* 13 (1965): 65–75; Stanley Parker, *The Future of Work and Leisure* (New York: Praeger, 1971), 55, 66, 72.

33. Stanley Parker, *Work and Leisure* (London: George Allen and Unwin, 1983), 87–91; Parker, *Future of Work and Leisure*, 109–10; for some corrective analysis see, Roger C. Mannell and Seppo E. Iso-Ahola, "Work Constraints on Leisure: A Social Psychological Analysis," in *Constraints on Leisure*, ed. Michael G. Wade (Springfield, Ill.: Charles C. Thomas, 1985), 161; Jiri Zuzanek, *Leisure and Social Change* (Waterloo, Ontario: University of Waterloo, 1976); Zuzanek and Mannell, "Work-Leisure Relationships," 330. For additional critiques of Parker and other analyses, see Rojek, *Capitalism and Leisure Theory*, 97–100; Boris Kabanoff and Gordon E. O'Brien, "Work and Leisure: A Task Attribute Analysis," *Journal of Applied Psychology* 65 (1980): 597; Mannell and Iso-Ahola, "Work Constraints on Leisure," 165–81; T. M. Kando and W. C. Summers, "The Impact of Work on Leisure," *Pacific Sociological Review* 14 (July 1971): 310–27. For an example of how respondents may not understand how leisure satisfies deeper needs, see Mannell and Iso-Ahola, "Work Constraints on Leisure," 172.

34. For evidence of no connection between work and leisure see, Edward M. Bruce, "An Empirical Examination of the Relationship between Work and Leisure" (master's thesis, University of Regina, 1975), 57–72; A. W. Bacon, "Leisure and the Alienated Worker: A Critical Reassessment of Three Radical Theories of Work and Leisure," *Journal of Leisure Research* 7 (1975): 188. For examples of how leisure should compensate for work, see Fritz Redlich, "Leisure-Time Activities: A Historical, Sociological, and Economic Analysis," *Explorations in Entrepreneurial History* 3 (fall 1965): 12; Karl Mannheim, *Freedom, Power, and Democratic Planning* (London: Routledge and Kegan Paul, 1951, 269; Joseph Levy, *Play Behavior* (New York: John Wiley and Sons, 1978), 162–64; Francis Abernethy, "Games and Recreation," in *Texas Toys and Games*, ed. Francis Abernethy (Dallas: Southern Methodist University Press, 1989), 23. David T. Herbert, "Exploring the Work-Leisure Relationship: An Empirical Study in South Wales," *Leisure Studies* 6 (May 1987): 160;

35. Steven M. Gelber, "Working at Playing: The Culture of the Workplace and the Rise of Baseball," *Journal of Social History* 16 (June 1983): 3–22; Steven M. Gelber, "Their Hands Are All Out Playing: Business and Amateur Baseball, 1845–1917," *Journal of Sport History* 11 (spring 1984): 5–27; Boris Kabanoff and Gordon E. O'Brien, "Relationships between Work and Leisure Attributes Across Occupational and Sex Groups in Australia," *Australian Journal of Psychology* 34 (August 1982): 165–82.

36. Brian Kinsley and Iris M. Bradley, "Participation in Leisure Activities and Its Relationship to Work Activity Level and Occupation: Compensation and Alienation," in *Proceedings of the Third Canadian Congress on Leisure Research* (Edmonton, Alberta: University of Alberta, 1983), 399–415; Mitchell, *Mountain Experience*, 186–87; Marylee Stephenson, "Mountain-Climbing: Experience

and Function," *Contemporary Leisure Research, Proceedings of the Second Canadian Congress on Leisure Research* (Toronto: Ontario Research Council on Leisure, 1979), 521–25.

37.   Boas Shamir, "Commitment and Leisure," *Sociological Perspectives* 31 (1988): 238–58.

38.   Super, *Avocational Interest Patterns*, 106–7; Arthur Adams and Thomas H. Stone, "Satisfaction of Need for Achievement in Work and Leisure," *Journal of Vocational Behavior* 11 (1977): 174–81; Lynn Miller and Richard M. Weiss, "The Work-Leisure Relationship: Evidence for the Compensatory Hypothesis," *Human Relations* 35 (1982): 763–71; Parker, *Leisure and Work*, 58–59; Sharon L. Hunt, "Work and Leisure in the Academic Environment: Relationships between Selected Meanings," *Research Quarterly* 50 (1979): 388–95; Graeme Salaman, *Community and Occupation: An Explanation of Work/Leisure Relationships* (Cambridge: Cambridge University Press, 1974), 110–13.

39.   Scott Meis, "The Effects of the Social Environment at Home and at Work on Solitary Discretionary Behavior," *Contemporary Leisure, Proceedings of the Second Canadian Congress on Leisure Research* (Toronto: Ontario Research Council on Leisure, 1979), 173–81; David K. Banner, "Towards a Theoretical Clarification of the Spillover and Compensatory Work/Leisure Hypotheses," *Omega* 13 (1985): 16; Martin Meissner, "The Long Arm of the Job: A Study of Work and Leisure," *Industrial Relations* (October 10, 1971): 239–60; Christopher Orpen, "Work and Nonwork Satisfaction: A Causal-Correlational Analysis," *Journal of Applied Psychology* 63 (1978): 530–32; Cosper, "Occupation and Leisure Participation," 429, 433; Kenneth Roberts, *Leisure* (London: Longman, 1970), 27–29

40.   Michael Young and Peter Willmott, *The Symmetrical Family* (New York: Pantheon, 1973), 219–21; Simon J. Bronner, *Chain Carvers: Old Men Crafting Meaning* (Lexington: University of Kentucky Press, 1985), 28–29, 56, 130–31; interviews with surgeons found in Csikszentmihayli, *Beyond Boredom*, 129–30.

41.   Joseph Harry, "Work and Leisure: Situational Attitudes," *Pacific Sociological Review* 14 (July 1971): 301–9; Roberts and Chick, "Human Views of Machines," 145.

42.   Joffre Dumazedier, *Toward a Society of Leisure* (New York: Free Press, 1967), 74–75; Fred H. Blum, *Toward a Democratic Work Process: The Hormel Packinghouse Workers' Experiment* (New York: Harper, 1953), 109–10.

43.   Clement Greenberg, "Work and Leisure under Industrialism," in *Mass Leisure*, ed. Eric Larrabee and Rolf Meyersohn (Glencoe, Ill.: Free Press, 1953), 41.

44.   Sharon Hunt and Kenneth Brooks, "Perceptions of Work and Leisure: A Study of Industrial Workers," *Recreation Management* 23 (1980): 31–35; Robert Allen Karasek, "The Impact of the Work Environment on Life Outside the Job" (Ph.D. diss., Massachusetts Institute of Technology, 1974), 294–95; Robert F. Musolino and David B. Hershenon, "Avocational Sensation Seeking in High and Low Risk-Taking Occupations," *Journal of Vocational Behavior* 10 (1977): 358–65; Doyle W. Bishop and Masaru Ikeda, "Status and Role Factors in the Leisure Behavior of Different Occupations," *Sociology and Social Research* 54 (1970): 199–202.

1 Occupations for Free Time

1. E. P. Thompson, "Time, Work-Discipline, and Industrial Capitalism," *Past and Present* 38 (February 1967): 60–61; Jeremy Cherfos and Roger Lewin, *Not Work Alone: A Cross Cultural View of Activities Superfluous to Survival* (Beverly Hills, Calif.: Sage Publications, 1980), 14–16; Garry E. Chick, "Leisure, Labor, and the Complexity of Culture: An Anthropological Perspective," *Journal of Leisure Research* 18 (1986): 158–59, 162; Peter Just, "Time and Leisure in the Elaboration of Culture," *Journal of Anthropological Research* 36 (1980): 109; For examples of play on the job, see Donald F. Roy, " 'Banana Time': Job Satisfaction and Informal Interaction," *Human Organization* 18 (winter 1959–60): 158–68.

2. U.S. Bureau of the Census, *Historical Statistics of the United States, Colonial Times to 1970, Bicentennial Edition* (Washington, D.C.: Government Printing Office, 1975), 134; for a romanticized description of traditional work and leisure, see Sarah Orne Jewett, "The Failure of David Berry," *Harper's New Monthly Magazine* 83 (June 1891): 56–62; Juliet B. Schor, *The Overworked American: The Unexpected Decline of Leisure* (New York: Basic Books, 1992), 53–56; the quotation is on p. 44.

3. Joseph Zeisel, "The Workweek in American Industry, 1850–1956," in *Mass Leisure,* ed. Eric Larrabee and Rolf Meyersohn (Glencoe, Ill.: Free Press, 1958), 146; Schor, *Overworked American,* 76–80; *Historical Statistics,* 168–73.

4. Catharine E. Beecher, A *Treatise on Domestic Economy for the Use of Young Ladies at Home and at School* (New York: Harper and Brothers, 1855), 256.

5. Henry T. Williams, *Fret-Sawing for Pleasure and Profit* (New York: Henry T. Williams, 1877), 54, 5; see also Thomas Seaton, *A Manual of Fret Cutting and Wood Carving* (London: George Routledge and Sons, 1875), iv; *Current [Chicago]* (October 4, 1884): n.p., reprinted in "Thoughts of 1884," *Hobbies* 53 (October 1948): 148.

6. Virginia F. Townsend, "Her Life in Bloom," *Arthur's Home Magazine* 48 (January 1880): 34; "Home Pastimes," *Godey's Lady's Book* 73 (September 1866): 261; *New York Times,* December 21, 1879, 10.

7. Andrew Wright, *The American Musical Miscellany* (Northampton, 1798), reprinted in William T. Utter, "An Old Hobbies Song," *Hobbies* 43 (May 1938): 118; a very similar use of the term in a song from 1806 can be found in J. M. Sewall "The Hobbies," *Hobbies* 42 (December 1937): 12; Samuel Johnson, *Dictionary of the English Language* (London: 1823), 314; Noah Webster, *An American Dictionary of the English Language* (Springfield, Mass.: George and Charles Merriam, 1856), 555; James Stormonth, *Dictionary of the English Language* (London: William Blackwood and Sons, 1876), 258. B. F. Tefft, "The Monomaniacs," *Ladies' Repository* 6 (October 1846): 311.

8. "Hobbies," *Arthur's Home Magazine* 8 (September 1856): 167; J. E. M'C, "Mrs. Niel's Hobby," *Arthur's Home Magazine* 22 (September 1863): 142; Nora Perry, "Held by a Thread," *Harper's New Monthly Magazine* 35 (September 1867): 492.

9. T. DeWitte Talmage, "Hobbies," *Hours at Home* 8 (December 1868): 131–41; A Cynic [Leslie Stephen], "Vacations," reprinted from the *Cornhill Magazine* 20

(August 1869): 205–14 in *Mass Leisure*, 288; Carroll West, "The Old Woman Who Lived in a Shoe," *Godey's Lady's Book* 93 (September 1876): 226; W. DeM. Hooper, "The Evolution of a Hobby," *Library Journal* 11 (1882): 225; "Hobbies and Their Riders," *Catholic World* 23 (1876): 413–420.

10.   For example, see Talmage, "Hobbies," 131.

11.   "Hobbies," *Godey's Lady's Book* 92 (May 1876): 432; Alfred C. Sayres, "One Old Bachelor," *Godey's Lady's Book* 89 (July 1874): 76; [T. S. Arthur], "Too Late," *Arthur's Lady's Home Magazine* 37 (March 1871): 150.

12.   "Hobbies and Their Riders," 413; Theodore F. Dwight, "Hobbies and Their Riders," *Overland Monthly and Out West Magazine* 7 (September 1871): 259; "Will It Last?" *Stamp Collector's Guide* 1 (April 1871), 18.

13.   "Hobbies and Their Riders," 414.

14.   For example, see George Eliot, *Middlemarch* (New York: Frank F. Lovell, 1889), 161.

15.   Stephen Constantine, "Amateur Gardening and Popular Recreation in the Nineteenth and Twentieth Centuries," *Journal of Social History* 14 (1981): 387–406.

16.   George Lakoff, *Women, Fire, and Dangerous Things: What Categories Reveal about the Mind* (Chicago: University of Chicago Press, 1987), 31–37.

17.   Willett Kempton, *The Folk Classification of Ceramics: A Study of Cognitive Prototypes* (New York: Academic Press, 1981).

18.   "Hobby Horses," *All the Year Round* 14 (September 9, 1865): 163.

19.   "About Hobbies," *All the Year Round* 67 (November 8, 1890): 441.

20.   Quoted in *New York Times*, December 21, 1879, 10; Janet E. Ruutz-Rees, *Home Occupations* (New York: D. Appleton, 1883).

21.   Bill Martin and Sandra Mason, *Where Shall We Take Our Leisure? Leisure, Tourism, and Social Change* (Dunfermline: Centre for Leisure Research, 1984), 23, 26.

22.   Leonard Reissman, "Class Leisure and Social Participation," *American Sociological Review* 19 (1954): 80; Sebastian DeGrazia, *Of Time, Work, and Leisure* (New York: Twentieth Century Fund, 1962), 460–62; Arthur Kornhauser, *Mental Health and the Industrial Worker: A Detroit Study* (New York: John Wiley and Sons, 1965), 200; Michael Young and Peter Willmott, *The Symmetrical Family* (New York: Pantheon, 1973), 212; Neil H. Cheek Jr. and William R. Burch Jr., *The Social Organization of Leisure in Human Society* (New York: Harper and Row, 1976), 17, 22; Graham Staines and David Pagnucco, "Work and Nonwork, part 2," in *An Empirical Study of the Effectiveness of Work Roles: Employee Responses to Work Environments*, vol. 1 (Ann Arbor, Michigan: Survey Research Center, 1977), 738; Michael Chubb and Holly R. Chubb, *One-Third of Our Time? An Introduction to Recreation Behavior and Resources* (New York: John Wiley and Sons, 1981), 266; Gene Bammel and Lei Lane Burrus-Bammel, *Leisure and Human Behavior* (Dubuque, Iowa: William C. Brown, 1982), 247; John C. Pollock et al., *Where Does the Time Go?* (New York: Newspaper Enterprise Association, 1983), 30–31; Janet E. Stockdale, *What Is Leisure? An Empirical Analysis of the Concept of Leisure and the Role of Leisure in Peo-*

ple's Lives (London: Sports Council and Social Research Council, 1985), 59; Jarmila Horna, "Desires and Preferences for Leisure Activities: More of the Same?" *World Leisure and Recreation* 27 (1985): 31; Rhona Rappoport and Robert Rappoport, *Leisure and the Family Life Cycle* (London: Routledge and Kegan Paul, 1975), 253.

23. Ronald Bagley, "A Study to Determine the Contribution of Industrial Arts to Leisure Time Activities of the Graduates of Northeast State Missouri Teachers College" (Ed.D. diss., Colorado State College, 1965), 118–23; Rabel J. Burdge, "Levels of Occupational Prestige and Leisure Activity," in *Sport and American Society*, ed. George H. Sage (Reading: Pa.: Addison Wesley, 1974), 243; Arthur Kornhauser, *Mental Health and the Industrial Worker: A Detroit Study* (New York: John Wiley and Sons, 1965), 200–204; Craig Ross, "The Relationship between Occupational Prestige and Leisure Participation Patterns of Selected Employees" (Re.D. diss., Indiana University, 1980), 163. These findings are contradicted, however, by two rather crude surveys that found no difference in social status among collectors and handicrafters over the course of the twentieth century: Francis P. Noe, "Leisure Life Styles and Social Class: A Trend Analysis, 1900–1960," *Sociology and Social Research* 58 (1973): 286–94; and Michele McLoughlin and Frank P. Noe, "Changing Coverage of Leisure in *Harper's, Atlantic Monthly,* and *Reader's Digest:* 1960–1985," *Sociology and Social Research* 72 (1988): 224–26.

24. John P. Robinson and Geoffrey Godbey, *Time for Life: The Surprising Ways Americans Use Their Time* (University Park: Pennsylvania State University Press, 1997), 125, 170, 179, 206, 211; *New York Times,* May 9, 1993, sect. 4, p. 2; "Day in the Life," *Maclean's* 106 (May 10, 1993): 6.

25. John R. Kelly, "How They Play in Peoria: Models of Adult Leisure," in *Meaningful Play, Playful Meaning,* ed. Gary Alan Fine (Champaign, Ill.: Human Kinetics Publishers, 1987), 36; John R. Kelly, *Leisure Identities and Interactions* (London: George Allen and Unwin, 1983), 16.

26. William C. Menninger, "Psychological Aspects of Hobbies," *American Journal of Psychiatry* 99 (June 1942); reprinted in *A Psychiatrist for a Troubled World: Selected Papers of William C. Menninger, M.D.,* ed. Bernard H. Hall (New York: Viking Press, 1967), 708–12.

27. Robert C. Pierce, "Dimensions of Leisure, 1: Satisfaction," *Journal of Leisure Research* 12 (1980): 5–12; Mihaly Csikszentmihayli and Eugene Rochberg-Halton, "Leisure and Work," *Leisure Information Newsletter* 8 (1981): 6.

28. Georges Friedmann, *The Anatomy of Work: Labor, Leisure, and the Implications of Automation* (New York: Free Press of Glencoe, 1961), 105; Dale Dannefer, "Neither Socialization nor Recruitment: The Avocational Careers of Old Car Enthusiasts," *Social Forces* 60 (December 1981): 395–413.

29. Maurice F. Ethridge and Jerome L. Neapolitan, "Amateur Craft Artists: Marginal Leisure Roles in a Marginal Art World," *Sociological Spectrum* 5 (1985): 68; John A. Bellingham Jr., "Assessing Sources of Intrinsic and Extrinsic Satisfaction in the Crafts Experience: Woodworking" (Ph.D. diss., Michigan State University, 1981).

30. Hyam I. Day, "Why People Play," *Loisir et Société/Society and Leisure* 2 (April 1979): 143; Hyam I. Day, "Leisure Satisfactions: Playfulness and Workfulness," *Proceedings of the Third Canadian Congress on Leisure Research* (Edmonton: University of Alberta, Canadian Association for Leisure Studies, 1983), 392; Robert A. Stebbins, "Amateurism in the Postretirement Years," *Journal of Physical Education and Recreation* 49 (1978): 40; Nancy J. Osgood and Christine Z. Howe, "Psychological Aspects of Leisure: A Life Cycle Development Perspective," *Loisir et Société/Society and Leisure* 7 (1984): 189; Jerome F. Singleton, "Activity Patterns of the Elderly," *Loisir et Societe/Society and Leisure* 8 (1985): 813; Michael Humphrey and Christine Lenham, "Adolescent Fantasy and Self-fulfillment: The Problem of Female Passivity," *Journal of Adolescence* 7 (1984): 295–304.

31. Max Weber, *The Protestant Ethic and the Spirit of Capitalism* (New York: Charles Scribner's Sons, 1958), 71; P. Hoggett and J. Bishop, "Leisure beyond the Individual Consumer," *Leisure Studies* 4 (1985): 35–36.

32. H. F. Moorhouse, "The Work Ethic and Leisure Activity: The Hot Rod in Post-War America," in *The Historical Meaning of Work,* ed. Patrick Joyce (New York: Cambridge University Press, 1987), 257.

33. Stanley Parker, *Leisure and Work* (London: George Allen and Unwin, 1983), 22–27; Ross McKibbin, "Work and Hobbies in Britain, 1880–1950," in *The Working Class in Modern British History,* ed. Jay Winter (London: Cambridge University Press, 1983), 142.

34. Horace Coon, *Hobbies for Pleasure and Profit: New Worlds of Fun and Relaxation for Everyone* (New York: New American Library, 1955), 9–11, 16, 196.

35. Russell Kirk, *A Program for Conservatives* (Chicago: Henry Regnery, 1954), 137–39.

36. John R. Kelly, "Situational and Social Factors in Leisure Distribution," *Pacific Sociological Review* 21 (July 1978): 325; John Child and Brenda Macmillan, "Managers and Their Leisure," in *Leisure and Society in Britain,* ed. Michael A. Smith, Stanley Parker, and Cyril Smith (London: Allen Lane, 1973), 111–24; Simon J. Bronner, *Chain Carvers: Old Men Crafting Meaning* (Lexington: University of Kentucky Press, 1985), 126, 130–31, 151.

37. *Historical Statistics,* 168; Witold Rybczynski, *Waiting for the Weekend* (New York: Penguin Books, 1991), 132–35.

38. Elise Hill, "Breaking in a Hobby," *Century Magazine* 85 (February 1913): 635–36; Costen Fitz-Gibbon, "A Collection of Old Watches," *American Homes and Gardens* 10 (November 1913): 397.

39. Arthur Christopher Benson, *Along the Road* (New York: G. P. Putnam's Sons, 1913), 368–69; *Papers of the Hobby Club* (New York: privately printed, 1912), 21; however, the lead of a long article on the Hobby Club in 1920 started with the premise that collectors are boring to everybody but other collectors, *New York Times,* August 1, 1920, sect. 7, p. 2.

40. *Papers of the Hobby Club; New York Times,* February 18, 1912, sect. 5, pp. 9–10; *New York Times,* February 18, 1912, sect. 5, pp. 9–10.

41. *New York Times,* February 18, 1912, sect. 5, p. 9.

42. William H. Tolman, *Social Engineering* (New York: McGraw Publishing, 1909); Lebert H. Weir, *Vocational Recreation in Indiana* (Bloomington: Extension Division of Indiana University, 1916); Mary K. Simkhovitch, *The City Worker's World in America* (New York: Macmillan, 1917).

43. H. C. MacDougall, "What Is Your Hobby?" *Musician* 18 (August 1913): 562.

44. "Hobbies and Health," *Independent* 66 (May 13, 1909): 1038–39; H. Addington Bruce, "Hobby Riding for Health," *Good Housekeeping* 65 (August 1917): 44.

45. For examples, see Fred W. Burgess, *Chats on Household Curios* (New York: Frederick A. Stokes, 1914), 21–22; Henry Van Dyke, *Days Off and Other Digressions* (New York: Charles Scribner's Sons, 1907), 10–11.

46. Perry Rule, "Pigeons as a Hobby," *Suburban Life* 16 (April 1913): 294; *New York Times*, December 16, 1911, 12.

47. "Laborious Leisure," *Living Age* 255 (1907): 812.

48. Quoted without citation in J. Shore, *Model Steam Engines: The Story of a Clergyman's Hobby* (Newcastle-upon-Tyne: Andrew Reid, 1911), 1.

49. Cornelia James Cannon, "The New Leisure," *North American Review* 223 (September 1926): 499; W. A. Bloedern, "Have You a Hobby?" *Hygeia* 4 (December 1926): 681; *New York Times*, September 9, 1927, 24.

50. Benjamin K. Hunnicutt, *Work without End: Abandoning Shorter Hours for the Right to Work* (Philadelphia: Temple University Press, 1988), 67–108; Gary Cross, *A Quest for Time: The Reduction of Work in Britain and France* (Berkeley: University of California Press, 1989), 179–91; *New York Times*, February 25, 1923, sect 2, p. 4; *New York Times*, November 12, 1929, 17; *New York Times*, September 2, 1929, 14.

51. Charles William Taussig and Theodore Arthur Meyer, *The Book of Hobbies; or a Guide to Happiness* (New York: Minton, Balch, 1924), xv, 46; J. K. Hart, "The Place of Leisure in Life," *Annals of the American Academy* 118 (1925): 111.

52. Samuel Crowther, "Henry Ford: Why I Favor Five Days' Work with Six Days' Pay," *World's Work* 52 (October 1926): 615; *New York Times*, April 15, 1925, 16; Irwin Edman, "An American Leisure," *Harper's Magazine* 156 (January 1928): 221, 225.

53. Amos Bradbury, "More Health for 1929," *Printers' Ink* 7 (January 1929): 41; Augusta Shuford, "The Other Side of Their Heads," *New York Times Book Review and Magazine* (July 29, 1923), 14; L. H. Robbins, "Riding Their Hobbies to the Fountain of Youth," *New York Times Magazine* (July 14, 1929): 12–13; Joseph K. Drake, "Hobbies of Credit Managers," *Credit Monthly* 29 (September 1927): 11; *New York Times*, July 29, 1923, sect. 3, p. 9; Alfred George Gardiner, *Windfalls* (New York: J. M. Dent, 1920), 85; Robert S. Lynd and Helen Merrell Lynd, *Middletown: A Study in American Culture* (New York: Harcourt, Brace and Co., 1929), 309.

54. Herbert R. Maxwell, "Is a Hobby a Business Asset?" *Systems* 50 (September 1926): 291–94; George W. Lee, "Hobbies: The How and Why of Bringing Them Up in a Sales Interview," *Printers' Ink* 18 (April 1929): 66.

55. *New York Times*, March 11, 1883, 5; W. L. Blair, "When Businessmen Retire," *Nation's Business* 16 (September 1928): 50; Bradbury, "More Health for 1929,"

41; Ernest Elmo Calkins, "Hobby Horses," *Atlantic Monthly* 151 (May 1933): 598; Coon, *Hobbies for Pleasure and Profit*, 195.

56. Hunnicutt, *Work without End*, 118–19.

57. Butler quoted in Arthur Dean, "Neither a Vocationist nor a Leisurist," *Industrial Education Magazine* 26 (1925): 255; Arthur Pound, *The Iron Man in Industry: An Outline of the Significance of Automatic Machinery* (Boston: Atlantic Monthly Press, 1922), 207; A. H. Reeve, "Leisure and the Home," *Playground* 20 (December 1926): 495

58. E. C. Warriner, "Report of Committee on Best Use of Leisure Time," *Michigan Educational Journal* 1 (1924): 347; *New York Times*, May 29, 1922, 10; *New York Times*, July 14, 1929, sect. 5, p. 12.

59. Mary Corrin Winston, "The New Leisure," *Playground* 22 (August 1928): 281.

60. "To Capitalize Hobbies Educationally," *Literary Digest* 101 (May 25, 1929): 24; Isobel Davidson, "Training in the Right Use of Leisure," *Journal of Rural Education* 3 (1924): 301; Hunnicutt, *Work without End*, 120–21; C. A. B. "The General Shop—Recreational Activity," *Industrial Education Magazine* 182 (1929): 276–77; W. T. Bowden, "Education for the Proper Use of Leisure Hours," *Manual Training Magazine* 22 (1920): 13.

61. The "threat of leisure" was the title of a book by the president of Colgate University, George Barton Cutten, *The Threat of Leisure* (Washington, D.C.: McGrath Publishing, 1926); John M. Cooper, "Do Play Traits Breed Life Traits?" *Playground* 19 (October 1925): 369; William M. Proctor, *Educational and Vocational Guidance: Guidance in the Worthy Use of Leisure Time* (Boston: Houghton Mifflin, 1925), 198.

62. For examples, see Eric Wood, *Hobbies* (New York: Funk and Wagnalls, 1923); Nellie E. Parham, "Hobbies," *Libraries* 31 (July 1926): 318.

63. Stuart M. Stoke and W. F. Cline, "The Avocations of One Hundred College Freshmen," *Journal of Applied Psychology*, 13 (1929): 259; "What is Your Hobby?" *Woman's Home Companion* 53 (January 1926): 40; George A. Kelly, "One Thousand Workers and Their Leisure" (master's thesis, University of Kansas, 1928), 269–76; O. D. Wyatt, "An Analysis of Leisure Time Activities of Adults in Fort Worth, Texas" (master's thesis, Colorado State Teachers College, 1929); "Hobby Riding, A Healthful Exercise," *Literary Digest* 78 (September 29, 1923): 24.

64. *Leisure Hours of Five Thousand People: A Report of a Study of Leisure Activities and Desires* (New York: National Recreation Association, 1934), 14–17; however, see contradictory data in Sebastian DeGrazia, *Of Time, Work, and Leisure* (New York: Twentieth Century Fund, 1962), 453–54; Marian Flad, "Leisure Activities of Four Hundred Persons," *Sociology and Social Research* 18 (1934): 271.

65. John F. Fox, "Leisure Time and Social Backgrounds in a Suburban Community," *Sociology of Education* 4 (1934): 499; Elmer W. Cressman, *Out of School Activities of Jr. High School Pupils in Relation to Intelligence and Socio-economic Status*, (State College, Pa.: Pennsylvania State College Studies in Education, no. 20, 1937), 34; *Leisure Hours of 5000 People*, 10–11; George Lundberg, Mira Konarovsky, and Mary A. McInery, *Leisure: A Suburban Study* (New York: Columbia University Press, 1934), 107.

66. Hunnicutt, *Work without End.*

67. Archibald Rutledge, "Here's a Job You Can't Lose," *American Magazine* 116 (November 1933): 80.

68. Austen Fox Riggs, *Play: Recreation in a Balanced Life* (Garden City, N.Y.: Doubleday, Doran, 1935), 103, 107; B. F. Morrow, "Time Out! The Psychology of a Hobby," *Avocations* 2 (July 1938): 307–10.

69. George E. Davis, "The Prevalence of Hobbies and Their Educational Significance" (Ph.D. diss., University of Iowa, 1937), 38–42; Erna D. Bunke, "My Hobby Is Hobbies," *Survey* 63 (February 15, 1930): 581.

70. Walter B. Pitkin, *Life Begins at Forty* (New York: Whettlesey, McGraw Hill Book Company, 1932); see also Walter B. Pitkin, introduction to Earnest Elmo Calkins, *Care and Feeding of Hobby Horses* (New York: Leisure League of America, [ca. 1934]); *New York Times*, May 29, 1932, sect. 3, p. 1.

71. Hunnicutt, *Work without End*, 174–75; "Teaching Hobbies in Public Schools Foreseen by Educational Director at Columbia University," *Hobbies* 38 (March 1933): 17.

72. Eugene T. Lies, *New Leisure Challenges the Schools* (Washington, D.C.: McGrath Publishing and the National Recreation and Park Association, 1933), 21–25; "Observations," *Leisure* (November 1935): 39; "Hobbies for Everyone," *Etude* 53 (November 1935): 633.

73. George E. Davis, "Riding a Hobby to School," *Hobbies* (January 1934): 169; Morris Fishbein, "Hobbies Play Important Part in Keeping Aged People Well," *Hobbies* 36 (May 1931): 97; Anne Jesty Rogers, "Advocates Hobbies for School," *Hobbies* 43 (October 1938): 120, reprint of "Voice of the People," *Chicago Tribune*, n.d., n.p.

74. *New York Times*, March 2, 1930, 6.

75. Blue Moon, member no. 63, "Hobbies," *Hobbies* 39 (March 1934): 126.

76. Fred Margaretten, "Physicians and Their Hobbies," *Avocations* 2 (June 1938): 229; Henry N. Moeller, "Following an Avocation as a Health Measure," *Avocations* 2 (June 1938): 240; John W. Shuman Sr., "Hobbies," *Avocations* 4 (June 1939): 173; O. C. Lightner, "Avoiding Undesirable Complexes," 36 *Hobbies* (July 1931): 10; Harold Lincoln Thompson, "Photography as a Hobby," *Avocations* 2 (June 1938): 275; "Hobby Riders Lead on to Utopia," *New York Times Magazine* (May 16, 1937): sect. 8, p. 21.

77. Ethel Peyser, *Fun with a Hobby* (n.p.: Home Institute, 1938), 4.

78. Dorothy Alofsin, "It's Fun to Have a Hobby," *St. Nicholas* 65 (April 1938): 38.

79. "Have You a Hobby?" *Hobbies* 36 (March 1931): 14; Gilbert C. Wrenn and D. L. Harley, *Time on Their Hands: A Report on Leisure, Recreation, and Young People* (Washington, D.C.: American Council on Education, 1941), 7.

80. "Teaching Hobbies," 17.

81. Orville Arthur Oaks, "Hobbies; or a Woodnut and His Boys," *Industrial Education Magazine* 37 (September 1935): 184.

82. C. H. Claudy, "Why Every Boy Should Have a Hobby," in *Pets, Hobbies, and Collections*, ed. Frank Hobart Cheley (New York: University Society, 1933), vi–xiii.

83. Davis, "Riding a Hobby to School," 20; *New York Times*, May 24, 1936, sect 10, p. 10; Max Chambers, "The Hobby and Peace of Mind," *Industrial Arts and Vocational Education* 23 (1934): 255.

84. C. Frances Loomis, "Hobbies as an Open Sesame to Community Interest," *Recreation* 28 (January 1935): 490–92.

85. Lies, "New Leisure Challenges," 300, 228, 198; *New York Times*, July 30, 1940, 16.

86. For an exception, see, Kenneth M. Swezey, "Worlds Champion Hobbyist," *Popular Science* 135 (November 1939): 72.

87. For example, see H. S. Card, "You'd Be Surprised," *Leisure* (November 1935): 6–8; "The Chase Bank Club Hobby Show" (New York, March 3–8, 1941, mimeographed).

88. "Observations," *Leisure* (November 1935): 39.

89. *New York Times*, February 18, 1934, sect. 2, p. 1.

90. O. C. Lightner, "The Publisher's Page," *Hobbies* 43 (October 1938): 123; Oaks, "Hobbies," 185–86; M. Chambers, "Aspects of National Avocationalism," *Industrial Arts and Vocational Education* 23 (April 1934): 144; Ross C. Cramlet, "Teacher and the Home Workshop," *Industrial Arts and Vocational Education* 24 (October 1935): 287–88.

91. *New York Times*, April 18, 1934, 21.

92. "Hobbies for Everyone," 633; *New York Times*, July 29, 1934, sect. 2, p. 2.

93. "The Hobby Guild," *Publishers' Weekly* 130 (November 28, 1936): 2113.

94. S. Jesse Robinson, "The Pursuit of Hobbies," *Hobbies* 41 (January 1936): 14–15.

95. Ruth Lampland, *Hobbies for Everybody* (New York: Harper, 1934), x.

96. *New York Times*, March 19, 1947, 62; there was a similar local show in Indiana in 1942, see "Radio Hobby Program Popular in Hoosier City," *Hobbies* 47 (February 1942): 119.

97. Ray Giles, "Hobbies with a Human Touch," *Reader's Digest* 34 (May 1939): 77–80; Louise Paine, "Do Men Have the Most Fun?" *Ladies' Home Journal* 56 (October 1939): 74; E. DeAlton Partridge and Catherine Mooney, *Time Out for Living* (New York: American Book, 1941), 499–521.

98. "Amusements and Hobbies," *Hobbies* 39 (May 1934): 115; "Hobby Riders Lead on to Utopia,"12; Dorothy Alofsin, "It's Fun to Have a Hobby," *St. Nicholas* 65 (April 1938): 38.

99. H. F. Kilander, "Hobbies," *Hygeia* 9 (September 1931): 820–21; Marion L. Faegre, "Hobbies," *Ladies Home Journal* 51 (October 1934): 90; Riggs, *Play*, 123–25; Rose Heylbut, "Music Is My Hobby," *Etude* 57 (December 1939): 824; Otto T. Mallery et al., "Avocational Education," *School and Society* 38 (August 19, 1933): 252.

100. "Hobby Riders Lead on to Utopia," 21.

101. Dorothea Brande, "Check Up On Yourself: Success is Fun; It May Be around the Corner," *Review of Reviews* (November 1936): 70, reprinted from *Cosmopolitan*, n.d.

102. Edgar A. Felix, "Share Your Boy's Hobbies," *Parents Magazine* 6 (March 1931): 79; Davis, "Riding a Hobby to School," 169.

103.   Jo Chamberlin, "A Hobby Can Pay You Dividends," *Nation's Business* 27
       (August 1939): 24.

104.   *New York Times*, May 25, 1932, 21: Robert Hoppock, *Job Satisfaction* (New York:
       Harper and Brothers, 1935), n.p., cited in William Virgil Nestrick, *Construc-
       tional Activities of Adult Males* (New York: Teachers College, Columbia Uni-
       versity, 1939), 11.

105.   Nestrick, *Constructional Activities*, 56; C. G. Suits, "How Engineers Spend
       Their Spare Time," *General Electric Review* 41 (November 1938): 478–83; see
       also, Bunke, "My Hobby Is Hobbies," 580.

106.   M. J. Poppenberg Jr., "A Survey of the Leisure Time Activities of Adults in
       Greeley, Colorado" (master's thesis, Colorado State College of Education,
       Greeley, 1940), 82; Irving Bacchus, "Hobbies for Defense," *Recreation* 35
       (March 1942): 704; Raymond J. Walker, "Hobbies in Wartime," *Hobbies* 47
       (September 1942): 116.

107.   *New York Times*, October 27, 1942, 21; *Technical Manual: Soldier Handicrafts*
       (Washington, D.C.: U.S. War Department, June 1945).

108.   Hunnicutt, *Work without End*.

109.   *Historical Statistics*, 169–70; Schor, *Overworked American*, 79–82.

110.   Harry Levine, "Psychological Problems of Increased Leisure," in *Personal
       Problems and Psychological Frontiers*, ed. Johnson E. Fairchild (New York:
       Sheridan House, 1957), 154–55; A. W. Zelmoek, *Leisure's Not for Loafing: A
       Changing America at Work and Play* (New York: John Wiley and Sons, 1959),
       80; Dorothy Barclay, "Time Out for Hobbies," *New York Times Magazine*
       (June 2, 1957): 48.

111.   Eleanor Doan, *Hobby Fun and Activities* (Grand Rapids, Mich.: Zondervan,
       1958), 4; Coon, *Hobbies for Pleasure and Profit*, 7; Edwin Teale, "America's Five
       Favorite Hobbies," *Popular Science* 138 (May 1941): 100–102.

112.   *New York Times*, May 26, 1949, 31; "There is Time for Hobbies, Too!" *Industrial
       and Engineering Chemistry* 49 (October 1957): 119–20; Harold D. Meyer, "The
       Adult Cycle," *Annals of the American Academy of Political and Social Science*
       313 (1957): 58–67; Geoffrey Mott-Smith, *Guide to Popular Hobbies: Photogra-
       phy, Stamp Collecting, Model Making, and Other Fascinating Pursuits* (Chica-
       go: J. G. Ferguson 1948); *New York Times*, September 11, 1954, sect. 6, p. 20.

113.   For example, see Ferdynand Zweig, *The British Worker* (Harmondsworth: Pen-
       guin, 1952).

114.   For example, see Dorothy Barclay, "Time Out for Hobbies," *New York Times
       Magazine*, June 2, 1957, 48.

115.   See, for example, Reed Millard, "Hobbies That Hold Your Family Together,"
       Coronet 31 (January 1952): 136–38; Martha Ruth Amon, "Home Is Where the
       Art Is," *American Vocational Journal* 56 (December 1955): 13–14; Richard S.
       Robbins, *Hobby Shop for Fun or Fortune?* (n.p.: Model Industry Association,
       1949), 19; Alexander Wiley, "Wisconsin Senator Promotes Hobbies," *Hobbies*
       55 (March 1950): 16–17.

116.   William C. Menninger, *Enjoying Leisure Time* (Chicago: Science Research
       Associates, 1950), 37; E. S. Bogardus, "Hobbies in War and Peace," *Sociology*

and Social Research 27 (1943), 221; *New York Times*, August 3, 1956, 23; "Noted Doctor Says High-Tension Personality Needs Hobby," *Hobbies* 55 (1950): 16; Bertha Beck, "You Say," letter to the editor, *Profitable Hobbies* 6 (January 1950): 4; Zweig, *British Worker*, 155.

117. Harry Zarchy, *Here's Your Hobby* (New York: Knopf, 1950), vii; "Answer to Pressure," *Chemical Week* 74 (May 8, 1954): 62; Jesse Wayne King, "Short Courses in Industrial Arts for Their Hobby Value" (master's thesis, Oregon State College, 1952), 41, 50.

118. Margaret Elizabeth Mulac, *Hobbies: The Creative Use of Leisure* (New York: Harper, 1959), 2.

119. Hildegarde Dolson, "Yoo-Hoo, Satan, I'm Idle," *New Yorker* 16 (February 8, 1941): 32.

120. Francis Marshall, "Are These Your Teen-agers?" *Better Homes and Gardens* 28 (April 1950): 269; James Gilbert, *A Cycle of Outrage: America's Reaction to the Juvenile Delinquent in the 1950s* (New York: Oxford University Press, 1986).

121. Dale Perkins, "A Study of Leisure Time and Recreational Interests of 982 Fifteen- and Sixteen-Year-Old Students" (Ph.D. diss., University of Houston, 1948), 49–50; Sister Mary Bernice, "Crafts, Leisure Time, and Adolescents," *Catholic Educational Review* 45 (January 1947): 30–34; King, "Short Courses," 33; Robert Bromley Harris, "Education for Leisure in the Secondary Schools of Dallas, Texas" (Ph.D. diss., University of Texas, Austin, 1952); Shirley Kessler, "Preparing for Life through Hobbies," *Today's Health* 33 (December 1955): 42.

122. Perkins, "A Study of Leisure Time and Recreational Interests," 51–55, 59.

123. Harold Don Allen, "Hobbies Teach and Discipline," *New Zealand Numismatic Journal* 10 (February 1961): 106.

124. *New York Times*, January 3, 1949, 6; *New York Times*, February 22, 1952, 29.

125. "Your Hobby Reporter," *Profitable Hobbies* 8 (September 1952): 13; there were fifteen news stories on hobby shows in the *New York Times* between the end of the war and 1954.

126. Helen Waterman, "Hobby Exhibit Builds Morale," *American Business* 25 (January 1955): 28–29; *New York Times*, May 1, 1941, 24.

127. "Hobbies Encouraged as Aid to Efficiency of Employees," *Printers' Ink* 231 (May 19, 1950): 42–43; Marion L. Briggs, "Employees Hold Hobby Show," *American Business* 23 (July 1953): 30–31; *New York Times*, May 13, 1947, 27; May 12, 1949, 33; May 8, 1952, 33.

128. *New York Times*, May 15, 1949, 62; May 13, 1947, 27; Fessenden Searer Blanchard, *Where to Retire and How; A Comprehensive Guide* (New York: Dodd, Mead, 1952), 34–37; "To Retire Happily, Get a Hobby First," *Business Week* (December 22, 1951): 36; "Have a Hobby for a Boredom-proof Retirement," *Banking* 46 (August 1953): 52; *New York Times*, May 7, 1950, 81.

129. Amy Loveman, "Cultivate a Hobby," *Saturday Review of Literature* 33 (July 29, 1950): 20; Ray Giles, "Why Not Rehearse Your Retirement," *Better Homes and Gardens* 24 (August 1946): 91.

130. Janet Rockwood Maclean, "An Analysis of Leisure Time Activities of Selected Aged Residents of Bartholomew City, Indiana" (Ph.D. diss., Indiana Universi-

ty, 1959), 129–32; Fred Darling, "A Leisure Time Analysis of Retired Public School Teachers in Kentucky" (Ph.D. diss., Indiana University, 1958), 93, 95.

131. "Handicrafts Are Both Hobbies and Big Business," *Domestic Commerce* 34 (December 1946): 65–66; American Handicrafts Company [catalog] (East Orange, N.J., 1949); *New York Times*, August 3, 1956, 23.

132. "Amateur Painting: It's a Craze," *Newsweek* 43 (January 11, 1954): 50; J. Stocker, "Bored? Be a Happy Dabbler!," *Rotarian* 84 (April 1954): 15–17; Daniel Rubin, "Thursday Night Is Railroad Night," *Popular Mechanics* 98 (December 1952): 112–15. For an example of hobbyists profiting from their hobbies, see "Handicraft on Manhattan," *Popular Mechanics* 95 (March 1951): 150–51.

133. Eric Larrabee, "What's Happening to Hobbies," in *Mass Leisure*, 268–74.

134. L. H. Brendel, "Hobby Club Builds Jobber Goodwill for Industrial Manufacturer," *Printers' Ink* 15 (January 30, 1942): 15; Margaret L. Jones, "Hobbies Develop the Executives," *Dun's Review and Modern Industry* 63 (March 1954): 56–59

135. Henry Bollman, "How to Market What You Make," *Profitable Hobbies* 8 (September 1952): 16–17.

136. Robert Behme and Charles Leonard, "At Seventy Engrossed in Engrossing," *Profitable Hobbies* 6 (October 1950): 38.

137. *Profitable Hobbies Handbook: Earn Spare Time Money with an Interesting Hobby* (Greenwich, Conn.: Fawcett Publications, 1949); Robert Scharff, *Handicraft Hobbies for Profit* (New York: McGraw Hill, 1952); Marguerite Ickis, *Handicrafts and Hobbies for Pleasure and Profit* (New York: Greystone Press, 1948); Celia F. Beck, "I Always Wanted to Work with My Hands," *Occupations* 25 (December 1946): 165–68.

138. "Personal Business," *Business Week* (September 22, 1956): 185; Coon, *Hobbies for Pleasure and Profit*, 16; Robert Hertzberg, "Their Small-scale Trains are Big-scale Business," *Popular Science* 162 (February 1953): 153.

139. "Hitching Post," *Profitable Hobbies* 6 (February 1950): 5–11; *Profitable Hobbies* 7 (January 1951).

140. "Hitching Post," 5–11.

141. "Hobby Huddle," *Profitable Hobbies* 6 (January 1950), 1; Bagley, "A Study to Determine the Contribution of Industrial Arts to Leisure Time Activities," 172–74.

142. Doris Ann Krupinski, "Birth of a Hobby Club," *Profitable Hobbies* 7 (September 1951): 16–19.

2 The Collectible Object

1. *New York Times*, January 9, 1994, 37.

2. See, for example, E. C. R. Hadfield, *The Young Collector's Handbook* (London: Oxford University Press, 1940), 263–78; Frederick P. Keppel, "Riding with a Purpose," *Journal of Adult Education* 1 (1929): 247, 252; "Shrines for the Tourist," *Hobbies* 53 (July 1948): 116; Douglas Rigby and Elizabeth Rigby, *Lock, Stock, and Barrel: The Story of Collecting* (New York: Lippincott, 1944), 346–48; Stephen R. Kellert, "Birdwatching in American Society," *Leisure Sciences* 7 (1985): 343–60.

3. For an example of primary collecting, see Maurice L. Zigmond, "Gotlieb Adam Steiner and the G. A. Steiner Museum," *Journal of California Great Basin Anthropology* 1 (1979): 322–30. For a different, but useful, scheme of categorizing collectibles see John Windsor, "Identity Parades," in *The Cultures of Collecting*, ed. John Elsner and Roger Cardinal (Cambridge, Mass.: Harvard University Press, 1994), 50.

4. Rigby, *Lock, Stock, and Barrel*, 262–69; Edwin Wolf II, "Great American Book Collectors to 1800," *Gazette of the Grolier Club* (June 1971): 2–70.

5. John M. Mulder, "William Sprague: Patriarch of American Collectors," *American Presbyterians* 64 (1986), 1–2; for European precedents, see Agnes Repplier, "Collection of Autographs," *Century* 92 (August 1916): 584; Joseph E. Fields, "A History of Autograph Collecting," in *Autographs and Manuscripts: A Collector's Manual*, ed. Edmund Berkeley Jr. et al. (New York: Scribner's, 1978), 44–49.

6. Theodore F. Dwight, "Autographomania," *Overland Monthly and Out West Magazine* 3 (October 1869): 345; "The Lumley Autograph," *Graham's Magazine* 38 (January 1851): 31–36, and 38 (February 1851): 97–101; T. F. Dwight, "Collectors and Collections," *Overland* 5 (August 1870): 143; "Hoarding Relics," *Godey's Lady's Book* 89 (August 1874): 144–45; "Autographs," *Godey's Lady's Book* 94 (April 1877): 372; Victor Rosewater, "Collecting Autographs Fifty Years Ago," *St. Nicholas* 63 (June 1936): 30; Charles Hamilton "The Old Fashioned Collector," *Hobbies* 56 (June 1951): 134; Mulder, "William Sprague," 2–8.

7. Alfred Edward Newton, *This Book Collecting Game* (Boston: Little Brown, 1928), 200–201; Mulder, "William Sprague, 10; Kenneth W. Rendell, "Who Collects Autographs, and Why: The Philosophy of Collecting," in *Autographs and Manuscripts*, 63–65.

8. Mulder, "William Sprague," 1, 10–13.

9. "The Fancy Card Mania," *Arthur's Home Magazine* 48 (July 1880): 437; Deborah A. Smith, "Consuming Passions: Scrapbooks and American Play," *Ephemera Journal* 6 (1993): 66.

10. Janet E. Ruutz-Rees, *Home Occupations* (New York: D. Appleton, 1883), 97–98; C. A. Montresor, *Some Hobby Horses* (London: W. H. Allen, 1890), 1–2; Smith, "Consuming Passions," 63–76; Frances Lichten, *Decorative Arts of Victoria's Era* (New York: Charles Scribner's Sons, 1950), 40–43, 188–89.

11. Kate Crombie, "Aunt Ruth Discourses on Business Cards," *Godey's Lady's Book* 103 (September 1881): 264–66.

12. Barbara Prince, "Spoons: A Special Kind of Gift," in *The Encyclopedia of Collectibles*, vol. 12, ed. Andrea DiNoto (New York: Time-Life Books, 1978), 75; Colleen McDannell, "Parlor Piety: The Home as Sacred Space in Protestant America," in *American Home Life, 1880–1940*, ed. Jessica H. Foy and Thomas Schlereth (Knoxville, Tenn.: University of Tennessee Press, 1992): 167.

13. *New York Times*, November 1, 1946, 20; Kim Moare, "Through the Years," *Hobbies* 49 (August 1944): 35; Thomas L. Elder, "Recollections of an Old Collector," *Hobbies* 40 (January 1935): 76.

14. Quotation from *New York Sun* is in Norman Waltz, "Cigar Bands and Labels: Pop Art from a Smoke," in vol. 4, *The Encyclopedia of Collectibles*, 47–48; A. E. Hotchner, *King of the Hill: A Memoir* (New York: HarperCollins, 1972), 14.

15. Gabriel Wells, "Evolution of a Book Collector," *Bookman* 51 (April 1920): 180; "Stamp News," *Collector's Journal* 3 (October–December 1932): 298.

16. Charles R. Lamb, "Sand Is My Hobby," *Hobbies* 55 (April 1950): 133; Barney Lefferts, "Who Collects and Why," *New York Times Magazine* (February 21, 1960): 78; John D. Knox, "Collect Pig Iron from Old Stone Furnaces as Hobby," *Steel* 108 (April 21 1941): 88.

17. Krzysztof Pomian, *Collectors and Curiosities: Paris and Venice, 1500–1800* (Cambridge: Polity Press, 1990), 9.

18. Oliver Impey and Arthur MacGregor, eds., *The Origins of Museums: The Cabinet of Curiosities in Sixteenth- and Seventeenth-Century Europe* (Oxford: Clarendon Press, 1985); Peter S. Dance, *A History of Shell Collecting* (Leiden: E. J. Brill, 1986), 10–11; Jan Toller, *The Regency and Victorian Crafts* (London: Ward and Lock, 1969), 9–20; Rosella Rice, "The Preacher's Daughters," *Arthur's Lady's Home Magazine* 38 (November 1871): 258; Cecil Henry Bullivant, *Every Boy's Book of Hobbies* (New York: Dodge Publishing, 1912), 286–96.

19. For examples of small museums open to the public, see Madeleine Miller, *My Hobby of the Cross: Stories of a Quest in Many Lands* (New York: Fleming H. Revell, 1939), 18–19; "Hobby House," *Hobbies* 47 (December 1942): 13; E. D. Collins, "The Collector and the Housing Crisis," *Hobbies* 52 (January 1947): 64. P. Martin, "Hobby House," *Saturday Evening Post* 217 (September 16, 1944): 24–51; "Great Alcazar Hotel at St. Augustine Becomes New Hobbies Museum," *Hobbies* 52 (August 1947): 10–11.

20. London *Saturday Review* article reprinted in *New York Times*, March 11, 1883, 5; *New York Times* September 28, 1890, 17.

21. "Collections," *Harper's Weekly* 46 (November 15, 1902): 1726–27; R. H. Van Court, "Arrangement of a Collection," *American Homes and Gardens* 10 (August 1913): ii; "Hobbies and Hobbyists," *Scientific American* 121 (August 23, 1919): 180.

22. H. Murdock, "Collector's Choice," *Ladies Home Journal* 63 (February 1946): 218–19; Martin, "Hobby House," 24–51.

23. Kenneth L. Roberts, *Antiquamania* (Garden City, N.Y.: Doubleday, Doran, 1928), 66–67; E. DeAlton Partridge and Catherine Mooney, *Time Out for Living* (New York: American Book, 1941), 201–5.

24. A. D. Olmsted, "Collectors and Collecting," paper presented at the Popular Culture Annual Meeting, New Orleans, 1988, 2.

25. Daniel Miller, *Material Culture and Mass Consumption* (Oxford: Basil Blackwell, 1987), 149–54.

26. *Annals of the Hobby Club* (New York: Hobby Club, 1920); Albert Beatty, "King of the Hobbies," *St. Nicholas* 58 (May 1931): 496; *New York Times*, April 22, 1934, sect 2, p. 3; "Avocations Starts," *Avocations* 3 (October 1938): 6.

27. A. M. Brooking, "A Cityful of Collectors," *Hobbies*, 36 (October 1931): 21; Jennie Spall Owen, "Collecting Hobbyists," *Scribner's* 99 (January 1936): 57–58.

28. Joseph Alsop, *The Rare Art Tradition* (Princeton: N.J.: Princeton University Press, 1982), 77. On collectors' foresight, see Holbrook Jackson, *The Anatomy of Bibliomania* (New York: Charles Scribner's Sons, 1932), 605.

29. Arjun Appadurai, introduction to *The Social Life of Things: Commodities in Cultural Perspective*, ed. Appadurai (Cambridge: Cambridge University Press, 1986), 21.

30. Reginal Brewer, *The Delightful Diversion: The Whys and Wherefores of Book Collecting* (New York: Macmillan, 1935), 12.

31. John Ahrens, "Beer Cans: Valued Empties," in vol. 2, *The Encyclopedia of Collectibles*, 22–24; Appadurai, introduction, 3–4; Susan Stewart, *On Longing: Narratives of the Miniature, the Gigantic, the Souvenir, the Collection* (Baltimore: Johns Hopkins University Press, 1984), 154.

32. Pomian's translator uses the term "semaphore" rather than "sign."Pomian, *Collectors and Curiosities*, 20–41; Jean Baudrillard, "The System of Collecting," in *The Cultures of Collecting*, 6–24; *New York Times*, February 19, 1879, 2.

33. Igor Kopytoff, "The Cultural Biography of Things: Commoditization as Process," in *The Social Life of Things*, 80–81; Alsop, *The Rare Art Tradition*, 49; C. R. Clifford, *The Junk Snupper: The Adventures of an Antique Collector* (New York: Macmillan, 1927), 130–31.

34. Appadurai, introduction, 16; Alsop, *The Rare Art Tradition*, 49; Kopytoff, "The Cultural Biography of Things," 72.

35. Observer, "Collecting Run Mad," *American Journal of Numismatics* 11 (January 1877): 54; Margaret Emerson Bailey, "Heirlooms," in *The Wild Streak* (New York: G. P. Putnam's Sons, 1932).

36. Clifford Geertz, *The Interpretation of Cultures* (New York: Basic Books, 1973), 433; Miller, *Material Culture*, 118–21; Brewer, *The Delightful Diversion*, 260.

37. Rigby, *Lock, Stock, and Barrel*, 47, 50.

38. Robert W. Chambers, "The Purple Emperor," in *The Mystery of Choice* (New York: D. Appleton, 1897); Stewart, *On Longing*, 159–60; Baudrillard, "The System of Collecting," 14; William Dana Orcutt, *The Magic of the Book* (Boston: Little, Brown, 1930), 267; Brewer, *The Delightful Diversion*, 11–12.

39. Richard G. Mitchell, *Mountain Experience: The Psychology and Sociology of Adventure* (Chicago: University of Chicago Press, 1983), 117–20; *New York Times*, April 3, 1929, 28.

40. Impey, *The Origins of Museums*, 3; the quotation is from Robert Shackleton and Elizabeth Shackleton, *The Charm of the Antique* (New York: Hearst's International Library, 1913), 5; Edward R. Byram, "Concerning Playbills," *New England Magazine* 18 (1905): 552–53.

41. Stewart, *On Longing*, 151.

42. W. A. Laughlin, "The Kind That I Collect," *Collectors' Journal*, 1 (August–September 1909): 250.

43. Walter Nelson Durost, *Children's Collecting Activity Related to Social Factors* (New York: Columbia University Teachers College, Contributions to Education, no. 535, 1932), 10; Werner Muensterberger, *Collecting: An Unruly Passion* (Princeton, N.J.: Princeton University Press, 1994), 74.

44. Stewart, *On Longing*, 156–58.

45. "Miscellaneous Collector: Old China," *House Beautiful* 28 (August 1910): 95; Gabriel Wells, "Evolution of a Book Collector," *Bookman* 51 (April 1920): 180; Philippe Jullian, *The Collectors* (Rutland, Vt.: E. Tuttle, 1967), 32.

46. *New York Times*, August 29, 1887, 2; Fostor Loso, ed., *Stamp Collectors' Round Table* (New York: F. A. Stokes, 1937), 47.

47. "Passion for Collecting," *American Journal of Numismatics* 24 (October 1889): 36; Frederick Litchfield, *Antiques, Genuine and Spurious* (London: G. Bell and Sons, 1921), 2.

48. William C. Menninger, "The Psychology of Stamp Collecting," *Weekly Philatelic Gossip* (May 3, 1941), reprinted in *A Psychiatrist for a Troubled World: Selected Papers of William C. Menninger, M.D.*, ed. Bernard H. Hall (New York: Viking Press, 1967), 758, 754.

3 Collectors

1. Gardner Teall, "The Joys of Collecting," *Independent* 109 (August 1922): 40. Joseph Alsop, *The Rare Art Tradition* (Princeton: N.J.: Princeton University Press, 1982), 16; Arjun Appadurai, introduction to *The Social Life of Things: Commodities in Cultural Perspective*, ed. Appadurai (Cambridge: Cambridge University Press, 1986), 44–45; Leora Auslander, "The Genesis and Gendering of Consumption," History Department, University of Chicago, typescript, 1990, 1–5; F. M. Bird, "An Hour among Hymn-Books," *Ladies' Repository* 24 (May 1864): 297.

2. A. D. Olmsted, "Collectors and Collecting," paper presented at the Popular Culture Annual Meeting, New Orleans, 1988, 3–4; Lillian Smith Albert, *A Button Collector's Second Journal* (Hightstown, N.J.: Lillian Smith Albert, 1941), 12; "Toy Mugs," *Hobbies* 54 (April 1949): 120; Holbrook Jackson, *The Anatomy of Bibliomania* (New York: Charles Scribner's Sons, 1932), 575.

3. Walter Raleigh, *The Letters of Sir Walter Raleigh* (New York: Macmillan, 1926), 182–83.

4. William A. Pearman, John Schnable, Aida K. Tomeh, "Rationalization and Antique Collecting," *Free Inquiry in Creative Sociology* 11 (May 1983): 55–58; Michael Berry, "Collector's Item," *Colliers* 131 (April 18, 1953): 77; Philippe Jullian, *The Collectors* (Rutland, Vt.: Charles E. Tuttle, 1967), 52.

5. Frederick Baekeland, "Psychological Aspects of Art Collecting," *Psychiatry* 44 (1981): 53.

6. Jackson, *Anatomy of Bibliomania*, 574; Carolyn Wells, "On Finishing Collector," *Atlantic* 138 (November 1926): 631.

7. John T. Winterich, *A Primer of Book Collecting* (New York: Greenberg, [ca. 1926]), x; Gelett Burgess, *The Romance of the Commonplace* (Indianapolis: Bobbs-Merrill, 1902), 78; H.C.V.P. [Major H. V. Porter], "I Would Rather be a Collector than the Owner of a Collection," *Seaby's Coin and Medal Bulletin* 382 (March 1950): 105.

8. Wilmarth S. Lewis, *Collector's Progress* (New York: Alfred A. Knopf, 1946), 8, 11–13; Douglas Rigby and Elizabeth Rigby, *Lock, Stock, and Barrel: The Story of*

Collecting (New York: Lippincott, 1944), 389; Margaret Elizabeth Mulac, *Hobbies: The Creative Use of Leisure* (New York: Harper, 1959), 139.

9.   Agnes Repplier, "Collection of Autographs," *Century* 92 (August 1916): 584.

10. John Ramsay, "The Luck of Collecting," *Hobbies* 52 (August 1947): 22.

11. J. W. Mackail, ed., "Collectors," *Modern Essays* (New York: Longmans, Green, 1915), 31–33.

12. "The Joy of Collecting and a Recent Great Sale," *Outlook* 115 (January 24, 1917): 134; Ruth Formanek, "Why They Collect: Collectors Reveal Their Motivations," paper delivered at the annual meeting of the Popular Culture Association, San Antonio, March 1991, 4–5.

13. Edmund Bergler, "Psychopathology of Bargain Hunters," *Journal of Clinical Psychopathology* 1 (1947): 626; Wells, "On Finishing Collector," 629–30.

14. Rupert Sargent Holland, "Boy's Hunt for Big Game," *St. Nicholas* 53 (December 1925): 156–59; Charles Hamilton, "The Old-Fashioned Collector," *Hobbies* 56 (June 1951): 134, 135; "Wrote to Lindberg Sixteen Times," *Hobbies* 38 (September 1933): 30.

15. Janet E. Ruutz-Rees, *Home Occupations* (New York: D. Appleton, 1883), 94.

16. Norman Sherwood, "The Walter P. Chrysler Collection of Old Mechanical Penny Banks," *Avocations* 3 (December 1938): 173.

17. Jackson, *Anatomy of Bibliomania*, 569–70; see also 582–83.

18. *New York Times*, February 18, 1912, 9; "Collections," *Harper's Weekly* 46 (November 15, 1902): 1726–27.

19. Gardner Teall, *The Pleasure of Collecting* (Boston: Century, 1920), vii; Olmsted, "Collectors and Collecting," 10; William C. Menninger, "Psychological Aspects of Hobbies," *American Journal of Psychiatry* 99 (June 1942): reprinted in *A Psychiatrist for a Troubled World: Selected Papers of William C. Menninger, M.D.*, ed. Bernard H. Hall (New York: Viking Press, 1967), 710; see also 712–13.

20. For example, see Chris Argyris "The Individual and Organization: An Empirical Test," *Administrative Science Quarterly* 4 (1959): 158.

21. A. D. Olmsted, "Morally Controversial Leisure: The Social World of Gun Collectors," *Symbolic Interaction* 11 (1988): 278.

22. Mary Douglas, *Purity and Danger: An Analysis of Concepts of Pollution and Taboo* (New York: Praeger, 1966).

23. Henry Clyde Shetrone, "Experiences of a Relic Hunter," *Stamp Collector* 1 (January 1910): 49; Mark Twain, "The Canvasser's Tale," in *Masterpieces of Fantasy and Enchantment*, ed. David G. Hartwell (New York: St. Martin's Press, 1988), 252–57.

24. John Walker Harrington, "Postal Carditis and Some Allied Manias," *American Illustrated Magazine* 61 (March 1906): 562; *New York Times*, February 18, 1912, 9; Barton Currie, *Fisher of Books*, vol. 1 (Boston: Little Brown, 1931), 21; E. R. Pennell, "My Cookery Books," *Atlantic* 87 (June 1901): 789.

25. Bill Carmichael, *Incredible Collectors, Weird Antiques, and Odd Hobbies* (Englewood Cliffs, N.J.: Prentice-Hall, 1971), 6–7; "Have You a Hobby?" *Hobbies* 37 (March 1931): 15; O. C. Lightner, "The Publisher's Page," *Hobbies* 55

(April 1950): 100; Charles Caldwell Dobie, "Wild Geese," *Arrested Moment and Other Stories* (New York: Day, 1927), 144.

26. Werner Muensterberger, *Collecting: An Unruly Passion* (Princeton: Princeton University Press, 1994), 11; Jackson, *Anatomy of Bibliomania*, 753; John Hill Burton, *The Book Hunter* (Philadelphia: J. B. Lippincott, 1863, 1900), 59; Jackson, *Anatomy of Bibliomania*, 572; Brander Matthews, "By Way of Introduction," *Recreations of an Anthologist* (New York: Dodd, Mead, 1904), 4.

27. *New York Times*, July 8, 1900, 17; Joseph Hergesheimer, "Fiddlebacks," *Saturday Evening Post* 199 (October 30, 1926): 18.

28. Louis E. Bisch quoted in "Hobbies: Collecting," *Literary Digest* (February 27, 1937): 31; Jones quoted in Formanek, "Why They Collect," 2; William C. Menninger, "The Psychology of Stamp Collecting," *Weekly Philatelic Gossip* (May 3, 1941), reprinted in *A Psychiatrist for a Troubled World*, 753.

29. William P. Cahill, "Intelligence and Compulsive Personality Traits as Mediators in the Contribution of the Collecting Hobbies to Academic Achievement for Eighth- and Ninth-Grade Students" (Ed.D. diss., Florida Atlantic University, Boca Raton, 1986), 25–26; Richard E. Matteson, "Purpose in Life as Related to Involvement in Organized Groups and Certain Sociocultural Variables" (Ed.D. diss., Northern Illinois University, 1975), 48–49; Stanley Cohen and Laurie Taylor, *Escape Attempts: The Theory and Practice of Resistance to Everyday Life* (New York: Penguin, 1978), 97–100.

30. Cahill, "Intelligence and Compulsive Personality Traits," 24–25.

31. For example, see Joseph Lister Rutledge, "Consider the Collector," *Canadian Magazine* 84 (November 1935): 14; Pierre Cabanne, *The Great Collectors* (New York: Farrar, Straus, 1953), viii; Bergler, "Psychopathology of Bargain Hunters," 626; Jullian, *The Collectors*, 45.

32. Walter A. Dyer, "One Collector's Hobbies," *Country Life* 34 (July 1918): 72.

33. Baekeland, "Psychological Aspects of Art Collecting," 50; John Forrester, " 'Mille e tre': Freud and Collecting," in *The Cultures of Collecting*, ed. John Elsner and Roger Cardinal (Cambridge, Mass.: Harvard University Press, 1994), 233; Abraham quoted in Formanek, "Why They Collect," 3.

34. Jean Baudrillard, "The System of Collecting," in *The Cultures of Collecting*, 18.

35. Baudrillard, "The System of Collecting," 10; Arnold Bennett, "Collecting," *Woman's Home Companion* 13 (May 1924): 84.

36. Charles Dickens, "About Hobbies," *All the Year Round* 67 (November 8, 1890): 444; Muensterberger, *Collecting*, 92; *New York Times*, July 27, 1886, 3.

37. A. S. W. Rosenbach, *The Unpublishable Memoirs* (New York: Mitchell, Kennerly, 1917), 155–60.

38. Eugene Field, *The Love Affair of a Bibliomaniac* (New York: Charles Scribner's Sons, 1896), vii.

39. Radclyffe Hall, "Lover of Things," in *Miss Ogilvy Finds Herself* (New York: Harcourt, Brace, 1934), 54–140.

40. Pearl Eley Seal, "Man with a Hobby," *Hobbies* 42 (April 1937): 8; Grace V. Sharritt, "He Has Collect-itis, but I Love Him," *Better Homes and Gardens* 16 (April 1938): 30; Frank Farrington, "The Bug and the Budget," *Hobbies* 40

(November 1935): 55; Harriet Pinkham, "Little Orphan Dannie," *Hobbies* 44 (July 1939): 63.

41. Roy S. Tinney, "The Gun Crank," *Hobbies* 40 (January 1935): 86; Jackson, *Anatomy of Bibliomania*, 579.

42. Bennett, "Collecting," 4.

43. Harry Earl Montgomery, "Why I Collect Coins," *Numismatist* 27 (March 1914): 138–39; Thomas Hamilton Ormsbee, *Collecting Antiques in America* (New York: Robert M. McBride, 1940), 21.

44. Harry B. Kossove, "Volume 1, Number 1," *Hobbies* 51 (November 1946): 150; Kenneth Griggs Merrill, "Hobby of a Traveling Man," *Atlantic* 139 (April 1927): 519–29; "Personality of a Collector," *Hobbies* 55 (March 1950): 77.

45. Johnson quoted in "On Collecting Things," *Living Age* 304 (January 31, 1920): 284–89. Besides being a collector, Brown was an orthographic reformer and his newsletter is written in his own phonetic system. This is a translation. William P. Brown, "Antikwiti or Dizain," *De Kuriositi Kabinet* 1 (November 1870): 1; Austen Fox Riggs, *Play: Recreation in a Balanced Life* (Garden City, N.Y.: Doubleday, Doran, 1935), 112.

46. James E. Boyle, "Be a Collector and Live Longer," *Nation's Business* 17 (May 1929): 168.

47. Edwin Wolf II, "Great American Book Collectors to 1800," *Gazette of the Grolier Club* (June 1971): 6; G. Stanley Hall, "Children's Collections," *Pedagogical Seminary* 1 (May 1891): 234–35; Caroline Frear Burk, "The Collecting Instinct," *Pedagogical Seminary* 7 (January 1900): 179–207.

48. A. S. W. Rosenbach, *Books and Bidders: The Adventures of a Bibliophile* (Boston: Little, Brown, 1927), 4, 11; Jackson, *Anatomy of Bibliomania*, 694–95.

49. William James, *The Principles of Psychology* (New York: Henry Holt, 1890), 293; see also, Paul A. Witty and Harvey C. Lehman, "Further Studies of Children's Interest in Collecting," *Journal of Educational Psychology* 21 (1930): 112–27.

50. Witty and Lehman, "Further Studies of Children's Interest"; Walter Nelson Durost, *Children's Collecting Activity Related to Social Factors* (New York: Columbia University Teachers College, Contributions to Education, no. 535, 1932); Ernest Beaglehole, *Property: A Study in Social Psychology* (New York: Macmillan, 1932), 120–21.

51. Matteson, "Purpose in Life as Related to Involvement," 33–38.

52. Harvey C. Lehman and Paul A. Witty, *The Psychology of Play Activities* (New York: A. S. Barnes): 49–53; Elmer W. Cressman, *Out of School Activities of Jr. High School Pupils in Relation to Intelligence and Socio-Economic Status* (State College: Pennsylvania State College Studies in Education, no. 20, 1937), 60; O. S. Ikenberry, "Leisure Activities in a Community" (Ph.D. diss., Colorado State College of Education, Greeley, 1941), 38; Jack R. Kudrna, "A Survey of the Out-of-School Activities of Senior High School Students" (master's thesis, Colorado State College, Greeley, 1943), 60.

53. *New York Times*, November 26, 1922, sect 9, p. 8.

54. "Is Your Child a Collector?" *Women's Home Companion* 69 (March 1942): 64.

55. "The Ornamental Artist," *Godey's Lady's Book* 1 (1830): 271; Catharine E. Beecher, *A Treatise on Domestic Economy for the Use of Young Ladies at Home and at School* (New York: Harper and Brothers, 1855), 253; Lydia Marie Child, *The Girl's Own Book* (New York: Clark Austin, 1833), 102; Witty and Lehman, "Further Studies of Children's Interest," 125; Bentley Bates, "The Making of Collections," in *Pets, Hobbies, and Collections*, ed. Frank Hobart Chelely (New York: University Society, 1933), 283–86.

56. E. DeAlton Partridge and Catherine Mooney, *Time Out for Living* (New York: American Book, 1941), 185, 200; Hildegarde Hawthorne, "Collections," *St. Nicholas* 48 (September 1921): 1012; Wheeler McMillen, *The Young Collector* (New York: D. Appleton, 1928), 11; "Three or Four Hobbies More than Equal One Career," *Hobbies* 36 (October 1931): 13; F. G. Bonser, *School Work and Spare Time* (Cleveland: Survey Committee of the Cleveland Foundation, 1918), 84, 98–107.

57. George Peak, "Does Your Child Collect? Make the Habit of Value to Him," *Delineator* 94 (February 1919): 40; Mary Blake, *Twenty-six Hours a Day* (Boston: D. Lathrop, 1883), 161; Emma Churchman Hewitt, *Queen of the Home: Her Reign from Infancy to Age, from Attic to Cellar* (Philadelphia: W. W. Houston, 1892), 186.

58. Hewitt, *Queen of the Home*, 186; Mary C. Quigley, "Book Collecting for Girls," *St. Nicholas* 65 (November 1937): 174; Shirley Kessler, "Preparing for Live through Hobbies," *Today's Health* 33 (December 1955): 46.

59. Baekeland, "Psychological Aspects of Art Collecting," 47.

60. A. D. Olmsted, "Collecting: Leisure, Investment, or Obsession," *Journal of Social Behavior and Personality* 6 (1991): 295; Olmsted, "Collectors and Collecting," 10–11.

61. Burk, "The Collecting Instinct"; E. Howe, "Can the Collecting Instinct Be Utilized in Teaching?" *Elementary School Teacher* 6 (May 1906): 466–71; Frank D. Boone, "A Study of Collecting among Children of Kansas in 1928" (master's thesis, University of Kansas, 1928), 34–37, 42; Witty and Lehman, "Further Studies of Children's Interest"; Paul A. Witty and Harvey C. Lehman, "The Collecting Interests of Town Children and Country Children," *Journal of Educational Psychology* 24 (April 1933): 170–84; Durost, *Children's Collecting Activity*, 31–32.

62. Burk, "The Collecting Instinct," 186; Mihaly Csikszentmihayli, *The Meaning of Things: Domestic Symbol and the Self* (Cambridge: Cambridge University Press, 1981), 107–9.

63. Burk, "The Collecting Instinct," 186, 193–94, 204; Bonser, *School Work and Spare Time*, 98–100; Dorothy L. Sayers, "The Dragon's Head," in *Sporting Blood*, ed. Ellery Queen (Boston: Little Brown, 1928), 342–43.

64. Boone, "A Study of Collecting," 48; M. Spottswood, "Hobbies for the Teen Age," *Recreation* 26 (February 1933): 523; Agnes Repplier, "The Pleasure of Possession," *Commonweal* 13 (December 17, 1930): 181.

65. Field, *The Love Affair*, 229–32; Vincent Starrett, *Penny Wise and Book Foolish* (New York: Covici Friede, 1929), 182–83; Richard Maass, "William Buell Sprague, Super Collector," *Manuscripts* 27 (1975): 255.

66. *New York Times*, October 9, 1921, sect. 2, p. 2; Louise Paine Benjamin, "Do Men Have the Most Fun?" *Ladies' Home Journal* 56 (October 1939): 74; Dorothy Brannan, "The Mounting Block for Hobby Horses," *Hobbies* 54 (May 1949): 123.

67. Prudence Crawford, "Buttons: Spin-offs from the Decorative Arts," in vol. 3 of *The Encyclopedia of Collectibles*, ed. Andrea DiNoto (New York: Time-Life Books, 1978), 7; Lillian Smith Albert and Kathryn Kent, *The Complete Button Book* (Garden City, N.Y.: Doubleday, 1949), ix.

68. Kim Moare, "Through the Years," *Hobbies* 49 (August 1944): 35.

69. "The Newest Society," *Hobbies* 50 (December 1945): 33.

70. Albert, *A Button Collector's Second Journal*, 11–12.

71. Polly de Steiguer Crummett, *Button Collecting* (Chicago: Lightner Publishing, 1939), 11; Grace Horney Ford, *The Button Collector's History* (Springfield, Mass.: 1943), 1.

72. Albert and Kent, *The Complete Button Book*, viii.

73. Pat H. Norwood, "Why I Collect Buttons," *Hobbies* 53 (March 1948): 46; "Hobby Groups," *Hobbies* 56 (February 1951): 12–13.

74. C. Ford, "I'm Collecting Myself," *Reader's Digest* 65 (October 1954): 100–102.

4 Constructing a Collector's Market

1. Arjun Appadurai, introduction to *The Social Life of Things: Commodities in Cultural Perspective*, ed. Appadurai (Cambridge: Cambridge University Press, 1986), 41–42; Augustine Birrell, *The Collected Essays and Addresses*, vol. 3 (London: J. M. Dent and Sons, 1922): 243; Jonathan Grant, "The Socialist Construction of Philately in the Early Soviet Era," *Comparative Studies in Society and History* 37 (July 1995): 476–93.

2. Andrew Lang, "The Humors of Collecting," *Independent* 68 (June 16, 1910): 1341.

3. Joseph K. Drake, "Hobbies of Credit Managers," *Credit Monthly* 29 (September 1927): 11.

4. A. Edward Newton, *The Amenities of Book-Collecting and Kindred Affections* (Boston: Atlantic Monthly Press, 1918), 123; "The Profit of Collecting," *American Journal of Numismatics* 15 (July 1880): 16.

5. George C. Williamson, *Everybody's Book on Collecting* (London: Herbert Jenkins, 1924): 13; Alfred Edward Newton, *This Book Collecting Game* (Boston: Little, Brown, 1928), 249, 11, 30, 196, 201.

6. William Dana Orcutt, *The Magic of the Book: More Reminiscences and Adventures of a Bookman* (Boston: Little, Brown, 1930), 266; Douglas Rigby and Elizabeth Rigby, *Lock, Stock, and Barrel: The Story of Collecting* (New York: Lippincott, 1944), 11–13; *New York Evening Post* quotation cited in "Collector's Fever," *Saturday Evening Post* 204 (May 18, 1931): 18; *Collecting for Profit* 2 (March 1932).

7. Harold Child, "The Future of Cartophily," *Essays and Reflections* (London: Cambridge University Press, 1948), 173–74; J. Zeitlin, "Art of Collecting the Common," *Saturday Review of Literature* 276 (September 4, 1943): 4.

8. Conway Bolt, "Collector to Numismatist," *Numismatist* 76 (April 1963): 481.

9.   C. L. Huntley, "Finds," *Hobbies* 36 (September 1931): 39; Morgan Towne, *Treasures in Truck and Trash* (Garden City, N.Y.: Doubleday, 1949); Alan Dundes, "Folk Ideas as Units of Worldview," *Journal of American Folklore* 84 (1971): 93–103; Patrick B. Mullen, "The Folk Idea of Unlimited Good in American Buried Treasure," *Journal of the Folklore Institute* 15 (1978): 209–20.

10. T. S. Arthur, "Owning a Picture," *Arthur's New Home Magazine* 28 (November 1866): 265.

11. Arthur, "Owning a Picture," 264–67.

12. Andrew Lang, *Books and Bookmen* (New York: George Coombs, 1886), 162–63, 171.

13. Barton Currie, *Fisher of Books*, vol. 1 (Boston: Little Brown, 1931), 254; Charles Rowed, *Collecting as a Pastime* (London: Cassell, 1920), 2.

14. A. S. W. Rosenbach, *The Unpublishable Memoirs* (New York: Mitchell, Kennerly, 1917), 1–16.

15. Rigby and Rigby, *Lock, Stock, and Barrel*, 411; Horace Annesley Vachell, *Quinney's Adventures* (New York: George H. Doran, 1924), 164; Russell N. Case, "Treasures May Hide in Old Pages," *Profitable Hobbies* 12 (January 1956): 23, 42; Wilmarth Lewis, *Collector's Progress* (New York: Alfred A. Knopf, 1951), 11–13.

16. C. R. Clifford, *The Junk Snupper: The Adventures of an Antique Collector* (New York: Macmillan, 1927), 171–76.

17. Susan Stewart, *On Longing: Narratives of the Miniature, the Gigantic, the Souvenir, the Collection* (Baltimore: Johns Hopkins University Press, 1984), 165, 167.

18. Barbara R. Mueller, *Common Sense Philately* (Princeton, N.J.: Van Nostrant, 1956), 4.

19. Alvin F. Harlow, *Paper Chase: The Amenities of Stamp Collecting* (New York: Henry Holt, 1940), 15–16; "Work Department," *Godey's Lady's Book* 101 (November 1880): 477; Charles James Phillips, *Fifty Years of Philately: The History of Stanley Gibbins, Ltd.* (London: Stanley Gibbins, 1906), 194.

20. Harlow, *Paper Chase*, 18, 25.

21. Gustav Schenk, *The Romance of the Postage Stamp* (Garden City, N.Y.: Doubleday, 1959), 146–47.

22. Theodore F. Dwight, "Hobbies and Their Riders," *Overland Monthly and Out West Magazine* 7 (September 1871): 265.

23. "Will It Last?" *Stamp Collector's Guide* 1 (April 1871): 18; Philo., "A Stamp's History," *Western Philatelist* 1 (August 1887): 8.

24. Robert Jay, *The Trade Card in Nineteenth-Century America* (Columbia: University of Missouri Press, 1987).

25. Ellen Gruber Garvey, *The Adman in the Parlor: Magazines and the Gendering of Consumer Culture, 1880s to 1910s* (New York: Oxford University Press, 1996), 18.

26. "Editorial: The Ladies' Number," *Pennsylvania Philatelist* 6 (June, 1894): 341; Lewis G. Quackenbush, "The Ladies—A Philatelic Toast," *Pennsylvania Philatelist* 6 (June 1894): 331.

27. Mame A. Keene, "A Plea for the Ladies," *Pennsylvania Philatelist* 4 (October 1893): 20.

28. Mame A. Keene, "The Silent Collector," *Pennsylvania Philatelist* 6 (June 1894): 340; Maud Charlotte Bingham, "My Stamp Album," *Pennsylvania Philatelist* 6 (June 1894): 334.

29. Keene, "The Silent Collector," 339.

30. Ernest A. Kehr, *The Romance of Stamp Collecting: Notes from the World of Stamps, Stamp Collecting, and Stamp Collectors* (New York: T. Y. Crowell, 1947), 282; Mueller, *Common Sense Philately*, 123.

31. Esther Schlosser, "Women and Philately," *Hobbies* 36 (September 1931): 50.

32. Harlow, *Paper Chase*, 2–3.

33. Lillie H. Murray, "Women and Philatelia," *American Collector* 2 (March 1897): 70; Lewis G. Quackenbush, "Philately as a Means of Education," *Southern Philatelist* 3 (November 1891): 40–41. Cundinamarca is a province in central Colombia and Nowanugger was a principality in nineteenth-century India.

34. Donald E. Super and Ralph L. Carlson, "What Adolescent and Adult Stamp Collectors Learn from Their Avocation," *Journal of Genetic Psychology* (1942): 99–108; "Stamp Collecting," *Stamp Collector's Guide* 1 (September 1871): 29; Blue Nose, "Philately's Benefits," *Eastern Philatelist* 9 (April 1892): 36.

35. Quackenbush, "The Ladies," 331; Keene, "A Plea for the Ladies," 102; Mame A. Keene, "A Plea for the Ladies—Second Paper," *Pennsylvania Philatelist* 4 (December 1893): 20; Edwin Christ, "The Adult Stamp Collector" (Ph.D. diss., University of Missouri, 1957), 90–96; D. J. McDermott, "She Stoops to Conquer," *Pennsylvania Philatelist* 6 (June 1894): 338; Luther W. Mott, "Phair Philatelists," *Pennsylvania Philatelist* 6 (July 1894): 361–62; Roy F. Greene, "The Charms of Annabel," *Pennsylvania Philatelist* 6 (June 1894): 330; William Blake, "A Philatelic Romance," *Collector's Journal* 10 (April 1920): 11–14; Guy W. Green, "How He Became a Collector," *Southern Philatelist* 2 (August 1891): 188; Guy W. Green, "A New Social Factor," *Eastern Philatelist* 7 (June 1891): 53; Clifford W. Kissinger, "The Fair Sex in Philately," *Pennsylvania Philatelist* 5 (January 1894): 173.

36. Mott, "Phair Philatelists," 361; Eva Earl, "Give the Girls a Chance," *Pennsylvania Philatelist* 4 (November 1893): 126.

37. Keene, "The Silent Collector," 339; Charlotte Matson, "Minneapolis Women's Philatelic Society," *Hobbies* 44 (May 1939): 66–67.

38. "Poetry of Philately," *American Journal of Philately* 2 (September 20, 1869): 104.

39. Iola, "The Postage Stamp Fiend," *Pennsylvania Philatelist* 11 (March 1897): 158.

40. Philo., "Philatelic Societies," *Stamp* 1 (February 1887): 9; Cleve Scott, "My Experience with a Public Crank," *Southern Philatelist* 4 (January 1893): 9.

41. G. A. Furse, "Philately in England," *Providence, R.I. Sunday Journal* (November 19, 1893): 10; Mauritz A. Hallgren, *All about Stamps: Their History and the Collecting of Them* (New York: A. A. Knopf, 1940), 181.

42. L. N. Williams and M. Williams, *The Postage Stamp: Its History and Recognition* (Hamondsworth: Penguin Books, 1956), 66–67.

43. Philo., "A Stamp's History," 47, emphasis added.

44. [Editorial], *Empire State Philatelist* (December 5, 1886): 92.

45. Eva Earl, "A Lady's Experience," *Pennsylvania Philatelist* 6 (June 1894): 337; Hallgren, *All about Stamps*, 314–20.

46. Walter N. Emerson, "Tendencies toward Sanity," *Hobbies* 42 (March 1937): 33–34; F. J. Melville, *Modern Stamp Collecting* (Toronto: Musson Book, 1940), 19.

47. Harlow, *Paper Chase*, 24.

48. Williams and Williams, *The Postage Stamp*, 75; Hallgren, *All about Stamps*, 290–94; Schenk, *Romance of the Postage Stamp*, 152.

49. For a slightly different categorization see Christ, "The Adult Stamp Collector," 223–31.

50. Dick Flint, "An Autobiography," *Southern Philatelist* 2 (June 1891): 165–67; I. B. Cohen, "How I Became a Collector," *Southern Philatelist* 1 (May 1890): 74–75; "Schoolboy's Collection," *American Journal of Philately* 1 (October 29, 1870): 69; Lewis, *A Collector's Progress*, 5.

51. Harlow, *Paper Chase*, 41–42; Guy W. Green, "The Philatelic Kindergarten," *Eastern Philatelist* 12 (October 1893): 21.

52. Philippe Jullian, *The Collectors* (Rutland, Vt.: Charles E. Tuttle, 1967), 31; Hallgren, *All about Stamps*, 180.

53. Sydney J. Eisenberg, "A Strange 'Change," in "Poetry of Philately," 105.

54. Philo., "The Bluffton Stamp Collector's Society," *Stamp World* 6 (March 1886): 65.

55. J. W. Longnecker, "Why I Collect Stamps," *Avocations* 1 (December 1937): 280–81; M. Iron, "The Philatelic Scarecrow," *American Collector* 4 (July 1898): 84–85.

56. Hallgren, *All about Stamps*, 281, 296–99; Lena Belle Shawen, *A President's Hobby* (New York: H. L. Lindquist, 1949); A. D. Cox, "Good as Wheat!" *American Collector* 4 (July 1898): 83.

57. Steele Penne, "Philatelic Missionary Work," *Eastern Philatelist* 14 (November 1894): 44; James L. Wright, "Ten Cents Grows into $10,000," *Hobbies* 36 (September 1931): 33.

58. Hallgren, *All about Stamps*, 25–55; Kehr, *The Romance of Stamp Collecting*, 193–95; Harlow, *Paper Chase*, 168–79; Williams and Williams, *The Postage Stamp*, 69–73.

59. M. J. Blackman, "Big Moments," *Hobbies* 38 (June 1933): 44–45; A. C. Townsend, "Call a Junk Man," *Hobbies* 40 (August 1935): 48–50; A. C. Townsend, "Consequences," *Hobbies* 41 (May 1936): 45–47; Paul Dore Burks, *Fireside Yarns — 1001 Nights: Reminiscences of an Old Coin Man* (Los Angeles: 1932), 14–25; Charles William Taussig and Theodore Arthur Meyer, *The Book of Hobbies; or a Guide to Happiness* (New York: Minton, Balch, 1924), 87; Harlow, *Paper Chase*, 162–65.

60. "Philatelic Liar," *Perforator* 1 (March 1897): 1.

61. Margaret Ford, "Philately," *Southern Philatelist* 4 (May 1893): 77–82.

62. Christ, "The Adult Stamp Collector," 238; Jack O'Donnell, "The Hobby of Kids and Kings," *Saturday Evening Post* 198 (November 14, 1925).

63. "The Moral Factor of Philately," *Southern Philatelist* 7 (February 1896): 20; Edwin B. Hill, "A Mender of Stamps," *Collector's Journal of Chicago* 6 (December 1915): 77–78; Homer Croy, "Trinidad Triangle," in *The Boy Scouts'*

Book of Indoor Hobby Trails, ed. Franklin W. Mathiews (New York: D. Appleton-Century, 1939), 227–38.

64. Kehr, *The Romance of Stamp Collecting*, 40–41; Harlow, *Paper Chase*, 28; Hallgren, *All about Stamps*, 183–84, 282–83.

65. Cox, "Good as Wheat!" 19–20; A. C. Townsend, "Diplomatic Entry," *Hobbies* 39 (December 1934): 30–31.

5 Deconstructing a Collector's Market

1. Elizabeth Stillinger et al., *The Antiquers* (New York: Knopf, 1980), 12, 8.

2. Rodris Roth, "The New England, or 'Olde Tyme,' Kitchen Exhibit at Nineteenth-Century Fairs," in *The Colonial Revival in America*, ed. Alan Axelrod (New York: W. W. Norton, 1985), 159–72.

3. Roth, "The New England . . . Kitchen," 174–77; Stillinger, *The Antiquers*, 8–16.

4. Clarence Cook, *The House Beautiful: Essays on Beds and Tables, Stools, and Candlesticks* (New York: Scribner, Armstrong, 1878), 59; Stillinger, *The Antiquers*, 52–54.

5. Francis Graham [editor, *Hobbies* magazine], typescript in possession of the author, ca. 1977, 6.

6. Cook, *The House Beautiful*, 161.

7. A. B. Frost, "The Rage for Old Furniture," *Harper's Weekly* 22 (November 16, 1878): 917.

8. Susan Prendergast Schoelwer, "Curious Relics and Quaint Scenes: The Colonial Revival at Chicago's Great Fair," in *The Colonial Revival*, 184–214; Stillinger, *The Antiquers*, 54–55; Roth, "The New England . . . Kitchen," 178–79; Graham, typescript, 7.

9. Alice Brown, "Righteous Bargain," *Meadow Grass: Tales of New England Life* (Boston: Houghton, 1895), 143–65.

10. Melinda Young Frye, "The Beginnings of the Period Room in American Museums: Charles P. Wilcomb's Colonial Kitchens," in *The Colonial Revival*, 217–40; Stillinger, *The Antiquers*, 124–32; John P. Gutenberg, "Vessels of History: American Flasks," *Art and Antiques* 4 (1981), 50–57; Jay E. Cantor, *Winterthur* (New York: Harry N. Abrams, 1985), 100; Esther Singleton, *The Furniture of Our Forefathers* (New York: Doubleday, Page, 1901).

11. Cantor, *Winterthur*, 100–101, 104; Charles Merz, *And Then Came Ford* (Garden City, N.Y.: Doubleday, Doran, 1929), 257; Stillinger, *The Antiquers*, 192–97; Walter Karp, "Henry Francis du Pont and the Invention of Winterthur," *American Heritage* 34 (1983): 86–97.

12. Joyce P. Barendsen, "Wallace Nutting, an American Tastemaker: The Pictures and Beyond," *Winterthur Portfolio* 18 (1983): 187–95; Margaret Kent, "The Show and the Showman: The Wallace Nutting Collection," *Early American Life* 17 (1988): 54; Wendell D. Garrett, "Wallace Nutting," in *Dictionary of American Biography*, ed. Edward T. James (New York: Charles Scribner's Sons, 1977), 567.

13. Wallace Nutting, *Wallace Nutting's Autobiography* (Framingham, Mass.: Old America, 1936), 94.

14. Quoted in Stillinger, *The Antiquers*, 190.

15. Joseph Hergesheimer, "Walnut," *Saturday Evening Post* 195 (June 2, 1923): 6.

16. Michael Wallace, "Visiting the Past: History Museums in the United States," *Radical History Review* 25 (1981), 76–77; Walter Karp, "My Gawd, They Sold the Town," *American Heritage* 32 (1981): 84–95.

17. Wallace, "Visiting the Past," 63–96.

18. James S. Wamsley, *American Ingenuity: Henry Ford Museum and Greenfield Village* (New York: Harry N. Abrams, 1985); C. R. Clifford, *The Junk Snupper: The Adventures of an Antique Collector* (New York: Macmillan, 1927), 129; Merz, *And Then Came Ford*, 257.

19. William Greenleaf, *From These Beginnings: The Early Philanthropy of Henry and Edsel Ford, 1911–1936* (Detroit: Wayne State University Press, 1964), 73, 77.

20. Walter Karp, "Greenfield Village," *American Heritage* 32 (1980): 103–4; Greenleaf, *From These Beginnings*, 78–85; Wallace, "Visiting the Past, 70.

21. Kenneth L. Roberts, *Antiquamania* (Garden City, N.Y.: Doubleday, Doran, 1928), 5; Helen Hill Miller, "The Joy of the Open Road," in *Essays and Essay Writing*, ed. William Maddux Tanner (New York: Little, Brown, 1933), 189; Allen Nevins and Frank Ernest Hill, *Ford: Expansion and Challenge, 1915–1933* (New York: Charles Scribner's Sons, 1957), 506.

22. Cantor, *Winterthur*, 104.

23. Roberts, *Antiquamania*, 53.

24. M. L. Law, "Collector's Pitfalls," *Saturday Evening Post* 198 (December 19, 1925): 79.

25. Marion Nicholl Rawson, *Country Auction* (New York: E. P. Dutton, 1929).

26. Merz, *And Then Came Ford*, 258.

27. Bernard DeVoto, "Letter from America," *Harper's Monthly* 177 (September 1938): 447.

28. O. C. Lightner, "The Publisher's Page," *Hobbies* 47 (February 1942): 121; "Market for Antiques Spirals," *Business Week* (August 1946): 74.

29. John T. Winterich, *The Grolier Club, 1884–1950: An Informal History* (New York: The Grolier Club, 1950), 6.

30. Alice Van Leer Carrick, *A Mother Goose for Antique Collectors* (New York: Payson and Clarke, 1927), 47.

31. Ring Lardner, "Ex Parte," in *A World of Great Stories*, ed. Hiram Haydn and John Cournos (New York: Crown, 1947); Clifford, *The Junk Snupper*, 1, 153–54.

32. Stephen Leacock, "Old Junk and New Money," *Laugh With Leacock* (New York: Dodd, Mead, 1926), 20; Sophie Kerr, "Old American," *Collier's* 76 (November 1925): 15.

33. Robert Shackleton and Elizabeth Shackleton, *The Charm of the Antique* (New York: Hearst's International Library, 1913), 2; Van Leer Carrick, *A Mother Goose*, 57; Leonard Falkner, "If You Must Collect," *Mentor* 22 (September 1930): 22–23; Walter Prichard Eaton, "Junk," *American Mercury* 4 (March 1925): 357;

34. Falkner, "If You Must Collect," 60; *New York Times*, August 24, 1941, 6.

35. Philippe Jullian, *The Collectors* (Rutland, Vt.: E. Tuttle, 1967), 22; Alain
     Corbin, "Backstage," in vol. 4 of *A History of Private Life*, ed. Michelle Perrot
     (Cambridge, Mass.: Belknap Press, Harvard University, 1990), 541–57.
36. Charles Messer Stow, "Antiques Collecting," in *Hobbies for Everybody*, ed.
     Ruth Lampland (New York: Harper, 1934), 10; Harold Donaldson Eberllein
     and Abbot Mcclure, *The Practical Book of American Antiques* (Garden City,
     N.Y.: Garden City Publishing, 1927), i.
37. Van Leer Carrick, *A Mother Goose*, 142.
38. Van Leer Carrick, *A Mother Goose*, 27.
39. Van Leer Carrick, *A Mother Goose*, 12.
40. Van Leer Carrick, *A Mother Goose*, 7, 13.
41. Thornton Wilder, *Three Plays: Our Town, The Skin of Our Teeth, The Match-
     maker* (New York: Harper and Row, 1938), 18–19; Falkner, "If You Must Col-
     lect."
42. Joseph Hergesheimer, "Of Ultimate Antiques," *Saturday Evening Post* 201
     (December 22, 1928): 9.
43. Nutting, *Autobiography*, 104, 117–18; Charles Messer Stow, "Antiques at Today's
     Prices, Sound Investment," *Hobbies* 37 (July 1932): 102; "About Antiques," *Col-
     lector's Journal* 3 (October-December, 1932): 310.
44. *New York Times*, October 14, 1956, sect. 2, p. 10.
45. "Woman Senator Enjoys 'Antiquing,' " *Hobbies* 56 (February 1951): 63; John
     Pirhalla Jr., "Wentworth's Hobby Museum," *Hobbies* 59 (March 1954): 30–31;
     New York Times, July 21, 1951, sect. 2, p. 16.
46. *New York Times*, July 8, 1900, 17.
47. Emily Clark, "Last Chips from an Old Block," in *Stuffed Peacocks* (New York:
     Knopf, 1927); Maxwell Aley, "Secret Sins of Mr. Pitt," in *Stories of the City*, ed.
     Henry Goodman and Bruce Carpenter (New York: Ronald Press, 1931).
48. Shackleton, *The Charm of the Antique*, 6.
49. Horace Annesley Vachell, *Quinney's Adventures* (New York: George H. Doran,
     1914): 129; Vachell, "Barbens of Barbens-Lacy," *Ladies' Home Journal* 38 (April
     1921): 11; Thomas Hamilton Ormsbee, *Collecting Antiques in America* (New
     York: Robert M. McBride, 1940), 25.
50. Van Leer Carrick, *A Mother Goose*, 31, see also 16, 24, 46.
51. Alice Van Leer Carrick, "Collecting Letters," *House Beautiful* 54 (July 1923): 25.
52. Miller, "The Joy of the Open Road," 168.
53. M. L. Law, "Collector's Pitfalls," *Saturday Evening Post* 198 (December 19,
     1925): 79.
54. Vachell, *Quinney's Adventures*, 60.
55. Vachell, *Quinney's Adventures*, 184–213; Joseph Crosby Lincoln, "The Anti-
     quers," *Cape Cod Stories* (New York: A. L. Burt, 1907), 228–29.
56. Roberts, *Antiquamania*, 57, 227; Clifford, *The Junk Snupper*, 20; Law, "Collec-
     tor's Pitfalls," 79; Van Leer Carrick, *A Mother Goose*, 9; see also 18, 26, 35, 42, 50,
     51, 64; "Wherein We Collect a Few Jokes," *Hobbies* 36 (April 1931): 31.
57. Cecil Roth, "Art and Craft of Jewish Collecting," *Commentary* 23 (June 1957):
     541; Shackleton, *The Charm of the Antique*, 100–101.

58. Clifford, *The Junk Snupper*, 147–52; Booth Tarkington et al., *The Collector's Whatnot* (New York: Houghton Mifflin, 1923), 32–33.
59. Tarkington et al., *The Collector's Whatnot*, 35–36; Roth, "Art and Craft of Jewish Collecting," 541.
60. Margaret Jones Peterson, "The Summer Hunt for Antiques," *Hobbies* 42 (June 1937): 59; Elsie Singmaster, "Man in the House," in *Bred in the Bone and Other Stories* (Boston: Houghton, Mifflin, 1925), 70–78; Vachell, *Quinney's Adventures*, 180; S. J. Perelman, "Going Around in Circles," *Reader's Digest* 51 (November 1947): 132.
61. Roberts, *Antiquamania*, 4.
62. Winfield Scott Moody, "The Pickwick Ladle," in *The Pickwick Ladle and Other Collector's Stories* (New York: Charles Scribner's Sons, 1907), 31; Moody, "The EMIB Lowestoft," in *The Pickwick Ladle*, 126–37. Lincoln, "The Antiquers," 375.
63. George B. Dexter, *The Lure of Amateur Collecting* (Boston: Little, Brown, 1923), 64–66; Moody, "The Black Hawthorn Jar," in *The Pickwick Ladle*, 182–85.
64. Joseph Hergesheimer, "Collector's Blues," *Saturday Evening Post* 199 (October 2, 1926): 14–15.

6 Crafts, Tools, and Gender in the Nineteenth Century

1. Ruth Ellen Levine, "Historical Research: Ordering the Past to Chart Our Future," *Occupational Therapy Journal of Research* 6 (September–October 1986): 262; Simon J. Bronner, *Chain Carvers: Old Men Crafting Meaning* (Lexington: University of Kentucky Press, 1985), 150.
2. Milton Gordon and Charles Anderson, "The Blue Collar Workers at Leisure," in *Blue Collar World: Studies of the American Worker*, ed. A. Shostak and W. Gomburg (Englewood Cliffs, N.J.: Prentice Hall, 1964), 415; Alfred C. Clarke, "The Use of Leisure and Its Relation to Levels of Occupation," *American Sociological Review* 21 (1956): 301; Jiri Zuzanek, "Social Differences in Leisure Behavior: Measurement and Interpretation," *Leisure Studies* 1 (1978): 276–77; Doyle W. Bishop and Masaru Ikeda, "Status and Role Factors in the Leisure Behavior of Different Occupations," *Sociology and Social Research* 54 (1970): 197; Rabel J. Burdge, "Levels of Occupational Prestige and Leisure Activity," in *Sport and American Society*, ed. George H. Sage (Reading: Pa.: Addison Wesley, 1974), 242–44.
3. Mihaly Csikszentmihayli, *The Meaning of Things: Domestic Symbol and the Self* (Cambridge: Cambridge University Press, 1981), 108–9.
4. Eric A. Grubb, "Assembly Line Boredom and Individual Differences," *Journal of Leisure Research* 7 (1975): 264–65; Margaret Andreasen and Leslie H. Steeves, "Employed Women's Assertiveness and Openness as Shown in Magazine Use," *Journalism Quarterly* 60 (1983): 45; Maria T. Allison, "Women, Work, and Leisure: The Days of Our Lives," *Leisure Sciences* 9 (1987): 154; the same held true for "blue-collar" farmwives, see Karla A. Henderson and Jean S. Rannells, "Farm Women and the Meaning of Work and Leisure: An Oral History Perspective," *Leisure Sciences* 10 (1988): 45

5. Elyce J. Rotella, *From Home to Office: U.S. Women at Work, 1870–1930* (Ann Arbor, Mich.: UMI Research Press, 1981), 3–38.

6. The expression "haven in a heartless world" is from Christopher Lasch, *Haven in a Heartless World: The Family Besieged* (New York: Basic Books, 1977); Eliza Woodworth, "Our Homes," *Arthur's Home Magazine* 26 (December 1865): 344; Angel Kwolek-Folland, "Gender, Self, and Work in the Life Insurance Industry, 1880–1930," in *Work Engendered: Toward a New History of American Labor*, ed. Ava Baron (Ithaca, N.Y.: Cornell University Press, 1990).

7. Lyman Abbott et al., *The House and Home: A Practical Book* (New York: Charles Scribner's Sons, 1896), 184; Alice B. Neal, "Finding the Leak: A Domestic Episode," *Godey's Lady's Book* 54 (January 1857): 31.

8. Susan Burrows Swan, *Plain and Fancy: American Women and Their Needlework, 1700–1850* (New York: Holt, Rinehart and Winston, 1977), 150.

9. E. B. Duffey, "Women's Work in the World," *Arthur's Home Magazine* 44 (October 1876): 568.

10. *Daughter's Own Book: or Practical Hints From a Father to His Daughter* (Boston: Lilly, Wait, Colman and Holden, 1834), 232.

11. Ann M. Spaulding, "Idle Hours," *Arthur's Home Magazine* 22 (October 1863): 270.

12. "Philosophy of Pastime," *Godey's Lady's Book* 57 (September 1858): 238; "Home Pastimes," *Godey's Lady's Book* 73 (September 1866): 261; *Daughter's Own Book*, 123.

13. Anne L. McDonald, *No Idle Hands: The Social History of American Knitting* (New York: Ballantine Books, 1988), 9.

14. Jan Toller, *The Regency and Victorian Crafts: or the Genteel Female—Arts and Pursuits* (London: Ward and Lock, 1969), 37, 56; Swan, *Plain and Fancy*, 69, 127.

15. Jonathon Barton, "Painted Furniture" in *The Encyclopedia of Collectibles*, vol. 9, ed. Andrea DiNoto (New York: Time-Life Books, 1979), 58; Frances Lichten, *The Decorative Arts of Victoria's Era* (New York: Charles Scribner's Sons, 1950), 9.

16. "The Toilet," *Godey's Lady's Book* 8 (January 1834): 25; ibid. (February 1834): 88; ibid. (March 1834): 132; ibid. (April 1834): 181; ibid. (May 1834): 271; Lydia Marie Child, *The Girl's Own Book* (New York: Clark Austin, 1833), 101–9, 121–23.

17. Louisa May Alcott, *Little Women; or, Meg, Jo, Beth, and Amy* (Boston: Little, Brown, [1868] 1915); Faye E. Dudden, *Serving Women: Household Service in the Nineteenth Century* (Middletown, Conn.: Wesleyan University Press, 1983), 130; "Amusement for Ladies," *Godey's Lady's Book* 3 (March 1831): 176; Ada Neil, "The Wife's Experiment," *Godey's Lady's Book* 5 (October 1856): 342–43.

18. Frances M. Trollope, *Domestic Manners of the Americans* (New York: Alfred A. Knopf, 1949), 284.

19. Quoted in Lichten, *Decorative Art*, 170.

20. Julia McNair Wright, *The Complete Home: An Encyclopaedia of Domestic Life and Affairs* (Philadelphia: P. W. Ziegler, 1879), 173–75; Janet E. Ruutz-Rees, *Home Occupations* (New York: D. Appleton, 1883), 5–6.

21. Ruutz-Rees, *Home Occupations*, 6.

22. Annie S. Frost, *The Ladies' Guide to Needle Work, Embroidery, etc.* (New York: Adams and Bishop, 1877), i; Swan, *Plain and Fancy*, 12; Alcott, *Little Women*,

257; Frances E. Wadleigh, "Their King it is Who Tolls," *Godey's Lady's Book* 104 (June 1882): 548.

23. *Needle and Brush: Useful and Decorative* (New York: Butterick Publishing, 1889), 113.

24. T. Webster and Mrs. Parkes, *The American Family Encyclopedia of Useful Knowledge; or the Book of 7,223 Receipts and Facts* (New York: Derby and Jackson, 1857), 263; Mrs. John A. Logan, *The Home Manual: Everybody's Guide in Social, Domestic, and Business Life* (Chicago: H. J. Smith, 1889), 162; Catharine E. Beecher, *A Treatise on Domestic Economy for the Use of Young Ladies at Home and at School* (New York: Harper and Brothers, 1855), 325–26.

25. For example, see Alcott, *Little Women*, 153–54.

26. Mrs. H. D. Conrad, "Our Minister's Wife," *Ladies' Repository* 16 (December 1856): 729–30.

27. "Parlor Work," *Godey's Lady's Book* 46 (June 1853), 571.

28. E.B.D., "A Plea for Knitting," *Arthur's Home Magazine* 33 (March 1869): 186.

29. Marion Harland, "Entirely at Home," *Godey's Lady's Book* 74 (January 1867): 30; Sarah Hart, "The Treasure Trunk," *Arthur's Illustrated Magazine* 43 (May 1875): 298.

30. T. S. Arthur, "The Quilting Party," *Godey's Lady's Book* 39 (September 1849): 185–86; Jane C. Nylander, *Our Own Snug Fireside: Images of the New England Home, 1760–1860* (New York: Alfred A. Knopf, 1993), 226–30; the quotation is from "Patchwork—The Artistic Side of the Question," *Arthur's Lady's Home Magazine* 38 (July 1859): 59; Dulcie Weir, "The Career of a Crazy Quilt," *Godey's Lady's Book* 109 (July 1884): 77–82.

31. Jennie June, "The Family Sewing Machine," *Arthur's Home Magazine* 27 (June 1866): 427; "Ladies Work Department, Knitting," *Godey's Lady's Book* 34 (March 1847): 170; Constance Cary Harrison, *Woman's Handiwork in Modern Homes* (New York: Charles Scribner's Sons, 1881), 8–9; "My Friend's Sewing-Machine Experience," *Ladies' Repository* 3 (January 1869): 49.

32. Rozsika Parker, *The Subversive Stitch: Embroidery and the Making of the Feminine* (New York: Routledge, 1984), 74; Swan, *Plain and Fancy*, 15.

33. S. Woodworth, "The Needle," *Godey's Lady's Book* 1 (March 1830): 328.

34. Emily B. Carroll, "Mary Grey," *Godey's Lady's Book* 60 (June 1860): 498.

35. "Art at Home," *Arthur's Home Magazine* 49 (August 1881): 487; Marian Ford, "Novelties in Fancy Work," *Potter's American Monthly* 16 (May 1881): 458–65; ibid. (June 1881): 554–63; ibid. (July 1881): 76–82: ibid. (July 1881): 363–68.

36. Marion Harland, "Rizpah's Idols," *Godey's Lady's Book* 72 (January 1866): 26.

37. Parker, *The Subversive Stitch*, 11.

38. For example, see *The Fancy Home Needleworker* (Milwaukee: Globe Circulation Agency, 1900), 12.

39. Katherine C. Grier, *Culture and Comfort: People, Parlors, and Upholstery, 1850–1930* (Rochester, N.Y.: Strong Museum, 1988), 268; Lichten, *Decorative Arts*, 11–13; Raymond Francis Yates and Marguerite W. Yates, *Early American Crafts and Hobbies* (New York: Funk, 1954), 73–75.

40. Yates, *Early American Crafts*, 80–81; Lichten, *Decorative Arts*, 186.

41. "Some of the Work in Which Women Are Deficient," *Godey's Lady's Book* 65 (September 1859): 221; Hollis Freeman, "Sally," *Godey's Lady's Book* 104 (May 1882): 445.

42. Quoted in Sandi Fox, *Wrapped in Glory: Figurative Quilts and Bedcovers, 1700–1900* (Los Angeles: Los Angeles County Museum of Art, 1990), 108.

43. C. M. Trowbridge, "Chapter about Indolence," *Arthur's Home Magazine* 1 (January 1853): 262.

44. Marion Harland, "Phemie Rowland," *Godey's Lady's Book* 76 (January 1868): 35.

45. Miss Leslie, *American Girl's Book; or, Occupation for Play Hours* (Boston: Munroe and Francis, 1831); "Fancy Work," *Arthur's Illustrated Home Magazine* 43 (September 1875): 474; Child, *The Girl's Own Book*, 202; A Lady, "Evening Employment for Boys," *Arthur's Home Magazine* 33 (February 1869): 114; M.D.R.S., "Mother's Needle," *Arthur's Home Magazine* 22 (July 1863): 43.

46. Alcott, *Little Women*, 441–42; Marion Harland, "Stumbling Blocks," *Godey's Lady's Book* 84 (April 1872): 329.

47. "Fancy Work," *Arthur's Illustrated Home Magazine* 43 (September 1875): 474; see also H. Effie Webster, "Keeping House, Two Ways," *Ladies' Repository* 26 (August 1860): 465.

48. Florence Hartley, *The Ladies' Hand Book of Fancy and Ornamental Work* (Philadelphia: John E. Potter, 1859); "The Ornamental Artist," *Godey's Lady's Book* 1 (1830): 282; ibid. 2 (1831): 81, 93, 149, 308; "Work Department," *Godey's Lady's Book* 93 (October 1876), 370–73.

49. Lucy Maynard Salmon, *Domestic Service* (New York: Macmillan, 1895), 12; "Instructions for Making Ornaments in Rice and Shell Work," *Godey's Lady's Book* 48 (January 1854): 22; "The Arts," *Graham's Magazine* 46 (May 1855): 484; "The Ornamental Artist," *Godey's Lady's Book* 1 (1830): 282; *Treasures of Use and Beauty: An Epitome of the Choicest Gems of Wisdom, History, Reference, and Recreation* (Detroit: F. B. Dickerson, 1883), 398; "An Elegant Cement," *Godey's Lady's Book* 43 (July 1851): 63.

50. Caroline E. Smith, *The American Home Book of In-door Games, Amusements, and Occupations* (Boston: Lee and Shepard, 1873), 336, 346; *Elegant Arts for Ladies* (London: Ward and Lock, 1860), 15.

51. "Ornamental Flower Pot Stands," *Godey's Lady's Book* 83 (April 1871): 371.

52. See the description of papier-mâché in Toller, *The Regency and Victorian Crafts*, 51; "Papier-Plastique, or Paper Modeling," *Graham's Illustrated Magazine* 52 (May 1858): 476; "The Danger of Modeling Wax," *Graham's Illustrated Magazine* 49 (July 1856): 80.

53. "The Ornamental Artist," *Godey's Lady's Book* 2 (1831): 149; E. S. Custard, "Pebble Work," *Godey's Lady's Book* (November 1861): 386; C. S. Jones and Henry T. Williams, *Ladies' Fancy Work: Hints and Helps to Home Taste and Recreations* (New York: Henry T. Williams, 1876), 227–48; "Work Department," *Godey's Lady's Book* 103 (August 1881): 178–79; "Work Department," *Godey's Lady's Book* 111 (December 1885): 617.

54. Lichten, *Decorative Arts*, 172.

55. *Treasures of Use and Beauty*, 407; "Decalcomanie," *Arthur's Home Magazine* 24 (August 1864): 87–88; Lichten, *Decorative Arts*, 172.

56. "The Ornamental Artist," *Godey's Lady's Book* 1 (1830): 271.

57. "Articles for Presents or Fancy Fairs," *Godey's Lady's Book* 60 (April 1860): 357; "The Ornamental Artist," *Godey's Lady's Book* 2 (1831): 308.

58. *Elegant Arts for Ladies*, 63.

59. For examples of both approaches, see Jones and Williams, *Ladies' Fancy Work*.

60. See illustrations in Toller, *Regency and Victorian Crafts*.

61. Quoted in Lichten, *Decorative Arts*, 119.

62. Smith, *The American Home Book of Indoor Games*; Jones and Williams, *Ladies' Fancy Work*; "Novelties in Straw Work," *Godey's Lady's Book* 96 (June 1878): 531; *Treasures of Use and Beauty*; *Elegant Arts for Ladies*; "Art of Painting on Glass," *Godey's Lady's Book* 54 (June 1857): 491–93; 107–12.

63. Emma Churchman Hewitt, *Queen of the Home: Her Reign from Infancy to Age, from Attic to Cellar* (Philadelphia: W. W. Houston, 1892), 255–56; Jones and Williams, *Ladies' Fancy Work*.

64. Marion Harland, "Poor and Proud," *Godey's Lady's Book* 80 (May 1870): 423; A Member, "Far and Near Club," *Godey's Lady's Book* 116 (April 1888): 381.

65. Margaret B. Harvey, "Fancy Work," *Arthur's Home Magazine* 48 (February 1880): 128–30.

66. "Ladies' Work Department," *Godey's Lady's Book* 34 (January 1847): 48; Parker, *The Subversive Stitch*, 155–56; "Embroidered Cigar-Case," *Godey's Lady's Book* 47 (August 1853): 176–77; Alcott, *Little Women*, 65–67.

67. W.M.F., "To My Watch Case — A Lady's Gift," *Godey's Lady's Book* 75 (December 1867): 514.

68. Kate Crombie, "Aunt Hetty's Room," *Godey's Lady's Book* 105 (August 1882): 155.

69. N. H. Snyder, "Women's Dainty Fingers," *Godey's Lady's Book* 130 (January 1895): 112; Cook, *The House Beautiful*, 135–36.

70. David P. Handlin, *The American Home: Architecture and Society, 1815–1915* (Boston: Little, Brown, 1979), 436–39; Constance Cary Harrison, "Woman's Handiwork," in *The House and Home*, ed. Abbot, 217–18; Jan Gordon and Jan McArthur, "Interior Decorating Advice as Popular Culture: Women's Views Concerning Wall and Window Treatments," in *Making the American Home: Middle Class Women and Domestic Material Culture, 1840–1940*, ed. Marilyn Ferris and Pat Brown (Bowling Green, Ohio: Bowling Green State University Popular Culture Press, 1988): 111–12.

71. Parker, *The Subversive Stitch*, 162–63; Macdonald, *No Idle Hands*, 46; Phillipa B., "Jack's Silhouettes," *Godey's Lady's Book* 112 (March 1886): 275; Jennie June, "What Is Going on in New York," *Godey's Lady's Book* 114 (March 1887): 196. For Civil War fairs see, Gordon and McArthur, "Interior Decorating Advice," 112; by the end of the decade they were being used to raise money for noncharitable clubs as well, Abbot, *The House and Home*, 204.

72. Stephen Nissenbaum, "Lighting the Freedom Tree," *New York Times*, December, 25, 1996, A17; Trollope, *Domestic Manners*, 281–82.

73. "Contributions to Fancy Fairs," *Godey's Lady's Book* 51 (August 1855): 167; Mac-donald, *No Idle Hands*, 110–12; Gussie, "Our Afghan," *Arthur's Lady's Home Magazine* 39 (February 1872): 100.

74. Alcott, *Little Women*, 317–29.

75. "The Fancy Fair," in *The Prose and Poetry of Europe and America*, ed George Morris Pope (New York: Leavitt and Allen, 1853), 416.

76. A. M. F. Annan, "The Fancy Fair," *Graham's Magazine* 21 (July 1842): 4–7; June, "What Is Going on in New York," 196.

77. *Treasures of Use and Beauty*, 208.

78. June, "What Is Going on in New York," 196.

79. L. A. Corry, "The Great Scamperton Fair," *Godey's Lady's Book* 113 (October 1886): 352–61.

80. Annie S. Frost, *Frost's Laws and By-laws of American Society* (New York: Dick and Fitzgerald, [ca. 1869]), 107–8; Frost, "The Daffodils at a Fancy Fair," *Godey's Lady's Book* 73 (August 1866): 145, 147, 149; Corry, "The Great Scam-perton Fair," 357–58.

81. "Wife's Lesson; or, Managing a Husband," *Graham's Magazine* 48 (March 1856): 254–57.

82. Grace Livingston Furniss, "Pogit Way," *Harper's New Monthly Magazine* 87 (June 1893): 113; Ellis A. Davidson, *Pretty Arts for the Employment of Leisure Hours: A Book for Ladies* (London: Chapman and Hall, 1879), vi, 1, 3, 23, 36, 118–19.

83. Wright, *The Complete Home*, 464; Logan, *The Home Manual*, 270–75; Cook, *The House Beautiful*, 143; Vander Weyde, " In Nature's Storehouse," 342–43.

84. Max Vander Weyde, "With Sounding Brass," *Godey's Lady's Book* 112 (February 1885): 176–81; Almon C. Varney, *Our Homes and Their Adornments; or, How to Build, Finish, Furnish, and Adorn a Home* (Chicago: People's Publishing, 1885), 230; [Harriet Beecher Stowe] "The Handy Man," *Arthur's Home Maga-zine* 34 (October 1869): 231; Catharine E. Beecher, *Miss Beecher's Housekeeper and Healthkeeper* (New York: Harper and Brothers, 1873), 289; "Hints on Home Adornment," *Godey's Lady's Book* 78 (February 1879): 184–85; Ruutz-Rees, *Home Occupations*, 79.

85. Grier, *Culture and Comfort*, 263–79; Mertie, "Home Made Furniture," *Godey's Lady's Book* 81 (September 1870): 273.

86. "Graining Wood," *Arthur's Home Magazine* 33 (February 1869): 115; Wright, *The Complete Home*, 465; Bissell Brooke, "Spring Decorating Ideas in the Gay Nineties," *Hobbies* 24 (May 1958): 24; Vander Weyde, "In Nature's Storehouse," 343; for do-it-yourself wallpapering for women, see Varney, *Our Homes and Their Adornments*, 226.

87. Constance Cary Harrison, *Woman's Handiwork in Modern Homes* (New York: Charles Scribner's Sons, 1881), 134.

88. Hewitt, *Queen of the Home*, 256–58; A Lady, "Evening Employment for Boys," *Arthur's Home Magazine* 33 (February 1869): 114; Robert Griffith, *Boys' Useful Pastimes* (New York: A. L. Burt, 1885), 6; Beecher, *A Treatise on Domestic Econo-my*, 254; Louisa May Alcott, *Little Men* (Racine, Wisc.: Golden Press, 1965), 43.

89.   "Workshop," *Godey's Lady's Book* 58 (March 1859): 285; "Boys! Boys!" *Arthur's Home Magazine* 40 (1872): n.p. [advertising section].

90.   John A. Bower, *How to Make Common Things for Boys* (London: Society for Promoting Christian Knowledge, 1893), 8.

91.   [Stowe,] "The Handy Man," 230; "House Repairs," *Leisure Hour* 25 (1876): 491, 494.

92.   F. M. L. Thompson, *The Rise of Respectable Society: A Social History of Victorian Britain, 1830–1900* (Cambridge, Mass.: Harvard University Press, 1988), 302; Dudden, *Serving Women*, 158; Claudia L. Bushman, *A Good Poor Man's Wife* (Hanover, N.H.: University Press of New England, 1981): 112–13, 116–17.

93.   Joan M. Seidl, "Consumers' Choices: A Study of Household Furnishing, 1880–1920," *Minnesota History* 48 (spring 1983): 183–97; M.E.G., "Frugal Arts Letters," *Godey's Lady's Book* 102 (March 1881): 256–57.

94.   Catharine E. Beecher and Harriet Beecher Stowe, *The American Woman's Home* (New York: J. B. Ford, 1869), 32; see also 89, 91; Nina H. Clark and C. A. Hazelton, "Holiday Knickknacks," *Godey's Lady's Book* 116 (January 1888): 79; "Hints on Home Adornment," *Godey's Lady' Book* 100 (February 1880): 183; Wright, *The Complete Home*, 9, 48.

95.   "A New Fancy Table," *Godey's Lady's Book* 42 (February 1851): 133; Holmes quoted in Harry J. Hobbs, *Working with Tools* (New York: Leisure League of America, 1935), 11.

96.   Cook, *The House Beautiful*, 124, 199.

97.   *Treasures of Use and Beauty*, 363–64.

98.   "A Useful and Instructive Christmas Present," *Arthur's Home Magazine Advertiser* 46 (1878): 2.

99.   Oliver Impey and Arthur MacGregor, eds., *The Origins of Museums: The Cabinet of Curiosities in Sixteenth and Seventeenth Century Europe* (Oxford: Clarendon Press, 1985), 2; Percival Marshall, *Mechanics in Miniature* (London: Percival Marshal, 1947), 4; L. F. Anderson, *History of Manual and Industrial School Education* (New York: D. Appleton, 1926), 136; "Hobbies," *Arthur's Home Magazine* 8 (September 1856), 167.

100. Thomas Seaton, *A Manual of Fret Cutting and Wood Carving* (London: George Routledge and Sons, 1875), 26–27; "Lester Saw," *Arthur's Home Magazine Advertiser* 46 (1878): 2; *Bowman's and Russell's Famous Scroll Saw Designs* (New York: Millers Falls Co., 1885), 28; Edward H. Moody, *Catalogue and Price List of Scroll Saws and Scroll Saw Material* (Hartford, Conn.: Star Job Printing, 1884), 5.

101. Henry T. Williams, *Fret Sawing for Pleasure and Profit* (New York: Henry T. Williams, 1877), 107; "Fleetwood Scroll Saw," *Arthur's Home Magazine* 17 (October 1874): n.p. [advertisements]; "Fleetwood Scroll Saw," *Godey's Lady's Magazine* 97 (1875), n.p. [advertisements].

102. *Bowman's and Russell's Famous Scroll Saw*, 28; Moody, *Catalogue and Price List*, 5; Charles Reichman, "The Tools that Fueled the Fretwork Frenzy," *Chronicle of the Early American Industries Association* 41 (March 1988): 1.

103. Julius Wilcox, "Fret Sawing and Wood Carving," *Harper's New Monthly Magazine* 54 (March 1878): 533.

104. Williams, *Fret Sawing*; Seaton, *A Manual of Fret Cutting*, 13; Wilcox, "Fret Sawing and Wood Carving," 533–35; Yates and Yates, *Early American Crafts*, 132; Lichten, *Decorative Arts*, 176.

105. Yates and Yates, *Early American Crafts*, 128.

106. Wilcox, "Fret Sawing and Wood Carving," 533; Seaton, *A Manual of Fret Cutting*; "Fleetwood Scroll Saw," *Godey's Lady's Magazine* 97 (1875), n.p. [advertisements].

107. *Bowman's and Russell's Famous Scroll Saw*, 4.

108. Williams, *Fret Sawing*, 107.

109. Williams, *Fret Sawing*, 55, 106–7.

7 Expanding the Boundaries of Crafts

1. Agnes Repplier, "Our Accomplished Great-Grandmothers," *A Happy Half-Century and Other Essays* (New York: Houghton Mifflin, 1908), 218–19; Addie E. Heron, *Fancy Work for Pleasure and Profit* (Chicago: Thompson and Thomas, 1894, 1905), 6.

2. Frank L. Hahn, *Collector's Guide to Burnt Wood Antiques* (Lima, Ohio: Golden Era, 1994); Carole Smyth and Richard Smyth, *The Burning Passion: Antique and Collectible Pyrography–Burnt Wood* (n.p.: Carole and Richard Smyth, 1995).

3. M. Cutler, "The Arts and Crafts Movement," *Harper's Bazaar* 40 (February 1906): 162–66; Cheryl Robertson, "House and Home in the Arts and Crafts Era: Reforms for Simpler Living," in *The Art That Is Life: The Arts and Crafts Movement in America*, ed. Wendy Kaplan (New York: Little, Brown, Boston Museum of Fine Arts, 1987), 350.

4. Eileen Boris, *Art and Labor: Ruskin, Morris, and the Craftsman Ideal in America* (Philadelphia: Temple University Press, 1986), 13–31; Anthea Callen, *Angel in the Studio: Women in the Arts and Crafts Movement* (London: Astragal Books, 1979), 3–4; [Gustav Stickley], "Small Farming and Profitable Handicrafts," *Craftsman* 14 (April 1908): 53; Katherine Louise Smith, "Revival of Fireside Industries," *New England Magazine* 29 (December 1903): 442–49; F. W. Coburn, "Handicraft in Massachusetts," *Nation* 78 (June 23, 1904): 489; F. W. Coburn, "The Revolt from the Machine," *National Magazine* 18 (April 1903): 58–63; Caroline Hunt, "More Pleasure for the Producer of Household Stuff," *Chautauquan* 37 (May 1903): 178; F. T. Carlton, "The Significance of the Arts and Crafts Movement," *Popular Science Monthly* 65 (September 1904): 415.

5. Ernest A. Batchelder, "Arts and Crafts Movement in America: Work or Play?" *Craftsman* 16 (August 1909): 547; Mary K. Simkhovitch, "Handcrafts in the City," *Craftsman* 10 (1904): 364.

6. "The Workroom That Is Taking the Place of Library, Study or Den," *Craftsman* 9 (December 1905): 378–79; "The Value of Making Things at Home," *Craftsman* 20 (May 1911): 226; Rollin Lynde Hartt, "Amateur Hand-Crafts That Pay," *World's Work* 14 (September 1907): 9368, 9370.

7. Hartt, "Amateur Hand-Crafts," 9369; Madge C. Jenison, "Defense of the Arts and Crafts Movement," *Independent* 60 (February 8, 1906): 325.

8. Mable Tuke Priestman, *The Handicrafts in the Home* (Chicago: A. C. McClurg, 1910), 3.

9. A. Sterling, "Plea for American Needlecraft," *Atlantic Monthly* 86 (November 1900): 558; "Pin Money Made with the Needle," *Ladies' Home Journal* 21 (January 1904): 22; May C. Moore, *100 New Money Making Plans for Untrained Women* (Atlanta: National Women's Exchange Publishing, 1904), 25, 53–54, 66; Priestman, *The Handicrafts at Home*.

10. H. P. Macomber, "The Craftsman Today: His Relation to the Community," *American Magazine of Art* 13 (October 1922): 331.

11. Eileen Boris, *Art and Labor: Ruskin, Morris, and the Craftsman Ideal in America* (Philadelphia: Temple University Press, 1986), 62–80, 101–2; Anthea Callen, *Women Artists of the Arts and Crafts Movement* (New York, Pantheon Books, 1979), 78–81. For examples of women operating small crafts businesses, see Robertson, "House and Home in the Arts and Crafts Era," 338; Karen J. Blair, *The Torchbearers: Women and Their Amateur Arts Associations in America, 1890–1930* (Bloomington: Indiana University Press, 1994): 84–85.

12. Moore, *100 New Money Making Plans*, 63–66; Charles Barnard "The Revival of Skilled Hand Work," *World's Work* 4 (July 1902): 2340; Lydia H. Littlefield, "The Quilting Bee Lives Again, First as a Socializing Influence, Then as a Paying Industry, *Modern Priscilla* 31 (November 1917): 9; E. O. Seabury, "The Family Venture," *Modern Priscilla* 23 (June 1909): 6; social worker quoted in *New York Times*, November 20, 1910, 10.

13. Helen R. Albee, "What Women in Your Town Can Do: How to Organize and Conduct a Home Industry," *Ladies' Home Journal* 33 (June 1916): 30.

14. *New York Times*, September 3, 1905, 9.

15. Barnard, "The Revival of Skilled Handwork," 2339–40.

16. Priestman, *The Handicrafts at Home*, 2; Louis J. Haas, "A New Vocation — Diversional Occupation," *Industrial Arts Magazine* 5 (December 1916): 516–21; Valentine C. Kirby, "Craftsmanship as a Preventive of Crime," *Craftsman* 8 (April-September 1905): 171, 178.

17. L. F. Anderson, *History of Manual and Industrial School Education* (New York: D. Appleton, 1926), 137, 144–45.

18. Quoted in Paul Hopkins Rule, "Industrial Arts in Education and Leisure" (master's thesis, University of Washington, 1940), 20.

19. Anderson, *History of Manual and Industrial School Education*, 155–87; Rule, "Industrial Arts in Education," 21–22.

20. Abby L. Marlatt, "Crafts in Secondary Schools," *Chautauquan* 38 (1903), 585; Eva V. Carlin, "A Salvage Bureau," *Overland Monthly and Out West Magazine* 36 (September 1900): 252.

21. K. E. Dopp, "Arts and Crafts in American Education," *Chautauquan* 38 (September 1903): 487–91; Dopp, "Forms and Limitations of Handwork for Girls in the High School," *National Education Association: Proceedings and Addresses* (n.p.: National Education Association, 1905), 580–90; Ruby M. Hodge, "Rela-

tion of Primitive Handicraft to Present-Day Educational Problems," *Journal of Proceedings and Addresses* (Winona, Minn.: National Education Association, 1907): 816.

22. Eva C. Carlin, "California's First Vacation School," *Overland Monthly and Out West Magazine* 35 (May 1900): 432.

23. Ella Bond Johnston, "The Democratic Art Movement," *Chautauquan* 36 (March 1903): 382; Anderson, *History of Manual and Industrial School Education*, 188–89; Boris, *Art and Labor*, 82–98; Rule, *Industrial Arts in Education*, 20–23; Johnston, "The Democratic Art Movement," 382; Edgar Morton, "The Home Workshop," *American Homes and Gardens*, 9 (October 1912): 18; Mary Corbin Sies, "American Country House Architecture in Context: The Suburban Ideal of Living in the East and Midwest" (Ph.D. diss., University of Michigan, 1987), 375, 377.

24. Ira S. Griffith, "Cabinet Making as a Handicraft," *American Homes and Gardens* 7 (September 1910): 346.

25. Quoted in Wendy Kaplan, "Spreading the Crafts: The Role of the Schools," in *The Art That Is Life*, 301.

26. Ira S. Griffith, "Three Things to Make in Your Own Workshop," *Suburban Life* 13 (November 1911): 269; Griffith, "Cabinet Making," 345–46.

27. Daniel C. Beard, *What To Do and How to Do It: The American Boy's Handy Book* (New York: Charles Scribner's Sons, 1905); Henry Wysham Lanier, "To Do Or How To Do," *The Bookman* 49 (July 1919): 587–88.

28. Lanier, "To Do," 588; A. Neely Hall, *Carpentry and Mechanics for Boys* (Boston: Lothrop, 1918), 235–55; A Neely Hall, *Handicrafts for Handy Boys* (Boston: Lothrop, 1911), 111, vi.

29. Hall, *Handicrafts for Handy Boys*, 135–59; A. Neely Hall, *Handy Boy* (Boston: Lothrop, 1913), 32–33, quotation on p. v; Hall, *Carpentry and Mechanics*, 1–13, 63–95.

30. Cecil Henry Bullivant, *Every Boy's Book of Hobbies* (New York: Dodge Publishing, 1912), 13; Hall, *Handicrafts for Handy Boys*, 103–4, 135–36.

31. Jane Ferrari, "Education in the Arts and Crafts," in *California Design, 1910*, ed. Timothy J. Anderson, Eudorah M. Moore, Robert W. White (Santa Barbara, Calif.: Peregrine Smith, 1980), 60; A. Neely Hall and Dorothy Perkins, *Handicrafts for Handy Girls* (Boston: Lothrop, 1916), vi, 1, 222–25.

32. Michael S. Kimmel, "The Contemporary 'Crisis' of Masculinity in Historical Perspective," in *The Making of Masculinities: The New Men's Studies*, ed. Harry Brod (Boston: Allen and Unwin, 1987), 138; Angel Kwolek-Folland, "Gender, Self, and Work in the Life Insurance Industry, 1880–1930," in *Work Engendered: Toward a New History of American Labor*, ed. Ava Baron (Ithaca, N.Y.: Cornell University Press, 1990), 176–77; Mark C. Carnes, "Middle-Class Men and the Solace of Fraternal Ritual," in *Meanings for Manhood: Constructions of Masculinity in Victorian America*, ed. Mark C. Carnes and Clyde Griffen (Chicago: University of Chicago Press, 1990), 38–39, 46–48; Mary Ann Clawson, *Constructing Brotherhood: Class, Gender, and Fraternalism* (Princeton: Princeton University Press, 1989), 174; Jeffery P. Hantover, "The Boy Scouts and the Vali-

dation of Masculinity," in *The American Man*, ed. Elizabeth H. Pleck and Joseph H. Pleck (Englewood Cliffs, N.J.: Prentice-Hall, 1980), 285–301.

33. Margaret Marsh, "Suburban Men and Masculine Domesticity, 1870–1915," *American Quarterly* 40 (1988): 166.

34. Octave Thanet, "The Blazing Hen-Coop," *Harper's New Monthly Magazine* 96 (January 1898): 210–11.

35. Lummis quoted in Eileen Boris, "Dreams of Brotherhood and Beauty: The Social Ideas of the Arts and Crafts Movement," in *The Art that Is Life*, 211; Michael Kimmel, *Manhood in America: A Cultural History* (New York: Free Press, 1996), 27–29; Clawson, *Constructing Brotherhood*, 153–54, 164.

36. Robertson, "House and Home in the Arts and Crafts Era," 341 n. 27.

37. Reproduced in Kaplan, "Spreading the Crafts," 299.

38. Robertson, "House and Home in the Arts and Crafts Era," 346; Gwendolyn Wright, *Building the Dream: A Social History of Housing in America* (New York: Pantheon, 1981), 131; Anthony D. King, *The Bungalow: The Production of a Global Culture"* (London: Routledge and Kegan Paul, 1984), 136; Jim Bettinger, "The Bungalow," *San Jose Mercury News, West* (July 10, 1994): 3; Robert Edwards, "The Art of Work," in *The Art That Is Life*, 234.

39. Olivier Zunz, *The Changing Face of Inequality: Urbanization, Industrial Development, and Immigrants in Detroit, 1880–1920* (Chicago: University of Chicago Press, 1982), 170–71; Richard Harris, "American Suburbs: A Sketch of a New Interpretation," *Journal of Urban History* 15 (November 1988): 98–103; Richard Harris, "Self-Building in the Urban Housing Market," *Economic Geography* 67 (1991): 1–21; John Bodnar, Roger Simon, and Michael P. Weber, *Lives of Their Own: Blacks, Italians, and Poles in Pittsburgh, 1900–1960* (Urbana: University of Illinois Press, 1982), 155; Richard Harris, "Working-Class Home Ownership in the American Metropolis," *Journal of Urban History* 17 (1990): 50–51; Richard Harris and Chris Hamnett, "The Myth of the Promised Land: The Social Diffusion of Home Ownership in Britain and North America," *Annals of the Association of American Geographers* 77 (1987), 173–90; Kenneth T. Jackson, *Crabgrass Frontier: The Suburbanization of the United States* (New York: Oxford University Press, 1985), 126.

40. A. L. Hall, "My Workshop at Home," *Suburban Life* 7 (November 1908): 256; George Frederick, "Play Confessions of a Busy Man," *Craftsman* 13 (February 1908): 565; Ira S. Griffith, "Recreation with Tools," *Suburban Life* 10 (June 1910): 22.

41. Edgar Morton, "The Home Workshop," *American Homes and Gardens* 9 (October 1912): 342.

42. Robertson, "House and Home in the Arts and Crafts Era," 342; Grier, "Culture and Comfort," 287–300; Katherine C. Grier, "The Decline of the Memory Palace: The Parlor after 1890," in *American Home Life, 1880–1930: A Social History of Spaces and Services*, ed. Jessica H. Foy and Thomas J. Schlereth (Knoxville: University of Tennessee Press, 1992), 63.

43. Hall, "My Workshop at Home," 256; Griffith, "Cabinet Making," 345.

44. Thomas J. Schlereth, "Conduits and Conduct: Home Utilities in Victorian America, 1876–1915," in *American Home Life*, 229; Grier, "Culture and Comfort," 28; Paul Ellsworth, "A Portable Workshop," *Suburban Life* 16 (March 1913): 133; Floyd H. Alllport, "This Coming Era of Leisure," in *These United States: Contemporary Essays for College Students*, ed. Louis Jones, William Huse Jr., Harvey Eagleson (New York: Richard R. Smith, 1933), 201–2; Hall, *Handicrafts for Handy Boys*, 3.

45. Frederick, "Play Confessions of a Busy Man," 563–66; Robert McCracken Peck, "The Cult of the Rustic in Nineteenth-Century America" (master's thesis, University of Delaware, 1976), 20–21; Jean-Christophe Agnew, "A House of Fiction: Domestic Interiors and the Commodity Aesthetic," in *Consuming Visions: Accumulation of Display Goods in America, 1880–1920*, ed. Simon J. Bronner (New York: W. W. Norton, 1989), 138–40; Joseph Corn, "Popular Mechanics, Mechanical Literacy, and American Culture, 1900–1950," typescript, 1989, 13–17.

46. Griffith, "Three Things to Make," 269.

47. Ira S. Griffith, "How to Make a Mission Seat," *Suburban Life* 16 (February 1913): 16; D. H. Culyer, "Making a Magazine Stand," *Circle* 2 (July 1907): 48; for knocked-down furniture advertisement see, "Whittelsey System Porch Swing," [advertisement] *Circle*, 2 (July 1907): 49; Marion Pitcher, "How I Improved Some Old Furniture," *House Beautiful* 42 (September 1917): 253.

48. Helen Campbell, *The American Girl's Home Book of Work and Play* (New York: G. P. Putnam's Sons, 1912), 339, 343; M. E. Griswold, "Home Made Summer Furniture," *American Homes and Gardens* 8 (August 1911): 290–92.

49. Hewitt, *Queen of the Home*, 81–82; "Making Box Furniture: Its Practical and Ethical Value," *Craftsman* 21 (November 1911): 218.

50. *New York Times*, November 29, 1910, 10; the quotation is from Louise Brigham, introduction to *Box Furniture: How to Make a Hundred Useful Articles for the Home*, (New York: Century, 1909), n.p; "Making Box Furniture," 219.

51. Louise Brigham, "Rugs and Baskets Which Cost Nothing," *Ladies' Home Journal* 27 (August 1910): 31; "Making Box Furniture," 219; *New York Times*, November 29, 1910, 10; Brigham, *Box Furniture*.

52. Louise Brigham, "How Boys Make Furniture from Boxes," *St. Nicholas* 42 (January 1915): 241–44; "Making Box Furniture," 220; Hall, *Handicrafts for Handy Boys*, 160–69; A. Neely Hall, *Carpentry and Mechanics for Boys* (Boston: Lothrop, 1918), 96–109; Brigham, *Box Furniture*; Brigham, "Rugs and Baskets," 70.

53. Edwin Makepeace, "A Home-Made House and Furniture," *Country Life* 19 (November 15, 1910): 123.

54. Pitcher, "How I Improved Some Old Furniture," 253–54; "Women Do Not Paint," [advertisement] *Suburban Life* 12 (April 1911): 259.

55. Garrett Winslow, "Practical Decoration for the Home Interior," *Suburban Life* 15 (October 1912): 187; Agnes Athol, "What a Woman Can Do with a Paint Brush," *Suburban Life* 15 (November 1912): 268.

56. U.S. Bureau of the Census, *Historical Statistics of the United States, Colonial Times to 1970, Bicentennial Edition* (Washington, D.C.: Government Printing

Office, 1975), 140; Phyllis Palmer, *Domesticity and Dirt: Housewives and Domestic Servants in the United States, 1920–1945* (Philadelphia: Temple University Press, 1989), 1–10; Agnew, "A House of Fiction," 141.

57. "The World of Art: Guild of the Needle and Bobbin Crafts," *New York Times Magazine* (July 11, 1920): 12.

58. "How Can I Earn a Little Money," *Needlecraft Magazine* 12 (July 1921): 3; W. Livingston Larned, "Melody of the Needles," *Needlecraft Magazine* 14 (January 1923): 3; *Sealing Wax Craft* (Framingham, Mass.: Dennison Manufacturing Company, 1926), 38; *Suggestions for Porch-time Decorating* (Chicago: Thayer and Chandler, summer, 1926), 2; Fannie Hurst, *Back Street* (New York: Cosmopolitan Book, 1930), 185.

59. Arthur Wakeling, *Fix It Yourself* (New York: Popular Science Publishing, 1929), 149; *Make It Yourself*, (n.p.: Popular Mechanics Press, 1927), 158

60. *Modern Priscilla Home Furnishing Book* (Boston: Priscilla Publishing, 1925), 215, 312–13; Helen Koues, *How to Be Your Own Decorator* (New York: Good Housekeeping, 1926), 199, 219; Edna Selena Cave, *Craft Work* (New York: Century, 1929): 3–32.

61. *Sealing Wax Craft*, 4; *Arcor Creative Handicraft Catalog* (New York: American Reedcraft, 1923), 30.

62. *Arcor Creative Handicraft Catalog*, 1, 47.

63. Alice Van Leer Carrick, *A Mother Goose for Antique Collectors* (New York: Payson and Clarke, 1927), 45.

64. *Make It Yourself*, 88–92; *Modern Priscilla Home Furnishing Book*, 313; Louis M. Roehl, *Household Carpentry* (New York: Macmillan, 1927); Joseph Hergesheimer, "The Art of Hoax," *Saturday Evening Post* 199 (November 1926): 136.

65. *Historical Statistics*, 646; Jackson, *Crabgrass Frontier*, 116–37, 157–71; Harris, "Working-Class Home Ownership," 54, 58; Samuel Crowther, "Henry Ford: Why I Favor Five Days' Work with Six Days' Pay," *World's Work* 52 (October 1926): 615; Rose C. Feld, "Now That They Have It," *Century* 108 (1924): 753, 756.

66. *Make It Yourself*; Walter J. Coppock, *Make Your Home Your Hobby* (Yellow Springs, Ohio: Antioch Press, 1945); "Rich and Poor Find Joy in Work with Hands," *Popular Mechanics* 42 (August 1924): 221–22.

67. W. A. Bloedorn, "Have You a Hobby?" *Hygeia* 4 (December 1926): 681; William Frederick Harris, "The Preacher's Hobby: Cabinet Work," *Homiletic Review* 96 (July 1928): 14; Henry H. Saylor, *Tinkering with Tools* (New York: Grosset and Dunlap, 1924): 3–11; Wakeling, *Fix It Yourself*, 5; Arthur T. Wakeling, "The Home Workshop," *Popular Science Monthly* 123 (December 1930): 1–2.

68. J. Tate, "Tools for the Home Mechanic," *Make It Yourself* (Chicago: Popular Mechanics Press, 1927), 2.

69. George M. Morris, "Relation of Instruction in Manual Arts to the Seven Cardinal Principles of Education," *Industrial Education Magazine* 29 (June 1928): 439.

70. Blanche Halbert, "Every Boy Needs Tools," *Parents' Magazine* 4 (September 1929): 26.

71. Mabel Hutchings Bellows, "Woodwork: Its Value and Purpose," *Normal Instructor and Primary Plans* 39 (December 1929): 18; A. King, "Hobbies for Young and Old," *Industrial Arts Magazine* 14 (February 1925): 56; George Peak, "Does Your Child Collect? Make the Habit of Value to Him," *Delineator* 94 (February 1919): 40; S. Mythaler, "Correlation between Academic Work and Woodwork," *Industrial Education Magazine* 31 (December 1929): 214; A. Neely Hall, *The Big Book of Boys' Hobbies* (Boston: Lothrop, 1929), v, vi.

8 Home Crafts in Hard Times

1. U.S. Bureau of the Census, *Historical Statistics of the United States, Colonial Times to 1970, Bicentennial Edition* (Washington, D.C.: Government Printing Office, 1975), 170; Alfarata Hilton, "The Hobby School," *Publisher's Weekly* 126 (November 1934): 1646; H. J. Hobbs, "51 Hours a Week," *Better Homes and Gardens* 12 (January 1934): 24; Doris Webster, *How to Spend Your Husband's Leisure* (New York: Maple Press, 1934), 7–8; Lester C. Smith, "Shopwork as Stimulating Recreation: A Healthful Hobby," *Hygeia* 11 (May 1933): 405; Arthur W. Wilson, "Home Hobbyists Offer a Market," *Printers' Ink* 163 (May 4, 1933): 69.

2. Anne D. Williams, "Leisure in the Great Depression: The Many Pieces of the Jigsaw Puzzle Story," *Ephemera Journal* 6 (1993), 99–115; George H. Copeland, "The Country Is Off on a Jig-Saw Jag," *New York Times Magazine* (February 12, 1933): 8; Williams, "Leisure in the Great Depression"; Clarence R. Buck, "Self Supporting Craft Projects," *Recreation* 27 (August 1933): 224; Mary Beimfohr, "Puzzling the Public," *Profitable Hobbies* 6 (May 1950): 42.

3. J. Y. Shambach, "Prepare for Retirement," *Recreation* 32 (September 1938): 328; John Hanley, "Collecting By-Paths," *Hobbies* 44 (June 1939): 118–19.

4. David C. Minter, *Modern Home Crafts* (New York: J. H. Hopkins and Sons, 1936): 253.

5. Stanley F. Morse, "Develop Home-work Industries," *Manufacturer's Record* 100 (September 1931): 27; Warren S. Thompson, "The Case for the Machine," *American Mercury* 25 (March 1932): 298; Allen H. Eaton, "Handicraft Work and the Worker," *Industrial Education Magazine* 40 (May 1938): 147.

6. Marjorie Barstow Greenbie, "Absorbing Art of Making Things," *The Arts of Leisure* (New York: McGraw Hill, 1935), 231–34.

7. Elizabeth McCausland, "Our Growing American Handicrafts," *Independent Woman* 18 (November 1939): 353; Greenbie, "Absorbing Art of Making Things," 233; *New York Times*, November 23, 1958, sect. 10, p. 14; Berta Crone, "Occupations, Today and Tomorrow," *New Outlook* 163 (March 1934): 4; G. A. McGarvey, "Home-made and Hand-made: Fireside Occupations in a Machine Age," *School Life* 19 (February 1934): 120.

8. Eve Chappell, "Imponderables and Money Returns form Handicrafts," *Journal of Adult Education* 11 (January 1939): 36–39; Eaton, "Handicraft Work and the Worker," 142; *New York Times*, August 2, 1953, sect. 2, p. 13; *New York Times*,

March 13, 1938, sect. 8, p. 13; Robert Stanley Russell, "The Southern Highland Handicraft Guild" (Ph.D. diss., Columbia University Teachers College, 1976).

9. Florence Seville Berryman, "Southern Mountain Handicrafts Touring the Unit-ed States," *Daughters of the American Revolution Magazine* 68 (1934): 91; Jane Stewart Becker, "Selling Tradition: The Domestication of Southern Appalachi-an Culture in 1930s America" (Ph.D. diss., Boston University, 1993); "New York State to Teach Homecrafts," *Newsweek* 2 (November 4, 1933): 24; Katharine Lee Grable, "A Rural Home Craft Movement in New York State," *Practical Home Economics* 12 (August 1934): 223–24.

10. "Sink or Swim," *Home Craftsman* 2 (May–June, 1933): 49; "Making the Jigsaw Pay You Profits," *Popular Mechanics* 59 (February 1933): 332–33; Conrad Hoover, "Spare Time Work," *American Builder and Building Age* 56 (January 1934): 34; "You Asked for It!" *Recreation* 32 (January 1939): 578; "Hobbies for Hire," *Nation's Business* 29 (December 1941): 85; Beula M. Wadsworth, "Cre-ation in Crafts Becomes an Elixir of Life," *School Arts* 40 (March 1941): 229–30; *Amateur Craftsman's Cyclopedia*, (New York: Popular Science Publishing, 1937), 27, 129, 5, 124.

11. "A Craft and Hobby Exhibit in San Diego," *Recreation* 35 (October 1941): 424; Ruby M. Palmer, "Promoting Art Hobbies," *Recreation* 26 (April 1932): 27–28; Margaret E. Mulac, "Hobby Craft Program for Cleveland," *Recreation* 33 (May 1939): 68; Ellick Maslan, "Recreation Through *Handicraft*," 31 (September 1936): 304; "Handcraft for the Women and Girls of Detroit," *Playground and Recreation* 22 (March 1929): 689; Chester Geppert Marsh, "Amateur Arts in a Machine Age," *Recreation* 25 (May 1931): 67–68; Marston Martel McCluggage, "Motivating Forces in the Development of Collectivized Forms of Leisure Time Activity (Ph.D. diss., University of Kansas 1941): 81; Eugene Lies, *New Leisure Challenges in the Schools* (Washington, D.C.: McGrath Publishing and Nation-al Recreation and Park Association, 1933), 228.

12. Edward Daniel Covington, "Three Saturdays; A Radio Playlet," *Industrial Edu-cation Magazine* 40 (November 1938): 255; Penelope Baldwin, "A Boy's Own Workshop," *Parents' Magazine* 7 (March 1932): 28; *Home Craftsman* 2 (Janu-ary–February 1933): back cover; Greenbie, "Absorbing Art," 237–38.

13. A. Dillon-Clarke, "Handicrafts in Adolescence," *New Era* 18 (December 1937): 317; Arthur Wakeling, *Home Workshop Manual* (New York: Popular Science Publishing, 1930), 1–2; Evanda Kraus Perry, *Crafts for Fun* (New York: William Morrow, 1940), 7.

14. Edward L. Thorndike, "The Right Use of Leisure," *Journal of Adult Education* 2 (1930): 31–32; Ethel Bowers, "A Home for Hobbies," *Recreation* 26 (July 1932): 179, 200; Boris Blai, "In Your Hands," *American Magazine* 129 (January 1940): 52.

15. Arthur L. Beeley, *Boys and Girls in Salt Lake City* (Salt Lake City: University of Utah, Publications of the Department of Sociology, 1935), 16–17; Bowers, "A Home for Hobbies," 179; Smith, "Shopwork as a Stimulating Recreation," 404; Palmer, "Promoting Art Hobbies," 30.

16. Hilton, "The Hobby School," 1646; Beeley, *Boys and Girls in Salt Lake City*, 17.

17. Harry J. Hobbs, "For Fathers Only," *Parents' Magazine* 32 (February 1935): 32.

18. Harry J. Hobbs, *Working with Tools* (New York: Leisure League of America, 1935): 75; "Building Tomorrow's Customers," *Printers' Ink* 153 (November 20, 1930): 10; J. J. Metz, "A Worth-while Youth Movement," *Industrial Arts and Vocational Education*," 25 (October 1936): 308; M. A. Powell, "A Survey of the National Home Workshop Guild" (master's thesis, Colorado State College of Education, Greeley, 1935), 21.

19. Joseph Corn, "Popular Mechanics, Mechanical Literacy, and American Culture, 1900–1950," typescript, 1989, 22.

20. *Amateur Craftsman's Cyclopedia*, 102–3, 114–15, 118–19.

21. Cartoon reproduced in E. J. Tangerman, *Whittling and Woodcarving* (New York: McGraw-Hill, 1936), 112; Robert J. Benson, "Model Yacht Building and Racing," *Industrial Arts and Vocational Education*," 22 (April 1933): 166–67; H. J. Hobbs, "For Fathers Only," 32; *New York Times*, February 24, 1936, 35.

22. Edgar Westbury, *The History of Model Power Boats* (London: Percival Marshall, 1950), 3–5; Anderson G. Orb, "Juvenile Aircraft Industry," *Scientific American* 143 (October 1930): 294–95.

23. "The Business of Building Model Planes," *Aero Digest* 16 (March 1930): 144; Orb, "Juvenile Aircraft Industry," 295.

24. Orb, "Juvenile Aircraft Industry," 294; "Models," *Fortune* 13 (June 1936): 30; "Rich and Poor Find Joy in Work with Hands," *Popular Mechanics* 42 (August 1924): 221; Peter G. F. Chinn, *Model Four Stroke Engines* (n.p.: P. G. F. Chinn, 1986), 12; John Allen Murphy, "Hobbies That Grew Into a Business," *American Business* 6 (July 1936): 10–12; John Allen Murphy, "Sales Boom in Hobby Goods," *American Business* 6 (May 1936): 16; *New York Times*, September 26, 1937, sect. 2, p. 1; *New York Times*, November 1, 1937, 23; *New York Times*, June 4, 1939, 51; *New York Times*, August 7, 1939, 17; *New York Times*, January 22, 1939, sect. 7, p. 23; Orb, "Juvenile Aircraft Industry," 295.

25. Paul Edward Garber, *Building and Flying Model Aircraft* (New York: Ronald Press, 1928), 3; Richard S. Robbins, *Hobby Shop for Fun or Fortune?* (n.p.: Model Industry Association, 1949), 23.

26. Verne H. Barnes, "The Miniature Airplane Club," *Industrial Education Magazine* 31 (February 1930): 294; *New York Times*, June 4, 1939, 51; *New York Times*, August 7, 1939, 17; Harold W. Kulick, "Everybody Loves a Model," *American Magazine* 130 (October 1940): 117–24; *The Boy Mechanic* (Chicago: Popular Mechanics Press, 1940), 98–99, 127–30; *Giant Home Workshop Manual* (New York: Popular Science Publishing, 1941): 308–9, 312–15.

27. Gustav Reder, *Clockwork, Steam, and Electric: A History of Model Railways* (London: Ian Allen, 1972), 83.

28. Hamilton Ellis, *Model Railways* (London: George Allen and Unwin, 1962), 13–17, 55, 59; Reder, *Clockwork, Steam, and Electric*, 6, 9–12, 17, 23, 162–67; Allen Levy, *A Century of Model Trains* (New York: Crescent Books, 1974), 7, 16, 51, 57.

29. W. F. McAllister, "It's Model Railroading, Hobby with a National Organization," *Standardization* 20 (July 1949): 169–70; Derham Groves, "Walt Disney's Backyard," *Exedra* 5 (1994): 29–38; "Miniature Trains," *Fortune* 6 (December 1932): 42, 110.

30. L. H. Robbins, "Casey Jones in Miniature," *New York Times Magazine* (October 15, 1939): 9; *New York Times*, January 24, 1937, 10; "Ten Million Dollars Worth of Fun on Model Rails," *Business Week* (January 13, 1951): 24; "Railroading for Men Only," *Popular Mechanics* 68 (December 1937): 882–84.

31. Reder, *Clockwork, Steam, and Electric*, 101, 103; "Railroading for Men Only," 884; "Models," *Fortune*, 30; Murphy, "Sales Boom in Hobby Goods," 16.

32. R. A. Hinderman, "Leisure Time Industrial Arts Activities," *Industrial Education Magazine* 36 (1934): 36–38; Ray Stombaugh, *A Survey of the Movements Culminating in Industrial Arts Education in Secondary Schools* (New York: Teacher College, Columbia University, 1936), 5–6; Paul Hopkins Rule, "Industrial Arts in Education and Leisure" (master's thesis, University of Washington, 1940), 100, 106.

33. John C. Kieffer, "Planning the Handicraft Program," *Recreation* 27 (June 1933): 141.

34. R. C. Cramlet and W. L. Hunter, "Home Workshop Organization," *Industrial Arts and Vocational Education* 25 (September 1936): 259.

35. Sylvan Austin Yager, "Creating an Interest in the Home Workshop," *Industrial Education Magazine* 40 (January 1938): 11–12; A. A. Cooper, "Stimulating Interest in the Home Workshop," *Industrial Arts and Vocational Education* 25 (November 1936): 329–30; Cramlet and Hunter, "Home Workshop Organization"; R. C. Cramlet, "The Home Workshop," *Industrial Arts and Vocational Education* 24 (February 1935): supplement 14; the shop teacher's quotation is from G. Barich, "Home Workshop Programs as a Hobby," *Industrial Arts and Vocational Education*, 31 (April 1942): 20A; Albert Neely Hall, *Craft Work and Play Things: A Handy Book for Beginners* (Philadelphia: J. B. Lippincott, 1936), v; the junior high school teacher's quotation is from L. E. Thurman, "The Home Workshop for Boys," *Industrial Education Magazine* 36 (November 1934): 252.

36. Smith, "Shopwork as Stimulating Recreation," 404; Hall, *Craft Work and Play Things*, 16–17; *Home Craftsman* 2 (January–February 1933): cover; *Popular Mechanics: What to Make* (Chicago: Popular Mechanics Press, 1939), cover; Yager, "Creating an Interest in the Home Workshop," 11; Dean Kittle, "The Activities and Equipment Found in the Home Workshops of Boys in Lima, Ohio" (master's thesis, Iowa State College, Ames, 1935), 8–9.

37. J. W. M. Rothney, "Interests of Public Secondary School Boys," *Journal of Educational Psychology* 28 (1937): 584–93; William H. Johnson, "A New Day for the Arts and Crafts in Chicago," *American School Board Journal* 94 (June 1937): 205; Earl L. Bedell and Ernest G. Gardner, *Household Mechanics: Industrial Arts for the General Shop* (Scranton, Pa.: International Textbook, 1937).

38. Joseph J. Corn, "Educating the Enthusiast: Print and Popularization of Technical Knowledge," in *Possible Dreams: Enthusiasm for Technology in America*, ed. John L. Wright (Dearborn, Mich.: Henry Ford Museum and Greenfield Village 1992); Kittle, "The Activities and Equipment Found in the Home Workshop," 24; Powell, "A Survey of the National Home Workshop Guild," 77; Elmer W. Cressman, *Out of School Activities of Jr. High School Pupils in Rela-*

tion to Intelligence and Socio-Economic Status (State College, Pa.: Pennsylvania State College Studies in Education, no. 20, 1937), 50; C. L. Page, "A Survey of Home Workshops in Ottumwa, Iowa" (master's thesis, Colorado State College, 1941), 41.

39. "National Homeworkshop Guild," *Popular Science* 123 (December 1933): 62–63; Orville Arthur Oaks, "Hobbies; or, a Woodnut and His Boys," *Industrial Education Magazine* 37 (September 1935): 186; Wakeling, *Home Workshop Manual*, v; Powell, "A Survey of the National Home Workshop Guild."

40. Powell, "A Survey of the National Home Workshop Guild," 15.

41. "Dreams on Paper: Home Sewing in America," museum exhibit, Museum at the Fashion Institute of Technology, New York (February 25-April 19, 1997); Anne L. Macdonald, *No Idle Hands: The Social History of American Knitting* (New York: Ballantine Books, 1988), 277–80; Christine Ferry, "Needlework is Definitely BACK!" *American Home* 12 (August 1934): 150–52.

42. "Institute Tests Plan to Revive Interest of Women in Sewing," *Sales Management* 42 (January 1938): 51; Janet Fowler Nelson, *Leisure-Time Interests and Activities of Business Girls* (New York: Woman's Press, 1933), 23; Rule, "Industrial Arts in Education for Leisure," 86.

43. "Our Return to the Art of Homemaking," *Needlecraft* 42 (February 1933): 3; Lucille W. Reynolds, "Leisure Time Activities of a Selected Group of Farm Women" (Ph.D. diss., University of Chicago, 1935), 79, 83

44. Harry E. O'Neal, "A Study of the Leisure Time Activities of Cincinnati Teachers" (master's thesis, University of Cincinnati, 1934), 23–24; Nelson, *Leisure Time Interest and Activities*, 22; Lucile E. Allard, "A Study of the Leisure Activities of Certain Elementary School Teachers of Long Island" (Ph.D. diss., Columbia University 1939), 31, 33, 90–91; Reynolds, "Leisure Time Activities," 79.

45. Dillon-Clarke, "Handicrafts in Adolescence," 318; Robert E. Dodds, *Handicrafts as a Hobby* (New York: Harper and Brothers, 1939); Edwin T. Hamilton, *Handicraft for Girls* (New York: Dodd, Mead, 1932); Minter, *Modern Home Crafts*; Harry Zarchy, *Here's Your Hobby* (New York: Knopf, 1950); Lester Griswold, *Handicraft: Simplified Procedure and Projects* (Colorado Springs, Col.: Out West Printing, 1942); Curtiss Sprague, *How To Make It: A Book of Crafts* (Pelham, N.Y.: Bridgman, 1941).

46. *Amateur Craftsman's Cyclopedia*, 10, 11, 16, 26; *Giant Home Workshop Manual*, 122, 213, 241; Wakeling, *Home Workshop Manual*, 122–25; *How to Make Lovely things of Wood for the House* (Chicago: Craftsman Wood Service, 1934); *Hammett's Material for Basketmaking, Weaving Materials, and Manual Arts Supplies* (Cambridge, Mass.: J. L. Hammett, [ca. 1935]).

47. Marge E. Staunton, "Marge Does It Herself," *American Home* 18 (August 1937): 42; Martha Wirt Davis, "Some Tips for Mrs. Fixit," *American Home* 15 (April 1936): 44.

48. J. C. Woodin, *Home Mechanics for Girls* (Wichita, Kans.: McCormick-Mathers, 1938), iii; W. Brewer, "Boys not Allowed," *Texas Outlook* 33 (December 1949): 16–18; Mabel Kitty Gibbard, *Hobbies for Girls* (Philadelphia: J. B. Lippincott, 1930), 201.

49. "If You Make It, She'll Paint It!" *Home Craftsman* 2 (March-April 1933): inside back cover.

50. *New York Times*, January 10, 1937, sect. 11, pp. 9, 12.

51. M. J. Poppenberg Jr., "A Survey of the Leisure Time Activities of Adults in Greeley, Colorado" (master's thesis, Colorado State College of Education, Greeley, 1940), 64; O'Neal, "A Study of the Leisure Time Activities of Cincinnati Teachers," 53.

52. C. G. Suits, "How Engineers Spend Their Spare Time," *General Electric Review* 41 (November 1938): 479–80.

53. William Virgil Nestrick, *Constructional Activities of Adult Males* (New York: Teachers College, Columbia University, 1939), 54, 56–57; Page, "A Survey of the Home Workshops," 13; Powell, "A Survey of the National Home Workshop Guild," 21.

54. P. H. Nicholson, "Adult Leisure Activities in a Colorado Rural School District" (master's thesis, Colorado State College of Education, Greeley, 1931), 22; Glen Charles Cook, *389 Things to Make for Farm and Home* (Danville, Ill.: Interstate Printer and Publishers, 1941).

55. Arthur W. Wilson, "Home Hobbyists Offer a Market," *Printers' Ink* 163 (May 4, 1933): 69; Edward Hobbs, *Home Carpenter's Practical Guide* (London: Cassell, 1933), 24; the quotation is from Hobbs, *Working with Tools*, 63.

56. "American Home Employment Plan," *American Home* 7 (November 1931): 81; Roger B. Whitman, *First Aid for the Ailing House* (New York: Whittlesey House, 1934), ix; Julian Starr Jr., *Fifty Things to Make for the Home* (New York, Whittlesey House, 1941), 3.

57. Julius Gregory, "Keep Your Garden from Slipping Back," *House and Garden* 64 (October 1933): 57; Godfrey Ernst, "Things That Make You Say Damn!" *House and Garden* 70 (July 1936): 38–39; *Handy Man's Home Manual* (Greenwich, Conn.: Modern Mechanix Publishing, 1936).

58. Hobbs, *Working with Tools*, 12.

59. C. T. Schaefer, *The Handy Man's Handbook* (New York: Harper and Brothers, 1931), xi, although a case could be made for Arthur Wakeling's collection of articles from *Popular Science*, which were published as Arthur Wakeling, *Fix It Yourself* (New York: Popular Science Publishing, 1929); for hybrid examples, see A. C. Horth, *101 Things for the Handyman to Do* (Philadelphia: J. B. Lippincott, 1938); Hawthorne Daniel, *The Householder's Complete Handbook* (Boston: Little, Brown, 1936).

60. Powell, "A Survey of the National Home Workshop Guild," 6; Schaefer, *The Handy Man's Handbook*, xi.

61. Cressman, *Out of School Activities*, 50; Kittle, "The Activities and Equipment Found in the Home Workshops," 24; Wakeling, *Home Workshop Manual*; *Handy Man's Home Manual*; *Amateur Craftsman's Cyclopedia*; *What to Make*; *Giant Home Workshop Manual*.

62. Wakeling, *Home Workshop Manual*, 318–19; *Amateur Craftsman's Cyclopedia*, 201.

63. Hobbs, *Home Carpenter's Practical Guide*, 156; "Furniture Surgery: Revamping Old Pieces," *House Beautiful* 77 (February 1935): 60–61; *What to Make and*

How to Make It (Chicago: Popular Mechanics Press, 1939), 65–66; William Longyear, "For the Home Craftsman: Nail Keg Furniture," *American Home* 11 (February 1934): 173; *Giant Home Workshop Manual*, 67.

64. Edwin T. Hamilton, *Boy Builder* (New York: Harcourt, Brace, 1933); Hobbs, *Home Carpenter's Practical Guide*; Hobbs, *Working with Tools*; William W. Klenke, *The Home Workshop* (Peoria, Ill.: Manual Arts Press, 1935); William W. Klenke, *Things to Make for the Home* (Peoria, Ill.: Manual Arts Press, 1935); Frederick A. Collins, *Working with Tools for Fun and Profit* (New York: D. Appleton-Century, 1937); Emanuele Stieri, *Home Craftsmanship* (New York: McGraw-Hill, 1935); Emanuele Stieri, *Woodworking as a Hobby* (New York: Harper, 1939).

65. Powell, "A Survey of the National Home Workshop Guild," 58, 62, 85; Kittle, "The Activities and Equipment Found in the Home Workshops," 20.

66. Klenke, *Home Workshop*, 1.

67. Ken F. Sheperdson, *Furnishing the Home Grounds* (New York: Bruce, 1936), 12; Starr, *Fifty Things to Make for the Home*, 139; Clay H. Tate, "I Made My Own Furniture," *American Home* 17 (May 1937): 58.

68. The quotation is from Klenke, *The Home Workshop*, 6; H. M. Flemming, "Fun for the Handy Man," *Better Homes and Gardens* 13 (March 1935): 38; Wakeling, *Home Workshop Manual*, 4; Klenke, *Things to Make for the Home*, 6.

69. Wakeling, *Home Workshop Manual*, 32; Edwin T. Hamilton, *Boy Builder* (New York: Harcourt, Brace, 1933), 237; W. T. R. Price, *It's Fun to Build Things* (New York: Hillman-Carl, 1937), viii; Collins, *Working with Tools*, 134.

70. "What's Your Hobby?" *American Home* 28 (August 1942): 13; Dick Ramsell, "Diary of a Desperate Daddy," *Better Homes and Gardens* 20 (May 1942): 22–23; *The Boy Mechanic* (Chicago: Popular Mechanics Press, 1940), 28; George A. Raeth, *Modern Homecraft* (Chicago: Frederick J. Drake, 1941); Clifford K. Lush, *It's Fun to Build Modern Furniture* (Milwaukee: Bruce Publishing, 1942).

71. Frank I. Solar, "Some Things to Make on Lazy July Afternoons," *Better Homes and Gardens* 9 (July 1931): 37; Hobbs, *Working with Tools*, 64.

72. Stieri, *Woodworking as a Hobby*, 1–3; *Amateur Craftsman's Cyclopedia*, 247; Horth, *101 Things for the Handyman to Do*, 2–7; *New York Times*, January 19, 1936, sect. 10, p. 8; Powell, "A Survey of the National Home Workshop Guild," 42; Kittle, "The Activities and Equipment Found in the Home Workshop," 15; Page, "A Survey of the Home Workshops," 26.

73. Wakeling, *Fix it Yourself*, 168–69; Daniel, *Householder's Complete Handbook*, 52–53; Starr, *Fifty Things to Make for the Home*, 3; Etna M. Kelley, "Millions for Hobbies: One of Today's Big Sales Opportunities," *Sales Management* 40 (January 1937): 81.

74. Wilson Follett, "Tools and the Hand," *Atlantic Monthly* 169 (April 1942): 469; Wakeling, *Fix It Yourself*, 233; Lush, "It's Fun to Build Modern Furniture," 4; John Allen Murphy, "Sales Boom in Hobby Goods," *American Business* 6 (May 1936): 51.

75. Murphy, "Sales Boom," 51, 55; Robert K. Leavitt, "Mr. Macy, Meet the Guppy, and Mr. Advertiser, Meet the Hobby," *Advertising and Selling* 21 (June

1933): 17; "Millions in Power Tools for Craftsman Hobbies," *Steel* 100 (May 17, 1937): 28–29; *What Others Have Done with "Delta" Tools in Hobby–Spare Time and Production Work* (Milwaukee, Wisc.: Delta Manufacturing, ca. 1933).

76. Garrot Barich, "The Home Workshop Program as a Hobby," *Industrial Arts and Vocational Education* 31 (April 1942): 20; Page, "A Survey of Home Workshops, 41; *Forty Power Tools You Can Make* (Chicago: Popular Mechanics Press, 1941), 3.

77. Kittle, "The Activities and Equipment Found in the Home Workshops," 26; Powell, "A Survey of the National Home Workshop Guild," 53; Page, "A Survey of Home Workshops," 32; "Millions in Power Tools," 28–29.

9 Kits: Assembly as Craft

1. Mary Mardison, "Fixing it Yourself," *New York Times Magazine* (March 7, 1943): 24; Earnest Elmo Calkins, "Hitting the Nail on the Head, or the Art of Puttering," *Atlantic Monthly* 172 (July 1943): 113; Bob Gilmore, "How to Tool Up Your Home," *Better Homes and Gardens* 23 (February 1945): 30; Harold J. Hawkins, "Fixing Things around the House," *Parents' Magazine* 17 (August 1942): 48–49; "Family's Day for Repairs," *Parents' Magazine* 16 (February 1941): 55; Dick Ramsell, "Diary of a Desperate Daddy," *Better Homes and Gardens* 20 (May 1942): 23.

2. Elizabeth Shaffer, "Tool Talk," *Household* 45 (July 1945): 12; S. S. Pheiffer, "Never Tell Your Wife," *House Beautiful* 86 (November 1944): 156; Calkins, "Hitting the Nail on the Head," 113.

3. Esther Boulton Black, "Confessions of a Hostess," *American Home* 28 (June 1942): 77; "Family's Day for Repairs," 55; Rachel McKinley Bushong, "Get Going! Not Brains, Not Talent, Not Skill—But Just Plain Work, Try It!" *American Home* 25 (March 1941): 30–31; Phyllis Krafft Newill, "They Also Serve," *Woman's Home Companion* 70 (May 1943): 114.

4. Sabina Ormsby Dean, "It Didn't Take a War to Make a Carpenter Out of Mother," *House Beautiful* 85 (October 1943): 118–19; Mrs. Robert C. Baker, "Everywoman's Primer of Home Repairs," *House and Garden* 83 (March 1943): 35–42; Janet Flanner, "Ladies in Uniform," *New Yorker* 17 (July 4, 1942): 21–29; "How to Fix It: Home Owners All over U.S. Learn to Make Own Repairs," *Life* 15 (July 26 1943): 87–95; Mardison, "Fixing it Yourself," 24; Baker, "Everywoman's Primer," 35–42; Arthur Bohnen, "Be Your Own Handyman: Maintenance—Not Repair," *American Home* 29 (January 1943): 36–38; Pheiffer, "Never Tell Your Wife," 160.

5. William H. Johnson and Louis V. Newkirk, "Crafts in the School and Home," *Industrial Arts and Vocational Education* 32 (December 1943): 399.

6. J. G. Fuller, "Hobbies May Help," *Industrial Arts and Vocational Education* 32 (December 1945): 454; Bonnie Malott, "Occupational Therapy," *School Arts* 43 (September 1943): 17; *New York Times*, January 25, 1943, 16; *New York Times*, February 5, 1943, 18; "Boom in Handcrafts," *House and Garden* 83 (April 1943): 17; *New York Times*, November 17, 1944, 16; "Repair of the Wounded," *Life* 15 (July

19, 1943): 36–42; *New York Times*, July 20, 1945, 34; *New York Times*, February 19, 1948, 48; *New York Times*, June 26, 1945, 16; John Gill, "Arts and Crafts: Their Role in Treating Tuberculosis," *California Journal of Secondary Education* 23 (May 1948): 280; Celia F. Beck, "I Always Wanted to Work with My Hands," *Occupations* 25 (December 1946): 167; E. Heeks, "Handwork May Solve Your Problems," *School* [elementary edition] 32 (March 1944): 614.

7.   W. T. Baxter, "Hobby Crafts for the U.S. Navy," *Industrial Arts and Vocational Education* 38 (January 1949): 15–18.

8.   *New York Times*, December 21, 1945, 19; "Make-it-Yourself Kit Seeks Market among Nation's Hobbyists," *Sales Management* 55 (December 15, 1945): 82; "Hobby Lobbying," *Modern Plastics* 22 (December 1944): 95–99; Alexander Reynolds, "Lobbying for Style," *Modern Plastics* 22 (March 1945): 113–15.

9.   Stephanie Coontz, *The Way We Never Were: American Families and the Nostalgia Trip* (New York: Basic Books, 1992), 27; Arlene Skolnick, *Embattled Paradise: The American Family in an Age of Uncertainty* (New York: Basic Books, 1991), 52; U.S. Bureau of the Census, *Historical Statistics of the United States, Colonial Times to 1970, Bicentennial Edition* (Washington, D.C.: Government Printing Office, 1975), 49; John Keats, *The Crack in the Picture Window* (Boston: Houghton Mifflin, 1956), 86, 95–97; M. J. S. Lockard, "Speaking for Handicrafts," *Practical Home Economics* 31 (September 1952): 23.

10. Fred Darling, "A Leisure Time Analysis of Retired Public School Teachers in Kentucky" (Ph.D. diss., Indiana University, 1958), 101, 104; Ralph C. Mayo, "Survey of Student's Needs and Interests," *Industrial Arts and Vocational Education* 46 (February 1957): 36; Dale Perkins, "A Study of Leisure Time and Recreational Interests of 982 Fifteen- and Sixteen-Year-Old Students" (Ph.D. diss., University of Houston, 1948), 74, 82, 323; "Suitable Stable for Hobby Horses," *Recreation* 38 (December 1944): 467; Margaret M. Holt, "Equipping a Craft Room," *Recreation* 46A (September 1953): 217–20; "Community Crafts Program," *Recreation* 47 (November 1954): 546; "Give Them a Hobby; Chicago Rotary Club Spearheads a City Wide Show," *Rotarian* 72 (May 1948): 34; *New York Times*, March 26, 1953, 33; R. J. Havighurst and K. Fiegenbaum, "Leisure and Life Style," *American Journal of Sociology* 64 (1958): 400–401; Barbara M. Kelly, *Expanding the American Dream: Building and Rebuilding Levittown* (Albany: State University of New York Press, 1993), 93.

11. Grier Lowry, "Teaching Handicrafts Stimulates Sales," *Hobby-Model Merchandising News* (November 1952): 10–11; Eva John Kuhn, "A Banker Turns Woodworker," *Profitable Hobbies* 12 (June 1956): 19; "Hobby Huddle," *Profitable Hobbies* 6 (February 1950): 1.

12. H. Miller, "Hobbies Can Make You Money," *Country Gentleman* 124 (November 1954): 102, 114–15; *New York Times*, July 18, 1946, 23; Marion Marzolf, "A Town's Craft Shop and How It Grew," *Profitable Hobbies* 12 (September 1956): 12–15.

13. "Earn Money on Things You Make at Home," *Changing Times* 7 (November 1953): 22; "Turn Your Art to Profit," *Design* 55 (November 1953): 85–86; Joseph Leeming, *Money-Making Hobbies: 100 Easy Ways to Earn Extra Money*

(Philadelphia: J. B. Lippincott, 1948); *Money-Making Hobbies* (Chicago: Popular Mechanics Press, 1949); "Hobby Parade," *Profitable Hobbies* 6 (February 1950): 12–13; C. Vernon Mobberly, "Attracting Tourist Trade," *Profitable Hobbies* 6 (June 1950): 38; Solange Strong, "A Bachelor's Buttons," *Profitable Hobbies* 8 (April 1952): 34; "Hobby Parade," *Profitable Hobbies* 8 (July 1952): 32–33; Weldon D. Woodson, "Novelties from Wood," *Profitable Hobbies* 10 (June 1954): 20–21; Mary Harvey, "Home Gift Shop," *Profitable Hobbies* 12 (June 1956): 28.

14. Michael Estrin, *Treasury of Hobbies and Crafts* (New York: Knickerbocker Publishing, 1946); Marguerite Ickis, *Handicrafts and Hobbies for Pleasure and Profit* (New York: Greystone Press, 1948); Jesse Wayne King, "Short Courses in Industrial Arts for Their Hobby Value" (master's thesis, Oregon State College, 1952), 32–52; an explicitly girl's hobby book had more sewing and less woodwork, but was otherwise similar, *Girl Book of Hobbies* (London: Hulton Press, 1958); Sybil Arata, "The Role of Fine Arts in Adult Education Programs," *California Journal of Secondary Education* 23 (May 1948): 276; Aino Jarvesoo, "Social and Educational Values of Handicrafts," *Journal of Home Economics* 45 (February 1953): 116.

15. *American Handicrafts* [catalog] (East Orange, N.J.: American Handicrafts, 1949).

16. "Playthings for Grownups," *House Beautiful* 100 (December 1958): 146–47; Ruth Schmidt, "Try a New Craft," *Farm Journal* 83 (January 1959): 67; Robert Gorman, *Hobby Tools and How to Use Them* (Long Island City, N.Y.: X-Acto Co., 1956), 5.

17. Edward L. Thorndike, "The Right Use of Leisure," *Journal of Adult Education* 2 (1930): 31–32; *New York Times*, November 28, 1954, 63.

18. Karal Ann Marling, *As Seen on TV: The Visual Culture of Everyday Life in the 1950s* (Cambridge, Mass.: Harvard University Press, 1994): 63; Richard Butsch, "Exploring the Relationship between Production and Reproduction in the Model Airplane Hobby Industry," *Arena Review* 9 (March 1985): 20; Deborah Nelles, "From Artisan to Courtesan: The Rationalization of Labour and Leisure" (master's thesis, McMaster University, 1978), 60–61.

19. Marky D. Pirie, "Behind Tandy's Tripled Sales," *Sales Management* 74 (April 15, 1955): 104–5; Nelles, *From Artisan to Courtesan*, 68–82.

20. "From Toys to Hobbies: Way to Men's Hearts," *Business Week* (January 28, 1956): 58; Nathaniel Benchley, "Insanity Ahoy," *Nation's Business* 41 (April 1953): 92–94.

21. Benchley, "Insanity Ahoy," 92; Barbara Humphrey, "Looking for a Hobby? Try Model Building," *Today's Health* 36 (February 1958): 37, 54.

22. Butsch, "Exploring the Relationship between Production and Reproduction"; "Hobby Show," *New Yorker* 32 (August 18, 1956): 16.

23. "Hobbies: Realism Is What Sells," *Business Week* (February 27, 1954): 59, 62; "From Toys to Hobbies," 56–61; *Hobbies Are Family Fun* [catalog] (New York: Polk's Hobby Department Store, [ca. 1960]).

24. *New York Times*, February 9, 1958, sect. 3, pp. 1, 3; "The Sap Is Running in Do-It-Yourself," *Business Week* (March 27, 1954): 122; "What's New in Do-It-Yourself," *Changing Times* 10 (February 1956): 37, 38.

10 Do-It-Yourself: Expected Leisure

1. *Workbench* 13 (March-April 1957); *Workbench* 13 (July-August 1957).
2. Margaret Mead, "The Pattern of Leisure in Contemporary America," *Annals of the American Academy of Political and Social Science* 313 (1957): 15; Robert L. Griswold, "Divorce and the Legal Redefinition of Victorian Manhood," in *Meanings for Manhood*, ed. Mark C. Carnes and Clyde Griffen (Chicago: University of Chicago Press, 1990), 207; Arlene Skolnick, *Embattled Paradise: The American Family in an Age of Uncertainty* (New York: Basic Books, 1991), 71; Peter G. Filene, *Him/Her/Self: Sex Roles in Modern America* (Baltimore: Johns Hopkins University Press, 1986), 173; Virginia Scott Jenkins, *The Lawn: A History of an American Obsession* (Washington, D.C.: Smithsonian Institution Press, 1994), 117–132.
3. Harry Zarchy, *Here's Your Hobby* (New York: Knopf, 1950); Janet E. Stockdale, *What Is Leisure? An Empirical Analysis of the Concept of the Role of Leisure* (London: Sports Council and Social Research Council, 1985), 103; Anne Swartzlander, "Consumer Characteristics Related to the Frequency of Do-It-Yourself Home, Auto, Appliance, and Electronic Equipment Maintenance and Repair" (Ph.D. diss., Ohio State University, 1984), 19–20.
4. Kevin Melchionne, "Of Bookworms and Busybees: Cultural Theory in the Age of Do-It-Yourselfing," *Journal of Aesthetics and Art Criticism*, forthcoming. "How-To-Do-It, a Hobby," *Science News Letter* 67 (June 25, 1950): 404; Robert Kingery, *How To Do It Books: A Selected Guide* (New York: R. R. Bowker, 1950); "Off the Editor's Chest: Do It Yourself Movement," *Consumers Research Bulletin* 34 (November 1954): 29; Darrell Huff, "We've Found a Substitute for Income," *Harper's* 207 (October 1953): 30.
5. Percival Marshall, *Mechanics in Miniature* (London: Percival Marshal, 1947), 19; Walt Durbhan, "Our House Is Different—Yours Can Be Too," *American Magazine* 157 (January 1954): 72, 75; Margaret Elizabeth Mulac, *Hobbies: The Creative Use of Leisure* (New York: Harper, 1959), 21–22; Phil Creden, "America Rediscovers Its Hands," *American Magazine* 156 (December 1953): 21, 112–113.
6. Viron Nelson Hukill, "The Do-It-Yourself Movement in Pulaski County, Arkansas, and Its Implications for Industrial Arts" (Ed.D. diss., University of Missouri, Columbia, 1958), 80.
7. "Hobby Lobbying," *Modern Plastics*, 97; "The Shoulder Trade," *Time* 64 (August 2, 1954): 62–63; "The New Do-It-Yourself Market," *Business Week* (June 14, 1952): 61.
8. "Personal Business," *Business Week* (April 2, 1955): 131; "The New Do-It-Yourself Market," 60–64, 70; "The Shoulder Trade," 63; for an earlier use of the term do-it-yourself see "The ABC of Home Repair" [advertisement], *American Home* 31 (September 1945): 43; "Do-It-Yourself Idea—On Parade," *Business Week* (March 21, 1953), 33; Robert J. Bond, "The Do-It-Yourself Market," in *Mass Leisure*, ed. Eric Larrabee and Rolf Meyersohn (Glencoe, Ill.: Free Press, 1953), 275; *New York Times*, September, 19, 1954, sect. 3, p. 7; U.S. Bureau of the Census, *Historical Statistics of the United States, Colonial Times to 1970, Bicentennial Edition*

(Washington, D.C.: Government Printing Office, 1975), 646; Creden cuts that figure in half; Creden, "America Rediscovers Its Hands," 111.

9. Hubbard Cobb, *The Home Owner's Complete Guide to Remodeling* (Boston: Houghton Mifflin, 1953), 3.

10. *San Jose Mercury-News*, January 5, 1994, *Extra* 3, 4; ibid., January 12, 1994, *Extra* 3, 5; ibid. January 19, 1994, *Extra* 3, 5; Jerry Ditto and Lanning Stern, *Design for Living: Eichler Homes* (San Francisco: Chronicle Books, 1995); Ruth Stumpf, "You Can Be Your Own Cabinetmaker," *Better Homes and Gardens* 30 (October 1952): 186; for examples of plans for modern furniture, see *Build It* (Greenwich, Conn.: Fawcett, 1950), 2, 18, 66, 104, 124.

11. *New York Times*, October 24, 1955, 24; "Is There a Handy Man in the House?" *American Home* 38 (November 1947): 38–39; Betty Pepis, "Home Handymen Tooling Up," *New York Times Magazine* (June 28, 1953): 28–29; Elizabeth Matthews and Guy Henle, "Young Designer Furniture You Can Build Yourself," *Woman's Home Companion* 81 (October 1954): 60–63; John Webster, "Handsome Furniture You Can Build," *Better Homes and Gardens* 29 (March 1951): 258–259; Bond, "The Do-It-Yourself Market," 277; Henry Humphrey, *Woman's Home Companion Household Book* (New York: P. F. Collier and Son, 1948): 501, 503.

12. Barbara M. Kelly, *Expanding the American Dream: Building and Rebuilding Levittown* (Albany: State University of New York Press, 1993), 12, 71–73; Gwendolyn Wright, *Building the Dream: A Social History of Housing in America* (New York: Pantheon, 1981), 248–254; Clifford Edward Clark Jr., *The American Family Home, 1800–1960* (Chapel Hill, N.C.: University of North Carolina Press, 1986), 221–225; "Houseful of Ideas with One Aim, Sell the Fixup Market," *Business Week* (February 14, 1953, 66–68; Karal Ann Marling, *As Seen on TV: The Visual Culture of Everyday Life in the 1950s* (Cambridge, Mass.: Harvard University Press, 1994): 57; Kelly *Expanding the American Dream*, 94.

13. Creden, "America Rediscovers Its Hands," 113.

14. Kelly, *Expanding the American Dream*, 76, 79; Herbert J. Gans, *The Levittowners: Ways of Life in a New Suburb* (New York: Vintage Books, 1967): 270; *New York Times*, May 1, 1954, 19; Jerome Parker, "I'm Proud of My All-Thumbs Craftwork," *Popular Science* 152 (March 1948): 194.

15. Hukill, "The Do-It-Yourself Movement in Pulaski County," 17–21; Ronald Bagley, "A Study to Determine the Contribution of Industrial Arts to Leisure Time Activities of the Graduates of Northeast State Missouri Teachers College" (Ed.D. diss., Colorado State College, 1965); U.S. Bureau of the Census, *Homeowners and Home Improvements: 1987*, Current Housing Reports, Series H121/92–1 (Washington, D.C.: Government Printing Office, 1992), 3–4, 9; David A. Cunningham et al., "Active Leisure Activities as Related to Occupation," *Journal of Leisure Research* 2 (1970): 109; Bagley, "A Study to Determine the Contribution of Industrial Arts to Leisure Time Activities," 124; Craig Ross, "Relationship between Occupational Prestige and Leisure Participation Patterns of Selected Employees" (Re.D. diss., Indiana University, 1980), 163; Swartzlander, "Consumer Characteristics," 19–20; Michael Young and Peter Willmott, *The Symmetrical Family* (New York: Pantheon, 1973): 212; Milton Gordon

and Charles Anderson, "The Blue Collar Workers at Leisure," in *Blue Collar World: Studies of the American Worker*, ed. A. Shostak and W. Gomburg (Englewood Cliffs, N.J.: Prentice Hall, 1964); David Halle, *America's Working Man: Work, Home, and Politics among Blue-Collar Property Owners* (Chicago: University of Chicago, 1984), 43; Pete Hamill, "Steel Memories from Father's Toolbox," *New York Times*, October 26, 1995, B1.

16.   *New York Times*, April 12, 1955, 22; *New York Times*, September 28, 1955, 32; *New York Times*, May 13, 1956, sect. 12, p. 20.

17.   Horace W. Greeley, "Do-It-Yourself Urge Takes Hold, Builds New Home Market," *Printers' Ink* 247 (May 21, 1954): 37; "Paint Gives Protection and Beauty" [advertisement], *American Home* (September 1945): 37; Bond, "The Do-It-Yourself Market," 277; *New York Times*, March 13, 1955, sect. 2, p. 28; *New York Times*, June 10, 1956, sect. 8, p. 1; *New York Times*, May 22, 1954, 18; "Homeowners Are Making Over Old Business," *Business Week* (January 1 1955): 72; Greeley, "Do-It-Yourself Urge Takes Hold," 37; Nathan Kelne, "Is Your Product Ripe for the Four Billion Dollar Do-It-Yourself Market?" *Printers' Ink* 245 (November 12, 1953): 46–48; Roger W. Babson, "Do It Yourself—A New Industry," *Commercial and Financial Chronicle* 177 (March 5, 1953): 1012.

18.   Bond, "The Do-It-Yourself Market," 278; *New York Times*, September 19, 1954, sect. 3, p. 7; Carolyn M. Goldstein, *Do It Yourself: Home Improvement in Twentieth-Century America* (New York: Princeton Architectural Press, 1998), 54–59; Hukill, "The Do-It-Yourself Movement in Pulaski County," 39; Creden, "America Rediscovers Its Hands, 111; Kelne, "Is Your Product Ripe?" 46; "Do-It-Yourself Gives America a New Look," *Senior Scholastic* 64 (April 7, 1954): 14; Emanuele Stieri, *The Complete Home Repair Handbook* (New York: Prentice Hall, 1950).

19.   Walter J. Coppock, *Make Your Home Your Hobby* (Yellow Springs, Ohio: Antioch Press, 1945), 3; Eric Hodgins, *Mr. Blandings Builds His Dream House* (New York: Simon and Schuster, 1946); Huff, "We Found a Substitute for Income," 26, 31–32.

20.   Huff, "We Found a Substitute for Income," 31; *New York Times*, April 7, 1957, sect. 8, p. 1; "Build It Yourself," *Business Week* (October 18, 1952), 52.

21.   "Do-It-Yourself Man," *Look* 17 (September 22, 1953): 114.

22.   David Dempsey, "Home, Sweet (Homemade) Home," *New York Times Magazine* (March 31, 1957): 26.

23.   William Astor and Charlotte Astor, "Private Associations and Commercial Activities," *Annals of the American Academy of Political and Social Science* 313 (1957), 96; "Answer to Pressure," *Chemical Week* 74 (May 8, 1954): 62; Bond, "The Do-It-Yourself Market," 275; Kelne, "Is Your Product Ripe?" 46; "Do It Yourself Gives America a New Look," 14; *New York Times*, January 3, 1955, 91; "The Shoulder Trade," 66; at the high end, this figure is double the one found by the Department of Commerce in the same period, U. S. Bureau of the Census, Housing and Construction Reports, Series H101, no. 1, *Alterations and Repairs*, "Expenditures on Residential Owner-Occupied Properties January to May 1954" (Washington, D.C.: Government Printing Office, 1954), 3, 5; "Off the Editor's Chest," 2; "For Handymen Only," *Newsweek* 43 (April 26, 1954): 77;

New York Times, September 19, 1954, sect. 3, p. 7; Ruth Schwartz Cowan, *More Work for Mother: The Ironies of Household Technology* (New York: Basic Books, 1983), 63–69, 99; Leonard A. Stevens, "America's Most Popular Gadget," *Collier's* 134 (July 9, 1954): 80.

24. "The New Do-It-Yourself Market," 72; Stevens, "America's Most Popular Gadget."

25. Hukill, "The Do-It-Yourself Movement in Pulaski County," 30; Stevens, "America's Most Popular Gadget," 82–83; *How to Use Power Tools* (Greenwich, Conn.: Fawcett, book no. 212, 1953): 116; Dean Kittle, "The Activities and Equipment Found in the Home Workshops of Boys in Lima, Ohio" (master's thesis, Iowa State College, Ames, 1935), 28; M. A. Powell, "A Survey of the National Home Workshop Guild" (master's thesis, Colorado State College of Education, Greeley, 1935), 53; "Hobby Huddle," *Profitable Hobbies* 6 (January 1950): 2; Bond, "The Do-It-Yourself Market," 276.

26. *How to Use Power Tools,* 3; "The New Do-It-Yourself Market," 69; Huff, "We Found a Substitute for Income," 31; Bond, "The Do-It-Yourself Market," 276; "What's New in Do-It-Yourself," *Changing Times* 10 (February 1956): 35–36; "Teach 'em to Run It, They'll Buy a Power Tool," *Business Week* (December 11, 1954): 50; Humphrey, *Woman's Home Companion Household Book,* 488.

27. Marshall, *Mechanics in Miniature,* 15.

28. *New York Times,* May 13, 1956, 32; *New York Times,* September 23, 1956, 117.

29. Morris quoted in Robert W. Winter, "The Arroyo Culture," in *California Design,* ed. Timothy Anderson et al. (Santa Barbara, Calif.: Peregrine Smith, 1980): 20; "Armory Show," *Harper's* 206 (May 1953): 93.

30. John Keats, *The Crack in the Picture Window* (Boston: Houghton Mifflin, 1956), 88–89; *New York Times,* November 18, 1955, 12.

31. "A New Look in Home Power Tools," *Business Week* (March 20, 1954): 152.

32. *New York Times,* March 8, 1953, sect. 8, p. 1; *New York Times,* March 22, 1955, 34; *New York Times,* April 6, 1955, 28.

33. Lenore Hailparn, "She Did It Herself," *Independent Woman* 32 (June 1953): 203.

34. Reed Millard, "Hobbies That Hold Your Family Together," *Coronet* 31 (January 1952): 137–138; Huff, "We Found a Substitute for Income," 28–29.

35. Stieri, *Complete Home Repair Handbook,* 354–355; Bond, "The Do-It-Yourself Market," 278–279.

36. Hukill, "The Do-It-Yourself Movement in Pulaski County," 65; Elaine Tyler May, *Homeward Bound: American Families in the Cold War Era* (New York: Basic Books, 1988): 195; "Do It Yourself Gives America a New Look," 15–16; Durbhan, "Our House Is Different," 73; Sprague Holden, "Education of a House Husband," *House Beautiful* 89 (September 1947): 128; "A New Approach to Do-It-Yourself," *American Magazine* 156 (December 1963): 19.

37. "Dressing Up the Old Yard for a New Market," *Business Week* (November 1948): 78.

38. Creden, "America Rediscovers Its Hands," 21.

39. Kelne, "Is Your Product Ripe?" 46–48; Creden, "America Rediscovers Its Hands," 21, 111.

40. "Home Owners Are Making Over Old Business," *Business Week* (January 1, 1955): 72.

41. "For Handymen Only," 77.

42. Rose McAfee, "A Lady and a Jig Saw," *Profitable Hobbies* 11 (February 1955): 24; *How to Use Power Tools*, 9.

43. *How to Use Power Tools*, 130; *New York Times*, March 22, 1955, 34; Creden, "America Rediscovers Its Hands," 114.

44. Mary Newlin Borton, "Hobbies Can Build Character," *Parents' Magazine* (May 1951): 46; William G. Poole, "Coeducation Wood Shop," *Industrial Arts and Vocational Education* 47 (September 1958): 205.

45. *New York Times*, December 21, 1954, 33; Elizabeth Krusell Hall, "My Wood Working Hobby Paid Off," *American Home* 57 (March 1957): 109–110.

46. *New York Times*, September 19, 1954, sect. 3, p. 7.

47. Keats, *The Crack in the Picture Window*, 52; "Do-It-Yourself Man," 115; Eugene Rachlis, "How Not to Do-It-Yourself," *New York Times Magazine* (August 15, 1954): 34.

48. Hukill, "The Do-It-Yourself Movement in Pulaski County," 85–86; Holden, "Education of a House Husband," 128; Edward C. Fisher, "You're Going to Make a Chair," *Profitable Hobbies* 7 (January 1951): 44–45.

49. "The ABC of Home Repair," [advertisement] *American Home* 31 (September 1945): 43.

50. For examples, see Webster, "Handsome Furniture You Can Build," 258–259; *Build It*, 2, 66, 104–5; Humphrey, *Woman's Home Companion Household Book*, 501; Gans, *The Levittowners*, 270; *New York Times*, October 24, 1955 24; *New York Times*, February 9, 1958, sect. 3, p. 1; "The Sap Is Running in Do-It-Yourself," *Business Week* (March 27, 1954): 122; "What's New in Do-It-Yourself," 37.

51. Holden, "Education of a House Husband," 128.

52. "Do-It-Yourself Man," 114.

53. Kelly, *Expanding the American Dream*, 71, 86; cover illustration reproduced in Derham Groves, "The Euphoric Coalface," *Exedra* 6 (1995): 9.

54. Rachlis, "How Not to Do It Yourself," 34; Babson, "Do-It-Yourself—A New Industry," 1012.

55. May, *Homeward Bound*, 146–147; Humphrey, *Woman's Home Companion Household Book*, 489; Kay Campbell, "And What's Your Hobby?" *American Home* 37 (April 1947): 36.

56. *New York Times*, March 15, 1952, 10.

57. Harry Levine, "Psychological Problems of Increased Leisure," in *Personal Problems and Psychological Frontiers*, ed. Fairchild E. Johnson (New York: Sheridan House, 1957), 163, 165; "Do-It-Yourself Gives America a New Look," 14–16; *New York Times*, September 19, 1954, sect. 6, p. 4.

58. Cited in Creden, "America Rediscovers Its Hands," 113.

59. Albert Roland, "Do-It-Yourself: A Walden for the Millions," *American Quarterly* 10 (spring 1958): 154; "Armory Show," 95.

60. Francis Coughlin, "Is There a Handyman Handy?" *Science Digest* 23 (March 1958): 71–73; Bond, "The Do-It-Yourself Market," 275; Creden, "America Redis-

covers Its Hands," 112; "The Weird Economics of the Washing Machine," *Business Week* (June 14, 1952), 79; *New York Times*, May 12, 1956, 18.

61.   *Historical Statistics of the United States*, 167; this conclusion is based on the assumption that the average earnings of employees in the construction industry can be used as a surrogate for professional home craftsmen, and the average earnings of local, state, federal, and public education workers as a surrogate for middle-class incomes.

62.   Hukill, "The Do-It-Yourself Movement in Pulaski County," 54.

63.   "What Not to Do Yourself," *House Beautiful* 96 (July 1954): 54; Rachlis, "How Not to Do It Yourself," 34.

64.   "The Shoulder Trade," 64, 66; Dempsey, "Home Sweet (Homemade) Home," 26; Huff, "We Found a Substitute for Income," illustrations by Kroll, 27, 29.

65.   Holden, "Education of a House Husband," 129.

66.   Cartoon reproduced in Goldstein, *Do It Yourself*, 44; Cobb, *The Home Owner's Complete Guide*, 8.

67.   Julian Starr Jr., *Fifty Things to Make for the Home* (New York, Whittlesey House, 1941), 3–5.

Index